JOURNAL FOR THE STUDY OF THE OLD TESTAMENT SUPPLEMENT SERIES
237

Sheffield Academic Press

The Archaeology of Israel

Constructing the Past,
Interpreting the Present

edited by
Neil Asher Silberman &
David Small

Journal for the Study of the Old Testament
Supplement Series 237

Copyright © 1997 Sheffield Academic Press

Published by Sheffield Academic Press Ltd
Mansion House
19 Kingfield Road
Sheffield S11 9AS
England

Printed on acid-free paper in Great Britain
by Bookcraft Ltd
Midsomer Norton, Bath

British Library Cataloguing in Publication Data

A catalogue record for this book is available
from the British Library

ISBN 1-85075-650-3

CONTENTS

FOREWORD

This volume, *The Archaeology of Israel: Constructing the Past, Interpreting the Present,* is the fifth based on conferences at the Philip and Muriel Berman Center for Jewish Studies at Lehigh University and is aimed at stimulating new thinking in the field of Jewish Studies broadly conceived. In gathering together an interdisciplinary group of scholars, the Center sought to foster dialogue and debate among people approaching the field of the archaeology of the land of Israel from diverse perspectives and disciplinary orientations. By incorporating discussion of the cultural, social, and political conditions and effects, we endeavored to broaden the framework within which the archaeology of Israel is conventionally discussed.

I would like to thank Richard and Susan Master for their generous contribution which helped to make the conference and the volume possible. I am likewise grateful to Philip and Muriel Berman, who contributed generously to the funding of the conference, and whose generosity and imagination made possible the establishment and continued operation of the Center. I thank Neil Silberman and David Small for agreeing to edit the volume and for contributing an illuminating introduction that locates the various issues addressed by the contributors within the context of the scholarly discussions in the field. They, together with Trude Dothan and Ephraim Stern of the Philip and Muriel Berman Center for Biblical Archaeology at the Hebrew University in Jerusalem, played a major role in conceptualizing and organizing the conference. Without their wise counsel, the conference could not have been held. Shirley Ratushny, assistant to the director of the Berman Center, was responsible for preparing the volume for publication and for supervising the administrative and logistical organization of the conference. Carol Sabo, administrative coordinator of the Berman Center, was responsible for coordinating transportation and housing for the participants and registrants, and for attending to numerous technical details which helped to ensure the success of the conference.

Laurence J. Silberstein, Director
Philip and Muriel Berman Center
for Jewish Studies, Lehigh University

ABBREVIATIONS

AASOR	Annual of the American Schools of Oriental Research
AB	Anchor Bible
AIA	*Archaeological Institute of America*
ANET	J.B. Pritchard (ed.), *Ancient Near Eastern Texts*
BA	*Biblical Archaeologist*
BAR	British Archaeology Reports
BARev	*Biblical Archaeology Review*
BASOR	*Bulletin of the American Schools of Oriental Research*
BASORSup	*Bulletin of the American Schools of Oriental Research,* Supplements
BSac	*Bibliotheca Sacra*
DJD	Discoveries in the Judaean Desert
HSM	Harvard Semitic Monographs
HUCA	*Hebrew Union College Annual*
IEJ	*Israel Exploration Journal*
JBL	*Journal of Biblical Literature*
JJS	*Journal of Jewish Studies*
JNES	*Journal of Near Eastern Studies*
JQR	*Jewish Quarterly Review*
JSOT	*Journal for the Study of the Old Testament*
JSOTSup	*Journal for the Study of the Old Testament,* Supplement Series
PEQ	*Palestine Exploration Quarterly*
RA	*Revue d'assyriologie et d'archéologie orientale*
RB	*Revue biblique*
SBLDS	SBL Dissertation Series
SWBA	*The Social World of Biblical Antiquity*
VT	*Vetus Testamentum*
VTSup	*Vetus Testamentum,* Supplements
ZAW	*Zeitschrift für die alttestamentiche Wissenschaft*
ZDPV	*Zeitschrift des deutschen Palästina-Verein*

LIST OF FIGURES

LIST OF CONTRIBUTORS

Amnon Ben-Tor, Yigael Yadin Professor for the Archaeology of Eretz Israel, Institute of Archaeology, Hebrew University of Jerusalem

William G. Dever, Professor of Near Eastern Archaeology and Anthropology, Department of Near Eastern Studies, University of Arizona

Trude Dothan, Professor of Archaeology and Director of the Philip and Muriel Berman Center for Biblical Archaeology, Hebrew University of Jerusalem

Amos Elon, Israeli author and journalist

Israel Finkelstein, Professor of Archaeology, Institute of Archaeology, Tel Aviv University

Baruch Halpern, Professor of Ancient History and Religious Studies, Pennsylvania State University

Brian Hesse, Professor of Anthropology, University of Alabama at Birmingham

Lee Levine, Professor of Archaeology and Jewish History, Hebrew University of Jerusalem

Burke O. Long, Professor of Religion, Bowdoin College

Amihai Mazar, Professor of Archaeology, Institute of Archaeology, Hebrew University of Jerusalem

Yaacov Shavit, Professor, Jewish History Department, Tel Aviv University

Neil Asher Silberman, author and independent scholar, Branford, Connecticut

David B. Small, Associate Professor of Anthropology, Department of Sociology and Anthropology, Lehigh University

Ephraim Stern, Bernard M. Lauterman Professor, Institute of Archaeology, Hebrew University of Jerusalem

Paula Wapnish, Research Associate, Department of Anthropology, University of Alabama at Birmingham

Benjamin G. Wright III, Associate Professor, Department of Religious Studies, Lehigh University

INTRODUCTION

Neil Asher Silberman and David B. Small

Presented in this volume are papers delivered at a conference of the Philip and Muriel Berman Center for Jewish Studies at Lehigh University entitled 'The Archaeology of Israel: Constructing the Past, Interpreting the Present' held on the Lehigh campus in Bethlehem, Pennsylvania, May 22–24, 1994. The conference organizers, coordinated by Laurence J. Silberstein, the Center's director, brought together scholars of many emphases and specialities. Their aim was to provide a forum for the discussion of some of the important theoretical and practical developments that have occurred in the archaeology of Israel over the last decade. It should be noted that many of the intellectual controversies and changes of theoretical orientation experienced in this field and discussed at the Berman Conference have been paralleled by similar active discussions in other branches and traditions of world archaeology.

The archaeology of the land of Israel, of course, possesses one of the longest traditions of excavation and scholarly investigation of any region in the world. That tradition had been blessed and often complicated by the vast literary and historical record of the Bible; indeed, issues connected with the study of the Bible have long set the agenda for the investigation of the country's ancient remains. In the sections that follow we highlight the increasingly wide range of approaches to the ongoing archaeological exploration and study of the land of Israel, some of which are represented by the contributors to this volume. They range in theoretical orientation from the entirely positive—seeing in the material remains straightforward evidence of the life and texture of past civilizations—to more critical ideological approaches, regarding archaeological evidence as encoded (yet decipherable) messages about the social structure and power relationships of ancient societies. In a concluding section we will describe the contributions dealing with the question of how text and artifact may be productively related, a question of enormous and immediate interest in the reconstruction of biblical history.

Archaeology, Contemporary Culture, and Ideological Discourse

The first set of contributors to this volume is primarily concerned with archaeology as a social and political activity in modern Israel, quite apart from its character as a purely intellectual pursuit. As such, these authors are contributing to a sociology of knowledge that seeks to understand the social and political strategies underlying archaeological research and the subsequent utilization of archaeological data, that is, how archaeology is used by modern institutions and nations to create a socially meaningful understanding of the past. This approach to archaeology as modern social behavior, taken up by Childe as early as the 1930s in his attacks against Nazi anthropology (1933, 1934), has gradually been applied by scholars in many parts of the world to the analysis of archaeology's role in such diverse areas as nationalism and state-building (Trigger 1984; Fowler 1987; Gathercole and Lowenthal 1990; Friedman 1992; Kohl and Fawcett 1995; Patterson 1995); the ideological function of museums and historical sites in modern industrial society (Lowenthal 1985; Leone, Potter, and Shackel 1987); the role of archaeology in justifying South African apartheid (Hall 1984); and the physical and intellectual control exercised by Euro-Americans over the native American archaeological record in the United States (Trigger 1980; 1985; McGuire 1992; Klesert and Powell 1993). The intellectual roots of this trend of analysis stem from several sources, including Neo-Marxist scholarship (Althusser 1971), critical theory (Geuss 1981), literary criticism and folklore studies (Landau 1991), and the general realization that much of our perceived knowledge of the world's cultural heritage lies within a Eurocentric frame (Wolf 1982; Bernal 1987; Amin 1989; Scarre 1990).

The political and social effects of archaeological research in Israel can be traced to the very foundations of the discipline, beginning with nineteenth-century European imperial competition for influence in the Near East (Silberman 1982) and continuing into the early twentieth century. The latter saw the rise of distinct archaeological traditions among the scholars of the Jewish community in Palestine in the context of the Zionist movement (Shavit 1987), and among American biblical scholars—led by W.F. Albright—who pioneered an approach to the excavation that stressed the historicity of the biblical record, in the context of contemporary theological debates (Dever 1993). With the establishment of the State of Israel, archaeology became both a major national undertaking and the source of rich historical imagery

(Silberman 1993; Zerubavel 1995). In recent decades, however, the various traditions have undergone far-reaching changes, with increasingly anthropological approaches gaining ground in both American and Israeli archaeological schools (Dever 1985). In addition, archaeology has taken on a new social significance among the Palestinian population of the West Bank and Gaza with the establishment of academic departments at Palestinian universities and with the establishment of an inspectorate of antiquities by the Palestinian National Authority.

At the Berman conference, the speakers who addressed issues of Israeli archaeology's political or sociological context were drawn from fields that were not strictly archaeological: literature, history, social criticism, and the history of ideas. From their external perspectives, they offered unique assessments of the social utility and impact of archaeology in the history of the State of Israel. Consciously removing themselves from a partisan polemic about the 'politicization' of the archaeology of a certain national or religious tradition, these authors recognize that all historical discourse possesses a deeper significance in the construction of modern social identities and philosophies. Though their viewpoints are diverse and, in certain cases, even contradictory, their papers form an enlightening foreword to the more specific works of archaeological research presented in the subsequent sections of this volume.

Amos Elon, whose path-breaking book *The Israelis* (1971) first highlighted the enormous power of archaeology and archaeological motifs in modern Israeli society, here paints a wise, vivid, and often poignant portrait of the role of digs and diggers in the modern Israeli consciousness. Today, nearly 25 years after his initial (and harsher) portraits of Yadin, Dayan, and the other dominating figures of Israeli society and culture, he looks back on the sweep of modern Israeli history and surveys the growth of the discipline from the earliest days of the 1920s through the high points of the 1950s to the present and comes up with the assessment that archaeology has been utilized by politicians and philosophers, but not really to the detriment of the basic objectivity of the scholars involved in research, and certainly not to a professional standard that is lower than that of other regions of the world. Looking toward the future, however, he sees public fascination with archaeology as a nostalgic frame of mind characteristic of an early period of state-building and he cautions us to remember that there are or should be timeless ideals about society and national identity that transcend archaeological ideologies.

The polemical accusation that Israeli archaeology is uniquely (and negatively) impacted by ideological factors is a subject that Professor Yaacov Shavit of Tel Aviv University addresses. As a distinguished historian, critic, and commentator on modern Israeli history and philosophy, he casts doubt on the validity of literary challenges to the 'facticity' of the biblical narrative and draws a sharp distinction between the objective value of archaeological sites for elucidating ancient Near Eastern and biblical history and their occasional utilization by nonscholars for political or ideological ends. While some might disagree with such a neat separation, Shavit suggests that would-be critics of the politics of archaeology in Israel may themselves be politically inspired, in their failure to reflect on the political aspects of other archaeologies in the region. Most important, he rejects the proposition that Israeli archaeology is in any sense monolithic and dismisses facile statements about the character and motivation of the entire discipline. Shavit insists that scholars must seek a more sophisticated reading of the interaction between artifact, tradition, and text.

In contrast to Shavit, Neil Asher Silberman sees all of archaeology as meaningful in social terms, constituting the structure of the past in both time and space, quite beyond the conscious intention of the excavator or historian. Noting the transformation in the significance of material remains in general, he argues that the subjective aspect is not always separable from the objective—from validation of European empires in the Middle East to the construction of Israeli and Palestinian national identity. Additionally, he suggests that worldwide trends of tourism and economics may soon have far-reaching implications for the shaping of the past in both public and academic spheres.

Professor Burke Long of Bowdoin College examines the theoretical and philosophical underpinnings of the work of the most important American exponent of traditional 'biblical archaeology', William Foxwell Albright. His analysis focuses on Albright's underlying mental structures and his concept of the essence of human cognition, that is, his scheme of hierarchies of thought and the median 'missing link' between savage and fully rational. As Long argues, Albright saw biblical (i.e., Jewish) thought as empirical and therefore an advance over the 'pre-logical' savages, but still far less than 'Western'. In Christianity, Long suggests, Albright saw the most sublime cognitive expression. Albright further held that archaeology's role was to illustrate this evolution, rather than to supply evidence for a possible alternative cognitive progression. No less important to Long's mind is the lingering impact of Albright's intellectual rationalization for the implicit superiority of Christian European culture which masquerades as modern scientism.

Peoples and Cultures of Ancient Israel: Recent Archaeological Discoveries

The ideological-critical analysis of scientific research is not the only or even the major trend in Israeli archaeology or historical studies today. A major session of the Berman conference was devoted to presenting the results of some of the major archaeological excavations underway under the auspices of the Philip and Muruel Berman Center for Biblical Archaeology in Jerusalem. Thus, in studies of the Bronze Age city-state society in Canaan, in the creation of a distinct Philistine polity in the Early Iron Age, and in the case study of Phoenician coastal culture, some of the basic questions of social complexity, ethnogenesis, and interaction of material culture with the abundant historic texts were addressed.

Professor Trude Dothan of the Hebrew University presented the results of the important new excavations at Tel Miqne, a site identified with the ancient Philistine city of Ekron. In fact, this site has proved to be the richest of all the early Philistine sites so far examined, in terms of the quantity of its own material culture as well as its clear connections to the material culture of the Aegean world. This evidence offers a new perspective on the beginnings of Philistine settlement, a historical phenomenon which was to have such a lasting effect on the settlement history of the southern coastal plain. At this site, the earliest states of Philistine presence are represented by an abundant quantity of Mycenaean IIIC:1b pottery, workshops, crafts, and characteristic hearths—which Dothan argues are all manifestations of an initial state of the transference of Aegean culture to the region, a culture that only gradually became acculturated to the neighboring societies of the Middle East.

The ancient Canaanite city-state of Hazor, known as 'head of all those kingdoms' in the book of Joshua, is both an important archaeological site and a landmark in the history of Israeli archaeology. Excavations at the site, now conducted as a memorial to Professor Yigael Yadin, who first directed the James de Rothschild expedition there from 1955 to 1958, are being carried out under the direction of Professor Amnon Ben-Tor of the Hebrew University. In his account of the renewed Hazor excavations, Ben-Tor describes the beginning of a new era in the study of the site, with the formulation of new research methods and priorities. Although the excavations are still at too early a stage to make final comparisons between the current excavations and their predecessors, Ben-Tor suggests that Yadin's Iron Age stratigraphy has been essentially validated through the connection of the casemate wall with the 'Solomonic' gate. Most exciting is the exploration of the Middle and Late Bronze Age palace complexes in area A, where the preliminary indications of the presence of a cuneiform archive lend hopes for a sudden and dramatic advance in reconstructing Canaanite economy and history before the Israelite settlement.

Professor Ephraim Stern of the Hebrew University presents important findings from the large-scale excavations at the major coastal site of Dor, which he has directed since 1980. Briefly excavated by the British School of Archaeology in Jerusalem in the 1920s, Dor's stratified levels from the Middle Bronze Age to the end of the Roman period are now providing important new details on the rise and development of maritime culture and commerce along the Mediterranean coast of Israel. Current evidence points to extensive cultural contact with the Aegean world and the apparent conquest and settlement by the Sea People known as the Sikils (mentioned in the eleventh-century BCE Egyptian chronicle of the Travels of Wen-Amun). Equally important is the evidence recovered from the Dor excavations pertaining to the early stages of Phoenician culture and its links with Cyprus, the resumption of direct communication between the Levant and the Greek world (particularly Corinth and east Greece) in the Iron Age, and the establishment of an apparent Athenian commercial monopoly. An unprecedented wealth of Greek finds and an orthogonal city plan established in the Hellenistic period offer evidence of Dor's urban continuity from the Persian to the Roman periods.

Another important site now being re-excavated is biblical Beth Shean/classical Nysa-Scythopolis, in a massive joint project of the Hebrew University and the Israel Antiquities Authority. The excavation of the Bronze and Iron Age tell and the the preclassical remains in the center of the city is being directed by Professor Amihai Mazar of the Hebrew University. Mazar here offers his preliminary findings, beginning with evidence for the rise of complex society in the northern Jordan Valley in the Early Bronze Age II and the subsequent arrival of northern immigrants with a distinctive material culture marked by Khirbet Kerak ware toward the end of the third millennium. Though it seems that the site was only modestly occupied in the Middle Bronze Age, it was dominated by a complex of important religious structures in the Late Bronze. Mazar suggests that the appearance of imported Mycenaean IIIC:1b pottery at the site is historically linked with the establishment of an Egyptian garrison of the Twentieth Dynasty in the twelfth century BCE. The destruction of that garrison was followed by a return to Canaanite occupation.

The Archaeology and Social History of the Second Temple and Rabbinic Periods

The archaeological investigation of the Hellenistic, Roman, and Byzantine periods, though carried out at many of the same sites and with similar techniques as the archaeology of the biblical periods, is often pursued as a distinctive discipline in Israel. Indeed, there is often a sharp division in programs of academic study in universities in Israel, Europe, and America between those dealing with the prehistoric, Bronze, and Iron Ages, and those concerned with the archaeology of the Hellenistic, Roman, and Byzantine periods (cf. the chronological boundaries of such standard textbooks as Mazar 1990 and Ben-Tor 1992). A major focus of research in the Second Temple and rabbinic periods has long been on art historical and architectural questions (as has also been the case with the archaeology of the classical periods in Italy, Greece, and Asia Minor, cf. Morris 1994 and Greene 1986), but with the increasing use of rabbinic sources and social-scientific approaches to reconstruct the spiritual and communal life of the Jews of Roman Palestine, scholars are now coming to question some interpretative categories that have been standard in the field, namely religious orthodoxy and ethnic identity. Though the future scholarly consensus on these matters is far from settled, the papers here offer some exciting new perspectives.

Surveying the history of archaeological research on synagogues since the turn of the century, Professor Lee Levine of the Hebrew University reflects on the areas in which there have been important advances in understanding the nature of Jewish history. He focuses on the increasing evidence for an intensive Jewish occupation in the Golan and southern-most Judea, areas long considered outside the core of Jewish settlement in this period. He also deals with the thorny problem of chronology, with the apparent preponderance of synagogues beginning in the third century and continuing strongly in succeeding periods. Levine also highlights the important evidence for the heterogeneity of Jewish culture in this period, which may reflect either regional traditions or perhaps internal social divisions.

One of the most important archaeological debates on the Early Roman period is the apparent Jewish concern with purity as manifested in the material record in the form of *miqva'ot* or ritual baths. The first challenge, argues Professor Benjamin Wright of Lehigh University, is to make all conceptual premises clear. He maintains that while purity was certainly an issue in the Second Temple period, it is not at all clear that cultic or physical impurity was universally believed to be achieved through the use of ritual pools. Comparing the positions of archaeological maximalists and minimalists in assessing the wide variety of plastered pools found in excavations, Wright argues that some must be understood in the context of wider Mediterranean bathing customs. He suggests further that this conceptual indeterminacy requires grappling with the question of 'normative' Jewish practices in the period, which has long been accepted without serious consideration of the diversity of both practice and expression in the material record.

Archaeology and Ethnicity: Peoples of Ancient Canaan/Israel

The question of group identification and, in particular, ethnicity has been the subject of a recent surge of interest in cultural studies (Williams 1989; R. Cohen 1978; Comaroff and Comaroff 1992; Eriksen 1993). These recent studies have moved away from an initial matching of ethnic identification with discrete groups and constellations of material culture styles to an appreciation that ethnicity is not a static concept, but created and constantly renegotiated within specific social contexts and survival strategies. Some scholars, such as Shennan (1989), Baldwin (1987), and Whitefield (1987), have looked into the problematic issue of how ethnic groups might be identified within the archaeological record and others (Pollard 1994; Brumfiel 1989; Brumfiel 1994) have concentrated on the strategic creation of ethnicity in the development of complex societies.

In the case of the archaeology of Israel, the connection between material culture and ethnic self-identification has often centered around the prominent role accorded to ethnic groups in the Bible and other ancient Near Eastern literature. Whether referring to Egyptians, Philistines, Hittites, Phoenicians, Canaanites, or Israelites, the ancient literary references have long been regarded as representing a normative picture of social identities, against which archaeological material is often arranged. Focusing on the search for the emergence of the early Israelites, the following contributors have highlighted important historical and methodological questions in presenting the study of ethnicity in the early stages of Israelite settlement. They further argue that these studies can supply compelling case studies for research into the archaeological identification of ethnicity all over the world.

Professor Israel Finkelstein of Tel Aviv University, whose regional surveys of the traditional tribal territory of Ephraim and whose excavations at the sites of Izbet Sartah and Shiloh have contributed significantly to the modern understanding of the Israelite settlement, offers some cautionary observations about making simple correlations between material culture traits and ethnicity—Israelite or otherwise. Noting that recent sociological and anthropological studies have stressed the fluidity and subjective quality of ethnic identifications, Finkelstein further observes how many of the artifact types long associated with the Israelites are distributed far beyond their purported area of settlement, echoing an earlier argument by Hodder (1982), whose ethnoarchaeological research demonstrated how some of the same items of material culture can be used in different social strategies by spatially separated groups. He suggests that many such artifact types can be far more easily associated with specialized function or trade connections, and concludes that perhaps only the subtle evidence of food taboos (and the characteristic belief system that motivates them) may offer sufficient archaeological grounds for the legitimate identification of ethnicity.

Indeed the issue of food taboos is precisely that which Drs Brian Hesse and Paula Wapnish of the University of Alabama, internationally recognized specialists in the analysis of ancient faunal remains, discuss in detail. Reviewing the evidence of the occurrence of pig bones at sites throughout the ancient Near East, they offer a series of cautious generalizations about swine production in the ancient world. Stressing contexts, contrasts, and social tendencies, they set forth parameters including climate, population density, agricultural methods, and economic class that would tend to make pork eating more or less practised among ancient social groups. Thus they urge that archaeologists utilize evidence for this particular food use (or taboo) not as a simple indicator of historically recorded ethnicity but as an index of a group's position within a complex social context.

This was a theme echoed by Professor David B. Small of Lehigh

University, who adopts a cross-cultural perspective in assessing the role of ethnicity in the rise of early Israel. Stressing a distinction between the anthropological understandings of ethnicity and totemism, Small joins Finkelstein and Hesse and Wapnish in challenging conventional group identification through classes of characteristic artifacts. He maintains that it is much more important to recognize various economic and social interactions as being the source of constellations of material culture traits, which may then be used in the construction of ethnic identity. In reviewing comparative archaeological evidence from Mesoamerica, Small highlights the common manipulation of ethnicity in state formation and strategies of economic domination. He points out that in contrast to Mesoamerican polities, the Israelite monarchy showed an apparent lack of strong ethnic constructions, providing a useful example for cross-cultural studies of the creation of ethnicity in archaic state formations.

Imagining the Past:
The Bible, Israelite History, and Archaeological Research

The discussion of research methodology in effectively combining archaeological and textual data has attracted recent interest among archaeologists and historians in several different areas of study (Small 1995; Little 1992; Beaudry 1988; Leone and Potter 1988). In the archaeology of ancient Israel, the Bible is obviously one of the chief textual sources of historical information about Late Bronze and Iron Age history of the land of Israel. Its tremendous impact upon archaeology in reconstructing Israel's past has been of considerable concern to archaeologists as well as historians (e.g., Dever 1990; Thompson 1992). The concluding contributors address what has long been the central concern of archaeology in Israel: the legitimate use of biblical literature in reconstructing ancient remains, and, conversely, the extent to which archaeological discoveries expand our understanding of the biblical narrative. Although the impact of a processually based archaeology has profoundly altered this orientation in the last two decades, with increasing interest displayed in purely economic, environmental, and demographic aspects of historic and prehistoric society in the land of Israel, the literary, religious, and historical (i.e., the nonfunctional) aspects of ancient society are finding legitimacy once again.

Professor William G. Dever of the University of Arizona has been one of the pioneers and leaders in the recent theoretical development of archaeology in Israel, and has expressed strong opinions on the effective combination of texts and archaeology (1972; 1990). In his paper he examines recent scholarly attitudes toward the possibility of reconstructing the history of ancient Israel and the role that archaeology may play in its coming years. Dever dismisses the value of what he describes as an exhausted philologically based approach to the biblical text. This has descended into historicist nihilism and the demise of Old Testament theology, which in its essential Christian context denies central importance to the history of Israel as a phenomenon independent of the ministry of Jesus. He instead calls for a new approach, with new questions to be answered. Basically he argues that the historical dimension of the study of ancient Israel must be asserted, and while late redactions and interpolations in the biblical text must be recognized, they do not preclude the existence of a genuine historical core. Eschewing calls for a non-textual history of Israel, Dever insists that approach to Syro-Palestinian archaeology is multifaceted, or, as he claims, Syro-Palestinian archaeology is 'history or nothing'. Archaeology, Dever maintains, can offer a broad historical perspective and it must be sensitively read with the texts, not shaped to conform with either artificial models or modern theology.

In the final paper presented at the Berman conference, Professor Baruch Halpern of Pennsylvania State University questions the conventional bases of biblical archaeology—both textual and archaeological. Halpern follows current arguments that archaeological and textual information must be recognized as stemming from independent sources (Carmack and Weeks 1981; Leone, Potter and Shackel 1987; Leone and Potter 1988; Small 1995; Kosso 1995), noting the differences and intellectual pitfalls of these two distinct academic 'cultures'. Applying himself to the specific question of the historicity of the biblical accounts of the united monarchy, Halpern suggests that the story is simply too detailed, too chaotic, and too implicitly political to have been an ideological construct, as some now argue. The vivid and often seamy tales of dynastic intrigues and political murders are, to Halpern's mind, reflections of an unfolding historical reality, not mythological creations dreamed up after the fact. What is needed, he concludes, is a sensitive and creative recognition by scholars of the tension between literary and archaeological evidence. These two sources of historical evidence contain different kinds of messages and it is only in seeing their interplay (rather than forcing them into strict conformity) that we may be able to gain a more enlightening understanding of the early history of Israel.

As readers of this volume will see, the Berman conference featured a wide variety of scholarly viewpoints. The papers collected here offer a cross-section of the current developments in the archaeology of Israel rather than a representative selection of a particular school of thought. As research continues in Israel in the coming years, with ever-greater contact and discussion between archaeologists working throughout the entire Middle East and Mediterranean basin, it is to be hoped that the diversity of perspectives will continue to grow and enrich the modern understandings of ancient culture and society. In that respect, this discussion of the construction of the past, both in theory and practice, must be regarded as only a first step to an ever-greater dialogue between archaeologists, historians, and biblical scholars in their quest for ever more sophisticated understandings of the mechanics and meaning of human culture in the land of Israel.

BIBLIOGRAPHY

Althusser, L.
1971   'Ideology and Ideological State Apparatuses', in *Lenin and Philosophy* (trans. Ben Brester; New York: Monthly Review Press).
Amin, S.
1989   *Eurocentrism* (New York: Monthly Review Press).
Auger, R. *et al.* (eds.)
1987   *Ethnicity and Culture* (Calgary: University of Calgary).
Baldwin, S.
1987   'Roomsize Patterns: A Quantitative Method for Approaching Ethnic Identification in Architecture', in Auger *et al.* (eds.) 1987: 163-74.
Beaudry, M. (ed.)
1988   *Documentary Archaeology in the New World* (Cambridge: Cambridge University Press).
Ben-Tor, A. (ed.)
1992   *The Archaeology of Ancient Israel* (trans. R. Greenberg; New Haven: Yale University Press).
Bernal, M.
1987   *Black Athena. I. The Fabrication of Ancient Greece 1785–1985* (New Brunswick, NJ: Rutgers University Press).
Brumfiel, E.
1989   'Factional Competition in Complex Society', in *Domination and Resistance* (ed. Daniel Miller and Michael Rowlands; London: Unwin Hyman): 127-39.

1994   'Ethnic Groups and Political Development in Ancient Mexico', in *idem*, *Factional Competition and Political Development in the New World* (Cambridge: Cambridge University Press): 89-102.

Carmack, R., and J. Weeks
1981   'The Archaeology and Ethnohistory of Utatlan: A Conjunctive Approach', *American Antiquity* 46: 323-41.

Childe, V.G.
1933   'Is Prehistory Practical?', *Antiquity* 7: 410-18.
1934   'Anthropology and Herr Hitler', *Discovery* (March): 65-68.

Cohen, R.
1978   'Ethnicity: Problem and Focus in Anthropology', *Annual Review of Anthropology* 7: 379-403.

Comaroff, J., and J. Comaroff
1992   *Ethnography and the Historical Imagination* (Boulder: Westview Press).

Dever, W.
1972   *Archaeology and Biblical Studies: Retrospects and Prospects* (Evanston: Seabury-Western Theological Seminary).
1985   'Syro-Palestinian and Biblical Archaeology', in *The Hebrew Bible and its Modern Interpreters* (ed. D.A. Knight and G.M. Tucker; Philadelphia: Fortress Press): 31-74.
1990   'Artifacts, Ecology, Texts, and the Bible', in *Recent Archaeological Discoveries and Biblical Research* (Seattle: University of Washington Press): 3-36.
1993   'What Remains of the House that Albright Built?', *BA* 56: 25-35.

Elon, A.
1971   *The Israelis: Founders and Sons* (New York: Holt, Rinehart, and Winston).

Eriksen, T.
1993   *Ethnicity and Nationalism: Anthropological Perspectives* (London: Pluto Press).

Fowler, D.D.
1987   'The Uses of the Past: Archaeology in the Service of the State', *American Antiquity* 52: 229-48.

Friedman, J.
1992   'The Past in the Future: History and the Politics of Identity', *American Anthropologist* 94: 837-59.

Gathercole, P., and D. Lowenthal (eds.)
1990   *The Politics of the Past* (London: Unwin Hyman).

Geuss, R.
1981   *The Idea of a Critical Theory* (Cambridge: Cambridge University Press).

Greene, K.
1986   *The Archaeology of the Roman Economy* (Berkeley, CA: University of California Press).

Hall, M.
1984   'The Burden of Tribalism: The Social Context of Southern African Iron Age Studies', *American Antiquity* 49: 455-67.

Hodder, I.
1982   *Symbols in Action* (Cambridge: Cambridge University Press).
Klesert, A. and S. Powell
1993   'A Perspective on Ethics and the Reburial Controversy', *American Antiquity* 58: 348-54.
Kohl, P.L., and C. Fawcett
1995   *Nationalism, Politics, and the Practice of Archaeology* (Cambridge: Cambridge University Press).
Kosso, P.
1995   Epistemic Independence between Textual and Material Evidence', in *Methods in the Mediterranean: Historical and Archaeological Views on Texts and Archaeology* (ed. D. Small; Leiden: Brill): 177-96.
Landau, M.
1991   *Narratives of Human Evolution* (New Haven: Yale University Press).
Leone, M., and P. Potter
1988   'Issues in Historical Archaeology', in *The Recovery of Meaning* (ed. Mark Leone and Parker Potter Jr; Washington: Smithsonian Institution Press): 1-23.
Leone, M., P. Potter, and P. Shackel
1987   'Toward a Critical Archaeology', *Current Anthropology* 28: 283-302.
Little, B. (ed.)
1992   *Text-aided Archaeology* (Ann Arbor: CRC Press).
Lowenthal, D.
1985   *The Past is a Foreign Country* (Cambridge: Cambridge University Press).
McGuire, R.
1992   'Archaeology and the First Americans', *American Anthropologist* 94: 816-36.
Mazar, A.
1990   *Archaeology of the Land of the Bible* (New York: Doubleday).
Morris, I.
1994   *Classical Greece: Ancient Histories and Modern Archaeologies* (Cambridge: Cambridge University Press).
Patterson, T.
1995   *Toward a Social History of Archaeology in the United States* (Fort Worth, TX: Harcourt Brace).
Pollard, H.
1994   'Ethnicity and Political Control in a Complex Society: the Tarascan State of Prehispanic Mexico', in *Factional Competition and Political Development in the New World* (ed. Elizabeth Brumfiel; Cambridge: Cambridge University Press): 79-88.
Scarre, C.
1990   'The Western World View in Archaeological Atlases', in *The Politics of the Past* (ed. P. Gathercole and D. Lowenthal; London: Unwin Hyman): 11-17.

Shavit, Y.
 1987 'The Truth Shall Spring Out of the Earth': The Development of Jewish Popular Interest in Archaeology in Eretz-Israel', *Cathedra* 44: 27-54 (Hebrew).

Shennan, S.
 1989 'Introduction: Archaeological Approaches to Cultural Identity', in *Archaeological Approaches to Cultural Identity* (ed. S. Shennan; London: Unwin Hyman): 1-31.

Silberman, N.A.
 1982 *Digging for God and Country* (New York: Alfred A. Knopf).
 1993 *A Prophet from Amongst You: The Life of Yigael Yadin* (Reading, MA: Addison-Wesley).

Small, D. (ed.)
 1995 *Methods in the Mediterranean: Historical and Archaeological Views on Texts and Archaeology* (Leiden: Brill).

Thompson, T.
 1992 *Early History of the Israelite People from the Written and Archaeological Sources* (Leiden: Brill).

Trigger, B.
 1980 'Archaeology and the Image of the American Indian', *American Antiquity* 45: 662-76.
 1984 'Alternative Archaeologies: Nationalist, Colonialist, Imperialist', *Man* 19: 355-70.
 1985 'The Past and Power: Anthropology and the North American Indian', in *Who Owns the Past?* (ed. I. McBridge: Oxford: Oxford University Press): 49-74.

Whitefield, D.
 1987 'History, Ethnography and Class Struggle', in Auger *et al.* (eds.) 1987: 5-14.

Williams, B.
 1989 'A Class Act: Anthropology and the Race to Nation across Ethnic Terrain', *Annual Review of Anthropology* 18: 401-44.

Wolf, E.
 1982 *Europe and the People without History* (Berkeley, CA: University of California Press).

Zerubavel, Y.
 1995 *Recovered Roots: Collective Memory and the Making of Israeli National Tradition* (Chicago: University of Chicago Press).

ARCHAEOLOGY, CONTEMPORARY CULTURE,
AND IDEOLOGICAL DISCOURSE

POLITICS AND ARCHAEOLOGY

Amos Elon

A story is told of some early Zionist pioneers of Beit Alpha, a communal settlement in the Esdraelon Valley. The settlement was founded in the early twenties by young men and women belonging to the socialist youth movement *Hashomer Hatzair* (Young Guard). They subscribed to a bizarre combination of utopian Marxism, Freudian psychoanalysis, and the then-fashionable German *Jugendkultur*, with its romantic worship of nature, cult of eroticism, and disdain for bourgeois values. In December 1928, some of them were digging an irrigation channel and suddenly struck the brilliantly colored mosaic of a sixth-century Jewish synagogue. Their first reaction was to keep the discovery secret, and possibly cover it up again—a natural impulse, perhaps, that field archaeologists often encounter. The main concern, after all, had been to dig an irrigation channel. The unexpected discovery complicated this task and threatened to hold it up, perhaps indefinitely.

But there was more to it: an antireligious attitude. The young kibbutzniks, full of the fervor of Russian radicalism, had only a year or two earlier come out of Eastern Europe with—as the saying went at the time—'no clothes, but with copies of *Das Kapital* and Freud's *Interpretation of Dreams* in their knapsacks'. A few were still teenagers. Others were in open rebellion against their Orthodox religious fathers. Some had actually run away from home to help build socialism and create the 'new Jew' in the historic land of their forefathers: a utopian community not unlike those of the late 1960s in which their identity would be redefined and based on socialism and love. Religion was the opium of the people. For this reason alone, it might be best if the synagogue mosaic were covered up again. Others argued that the mosaic was not necessarily religious but rather political, a Zionist monument. It was important, so the argument went, to uphold every archaeological remnant that testified to the Jewish presence in the land, and confirmed the legitimacy of the Zionist claim. A debate took place. The conserva-tionist view prevailed over the iconoclastic.

The story may be apocryphal but it sums up, as such stories some-times do, the central facts of the case. A Jewish archaeologist, Eliezer Lipa Sukenik (the father of Yigael Yadin), was consulted. He proposed to conduct a scientific excavation of the site. It would be his first. Sukenik, formerly a high school teacher of mathematics and geography in Jerusalem, had spent a year studying archaeology at the University of Berlin at a time when the leading archaeologists and ethnologists at that university were obsessed with *Volk* and other ethnocentric prejudice. He never graduated in Berlin. His great ambition was the creation of a 'Jewish archaeology'. His view of history was narrowly Zionist or, if you like, Hegelian. He thought he recognized its spirit in Jewish longings for Zion throughout the ages. In his view Jewish history during the past eighteen centuries was only an insignificant interval between national independence lost in the first century and national independence to be regained in the twentieth. Sukenik lectured the young kibbutzniks on Jewish history, modern archaeology, and memory. Jews were a com-munity of memory. In his enthusiasm for digging up remnants and relics of the glorious Jewish past, he won over most of the kibbutzniks, who until that moment had been less interested in digging up the past than in building a utopian future. The site was solemnly excavated to much acclaim throughout the Jewish world. A story in *The New York Times* reported that Jewish workers in Palestine were excavating Jewish history—in the Holy Land.

It was probably no accident that this first recorded outbreak of a popular passion for Jewish archaeology occurred at a time of relatively low morale among the settlers, owing to the economic crisis and the mounting Arab opposition to Jewish settlement. Among the more sensi-tive pioneers there might even have been something like nagging guilt at being intruders in a country populated by another people that bitterly resented their arrival. For them, Sukenik's Jewish archaeology had a kind of cathartic effect. Word of Sukenik's dig at Beit Alpha spread quickly. Volunteers streamed to Beit Alpha to work on the dig. The richly colored mosaic was uncovered in a remarkably good state of preservation. It included not only Hebrew inscriptions and common Jewish religious symbols but also a surprising representation of Helios, the pagan Greek sun god—highlighting the eclectic nature of Jewish religious worship at that time.

Contemporary reports stress the festive atmosphere among the participants at the dig. Reading these accounts today you get the feeling they were participating in a kind of communion. By digging up the hard ground they were retrieving memory—one is tempted to say—as though they were recovering checked baggage from a storage room.

Sukenik later recalled the event in glowing terms:

> Suddenly people could see things that had never been so tangible before... There was a feeling that this piece of ground, for which people had suffered so much, wasn't just any plot of land but a piece of earth where their forefathers had lived fifteen hundred to two thousand years ago. Their work in the present was cast in a different light. Their history was revealed to them and they saw it with their own eyes (quoted in Silberman 1993: 26).

The enthusiasm at Beit Alpha, from all we know, was unprecedented in the history of the Zionist enterprise. Earlier pioneers—in the first and second wave of immigration—had barely been moved by the charm of antique sites or objects. They felt little need for buried proofs of the past to uphold their claims of the present. Self-conscious about their historic roles, many of them were men of letters, inveterate diarists, polemicists, endlessly writing editorials, manifestos, essays, and pamphlets. It was said of the men and women of the second wave that never was so much written about so many subjects by so few in so short a time. Yet even though their first years in Israel coincided with the first great excavations of important biblical sites by leading Protestant archaeologists, including Sir William Sellin, Sir Flinders Petrie, and R.A.S. Macalister, in their extensive writings there is hardly a word to suggest that any discoveries touched them even peripherally. The sudden outbreak of enthusiasm for Jewish archaeology at Beit Alpha in 1928 was unique. It anticipated the fervor of future years, and the political uses of archaeology in what was later hailed—or decried—as a 'national syndrome': a popular craze for archaeology, a *bulmus* in Hebrew. *Bulmus* is an old Talmudic term. It denotes a fit, a rage, a craze, a mania, a ravenous hunger resulting from prolonged fasting.

Archaeology often converged with nationalism in the new nation-states created in Europe after the Great War, but perhaps nowhere else did archaeology loom so large, or for so long, as in Israeli life until the early seventies. In Czechoslovakia, Turkey, Finland, Poland, and the Baltic states, archaeology was used politically to provide and occasionally fabricate material evidence of unbroken historical continuity. And let us not forget the Byzantine Queen Helena. I remember the late Yigael Yadin once calling her, a little wistfully perhaps, 'the most successful archaeologist in history'. Whatever she looked for she promptly found hundreds of years after the event: the stable where Mary had given birth to Christ, the twelve stations of the cross, Calvary, the true cross, the nails, the lancet, the Holy Sepulchre, and so on and on. In our own time we have seen elaborate celebrations at Persepolis staged by the Shah, a few years before his fall, to commemorate the 2500th anniversary of 'his' empire. In Iraq, Saddam Hussein proclaims himself a worthy successor of the ancient Babylonians. The Serbs venerate Kosovo, which, like Masada, is not the site of a victory but of a defeat.

Archaeological finds have inspired nearly all the Israeli national symbols, from the State Seal to medals and coins and postage stamps. (Walter Benjamin claimed that postage stamps were the visiting cards left by governments in children's playrooms.) Since independence, Israeli coins have been stamped with motifs copied from first-century Jewish silver shekels. (Many years ago I remember seeing in the shop window of an antique dealer on Allenby Road in Tel Aviv a display that attracted some attention: a few modern Israeli coins were placed there in a row next to the ancient Jewish coins that had inspired them. It was obvious to anyone looking that the ancient coins were considerably more accomplished and more beautiful in design, more aesthetic generally, than those of the modern.) And I remember a television interview with Prime Minister Menachem Begin at the peak point of hyperinflation in Israel in 1980 when a pack of cigarettes cost in the thousands, and cash registers could no longer cope with so many digits, and the economy was grinding to a halt because of a sudden drop in investments. Begin was expected to announce cuts in public spending, a wage-and-price freeze, and other anti-inflation measures. He didn't. He only proclaimed that the name of the monetary unit would be changed from the foreign name *lira* (i.e., 'pound') to shekel, a Hebrew name of ancient renown that by its historic weight alone, as Begin put it, would make it one of the world's hard currencies on par with the American dollar.

How did all this come about? In the years of struggle leading up to the establishment of the new state and during its first two decades or so, the cult of archaeological relics did much to determine the direction of Israeli culture. It was widely thought to provide an immigrant society with a common culture. There was, of course, also a calculated effort at public relations aimed at Bible-minded Gentile customers abroad. In a deeper sense, however, the apparent obsession with ancient Jewish sites and artifacts grew out of the feverish search for identity—a secular identity—which was characteristic of that period. The Dead Sea Scrolls thrilled *secular* Israelis; most Orthodox Jews were and still are indifferent to them. In the ethnocentric atmosphere of these early years there was a rush to identify Jewish sites, an overemphasis on digging them up, and a tendency to expose to public view the Jewish strata of a site even where other layers may have been historically or artistically more significant or revealing. The task of archaeology was to prove a point about Jews in the Holy Land and not always, as it probably should have been, to explore material remains in order to determine the circumstances of ancient cultures and civilizations in a country where they have been so varied and so many. There was even a somewhat comic attempt, fortunately short-lived, by the then director of antiquities to impose a nationalistic nomenclature. He asked that the Iron Age be referred to henceforth as the Israelite period, the Hellenistic as Hasmonean, the Roman as the Mishnaic, and the Byzantine as the Talmudic periods.

In our own time, a new post-Zionist generation of younger archaeologists has come to question the patriotic oversell and single-mindedness of their predecessors, their arbitrary choice of terms of subjects of study, their seeming haste, occasionally, to identify this or that site as unfailingly Jewish on the basis of partial or insufficient evidence. There is even a movement to discard the very term 'biblical archaeology' as a misleading and ethnocentric term. This is, perhaps, as it should be. And yet mistakes in attribution are common in art, too. The big question we must always ask is, Was the mistake caused by ideology? Excessive claims are also made in physics and in all other exact sciences. They are often made in order to raise money to support further research. In the philosophy of science it is common to distinguish between contexts of discovery and justification. We all have the right to pursue what we want to pursue, and to explore the buried past and eventually dig it up—the discovery. That we do so may be a personal or even a nationalistic choice or prejudice. But making a choice as a result of personal interest or ideology is common and natural in every field and as such is not objectionable. The problem arises when the justification or proof of our discovery is prompted not by evidence but by ideology. I may decide to study the history of my own family rather than that of someone else. But I may present my grandmother as a Balkan princess only if I can provide exact and irrefutable proof.

To judge them on this basis, I should say, most Israeli archaeologists, even of the early period, come out rather well. They were digging not only for knowledge but for the reassurance of roots, which they found in the Israelite ruins scattered throughout the country. They may have been prejudiced in their choice of study but not, in most cases, in their analysis of the results. They oversold their discoveries as other scientists do. The difference lay in the effects of their work on the culture as a whole, and in the manner in which its results were heralded in the press and on television, adopted by patriotic fan clubs, and popularized by eager schoolteachers, nationalist historians, tour guides, Bible nuts, youth leaders, and politicians. I am not saying that the archaeologists themselves had nothing to do with this manipulation. I am suggesting that their role in it was minor in comparison to, say, the powerful lobby of elementary and high school Bible teachers.

There were political and, I assume, psychological reasons why Israeli archaeology had at that time a distinctive, even chauvinistic, air. Several amateur archaeologists among the generals and the politicians imbued archaeological discoveries with a current 'meaning'. Moses Finley, reviewing Yadin's book on Masada in 1966, suggested that there was 'a large and interesting book to be written about the politics of modern archaeology in which Masada will be a centerpiece'. This has now been done by Neil Asher Silberman in his very revealing biography of Yadin, *'A Prophet from Amongst You'—The Life of Yigael Yadin: Soldier, Scholar and Mythmaker of Modern Israel* (1993). As Silberman puts it, very succinctly I think, under Yadin archaeology in Israel was not strictly an academic activity but 'a tangible means of communion between the people and the land'. The religious term *communion* is very well chosen here. Yadin himself often suggested that for young Israelis a 'faith' in history and archaeology was a kind of 'religion'. Its high priests were schoolteachers, youth leaders, and army education officers. They and the mass media combined to give archaeology—a certain kind of archaeology—a cultic aspect, and a prominence it never had, as far as I know, in another culture.

As Silberman writes, archaeological discoveries of ancient Jewish sites offered 'poetic validation for modern Jewish settlement. Artifacts came to possess the power of sacred relics in a new cult of veneration for the ancestors' (1993: 238). Now Yadin was certainly a very serious scientist. I am told that in his archaeological digs he followed the strictest scientific rules. And he kept insisting that archaeology and politics must be scrupulously kept apart. Yet, as Silberman shows, there was always an extrascientific message afterward, in the oversell.

He notes Yadin's reluctance or inability to define precisely the modern significance of Masada, if there was one. This is only partly true. Yadin initiated the practice of swearing in troops on the top of Masada. He attended these bizarre ceremonies himself. In one often-quoted speech he told the young recruits during the ceremony:

> When Napoleon and his troops stood by the pyramids of Egypt he told them that four thousand years of history were looking down on them. What would he not have given to be able to say: Four thousand years of *your own* history look down on you... The echo of your oath this night will resound throughout the encampments of our foes. Its significance is not less powerful than that of all our defensive armaments (quoted in Elon 1971).

In his 1957 book *The Message of the Scrolls* Yadin gave a special symbolic meaning to the date on which his late father had purchased the first of the Dead Sea Scrolls—

> ...at the (very) moment of the creation of the state of Israel. It is as if these manuscripts had been waiting in caves for two thousand years, ever since the destruction of Israel's independence until the people of Israel returned to their home and regained their freedom. The symbolism is heightened by the fact that the first three scrolls were brought to my father for Israel on 29 November 1947 the very day the United Nations voted for the re-creation of a Jewish state in Israel after two thousand years.

He had, when he spoke, the rare knack for drama that allows some men to endow dumb stones with the quality of speech. Speak they did in his hands, on his lecture tours through five continents, where he did more for Israel than all its hack government propagandists put together; and, in Israel, on a highly successful TV quiz program on archaeology that he hosted for two years every fortnight. After finding a series of ancient papyri in a Judean desert cave, including dispatches from Bar Kokhba, the fabled leader of the last Jewish uprising against the Romans in 120 CE, he arranged for the entire government to assemble at President Ben Zvi's residence without, however, giving them notice of what he had unearthed. At one point he turned to the President and announced, 'Excellency, Mr President of the State of Israel. I have the honor to present to you letters dispatched by the last president of the state of Israel: Bar Kokhba'. The event, if I remember correctly, was broadcast live on radio.

I remember hearing Yadin argue, on one private occasion, that he could not be held responsible for the immense publicity emanating from his digs, or for the popular message of Masada that had registered so powerfully and on occasion incorrectly in the public mind ('the Masada Complex'). It is also true that he never conducted excavations in the occupied territories, or even in East Jerusalem, as he might have done after 1967. Moreover, after 1967 he publicly decried the spreading worship of national and religious relics as an 'idolatrous' practice. Judaism was an abstract religion, he claimed, not given to the worship of saints and dead stones. And he ridiculed those who in 1968 had forced their way into the Muslim mosque within the cave of the Makhpela at Hebron, where Abraham, Isaac, Jacob, and their spouses are supposed to be buried, and had turned parts of the mosque into a Jewish synagogue. (The awful massacre took place there in 1994.) He mocked the entire idea and the worshipers too, and claimed he did not see why they were making so much fuss over the tombs of a couple of Arab sheiks.

He demonstratively refused to attend the bizarre state funeral Prime Minister Begin staged before television cameras for some obscure bones that had been found 20 years earlier in a Judean desert cave and were said to be the remains of Bar Kokhba's heroic soldiers, who had died in battle for Israel. By then Yadin was Begin's deputy prime minister. Begin insisted on staging the event as one of great contemporary relevance. The coffin containing the bones (several were of women and children) was draped in flags and carried to a tomb on the shoulders of four generals. Yadin's protests against this kind of political theater were in vain. The images he had helped to imprint on the nation's mind had taken on a life of their own.

In the 1950s, thousands of Israelis became ardent amateur archaeologists. Archaeology—by now a national cult—became a popular movement, as well as a sport of kings: politicians, socialites, top civil servants, famous army generals were known as ardent collectors. It was a cult quite unknown in this form in other countries, a national sport almost— not a spectator sport, but an active pastime. It turned into a movement that included tens of thousands of people, as perhaps fishing or hunting or bowling does elsewhere. In many a suburban private garden, flowerpots appeared on florid ancient marble pedestals. In middle-class houses one could see sizable archaeological collections assembled in bookshelves and glass cases through purchase or illicit digging by enthusiastic amateurs.

Government attempts to curtail illegal digging in the interests of science and the public museums were half-hearted and generally futile. The best-known amateur archaeologist was General Moshe Dayan. His life-long pursuit of archaeology nearly cost him his life in 1968, when a tunnel he was digging through a wet Philistine mound near Tel Aviv collapsed and he broke several of his ribs. He was asked in an interview what exactly he had been looking for underground. His answer was, 'The ancient land of Israel. Everything that ancient Israel was. Those who lived here then... I sometimes feel I can literally enter their presence.'

Dayan was a man of great personal magnetism. Apart from his military victories, he had an enormous collection of ancient artifacts, fast cars, numerous mistresses, and a highly developed business sense. His fame vastly contributed to the popular macho appeal of archaeology as a bloodless field sport. His private collection included one of the world's largest hoards of ancient Near Eastern artifacts, some of them dug up with his own hands. The most dramatic items were sarcophagi and burial urns. Here was a man, the darling of the local and foreign electronic news, the favorite guest star of all the Barbara Walterses of the world, who in the eyes of millions had come to symbolize the sabra, the new Jew, an ancient people's newly found vitality in modern times. Yet at home he lived in a morbid decor, among his burial urns, funeral plaques, death offerings, and sarcophagi.

In the fifties and sixties, the annual conventions of the Israel Exploration Society—a get-together of patriotic Bible and geography-of-Israel teachers—were regularly attended by more than a thousand spectators. This was almost one per thousand of the total Jewish population at that time. (Imagine about 150,000 people attending a similar seminar in the United States.) Long before the cable car to the top of Masada was built, scout leaders regularly led their young followers up the steep serpentine path to spend the night there. Lit by blazing torches, the dramatic nocturnal setting on Masada—much like Barbarossa's mountain—invited mythic interpretations. Gathering around camp fires the youngsters recited the grisly tale of the mass suicide and intoned the well-known refrain of Lamdan's poem 'Masada Shall Not Fall Again'. Masada, Hatzor, and Megiddo—all excavated by Yadin and popularized thanks to his marvelous gift of communication—were part of a young person's political education at that time.

So were the Dead Sea Scrolls, displayed in the specially built 'Shrine of the Book' in the grounds of the Israel Museum in Jerusalem. Archaeology and nationalism were perfectly matched in the 'Shrine of the Book', shaped like a chapel over a round altar where the main scroll was displayed like the relic of a saint. A ten-year-old schoolboy or girl could easily read it, as guides did not fail to point out. (Can a ten-year-old in Athens or Rome read ancient Greek or Latin inscriptions? In Greece and Italy, the language is no longer the same. In Jerusalem it is.) In an immigrant country, among a hybrid people from over a hundred countries of origin, the cult of archaeology reflected an obsessive search for common roots. It also promoted a kind of historical amnesia that assured that events that had taken place two thousand years ago were grasped more vividly than anything since, until the present. Joshua Kenaz, one of Israel's foremost novelists, vividly portrayed this in his fine novel *Hitganvut Yekhidim* (Individual Stealth). Here is the monologue of Alon, a training sergeant haranguing a couple of *nebbish* recruits in an army auxiliary unit:

> Imagine a shepherd of kibbutz Megiddo with his flock of sheep on the slope of an ancient mound. He suddenly discovers a tablet. It's inscribed in cuneiform letters. He passes this on to the archaeologists. They decipher it. They discover it's part of the epic of Gilgamesh. Someone wrote it 3500 years ago... D'you understand?... Here's a tale from ancient Babylon. It's suddenly discovered here. In the Land of Israel. Next to your house. In the yard outside they discover Herod's palace. In Nahal Hever near Ein Gedi they find a cave. Close to the remains of the Roman encampments there. A cave full of skeletons. Women's and children's bones. They all starved to death during the siege. Next to them shoes. Rags of clothes. Remains of foodstuff. And the big shard of a jar with Hebrew letters. As though waiting for us. For us to come and discover it. And now it all overflows and explodes. As the earth has saved it all just for us. As our roots... It's amazing. It's not like reading about it in the Bible... These men... they were like Arik Sharon's guys... men who know every wadi and don't know what fear is...

But it wasn't all politics, of course. Archaeology was more than politics, roots, or romantic yearnings for a distant barbaric past. There was an easy attraction in archaeology: unlike other outdoor sports, it combined fresh air with bookish toil and adventure. In Tel Aviv, where I grew up, we were never more than 15 minutes away from three or four known but not yet fully excavated sites—Roman, Jewish, or Hellenistic—each of them so rich in all kinds of fantastic finds that we rarely returned from an outing without a nice coin, or a shining piece of

wonderful blue Phoenician glass, or an oil-lamp or the interesting fragment of one, or a potsherd or a lump of sculptured marble.

As we grew older, we occasionally had a sense in Israel of living inside
a time machine. The mixture of ancient and modern history, the relent-
less intensity of daily life coupled with a notion, perhaps not always quite
conscious, of a national legitimacy widely contested and by our nearest
neighbors in the region—all that was likely to reinforce a life-long fascination with antiquities of all kinds. You did not have to be an Israeli to
share in it. Edmund Wilson, who by inclination was a shrinker of myths,
succumbed to it very willingly, as his recently published diaries, *The
Sixties*, clearly show.

Later on when the Old City of Jerusalem became accessible, the
forces and physical presence of the past were so palpable that it sometimes seemed the city failed to have a present. The ancient past and the
present intersected but almost never met. Everything was tight,
crowded, old, ruined, and intertwined. Under a stone parapet placed
there by a British engineer after the First World War lies a Mamluk
doorway built over a Hasmonean tower standing on foundations from
the time of the Judean kings. A Roman arch of the first century spans
an early Jewish pavement that connects the apses of a Byzantine church
with the top of a Muslim mosque. The Western Wall, the Church of the
Holy Sepulchre, and the mosques on the ancient Temple Mount are
within a stone's throw of each other—no pun is intended here—I simply
wish to emphasize the oppressive proximity of things, the way they
overhang and overlap.

A young person growing up in this milieu would frequently hear it
said that the present in Israel reflected the distant past (and vice versa).
Ben Gurion himself drew the analogy between Joshua, conqueror of
Canaan 'in storm' (to quote Tshernichovsky's famous poem), and
General Yadin himself. Such rhetoric highlighted the mirroring of past
and present. It stressed myths and symbols. We all turn history into
myth and ritual and into symbols that give meaning to life. This is why
we celebrate birth, and have mourning rites and funerals. The rhetoric
was convoluted at times, but it had its appeal and sometimes it almost
caused the time zones to overlap, as in those historic paintings in Italy or
France where one sees Dante holding hands with Virgil, or Charlemagne
in animated conversation with Napoleon.

Today, more than a century since the beginning of the Zionist settlement, Israel is often said to be the most excavated country in the world.

Last year, according to official figures, some 250 excavations took place within Israel proper (plus over 50 in the occupied territories). And yet archaeology seems no longer so large an enterprise as it was in years past. It is no longer the popular field sport of two or three decades ago. The trend has been noticeable for some years. The great stars are gone too. There has been a dramatic decline in public interest in archaeology. The army, for reasons of economy, I am told, no longer stages spectacular swearing-in ceremonies on Masada. Native Israelis—they are the large majority now—appear to have less need to search for roots; those who do turn rather to religion. The secular majority appears self-assured enough to accept a historical compromise with the Palestinians in a pragmatic mood of post-Zionist open-mindedness.

During the past decade a younger generation of archaeologists and historians has deconstructed the Masadan myth of patriotic suicide into what might have been, at best, the calculated invention of the first-century historian Josephus Flavius, and, at worst, a senseless mass hysteria, a kind of Jewish Jamestown. (Oddly enough, this may well have been the view at the time of the Jewish religious establishment. If indeed the mass suicide had taken place at Masada, as Josephus claimed, the rabbis must have preferred to suppress all memory of it. In the vast body of rabbinic literature there isn't a word about Masada.)

In a population almost six times larger than it was in 1952 the number of those attending the annual conventions of the Israel Exploration Society is still roughly the same as it was then. University statistics indicate a parallel drop, relatively speaking, in the number of archaeology students and a truly dramatic decline in Jewish and Hebrew studies generally, from Talmud to Jewish history and Hebrew literature or language. At the Hebrew University—in the fifties the center of Jewish, Land of Israel, and related studies—504 students registered this year in the Department of Japanese and Chinese studies. Only 19 are in the Department of Talmud (one of them is a Japanese).

Peace, if it comes, will accelerate this openness. It may not necessarily bring an end to the political uses of archaeology. Following the Oslo agreement between Israel and the PLO, a first exchange of views on 'archaeology' was marked by intransigence on both sides. Israel was ready to grant the Palestinians control only over 'Muslim' or 'Arab' archaeological sites on the West Bank; PLO representatives insisted on control of all sites, including Jewish ones, and furthermore demanded the restitution, among others, of the Dead Sea Scrolls (which were bought by Israelis in New York and elsewhere or seized during the 1967 War). They argued that the authors of the Dead Sea Scrolls, the Essenes, had been an 'ancient Palestinian sect'. Jesus Christ too is being claimed nowadays by Palestinian intellectuals as an 'ancient Palestinian'. Palestinian nationalism, which has so often in the past taken cues from Zionism, seems nowadays to be in need of archaeology to assist in nation building.

It may well be that both Israeli and Palestinian claims on archaeological sites are merely opening positions in what is bound to be a long-lasting negotiation. Except when it comes to Jerusalem, which is a hypersensitive subject for everyone, those claims are not likely to jeopardize a future settlement in the name of the past, however evocative or important the sites may be for the sense of identity on both sides.

We have all heard the old saying that archaeology thrives on ruins and war. There are more known ancient sites per square mile in Israel than in any other country. In Jerusalem alone we know of some 50 major sieges, sacks, captures, and destructions during the past 30 centuries (three in this century alone), and of at least ten more or less violent changes in the ruling religion. Jerusalem is a veritable outdoor Louvre of the history of warfare. A short time before his death W.H. Auden visited Jerusalem. I saw him standing one afternoon on the terrace of Mishkenot Saanim, the municipal guest house, admiring the magnificent view of the Old City. The mayor, Teddy Kollek, was standing there, too. They were both looking out across the valley of Hinnom, at the battlements and the tombs, and the mayor said in a laconic tone that Jerusalem would be a beautiful place if it weren't for the wars, and the orthodox of all faiths, and their squabbles and their riots. He said this, Auden recalled later, as one would say in London that it would be a lovely place except for the weather. Shortly after this Auden wrote the following lines in one of his poems before he died in 1973:

> From Archaeology
> one moral, at least, may be drawn
> to wit, that all
>
> our school text-books lie.
> What they call History
> is nothing to vaunt of,
>
> being made, as it is
> by the criminal in us:
> goodness is timeless.

BIBLIOGRAPHY

Auden, W.H.
    1991   *Collected Poems: W.H. Auden* (ed. Edward Mendelson; New York: Vintage Books).

Elon, A.
    1971   *The Israelis: Founders and Sons* (New York: Holt, Rinehart and Winston [repr.; Penguin: Harmondsworth, 1983]).

Kenaz, Y.
    1986   *Hitganvut Yehidim* (Individual Stealth) (Tel Aviv: Am Oved).

Silberman, N.A.
    1993   *A Prophet from amongst you: The Life of Yigael Yadin* (Reading, MA: Addison–Wesley).

Wilson, E.
    1994   *The Sixties: The Last Journal, 1960–1972* (New York: Noonday Press).

ARCHAEOLOGY, POLITICAL CULTURE, AND CULTURE IN ISRAEL

Yaacov Shavit

I

How come that in spite of their devotion to their homeland, they leave it
for us, the Christians, to dig after the hidden-treasures of the ancient
Hebrew past in the rubbish heaps of their ruined cities?

Thus wondered the Scottish adventurer John MacGregor after visiting
Tiberias and sailing his canoe, the 'Rob Roy', down the River Jordan in
1869.[1]

Jewish writers speculated about this as well. In 1912, for instance,
David Smilanski wrote his readers in Russia from nascent Tel Aviv
about a lecture by German archaeologist Carl Watzinger, in which
Watzinger discussed his own excavations in Jericho and some synagogues
in the Galilee recently discovered by E. Sellin and G. Schumacher:

thus Christian-Germans are working in our historical homeland. Both
religious and scientific interests are the driving forces behind their activities. And we, who should be the most interested party in the success of
these archaeological excavations, do almost nothing in this field and leave
it to whoever else wants it: Germans, Americans, British.[2]

Eight years later, upon the founding of the 'Hebrew Society for the
Study of Palestine and Its Antiquities' in Jerusalem in 1920, its secretary,
Yeshayahu Peress, declared that the establishment of such an institute
was imperative for both cultural and national-political reasons. He found
it scandalous that Jews stood by idly as various nations conducted

1. John MacGregor, *The Rob Roy on the Jordan* (Hebrew) (Tel Aviv, 1982),
p. 228. Since I was unable to obtain the original, I used the Hebrew translation of
this book.

2. David Smilanski, *A Town is Born* (Hebrew), ed. Yossi Katz (Tel Aviv,
1981), p. 134. This is a collection of articles published in Russian newspapers
between 1906 and 1913. German scholarship used the term '*Hebräische Archäologie*'.

archaeological research on the Holy Land via their respective institutions in Jerusalem. Peress called the creation of a corresponding Hebrew institution surveying the land's antiquities 'in the spirit of Israel' a 'holy duty'.[3]

Many of the Jews arriving in Palestine in the late nineteenth century and after showed no interest in ancient monuments and artifacts and even opposed archaeological exploration. Conservative in temperament, they felt that the Jewish people could do without stone carvings as a propaedeutic for the understanding of Judaism and Jewish links to the Holy Land. Nevertheless, from the late nineteenth century onward, the majority of the Jewish public in Palestine accepted biblical and post-biblical archaeology as a legitimate and useful discipline. Moreover, local interest in archaeology shifted from a purely intellectual interest to an active one.

What did proponents of Hebrew archaeology mean by encouraging archaeology 'in the spirit of Israel'? Nahum Schloucz, supervisor of the first 'Jewish' excavation in Hamat-Tiberias in 1920, opined that the aim of Hebrew archaeology was to reveal the deep roots of Jewish existence in the land of Israel and 'resolve the riddle of its creative forces'. More specifically, he wrote that archaeology could help recover important chapters in Jewish national and spiritual history in Palestine that had been literally forgotten and buried. He cited, by way of example, the history of the Galilee in the Late Roman and Byzantine period.[4] In this conception, Hebrew archaeology was 'national' because its main or even sole interest was the Jewish people.

One aspect of this 'nationalization' process was the inception of a Jewish periodization instead of the 'objective' one. Jews, wrote Y. Ben-Zvi in 1953, should use terms such as the 'period of the Patriarchs' or the 'First Temple period' that stress the 'Jewish character of the land'. By using Hebrew terminology, he concluded, 'we will compensate for the poor history of our nation and, at the same time, we will be more

---

3. *Collection of the Hebrew Society for the Study of Palestine and its Antiquities* (Hebrew), I, 1921. See also A.Y. Brawer, 'From the Early Days of the Hebrew Study for the Study of Palestine and its Antiquities', in *Galilee and the Coast of Galilee: The 19th Archaeological Convention of the Israel Exploration Society* (Hebrew) (October 1963; Jerusalem, 1965), pp. 228-36.

4. 'The Excavations at Hammath Tiberias' (Hebrew), *Hashiloach* 38 (1930), pp. 546-51. A stone lamp was found and Schloucz invited the High Commissioner, Herbert Samuel, to visit the excavation, but he declined.

precise'.[5] Another feature of this 'nationalization' was the claim that only Jewish scholars were acquainted with the Jewish sources and therefore only they were competent to work with them. Moreover, it was argued that Christian scholars were interested only in findings relevant to a narrow, Christian theological perspective, whereas Jewish scholars were curious about the totality of Palestine's past.

In the first years of the State of Israel, broad public interest in archaeology intensified and was quickly institutionalized by state and public bodies. The old lament about 'foreigners' handling the archaeological recovery of the Jewish past in Palestine faded into the dim recesses of memory, but a new complaint was aired: Israeli society chose to live in the shadow of ancient spirits, as it permitted ghosts from the past to shape its consciousness and lord over it. Archaeology, it was argued, had become a popular national cult, a cornerstone of Israel's civic religion, and a formidable component in its symbolic repertoire. Ancient excavated sites became objects of secular-national pilgrimage. Collectively, they constituted a new mandatory touring itinerary, tantamount to a remapping of the land, both symbolic and real. This new map was conveniently stretched over the pre-1948 map of non-Jewish settlement in Palestine.

Another critique leveled at the cult of archaeology alleged its deleterious effects on Jewish religion and spiritual engagement with modernity. The worship of monuments from the past became, in this view, a spur in the 1950s to religious and secular fundamentalism, territorial nationalism, and messianism. The sort of relation between Israel's past and present that the archaeological discourse encouraged was, for the critics, a fanciful one, as archaeology influenced politicians to indulge in a 'politics of the past'.[6]

---

5. Y. Ben-Zvi, *In the Caves of the Cliffs and the Crevices of the Boulders* (Hebrew) (Tel Aviv: Molad, 1953), pp. 237-41.

6. The literature on this subject is quite extensive. Examples include: Amos Elon, *The Israelis* (New York, 1971), pp. 365-78; Aharon Kempinski, 'Die Archäologie als bestimmender Faktor in der israelischen Gesellcaft und Kultur', *Judaica* 45 (1989), pp. 2-20; N.A. Silberman, 'Desolation and Restoration: The Impact of a Biblical Concept on Near Eastern Archaeology', *BA* 54.2 (June 1991), pp. 76-87; Magen Broshi, *Israel Museum Journal* 6 (Spring 1987), pp. 17-28; Leslie J. Hoppe, 'Archaeology and Politics in Palestine', *The Links* 20.1 (January–March, 1987), pp. 2-14. To put this in comparative context, see also the modes of acceptance of archaeology among other Near Eastern nations in such works as Israel Gershoni and James P. Jankowski, *Egypt, Islam and the Arabs: The Search for*

I will review such assessments of the role of archaeology in the state of Israel, starting with some definitions.

II

By 'culture', I mean a system of values and symbols and their creative product in a given society; by 'political culture', I mean the sphere of political and ideological polemics that appropriates the past for ideological ends, taming it into a mytho-allegorical or utilizable past. By 'archaeology', I refer both to 'greater' and 'lesser' archaeology. Since the 1920s, archaeology for most has practically been synonymous with excavations.[7] In Israel (and elsewhere), however, 'archaeology' never meant only sites, ruins, or the various material findings. It meant 'greater archaeology': an archaeology that renders new pictures of the past (*Geschichtsbilder*), a new concept and a new narrative of history. Of course, every evaluation of the role of archaeology must view it in proper context as but one element in a complex value system. Only as an addendum to a constellation of historical, linguistic, geographical, and literary dimensions does archaeology figure as a stimulus for visions of the past and, consequently, the present. We cannot specify the location, task, and utility of archaeology in a given culture without regard for the overall cultural system, with its many layers, determining historical narrative, historical myths, and collective memory. Archaeology constitutes the most fundamental stratum in the narrative of the people's historical emergence and of the land's development. In this sense, archaeology underwrites and validates all segments of the narrative layered above it. In the Jewish case, it serves to verify the historicity of biblical accounts,

Egyptian Nationhood, 1900–1930 (Oxford: Oxford University Press, 1986). For a good survey of Egyptology with an extensive bibliography, see Brian M. Fagan, *Rape of the Nile* (London: Moyer Bell, 2nd edn, 1992). There is, naturally, a greater spiritual attachment between Israelis and biblical history than between modern Muslim Egyptians and pharaonic history. See recently, Peter R. Schmidt and Thomas C. Patterson (eds.), *Making Alternative Histories: The Practice of Archaeology and History in Non-European Settings* (Advance Seminar Series; Santa Fe, NM: School of American Research Press, 1996); and Philip L. Kohk and Clarke Fawcett (eds.), *Making Alternative Histories: The Practice of Archaeology* (Cambridge: Cambridge University Press, 1995).

7. Kenneth Hudson, *A Social History of Archaeology* (London: Macmillan, 1981). On different categories of archaeological theories, see Bruce G. Trigger, *A History of Archaeological Thought* (Cambridge, reprint 1990), pp. 20-26.

thus validating the ancient history of the Jews. Translating received chronicles of history into authorized citations of historical fact, archaeology also provides Jews with a post-biblical link to the land of Israel by substantiating Jewish habitation in the land of Israel after the exile had begun.

In light of this, I will argue that for the past century 'greater archaeology' contributed much to what Redfield and Singer call the new 'Great [Jewish] tradition', meaning the system of values and codes by which (Jewish) culture interpreted and reinterpreted its old sacred texts and potentially produces new ones.[8] Lesser archaeology became an integral agent of modernization, shaping Judaism these last two hundred years, though in the Jewish context, modernistic elements combined with romantic ones.

III

Against this background, it is important to ask whether there is any truth to the maxim that 'in no country does archaeology loom so large as in Israel'. As supporting evidence, one might cite Israel's status as one of the most excavated countries in the world; the astounding numbers of professional and amateur archaeologists; the way the public stays abreast of archaeological discoveries; the ubiquity of archaeological museums in Israel; and such phenomena as the popularity of stamps with archaeological motifs.[9] These indeed indicate public interest and an archaeologically saturated culture, but such data do not specify the manner of archaeology's impact on historical consciousness. Other criteria are needed in order to evaluate archaeology's impact on the collective awareness of the past.

In fact, it is hard to say what determines intellectual interest in archaeology as opposed to an interest motivated by nationalist ideology. A visitor to Masada, for example, may be 'nationalistically' inspired,

8.   Milton Singer, *When a Great Tradition Modernizes: An Anthropological Approach to Indian Civilization* (New York: Prager Publishers, 1972), pp. 4-10.

9.   Magen Broshi, 'Archaeological Museums in Israel: Reflections on Problems of National Identity', in Flora E.S. Kaplan (ed.), *Museums and the Making of 'Ourselves': The Role of Objects in National Identity* (London: Leicester University Press, 1994), pp. 314-29. Ninety-four out of slightly more than a thousand stamps issued by the State of Israel in its first 40 years have borne archaeological motifs (Tsachor, *Israeli Postage Stamps, 1948–1980* [Jerusalem: Israeli Philatelic Authority, 1989]).

whereas a visitor to Caesarea, Beit Shean, or even Gamla will be impressed primarily by the 'archaeological merits' of the sites. In other words, we must distinguish between the function of archaeological sites or monuments as ideological agents, on the one hand, and the non-tendentious history that archaeology helps tell or retell, on the other.

The ancient past suffuses the Israeli landscape, but grasping the past's impact on the present is an elusive task. The popular Israeli guidebook *Every Place and Site* details each last tell and *hirbe* (ruin). These witness the past silently: most such ancient or not-so-ancient places impact not at all on the collective consciousness. They might interest tourists or even go entirely unnoticed, regarded merely as the 'archaeological furniture' that comes with the landscape. Only select monuments, holy places, sites serving national myths, and certain major documents (such as the Dead Sea Scrolls) have the potential to figure as part of general culture and perform some active cultural or political role because the historical or symbolic message they bear suits the mytho-poetic exigencies of the nation.

From all this, it is clear that it is not enough to dig and restore, for this in itself does not guarantee that the sites or monuments will impress themselves on national self-perception. And real remembrance, in the words of the sages, is remembrance that spurs action. A site's capacity to evoke emotive reaction is in itself insufficient; (greater) archaeology truly impacts the Israeli consciousness or collective behavior through school textbooks and popular and scholarly works, especially when the intention is to bestow symbolic significance. Only the strategic packaging of sites can result in new images of the past; the sites per se are powerless to do so.

In an article entitled 'Truth Shall Spring out of the Earth: The Development of Jewish Popular Interest in Archaeology in Eretz-Israel',[10] I suggested an outline of early Jewish interest in Palestine and Near Eastern archaeology, since the mid-nineteenth century. This interest began with the Jewish encounter with biblical criticism and the history of the ancient Near East. Against the background of this intensive encounter, it is important to distinguish between approaches to the history and the development of Jewish faith and religion, and approaches toward the political, social, and cultural history of the Jewish people.

10. Yaacov Shavit, 'Truth Shall Spring out of the Earth: The Development of Jewish Popular Interest in Archaeology in Eretz-Israel' (Hebrew), *Cathedra* 44 (June, 1987), pp. 27-54.

The first issue, Judaic faith, prompted attention to archaeology throughout the ancient Near East, primarily to that of Egypt and Mesopotamia, since events in the Bible are closely connected to them and indeed often transpired within these civilizations. The second issue—the political, social, and cultural identity of the Jews—mandated that attention be paid to the archaeology of the land of Israel, because it had been the national arena of the people of Israel. One must, then, distinguish between historical literature whose writing was influenced by archaeological findings in the Near East generally, and history whose writing was influenced by findings within the land of Israel.

This dual rapport with archaeology reveals a cleft in modern Jewish historical awareness. Given the disparate religious and secular interests in archaeological findings, many secular-national scholars maintained that Orthodox Jews rejected archaeology out of a fear that it undermined tradition. Secular Jews furthermore claimed that, for their own part, they did not ignore the religious dimension of archaeology, for they drew a distinction between the Torah as moral guidebook and the Torah as historical account. Accordingly, they pointed out that archaeology was superfluous for moral aspects of the Bible—the Ten Commandments do not need the validation of the Mesha Stele—whereas consideration of the Israelite monarchy does need this sort of historical verification.[11]

Secular proponents of archaeology did appreciate aspects of biblical morality, such as what they identified as 'biblical socialism' and the lessons of the Prophets, but argued archaeology's irrelevance for these elements. Archaeology could provide nothing more than a backdrop to prophecy, containing nothing that might validate the message of such prophecy. Joshua was in urgent need of archaeological corroboration, but the visions of Isaiah and Jeremiah, like biblical laws, did not require any such reinforcement in order to fulfill their crucial task in molding the Jewish ethical outlook.

Archaeology increasingly won over larger sectors of the Israeli public, as secular boosters of archaeology managed to sell their thesis that appreciation of archaeology did not require religious identification with the sites, on the one hand, yet permitted a hazy sympathy for biblical morality, broadly conceived, on the other, all the while nurturing the nationalist enthusiasm for ancient roots. Such an approach might be termed the public's 'secular biblical scriptualism', and it appears to

11. M. Soloweitshik, *Outlines of Biblical Sciences* (Hebrew) (Odessa: Moriah Publishing House, 1914).

characterize the relationship most Israelis have with the Bible as well as with archaeology. The public more or less accepts the historicity of biblical accounts as validated by archaeology. Religious Jews also avail themselves of such external evidence verifying the biblical narrative, which creates a common albeit tense ground with secular Jews.

It is clear, then, that archaeology helped revolutionize modern Jewish national awareness. It lent extra credibility to history (and not only to early sacred history) and, as a corollary, it legitimized the introduction of outside certification in discussions of biblical topics. Furthermore, it reconstructed old–new models of Jewish nationhood by recovering long-forgotten images of Israel's past: antique images that henceforth became decisive components of Jewish modernity. Archaeology's contribution to the overall Jewish modernist sensibility is often obscured by its purely nationalist uses.

IV

In the Yishuv or Jewish community in Mandatory Palestine, archaeology inspired popular study of the land of Israel (*Yediat Ha'aretz/Moledet*) and a new historical-geographical awareness. Ancient sites became stations along the route of organized tours (*tiulim me'urganim*) of national-secular pilgrimage, like medieval *hakafot* or *sibuvim*.[12] This interest in ruins and ancient objects grew as Judaism became less a religion of halakhic practice.[13] The historicity of sacred events and the palpability of the landscape in which they occurred became more central to the faith—myths, the Law, and record of the prophecies, but also a national history in the broad sense: the source of Jewish national existence and its foremost spiritual-cultural product. Zionism was a 'return to the Bible' no less than a return to the land of Israel.

Nevertheless, for secular nationalists, the Bible was not important as the repository of a theological claim to Palestine; the Bible's value consisted in the objective historical account of the Jews' title to the land, borne out by archaeological evidence.[14] Given the historical, nontheological use

12. See Saul Katz, 'The Israeli Teacher-Guide: The Emergence and Perpetuation of a Role', *Annals of Tourism Research*, vol. 12 (1985), pp. 49-72.

13. See Jacob Neusner, *Writing with Scripture* (Minneapolis: Fortress Press, 1989), pp. 166-82.

14. Gaalya Cornfeld and David Noel Freedman (eds.), *Archaeology of the Bible: Book by Book* (San Francisco: Harper and Row, 1976), p. 18. See M. Soloweitshik, *Gems of the Bible: A Treasury of Pictures for the Scriptures and their Times*

to which the Bible was put, it was part and parcel of Jewish modernity, and thus stood in the foundation of secular Israeli society, exerting a romantic and conservative influence simultaneously. Archaeology's transformation of biblical stories from the theological, literary, and allegorical realms into reality, fueled a cyclical process: the more credible the Bible became as a historical account, the more it served historical-national ends, increasing demand for yet more archaeological verification. Biblical history was not the only subject spun about like this. Almost every known trace of the periods of the First and Second Temple and of the Mishnah-Talmud era was unearthed and installed prominently in the new historical-national awareness. Of course, there was nothing fabricated about the artifacts and history emerging from the ground. What was manufactured was the linkage between them and the present, between ancient Hebrew history and modern Israel.

During that period, archaeology served mainly intra-Jewish ideological needs. The Arab challenge to Jewish historical claims to the land was of lesser importance. This internal Jewish discourse helped normalize Jewish existence in Palestine by recalling a time in which Jewish sovereignty was taken for granted, banishing ingrained Diaspora dissonance over the notion of Jewish national autonomy in the land of Israel. It provided young Jewish immigrants with local historical roots to replace the pseudo-roots of the Diaspora. It also supplied a local folklore (*Volkskultur*). As a result, secular Jews marveled over discoveries of synagogue mosaics and ancient cemeteries such as those at Beit Alpha and Beit She'arim.[15] The Beit Alpha mosaic, a copy of which was displayed in Tel Aviv, was celebrated as 'more decisive proof that many hundreds of years after our loss of sovereign freedom, Jewish settlement in the land endured'.[16]

Not only did archaeological findings nurture a sense of continuous Jewish habitation of the land, but also served to mirror the spread of Jewish settlement as the Mandate era drew to a close. Since both

(Hebrew) (Berlin: Dvir-Mikra, 1925). He writes that by means of archaeology, the Bible leaves the realm of mere literature and springs fully to life. He accomplishes this, in part, by ranging beyond the history of the people Israel, and discusses general knowledge regarding the development of human culture.

15. These sites were not given any religious significance but were considered to be manifestations of Jewish culture of that period.

16. *Ha-Poel HaTzair* 5 (April, 1939). On the consequences of the discovery of burial caves at Beit She'arim, see Bracha Habas, *Alexander Zayd* (Hebrew) (Tel Aviv: The Center for Youth of the Workers Federation, 1938), pp. 85-95.

religion and national culture need their *verba visibilia*, monuments were enlisted, satisfying what A.D. Smith calls a 'desire for physical tangibility' and for 'stations in time'.[17] He elaborates:

> For Jews archaeology has been allied to religious zeal in defining the homeland of Israel, in demarcating its boundaries... and in fusing the human monuments with 'their' landscape, thereby uniting the people to 'its' homeland... By naturalizing the monuments, the community is defined in space and time. We are told 'where we are'.[18]

It is important to note that unlike in Europe, archaeology in the land of Israel had no antimodern dimension. Serving various sectors of the population and corresponding to their sundry needs, it was essentially an agent of liberalism, conveying Jewish cultural history in all its plurality and diversity, nor did it ignore non-Jewish neighbor peoples whose histories impinged on the Hebrews.

V

Conventional wisdom has it that during the early years of the State, archaeology became a vital component of the civil religion, as it continued to provide Jews with roots. Both before and after 1948, archaeology did much more than merely disclose data about the past; it outfitted the past with specific images and meaning. In reality, very few findings became objects of public enthusiasm, and not every ruin met criteria to warrant attention by the State. Ben-Gurion was especially selective. He regarded the Bible as the *sola scriptura* of Judaism and, moreover, showed only scant interest in archaeology.[19] He displayed no affinity at all for the Second Temple era, and the State assistance he permitted for excavations at Masada and for the Bar-Kochva caves are exceptional cases. Support for these projects did not derive from any archaeological bent on his part, as many claim. There is no basis to the view that he saw the cult of archaeology as integral to modern Israeli identity, nor did

17. Anthony D. Smith, *The Ethnic Origins of Nations* (Oxford: Basil Blackwell, 1988), p. 181.

18. Smith, *Ethnic Origins*, p. 188.

19. Although supportive of Yadin, Ben-Gurion did not make a point of touring the excavations. He was far more interested in the biblical text itself: its historical narrative and moral-prophetic message. On this, see Michael Keren, *Ben-Gurion and the Intellectuals: Power, Knowledge, and Charisma* (De Kalb, IL: Northern Illinois University Press, 1983), pp. 100-14.

he believe that the new immigrants were in any way inspired by archaeological findings.

That there were powerful aficionados of archaeology who offset Ben-Gurion's apathy, such as Moshe Dayan, did not ensure the cultural ascendance of archaeology in the post-1948 era. Even the stir created by the discovery of ruins at Masada and documents in the Judean Desert only affected certain sectors of the public, and moreover, archaeology per se did not move even them. It was always part of a broader context and discourse, and certainly not the principal part.

For those whom archaeology did impress between 1949 and 1967, it conferred self-assurance based on continuity and affinity with the past, just as it had before 1948. (It was somewhat problematic that the Hebrew past with which archaeology helped Israelis to identify was primarily that of Judea and Samaria: the 'West Bank'.) To reach the general public beyond those by nature inclined toward archaeology, promoters of archaeology emphasized finds particularly evocative of Jewish continuity and belonging in Israel.

While this meant that certain finds and symbols were stressed and others marginalized or neglected, those highlighted were still only part of a more comprehensive and more complex network of symbols and motifs. In the sphere of creative activity, while providing a backdrop for some historical novels and contributing models to the fine arts, mainly in painting and sculpture (and stamps), archaeology's impact was minimal in comparison to other sources of artistic inspiration. Canaanite art was far less influential than the monumental art of Mesopotamia, whereas the Jewish-Hellenistic and Byzantine art that had flourished in Palestine was not even considered true Palestinian art. In any event, all the so-called ancient elements that had been absorbed into Israeli visual arts did not render Israeli art any less modernist. Archaeology certainly had a place in Israeli high culture, but left its modernist (and often 'Diaspora Jewish') nature intact.[20]

In the sphere of political culture, the situation was different. Attitudes toward archaeology were used by political camps as shibboleths demarcating battle lines in a *Kulturkampf*. After 1967, the symbolism and mytho-allegorical value of certain archaeological sites became more highly charged than ever as holy justifications for national ownership. On the other hand, many archaeological excavations in Jerusalem incited

20. Amos Kenan (ed.), *Sculpture in Israel: In Search of Identity* (Hebrew) (Tefen: Open Museum Press, n.d.).

the ultra-Orthodox to take to the streets in opposition, while secular-liberal 'post-Zionist' critics voiced their own objections against the Israeli cult of archaeology.

The ultra-Orthodox attitude had undergone some interesting transformations. From early indifference, it had evolved into conditional acceptance. Archaeology of the Second Temple period was particularly appreciated for offering evidence of Jewish observance and for disclosing data that helped one to understand the genesis and rationale behind many *halakhot* that liberal Jews pointed out with alacrity.[21] However, the orthodox position on archaeology is nuanced. Findings from the Second Temple period are welcomed, while First Temple period excavations often prompt anxiety. A large segment of the orthodox population is implacably averse to digs disturbing grave sites, and the violent demonstrations in which they express their disapproval testify to the radicalization of the ultra-Orthodox in Israel. Their rage against excavations is only secondarily about the excavation, and primarily about announcing to secular Israel that they have become emboldened and are willing to use new measures to promote their agendas.

The most important novelty in archaeology's status in political culture these last 30 years is the convergence of nationalist ideology, scholarship, and pseudoscholarship in the Gush Emunin camp. Gush members' historical writings on the land of Israel and its antiquities reveal the modern, secular means which some religious spokespersons are willing to wield in order to further their brand of messianic Judaism.[22]

The appropriation of archaeology by national-religious Jews such as these evoked a negative response by the secular public, which in large part turned against archaeology itself rather than against its uses and abuses. Many seculars impugned archaeology in Israel as a 'pagan-national' cult intrinsically amenable to nationalist-territorial manipulation. They agree with the traditional-Orthodox approach we encountered above in terms of claiming that spiritual values need no validation by artifacts. A more extreme secular wing argued that national culture, too, can dispense with possession of its material heritage. Previously,

---

21. Israel L. Levine, *The Rabbinic Class in Palestine during the Talmudic Period* (Hebrew) (Jerusalem: Yad Ben Zvi, 1986). Yoram Tsafrir, *Eretz Israel from the Destruction of the Second Temple to the Muslim Conquest*, vol. 2: *Archaeology and Art*. 'Discussions with Avraham Shapira', *Yediot Achronot* 23 (September, 1983).

22. On territorial aspects in historical perspective, see W.D. Davies, *The Territorial Dimension of Judaism* (Berkeley: University of California Press, 1982).

however, secular enthusiasts of archaeology drew the distinction between religious investment in unearthed artifacts and their national value, precisely in order to win over portions of the secular public that might recoil from archaeology because of the religious association with ancient sites; now, the argument was made in order to dissuade the secular public from supporting archaeology.

This argument was revived for the opposite purpose out of the desire to damage the national-religious camp at any cost, often spearheaded by ultraliberal 'post-Zionist' activists. Their goal is not so much to detach Israel from its past entirely—for they do endorse the moralistic, prophetic tradition of the Scriptures—as it is to discredit their rivals' specific discourse of the past. And since their rivals rely heavily on archaeology, they feel they must muster an assault expressly against archaeology. Once again, attitudes toward archaeology are an over-simplified reflection of cultural and political trends.[23]

It is worth noting that after the destruction of the Second Temple, opposition grew in Judaism to the adoration of graves. Nevertheless, in the Middle Ages, a cult of 'holy graves' and holy places developed, principally around tombs of patriarchs, which served as tangible signs of ownership over the land despite foreign suzerainty.[24] Ironically, the chief reason after 1967 for the intensification of the West Bank cult of holy places was not a religious renaissance in Israel, nor even the natural result of regained access to the places after years of denial; rather, the political-cultural debate in Israel increased the need for religious-historical symbols of ownership over the land. Secular exigencies of the society provoked a sharpening of the cult of holy symbols precisely when Israel's sovereignty over the West Bank might be expected to have reduced the need for the symbolic.[25]

23. For example, it is an open question whether the critique of the Masada myth is targeted specifically at the act of heroism at Masada or is addressed to the manner of fabrication of all myths of heroism in ancient and modern Israel.

24. Elchanan Reiner, 'Pilgrims and Pilgrimage to Eretz Yisrael, 1099–1517' (PhD thesis, Hebrew University, 1988).

25. Jehoshua Prawer, 'The Hebrew Itineraries of the Crusader Period' (A), *Cathedra* 40 (July, 1986), p. 34. It should also be noted that in recent years popular religion in Israel has sprouted hundreds of new 'holy places' that are the destinations of pilgrimage and sites on which miracles are requested.

VI

No group in Israel has a monopoly on the historical knowledge divulged by archaeology. Archaeology supports different historical visions, and it is possible to deduce virtually any desired conclusion concerning the development of Judaism, the character of the Jewish monarchy, or such other subjects as the 'open' or 'closed' propensities of Jewish culture.[26] Or taking a less traditional track, it is possible to use archaeological finds to stress the metahistorical character of Jewish history, even to offer a pagan view or to emphasize the commonalities among the various peoples that lived in the land of Israel.

In other words, archaeology is irreducibly nonmonolithic, accommodating rather diverse hermeneutic strategies. All in all, however, it seems that the public tended toward one stance: 'scriptural fundamentalism', the belief that archaeology's task is to verify biblical tradition. Consequently, this was archaeology's main contribution to the discourse of self-understanding in Israel's previous generation, in contradistinction to critical historiography and liberal, post-Zionist trends. But if Israeli political culture continues to evolve in this liberal direction, archaeology might find itself relegated solely to the domains of scholars and tourists, losing its traditional grip on the popular imagination and on the nation's collective consciousness.

26. Thus, there are a number of schools of Israeli Bible research—some traditional, others critical and radical. For an example of the way the critical and radical schools approached the problem in the previous century, see Nadav Na'aman and Itamar Zinger (eds.), *From Nomadism to Monarchy* (Jerusalem, 1994).

STRUCTURING THE PAST:
ISRAELIS, PALESTINIANS, AND THE SYMBOLIC AUTHORITY
OF ARCHAEOLOGICAL MONUMENTS

Neil Asher Silberman

Despite scientific pretensions and unspoken intellectual assumptions, the public function and social significance of archaeological sites—I would argue—rarely begin or end with the conscious intentions of archaeologists. As recent studies of the history of the discipline have conclusively shown, archaeology, in both its processes and its outcomes, must be seen as both a scholarly and a social activity with perceptible political contexts and effects (Trigger 1989; Patterson 1995; Kohl and Fawcett 1995). My aim in this paper will be to examine some of the cultural, political, and economic implications of archaeological activity in the land of Israel—quite apart from the philosophical nuances of scholarly discourse, or the history of academic research. In particular, I want to examine how over the last two centuries certain landscape elements—identified as 'archaeological sites' and, in a few special cases, 'archaeological monuments'—have been given a special status and have often assumed special symbolic power in the molding of the modern social and political landscape of the land of Israel. I intend to explore the changing modern function of archaeological sites from religious shrines to imperial treasure troves to national treasures. And with all due respect to the physical distance of Jerusalem, Masada, Megiddo, and Hazor from Colonial Williamsburg and Plimoth Plantation, I will discuss how some worldwide trends in the use of the past as entertainment threaten to alter forever the character of some of the most important archaeological sites in Israel and the West Bank today.

I must, first of all, make a basic terminological distinction lest professional scholars and excavators take exception to what may seem a glib reduction of all of modern archaeological history to imperial competition, nationalist mythmaking, and the establishment of popular tourist spots. This paper will *not* deal with the hundreds of archaeological sites all over the country known only or even primarily to scholars, and whose finds are disseminated and discussed primarily in the scholarly literature. Even though the interpretations of even the most obscure or ephemeral archaeological sites can be seen to possess an ideological or political significance (for example, Landau 1991; Silberman 1995), what I *am* interested in discussing, however, is the archaeological landscape as it is molded in the broad public consciousness by tourist traffic, school field trips, and the continual communication of archaeological findings to the general population who are aware of and regularly visit a relatively restricted number of sites. And in assessing the social impact of the limited number of Israeli archaeological sites that are known widely to the public (the approximately 50 sites that are administered by the Israel Parks Authority) it may be possible to see them as reflections of a larger public ideology.

More specifically, I will discuss the authority of widely known and visited archaeological monuments in their power to make modern logical assumptions, attitudes, and power relations seem natural, timeless, and inevitable (Leone 1981; Gero 1985; Patterson 1987). Through the routinized experience of visiting archaeological sites, open-air museums, and historical monuments, the public's shared perception of the past is shaped by a wide range of presentational elements including selected reconstructions of destroyed structures, informational brochures and signposts, and the explanations of tourist guides (see, for example Blatti 1987; Leon and Rosenzweig 1989). I would argue that all these elements combine to present the public with a composite historical 'story' or narrative that is far more sweeping in its conclusions and implications than the specific archaeological data on which it is ultimately based (as illustrated in Handsman and Leone 1989).

Often the officially sponsored narratives are highly political in their message, supporting the power of modern forms of government, specific territorial claims, or the current political supremacy of a particular ethnic group (cf. the essays in Kohl and Fawcett 1995). Yet far from being unique to the archaeology of the land of Israel, the politicization of archaeology can be observed from the very beginnings of the modern discipline (Trigger 1989), and particularly in the romantic connection of the archaeological sites and artifacts with modern nation-states (Lewis 1975; Sklenar 1983; Anderson 1983). Thus the search for the ruins and relics of the Celts, the Indo-Europeans, the Moundbuilders, the architects of Great Zimbabwe, or even for the 'Children of the Sun' of the hyper-diffusionist Manchester School of the early twentieth century (Renfrew 1967) all display the same tendency to impose on the historical or archaeological landscape the roots of a current political reality. Likewise, contesting 'counter-stories' that are the product of modern political resistance and that attempt to refute dominant scholarly hypotheses and the political assertions that derive from them must also avoid be seen not only in the context of intellectual discussion but also as elements in an ongoing political dispute (for examples, see Barkan 1988; Silberman 1995).

The authority and popularity of archaeological sites can also be seen to be affected by more subtle cultural and economic concepts, such as gender, profit, progress, and efficiency (Lowenthal 1985; Leone *et al.* 1987). These elements of interpretation reflect the larger conceptual universe not only of the particular nation-state but of the ideological foundations of modern transnational industrial capitalism whose perva-sive cultural effects and trappings had come to supersede or at least challenge the prerogatives of national sovereignty in many parts of the world by the closing decades of the twentieth century (Hobsbawm 1994: ch. 14). In many respects a modern tourist's visit to an archaeological site can be seen as parallel to the earlier practices of pilgrimage, in which religious rituals are enacted and wider social lessons are illustrated (and presumably learned). But here I must stress that the direction of the communication is not always unidirectional, from the intellectual or polit-ical establishment to a docile public. The rhetorical form of archaeologi-cal narratives is always shaped to a certain extent, I would suggest, by the public reaction to, and acceptance of, archaeological stories. And I will argue in the sections that follow that the archaeological history of the land of Israel has reached a stage where nonscholarly reactions and incentives have become central to the pace and funding of archaeologi-cal projects. And the implications of that socioeconomic development have far-reaching and ominous implications for the continuing interpre-tation of Israel's history and archaeology.

From Pilgrimage Shrines to Pageants of Progress: The Creation of the Christian Holy Land

The social authority of the landscape elements in the land of Israel that we might today call archaeological sites was, for centuries, if not millen-nia, closely connected with pilgrimage traditions and rituals. Although the earliest examples of the selective preservation or historical veneration of ancient tombs and ruins are known from the Old Testament (e.g., the Tomb of Rachel, Gen. 35.20; the ruins of Ai, Josh. 8.29) and even though the practice of pilgrimage to both Israelite and pagan shrines continued and even expanded throughout the Persian, Hellenistic, and Early Roman periods, a decisive transformation occurred with the adoption of Christianity as the official religion of the Roman Empire in the fourth century CE (Hunt 1982; Wilken 1992; Taylor 1993). While Jewish visits to Jerusalem continued on a relatively small scale, as conditions permitted (Mazar 1975: 94, 257, 285), the search for biblical (particularly New Testament) sites, their preservation and embellishment, and their incorporation into networks of regional and international pilgrimage routes had far-reaching implications for the place of the Byzantine provinces of Palaestina Prima, Secunda, and Tertia in the imperial consciousness, not to mention the imperial economy. From the seventh century CE, the Muslim rulers of Palestine gave their blessing to the establishment and encouragement of new pilgrimage traditions (Duri 1990), and many of the important Christian sites continued to attract visitors (Schick 1988). In fact, the competition between rival religious groups and political entities for *control* of the various pilgrimage sites, rather than any religiously based opposition to the practice, came to be a central element in international conflicts over the Holy Land throughout the Middle Ages and Ottoman period (Simon 1980).

A major change in Christian attitudes toward and understandings of the ancient sites of the Holy Land came with the Reformation. While Catholic pilgrimage continued, much of the Protestant world rejected the formalized pilgrimage traditions and, in preferring a spiritualized, metaphorical reading of the Bible, developed an abstracted and often dreamlike conception of biblical geography and history (cf. Lowance 1980). Yet this idealized image of the Holy Land was to clash unpleasantly with the realities of modern Palestine, when the first Protestant explorers began to arrive there in the early nineteenth century (Silberman 1991). The consequence was the creation of a new 'biblical archaeology', thanks largely to the conceptual innovations and tireless explorations of the American scholar, Dr Edward Robinson. Although Robinson was preceded by a number skeptical inquirers of various nationalities and religious orientations who had earlier questioned the historical reliability of the traditional pilgrimage sites (Silberman 1982), Robinson skillfully utilized his familiarity with the Bible and classical sources, on the one hand, and current Arabic geographical terminology, on the other, to reconstruct what he considered to be the authentic historical landscape of the country (Robinson 1841). No longer content with the traditional shrines and the time-honored methods of ecclesiastical validation, Robinson pioneered a means of identifying important ancient sites in which empirical evidence, not accorded sanctity, would henceforth be the key. This opened the door to a remaking of the Holy Land's geography through largely secular scholarship. And as it happened, this new intellectual project to transform the spiritual significance of certain landscape elements was soon to be subsumed in the contemporary territorial ambitions of the various European powers in the Middle East.

As I have described at length elsewhere (Silberman 1982), the race for choice fields for exploration and for the possession of newly discovered biblical activities eventually became an index of diplomatic prestige for rival European powers as the disintegrating Ottoman Empire became an attractive target for economic, cultural, and political penetration from the West. Through the second half of the nineteenth century, archaeological exploration became one of a number of highly visible European endeavors (others including education, health, missionary work, and civil engineering: see Kushner 1986, for example). Permanent national societies for the exploration of Palestine were founded in Britain (1865), the United States (1870), Germany (1877), and France (1890). Competition between scholars of the various Western nations could sometimes be bitter, seeing the important archaeological sites of the country not so much as sacred shrines as valuable sources of prestige-giving antiquities. In the aftermath of the bitter British–French–German competition for the 'Mesha Stele', archaeological spheres of influence were established in various parts of the country, with the Ottoman authorities granting virtual 'concessions' for excavations by the British in the south, the French in Jerusalem and its environs, and the Germans in the north (Silberman 1982). Far more important than the specific claims, however, was the cumulative effect of this archaeological activity on the perception of the modern landscape. In many cases, ancient sites were accorded an historical weight far greater in political terms than modern villages; the territorial shape of the Holy Land (long left hazy and undefined, but which ultimately became the legal boundaries of the post-World War I Palestine Mandate) was determined not by census or political debate, but primarily by the work of the archaeological surveyors of the British-sponsored Survey of Western Palestine (Ra'anan 1976).

Beyond the specific national competitions, however, there was a larger, shared concept that transformed the potential significance of each and every archaeological site in the Holy Land. Toward the end of the nineteenth century, the political and economic disintegration of the Ottoman Empire made the direct European rule over its territories and peoples seem increasingly likely. Western explorers—as self-identified participants in the conquering, civilizing 'crusade' that the European advance represented (as typically expressed in Macalister 1912)—began to disassociate the modern peoples of the region from the achievements of its ancient civilizations, in a manner strikingly reminiscent of the other kinds of colonialist archaeologies described so effectively by Bruce Trigger (1984). In the case of Palestine, the superimposed strata of archaeological deposits in the tells of the country were interpreted as both illustrating and embodying a continuous process of racial conquest, in which more 'vigorous' races had always overcome the more 'passive' ones (Silberman 1993a). There was, of course, little question in the minds of most Western explorers as to the 'vigorous' character of their own race. Thus beginning with the pioneering excavations of W.M.F. Petrie at Tell el-Hesy in 1890 and continuing through the great stratigraphic excavations of the interwar years, the excavated sites of the Holy Land came to possess a double significance: both illustrating the veracity of the specific historical narratives of the Old Testament and confirming the timelessness (and historical inevitability) of Palestine's conquest by the great empires of the world.

It could be argued that the most fundamental transformation in the social meaning of the ancient sites of the Holy Land came with the administration of the country by the British Mandatory authorities. With the establishment of a modern, bureaucratic Department of Antiquities and the enactment of laws protecting a recognized list of antiquities sites (Government of Palestine 1929), the various tells, ruins, tombs, and ancient village sites of the country acquired a special legal status that superseded any local religious or magical significance they might have possessed. The frequent mentions of disputes between the Jewish, Christian, and Muslim inhabitants of the country, on the one hand, and arriving archaeological expeditions on the other, over property rights to ancient sites, underline the new relations of power (for an example, see Silberman 1993b). While the traditional religious shrines of the country were maintained by the representatives of the various sects and denominations according to the time-honored status quo of the Ottoman period, the ancient sites of Palestine now became a field of active historical reinterpretation, ideological identification, and political legitimation. Digging, like war, had become politics pursued by other means.

The Rise of Israeli Archaeology

The spiritual relationship of the Jewish people to the physical monuments and ancient landmarks of the land of Israel adhered to the classical pattern of pilgrimage during the many centuries that followed the suppression of Judean autonomy by the Roman Empire. As already mentioned, the ruins of the Temple of Jerusalem retained their importance to the Jews as a tangible symbol of their former national independence, and, in time, sites associated with the real or legendary activities of the early rabbis and sages became the foci of new pilgrimage rituals, primarily, though not exclusively, in the Upper Galilee (Rusof 1992). Though sources for Jewish maintenance of pilgrimage sites through the Middle Ages are limited (Ben-Sasson 1975 and Prawer 1986), by the late Ottoman period, the responsibility for preservation of the sanctity of traditional sites of veneration and sometimes their physical maintenance had been assumed by the various charity funds and rabbinical associations of Jerusalem and Safed (Ben-Arieh 1986: 16-31; Schur 1983). Therefore, for the Jews of the Ottoman provinces of Palestine, the inexplicable yet defiling actions of European archaeologists in digging among the monuments and even remains of Israelite ancestors was often a cause for public protest and outrage (Silberman 1982: 72, 184).

Yet as Yaacov Shavit has shown in enlightening detail (1987), an interest in what might be called modern archaeology eventually dawned among the Jewish intelligentsia of central Europe—in a long and gradual process deeply connected with trends in the acculturation and social development of European Jewry itself. With the diffusion of modern nationalistic ideologies throughout Europe came the concomitant romantic yearning for historical novels, antiquarian collections, and the 'invention of tradition' among many peoples, in varying political and economic circumstances (Hobsbawm and Ranger 1983). And thus it was with the transformation that occurred in Jewish culture in Europe, with new concepts of secular history and political identity being absorbed into educational programs (Elboim-Dror 1986) and popular literature (Shenfeld 1986). Through the nineteenth century, the news of Western archaeological discoveries in Mesopotamia and Egypt that tended to confirm or elucidate biblical history was enthusiastically transmitted in the Hebrew press. Local interest in the antiquities and historical geography of the land of Israel eventually resulted, in 1912, in the establishment of the Jewish Palestine Exploration Society (Brawer 1965). In some circles, at least, the structure of Jewish history was being changed from a God-driven narrative of covenant, exile, and redemption, to a less spiritual, political epic of national character and national destiny. Thus the early excavations of the Jewish Palestine Exploration Society directed by Nahum Slouscz at the ancient synagogue of Hammat Tiberias in 1920 and of the Hebrew University at the ancient synagogue at Beth Alpha directed by Eleazar Sukenik in 1929 further cemented the connection between excavated archaeological sites and Jewish heritage in the land of Israel (Silberman 1993c: 19-27).

During the years of the British Mandate, excavation remained primarily the prerogative of large foreign excavations, due to the necessary expense and logistical difficulties. Although the Department of Archaeology at the Hebrew University undertook several small excavations throughout the 1930s and 1940s, the archaeological interest of the Jewish community in Palestine was expressed primarily through the exploration of the countryside and geographical study, rather than the veneration of particular archaeological sites. The development and diffusion of what was known to generations of schoolchildren and youth groups as *yediat ha-aretz*, 'knowledge of the land' (Shavit 1987), in many ways pioneered the much later archaeological developments of ethnoarchaeology and regional survey. Yet there was also an important, if unspoken, ideological significance to the identification of modern Arab villages with previously unidentified biblical localities and the study of the modern Palestinian Arab lifeways and material culture as a means of understanding the function of excavated artifacts. The traditional culture of the fellahin was implicitly identified as stagnant and therefore valuable primarily as a fossilized relic of the past. The intellectual implications of such an equation have in recent years been explored by various scholars (among them, Glock 1985: 468-69, with bibliography); the social and political effects were even more pervasive in the creation of an essential dichotomy on the physical landscape of the land of Israel between past and present; modern and primitive; Arab and Jew (cf. Gratz 1989).

As I have suggested elsewhere (Silberman 1993c: 230-31), one of the overlooked effects of the far-reaching military and political developments of 1948 was the profound altering of the physical historical landscape. In the 6 months between May and November, much of the element that had been identified as 'ancient' on the physical landscape of the newly created State of Israel was removed through a combination of military operations, mass migration, resettlement, and mechanical reshaping of the terrain (Morris 1987; Golan 1992). In addition, the eastern section of Jerusalem, with its icon-like Dome of the Rock, 'David's Tower', and tombs in the Kidron Valley were removed from the physical sphere of Israeli religious and educational activity. While recent considerations of the implications of the post-1948 territorial arrangements have all concentrated on political and diplomatic issues, I want to argue that this state of affairs also created something of an unnatural cultural situation—at least as far as the historical landscape of the newly established State of Israel was concerned. Much of what had come to be identified as 'ancient' (i.e., Arab villages and Jerusalem's most famous ancient landmarks) were suddenly either removed or placed out of reach, thus leaving a profound imbalance in the relationship of 'modern' and 'ancient' in the national landscape (cf. Lowenthal 1985: 35-73). Thus I would argue that archaeological sites began to take on an enormously important aspect in Israeli society in the 1950s and early 1960s—not only as a search for personal 'roots' as many have suggested (e.g., Dayan 1978), but also as a concerted attempt by cultural and intellectual institutions to restore chronological balance to a living landscape.

The story of the rise of Israeli archaeology has been narrated by participants, supporters, and critics and there is no point here in retracing the intellectual and social history of the archaeology-as-national-religion movement, except to note how in the initial stages the illustrations of Bronze Age pottery and architecture quickly replaced Arab villages and fellahin as the primary means of illustrating the past in a wide range of public media including travel posters, Passover *hagadot,* and school textbooks. Quite beyond the conflicting scholarly views of specific archaeological issues (cf. Bunimovitz 1995) or excavation methodology (beginning with Dever 1973), archaeology and its visual products became the chief medium of illustration for national historical self-definition. It is important to stress that the messages were not all purely nationalistic; modern social concepts of technological progress, efficiency, and even gender relations were also conveyed in the interpretation and reconstruction of archaeological sites. Israeli archaeology came to convey a wide variety of public messages—from the noble martyrdom of the Masada and Bar Kokhba rebels to the splendid (and ironically contradictory) Roman-style opulence of the Herodian temple and palaces, and the villas in the Upper City of Jerusalem. Indeed, the common Israeli perception of the past had so decisively shifted to a modernist, materialist perspective that Israeli archaeologists were sometimes seen as blasphemous interlopers and treated with contempt and hostility by ultra-orthodox religious and political factions throughout the Jewish world (for the famous case of the City of David excavations, see Meshi-Zahav and Meshi-Zahav 1985).

The Palestinian Version

Like the Jews and Christians of the Ottoman provinces of Palestine, the Muslim inhabitants of the various regions of the country developed a physical, landscape-based relationship to the past through the veneration of selected ancient ruins and tombs of holy men (Canaan 1927). For the most part, the Palestinian Muslim relationship to the past was a combination of pan-Islamic and highly localized traditions. Yet certainly by the Ottoman period, the repeated reconstructions and embellishments of a central shrine, the Dome of the Rock in Jerusalem, subtly expressed changing political connections and a protonational consciousness, even if they did not challenge or threaten earlier historiographical frameworks. Thus as St Laurent (1993) and St Laurent and Riedlmayer (1993) have demonstrated, the successive rebuildings and restorations of the Dome of the Rock by sultan Süleyman I (1545–66); by Ahmed I (1720–22); Mahmud II (1817); Abdulmecid (1853); Abdulaziz (1874–75); by the British mandatory authorities (1918–28); and by the Hashemite Kingdom of Jordan (1960–67 and 1992–present) have all utilized architectural elaboration and the placement of commemorative markers as visual, political rhetoric about both present and past. In fact, the traditional sanctity and political sensitivity of the Haram esh-Sharif enclosure compound are still strong enough to lead Islamic authorities to conceal or remove recently discovered archaeological remains (Adler 1991).

Until recently, archaeology played an insignificant role in the crystallization of Palestinian Arab national consciousness. From the early stages of the national movement at the turn of the century, most Palestinian Arab intellectuals concerned with the history of their people preferred literary studies and ethnology (Muslih 1988), leaving excavation to foreign scholars or participating in archaeology in strictly logistical or technical capacities. And for most rural Palestinians, archaeology provided—at most—temporary employment between harvest seasons (cf. Silberman 1993b). In fact, the relations between early European archaeologists and the rural population of the country was often openly hostile or coldly instrumental. In the case of the excavations of R.A.S. Macalister at Gezer at the turn of the century, the Palestinian peasantry was itself seen as the source of the country's modern stagnation (Macalister 1912: 121-29), and the subsequent employment of fellahin for the large-scale archaeological enterprises of Germans, Americans, British, and French did little to engage the interest of the Muslim public in archaeology as a means of national self-definition. Although Palestinian Christians and Arabs filled many clerical and enforcement positions in the British Mandatory Department of Antiquities, no independent excavations were conducted by Palestinian cultural or educational institutions.

The role of archaeology in the shaping of Palestinian national consciousness did not substantially increase during the administration of the West Bank by the Hashemite Kingdom of Jordan, from 1948 to 1967. All available resources for local archaeological activity were directed toward an integration of the antiquities recovered from both sides of the Jordan into a single Jordanian history. Within months of the end of the 1948 Arab–Israeli War, the Palestine Archaeological Museum (today generally known as the Rockefeller Museum), though intended as a center for the study of the archaeology of Palestine and maintained by an international board of trustees, became a secondary headquarters of the Jordanian Department of Antiquities. It was headed until 1956 by Gerald Lankester Harding, a former British colonial administrator and archaeologist. Throughout the 1950s and 1960s, archaeological work flourished in the West Bank under Jordanian auspices (King 1983), yet the activity can be seen as a continuation of the practice of the Mandate Period with the largest projects (Qumran, Tell el-Farah [N], Shechem, Taanach, Beth Zur, Dothan) all conducted by foreign institutions, concentrating on biblical connections, with virtually no participation by local scholars or graduate students at the highest staff levels of the dig. The value to the Kingdom of Jordan of these excavations and the occasional lasting historical monuments they produced was primarily limited to tourism and international prestige.

Even though the appointment of a Palestinian scholar, Awni Dajani, in 1960 as director of the Department of Antiquities of Jordan marked the start of a new era (King 1983: 200), little progress in cultivating a local archaeological interest was made before the 1967 war. The administrative archives of the Rockefeller Museum through the 1950s and 1960s are filled with repeated suggestions about ways to encourage museum attendance by school groups and private citizens—and with repeated reports of disappointing attendance figures. Yet by the 1980s, under the pressure of Israeli administration and with the tremendous expansion of higher education in the various Palestinian universities, the first steps were being taken toward the creation of a uniquely 'Palestinian' archaeological past. While the early attempts at such a project were transparently polemical (e.g. Baramki 1969), later efforts centered on the creation of new archaeological approaches that highlighted historical and cultural continuity (Ziadeh 1987). In an ironic ideological transformation of the *yediat ha-aretz* of earlier Jewish Palestinian scholars, the elements of traditional Palestinian village culture were now prized for their enduring embodiment (not fossilization) of the egalitarian social relations and even stylistic expression of ancient Palestinian societies.

No less important was the increasingly conscious connection between the study of material culture and modern political assertions of Palestinian Arab territorial sovereignty. A systematic (and at least partly archaeological) attempt to record the locations and character of the destroyed remains of pre-1948 Arab villages within the boundaries of the State of Israel was explicitly aimed by its editor to be both an important work of scholarship and 'of some relevance today in the search for an honorable and peaceful resolution of this century-old conflict' (Khalidi 1992: xxxiv). Thus, long-overlooked tumbles of stone walls and stripped foundations of houses began to take on a potent political significance as both archaeological data and physical embodiments of a national history. On a more practical, legal level, the 1993 negotiations between Israel and the newly constituted Palestinian Authority led to a fierce debate over the future of archaeological sites in areas from which the Israelis were prepared to withdraw (cf. Shanks 1994). Sites of antiquities, particularly in the Jericho district, became an important if short-lived international cause celèbre. Whether or not the sites and artifacts in question—ancient Hebrew and Aramaic manuscript finds and the Herodian winter palaces, for example—could be meaningfully linked to the historical narrative of the Palestinian people was less important than the assumption of all modern nations that control over the antiquities of a certain territory was an unalienable prerogative of sovereignty (as expressed in Haberman 1993). Thus, as had occurred before with so many other nations, the shift in the Palestinian consciousness from traditional approaches to the past to recognition of the value and importance of nonreligious archaeological monuments began to gain momentum with the emergence of the prerogatives and institutions of a nation-state.

Disneyland in the Holy Land?

By the final decade of the twentieth century, an important new element could be discerned in the construction of the past in the land of Israel. While conflicting ideological images of national heritage and territorial inheritance continued to inform standard presentations and popular interpretations, an instrumental (one might even say 'post-ideological') consciousness became increasingly influential in the allotment of resources for archaeological work. With the reorganization of the Israel Department of Antiquities in the spring of 1990 as an independent Antiquities Authority, under the direction of an energetic director and with the statutory ability to retain independently earned revenues and expand its administrative and professional apparatus (Rabinovich 1994), the governmental component of archaeological activity reached unprecedented levels. Between 1990 and 1994, the Authority's full-time staff quadrupled in number and its annual operating budget increased by a factor of ten (from $2 million to $22 million, according to Rabinovich 1994: 44). Forging active alliances with other governmental bodies such as the Ministry of Tourism and the Ministry of Labor, the Antiquities Authority embarked on an ambitious program of large-scale excavation throughout the country, particularly the highly visible, tourist-oriented projects at the large Graeco-Roman sites of Beth Shean, Caesarea, and Banias.

In contrast to the small salvage excavations and the 'pet' projects of earlier directors and deputy directors of the once small and sleepy Department of Antiquities, these new archaeological undertakings were meant to respond to modern economic and social problems (in addition to, or perhaps independent of, scholarly questions). In the case of Beth Shean, in particular, the problems of local unemployment and the desirability of developing a local tourist industry were important and perhaps decisive factors in the initial organization of the dig (Shanks 1990: 18). These objectives had, of course, been present in earlier Israeli excavations. Yadin's pioneering dig at Hazor in the 1950s employed a labor force primarily of new immigrants to Israel resettled at Rosh Pinna and his excavations at Masada in the 1960s resulted in the creation of one of Israel's most heavily visited tourist sites (Silberman 1993c). But until the recent developments, these factors were all secondary to the main object of the enterprise, which was generally the selection of sites for the light they could shed on specific historical questions and/or their selective incorporation into the Israel National Parks Authority, which *in aggregate* presented a material narrative of the history of the people of Israel and the rise of the State of Israel (for a similar process of incorporation in presenting the 'official' history of the United States, see Bodnar 1992).

The massive new projects, however, remained strangely *outside* (and largely unrelated to) traditional archaeological narratives in the land of Israel, stressing a uniquely denationalized admiration for classical architecture, ancient technology, and urban life. While the large Graeco-Roman sites now being developed as tourist showpieces harbored in their histories unpleasant episodes of imperial despotism (Caesarea), Herodian paganism (Banias), and mass murder of innocent Jewish citizens (Caesarea and Beth Shean), these stories were usually left unmentioned—and certainly not stressed as the central reasons for a historical commemoration of those sites. The choice of archaeological projects at Graeco-Roman cities should instead be seen as part of an international trend toward the exploitation of monumental archaeological remains as income-generating entertainment venues. Far more important in this selection are vistas and pleasant 'interactive' experiences for visitors than edifying or inspirational narratives (cf. Silberman 1994).

With the funding for academic and cultural projects progressively restricted the world over in an age of budget cutbacks and downsizing, archaeological authorities (as well as protectors of natural wonders and idyllic landscapes) are increasingly called upon to mobilize independent sources of funding for their activities. Strategies of economic exploitation of archaeological sites are becoming increasingly common, particularly in connection with the World Bank's 'World Heritage List', which since the 1980s is being taken all over the world, as the 1980s World Bank has identified important archaeological sites as the nucleus of development projects. This form of economic planning is already familiar in the United States and Europe, where national antiquities authorities, often in co-operation with private firms, have developed complex networks of edifying tourist attractions, new pilgrimages to be traversed not by penitents but by vacationing families and holiday-makers in air-conditioned coaches, rented cars, and campers (for some representative studies see Leon and Rosenzweig 1989 and Blatti 1987). Yet even more important than the infrastructure and the method of presentation of the past at these sites is the subtle shaping of the content: since the success or failure of many of these projects is judged by the volume of visitors (and the revenues that it brings), the desires and expectations of the potential audience must be taken into account. And in a situation where market share and market appeal become prime motivations for the planning of archaeological presentations, only the most foolhardy park planner will choose to highlight the pain, inequality, racism, and suffering, which— though certainly a part of history worth mentioning, even stressing— may not particularly appeal to vacationers or tourist agents in the planning of itineraries.

Whether a Walt Disney style 'Roman World' or 'Bible Land' in Israel or under the auspices of the Palestinian Authority can be far off is a question. Yet cadres of professional park designers, public relations consultants, and tourism promoters are already playing an important role in shaping of the historical landscape of the land of Israel. As elsewhere in the world, archaeologists are increasingly faced with the practical choice of being willing accomplices to economically inspired development projects or being regarded as obstructionists to progress and development. The transformation of the authority and meaning of archaeological sites in the land of the Bible has come a long way since the patriarch Abraham purchased the Cave of Machpelah. For centuries, many of them were invested with religious meaning; in modern times, they became foci of political power as well. Yet in this new post Cold War, post-ideological world of transnational investment and consumption, the tourist public may get precisely the kind of history it *wants* to see. And if current trends continue, the result will be hardly more aesthetically or morally appealing than earlier instances of religious or nationalistic archaeological chauvinism. The past predicated on profit will, of necessity, tend to become a sad parody: popular cartoon-like images of Ben-Hur and Spartacus will shoulder aside older images of Joshua, Umar Ibn al-Khattab, and Eleazar Ben-Yair. And tragically we may all be poorer, not richer, for the fact that some of Israel's historical landscapes, once considered sacred, then transformed to structured images of nation and progress, can be transformed so easily and profitably into the dehistoricized theme parks of the twenty-first century.

BIBLIOGRAPHY

Adler, S.J.
    1991   'The Temple Mount in Court', *BARev* 17/5: 60-68, 72.

Anderson, B.
    1983   *Imagined Communities: Reflections on the Origins and Spread of Nationalism* (London: Verso).

Baramki, D.C.
    1969   *The Art and Architecture of Ancient Palestine* (Beirut: Palestine Liberation Organization Research Center).

Barkan, E.
    1988   'Mobilizing Scientists Against Nazi Racism, 1933–1939', in *Bones, Bodies, Behavior* (ed. George W. Stocking; Madison, WI: University of Wisconsin Press).

Ben-Arieh, Y.
    1986   *Jerusalem in the Nineteenth Century: the Emergence of the New City* (Jerusalem: Yad Izhak Ben-Zvi).

Ben-Sasson, H.H.
    1975   'The Image of Eretz-Israel in the View of Jews Arriving There in the Late Middle Ages', in *Studies on Palestine During the Ottoman Period* (ed. Moshe Ma'oz; Jerusalem: Magnes Press).

Blatti, J. (ed.)
    1987   *Past Meets Present: Essays about Historic Interpretation and Public Audiences* (Washington: Smithsonian Institution Press).

Bodnar, J.
    1992   *Remaking America: Public Memory, Commemoration, and Patriotism in the Twentieth Century* (Princeton, NJ: Princeton University Press).

Brawer, A.
    1965   'From the Early Days of the Israel Exploration Society', in *Western Galilee and the Coast of Galilee* (ed. Joseph Aviram; Jerusalem: Israel Exploration Society).

Bunimovitz, S.
    1995   'How the Mute Stones Speak', *BARev* 21.2: 58-67, 96-100.

Canaan, T.
    1927   *Mohammedan Saints and Sanctuaries in Palestine* (Jerusalem: Palestine Oriental Society).

Dayan, M.
    1978   *Living with the Bible* (New York: William Morrow).

Dever, W.G.
    1973   'Two Approaches to Archaeological Method—The Architectural and the Stratigraphic', Eretz-Israel 11: 1-8.

Duri, A.A.
    1990   'Jerusalem in the Early Islamic Period', in *Jerusalem in History* (ed. K.J. Asali; New York: Olive Branch).

Elboim-Dror, R.
    1986   *Hebrew Education in Eretz-Israel* (Hebrew) (Jerusalem: Yad Izhak Ben-Zvi).
Gero, J.M.
    1985   'Socio-politics and the Woman-at-home Ideology', *American Antiquity* 50: 342-50.
Glock, A.E.
    1985   'Tradition and Change in Two Archaeologies, *American Antiquity* 50: 464-77.
Golan, A.
    1992   'The Transfer of Abandoned Rural Lands to Jews During Israel's War of Independence' (Hebrew), *Cathedra* 63: 122-54.
Government of Palestine
    1929   'Provisional Schedule of Historic Sites and Monuments', *Official Gazette* (15 June 1929).
Gratz, N.
    1989   'The War of Independence: The Conflict of Models in Israeli Culture' (Hebrew), *Tsiyonut*, Supplement 14: 9-50.
Haberman, C.
    1993   'Israel Hunts Antiquities, Angering Arabs', *New York Times* (15 November 1993).
Handsman, R.G., and M.P. Leone
    1989   'Living History and Critical Archaeology in the Reconstruction of the Past', in *Critical Traditions in Contemporary Archaeology* (ed. Valerie Pinsky and Alison Wylie; Cambridge: Cambridge University Press).
Hobsbawm, E.
    1994   *The Age of Extremes: A History of the World, 1914–1991* (New York: Pantheon Books).
Hobsbawm, E., and T. Ranger
    1983   *The Invention of Tradition* (Cambridge: Cambridge University Press).
Hunt, E.D.
    1982   *Holy Land Pilgrimage in the Later Roman Empire, AD 312–460* (Oxford: Clarendon Press).
Khalidi, W. (ed.)
    1992   *All That Remains: The Palestinian Villages Occupied and Depopulated by Israel in 1948* (Washington: Institute for Palestinian Studies).
King, P.J.
    1983   *American Archaeology in the Mideast* (Philadelphia: American Schools of Oriental Research).
Kohl, P.L., and C. Fawcett (eds.)
    1995   *Nationalism, Politics, and the Practice of Archaeology* (Cambridge: Cambridge University Press).
Kushner, D. (ed.)
    1986   *Palestine in the Late Ottoman Period: Political, Social, and Economic Transformation.* (Jerusalem: Yad Izhak Ben-Zvi).
Landau, M.
    1991   *Narratives of Human Evolution* (New Haven: Yale University Press).

Leon, W., and R. Rosenzweig
1989   *History Museums in the United States: A Critical Assessment* (Urbana: University of Illinois Press).

Leone, M.P.
1981   'Archaeology's Relationship to the Present and the Past', in *Modern Material Culture: The Archaeology of Us* (ed. Richard A. Gould and Michael A. Schiffer; New York: Academic Press).

Leone, M.P., P.P. Potter, and P.A. Shackel
1987   'Towards a Critical Archaeology', *Current Anthropology* 28: 283-302.

Lewis, B.
1975   *History: Remembered, Recovered, Invented* (New York: Simon and Schuster).

Lowance, M.I.
1980   *The Language of Canaan: Metaphor and Symbol in New England from the Puritans to the Transcendentalists* (Cambridge, MA: Harvard University Press).

Lowenthal, D.
1985   *The Past is a Foreign Country* (Cambridge: Cambridge University Press).

Macalister, R.A.S.
1912   *A History of Civilization in Palestine* (Cambridge: Cambridge University Press).

Mazar, B.
1975   *The Mountain of the Lord* (Garden City, NY: Doubleday).

Meshi-Zahav, Z., and Y. Meshi-Zahav, (eds.)
1985   *The Slope of the Temple Mount: Battle Diary* (Jerusalem: Meshi-Zahav).

Morris, B.
1987   *The Birth of the Palestinian Refugee Problem* (Cambridge: Cambridge University Press).

Muslih, M.
1988   *The Origins of Palestinian Nationalism* (New York: Columbia University Press).

Patterson, T.C.
1987   'Development, Ecology, and Marginal Utility in Anthropology', *Dialectical Anthropology* 15: 15-31.
1995   *Toward a Social History of Archaeology in the United States* (Fort Worth, TX: Harcourt Brace).

Prawer, J.
1986   'The Hebrew Itineraries of the Crusader Period' (Hebrew), *Cathedra* 41: 65-90.

Ra'anan, U.
1976   *Frontiers of a Nation* (Westport, CN: Hyperion Press).

Rabinovich, A.
1994   'Inside the Israel Antiquities Authority', *BARev* 20/2: 40-45.

Renfrew, C.
1967   'Colonialism and Megalithismus', *Antiquity* 41: 276-88.

Robinson, E.

1841   *Biblical Researches in Palestine, Mount Sinai, and Arabia Petraea: A Journal of Travels in the Year 1838* (Boston: Crocker and Brewster).

Rusof, D.

1992   *Sha'arei Meiron* (Hebrew) (Jerusalem: Sha'arei Ziv Institute).

St Laurent, B.

1993   'The Dome of the Rock: Restorations and Political Implications, 1720 to the Present' (unpublished paper presented at the Annual Meeting of the American Schools of Oriental Research).

St Laurent, B., and A. Riedlmayer

1993   'Restorations of Jerusalem and the Dome of the Rock and their Political Significance, 1537–1928', *Muqarnas* 10: 76-84.

Schick, R.

1988   'Christian Life in Palestine during the Early Islamic Period', *BA* 51: 218-21, 239-40.

Schur, N.

1983   *History of Safed* (Hebrew) (Tel Aviv: Dvir).

Shanks, H.

1990   'Glorious Beth Shean', *BARev* 16.4: 16-31.

1994   'Peace, Politics, and Archaeology', *BARev* 20.2: 50-57, 94.

Shavit, Y.

1987   ' "Truth Shall Spring Out of the Earth": The Development of Jewish Popular Interest in Archaeology in Eretz-Israel' (Hebrew), *Cathedra* 44: 27-54.

Shenfeld, R.

1986   *From King Messiah to Messiah of Flesh and Blood* (Tel Aviv: Papyrus Publishing House).

Silberman, N.A.

1982   *Digging for God and Country* (New York: Knopf).

1991   'Desolation and Restoration: The Impact of a Biblical Concept on Near Eastern Archaeology', *BA* 54: 76-87.

1993a   'Petrie and the Founding Fathers', in *Biblical Archaeology Today, 1990* (ed. Avraham Biran and Joseph Aviram; Jerusalem: Israel Exploration Society).

1993b   'Visions of the Future: Albright in Jerusalem, 1919–1929', *BA* 56: 8-16.

1993c   *A Prophet from amongst you: The Life of Yigael Yadin* (Reading, MA: Addison-Wesley).

1994   'The Battle that Disney Should Have Won', *Lingua Franca* 5.1: 24-28.

1995   'Promised Lands and Chosen Peoples: The Politics and Poetics of Archaeological Narratives.', in Kohl and Fawcett, 1995: 249-62.

Simon, R.

1980   'The Struggle for the Christian Holy Places in Eretz-Israel in the Ottoman Period, 1516–185' (Hebrew), *Cathedra* 17: 107-26.

Sklenar, K.

1983   *Archaeology in Central Europe: The First 500 Years* (New York: St Martin's Press).

Taylor, J.E.
1993   *Christians and the Holy Places: The Myth of Jewish-Christian Origins* (Oxford: Oxford University Press).

Trigger, B.G.
1984   'Alternative Archaeologies: Nationalist, Colonialist, Imperialist', *Man* 19: 355-70.
1989   *A History of Archaeological Thought* (Cambridge: Cambridge University Press).

Wilken, R.L.
1992   *The Land Called Holy: Palestine in Christian History and Thought* (New Haven: Yale University Press).

Ziadeh, G.
1987   'The Present is Our Key to the Past', *Bir Zeit Research Review* 4: 40-65.

HISTORICAL IMAGININGS, IDEOLOGICAL GESTURES:
W.F. ALBRIGHT AND THE 'REASONING FACULTIES OF MAN'

Burke O. Long

At mid-career, during the early days of World War II, William Foxwell
Albright published two books of intellectual history, really histories of
theism in the West, that were to solidify his reputation as a foremost
interpreter of the ancient Near East. In part, the books were conceived
as successors and correctives to the strictly humanistic works of James
Henry Breasted, especially *The Dawn of Conscience*.[1] Albright wrote as
a Christian, opposing what he would later call Breasted's 'non-religious
teleology', and yet he embraced a Breasted-like ambition to create a
unified history of Western religion from its prehistoric beginnings down
to early Christian times.[2]

Underlying the evolutionary narrative of these two books was a
typology of 'mental phenomena', which Albright used to describe both
the development of human cultural achievement in the ancient Near
East, and the inherent, natural possibilities of human reasoning.[3]
Whereas Albright saw these processes under three aspects—that is, the
aesthetic, affective, and conceptual—in fact he concentrated on the third

1.   New York and London: Charles Scribner's Sons, 1933.
2.   *From the Stone Age to Christianity* (Baltimore: The Johns Hopkins
University Press, 1940); *Archaeology and the Religion of Israel* (Baltimore: Johns
Hopkins, 1942). Albright greatly admired Breasted, but was troubled by his
'meliorism', his strong humanistic faith in a natural order which through human
effort becomes better and better. See Albright's memorial tribute, 'James Henry
Breasted, humanist', in *American Scholar* 5 (1936), pp. 287-99. I have been unable
to locate among Albright's papers a document in which, as David Noel Freedman
reported to me, Albright had compared his own accomplishments with those of
Breasted.
3.   The typology was outlined in the second chapter of *Stone Age*, described
more fully in *Religion of Israel*, and was a mainstay in his later essays, *History,
Archaeology, and Christian Humanism* (New York: McGraw–Hill, 1964).

dimension, those powers of conceptual reasoning that make human beings rational creatures.

I will limit my remarks accordingly. I wish to analyze Albright's notions of 'pre-(or proto) logical thought' (associated mostly with what he called 'primitive' societies), 'empirico-logical' thinking (in the ancient Near East exemplified best among the biblical Israelites), and finally, 'logical or philosophical-rational' thought (most perfectly achieved by the philosophers in classical Greece).

My main interest is to investigate the ideological and political contexts in which these claims were generated and announced. I will argue that this three-phased developmental schema disguised a program of religious and cultural apologetics. The program took on additional urgency around 1940 as Albright, along with many other intellectuals at the time, began to present the Christian and Jewish traditions, blended into what he called a Judeo-Christian yet dominantly Christian mix, as a bulwark against Fascism and Marxist Communism.

I offer this contextualization of Albright's work to suggest that historical imaginings, the ways we construct the 'facts' about the past, inevitably involve some such ideological gestures. Speaking about these in all their particularity ought to be a more routine part of our critical discourse than it is, both as we write the 'facts' of history, and as we write the history of past attempts to write history.

I make no claim to analysis that is devoid of vested interest. I pose specific questions arising out of my own philosophical orientation and social situation, and out of my desire to expand conventional notions of what constitutes critically aware biblical and archaeological scholarship. I inquire about ideology, which I understand as the creation of meaning in the maintenance and reproduction of social power.[4] I ask how this dimension of human experience shaped the scholarly theories and practice of Albright; by implication the question might be put to all other scholars who construct pictures of the past.

The Typology of Reason

Albright described proto-logical thought as lacking 'a clear conception of the logical principles of identity and contradiction'. It makes no fixed

---

4. See Terry Eagleton, *Ideology: An Introduction* (London/New York: Verso, 1991); Jorge Larrain, *The Concept of Ideology* (Athens, GA: University of Georgia, 1979).

empirical distinctions among human beings, animals, and plants. Proto-logical thought has no modern idea of causation for which one is just as likely to find 'explanation by accidental concomitance or sequence, or by superficial resemblance'. With such conceptions of reality (*unfounded* conceptions, Albright implied), 'primitive man', who lacks a sense of individuality, feels 'impersonal power or force all around him' and seeks to manipulate it through 'sympathetic magic'.[5]

In contrast, or I should perhaps say, in marked evolutionary advance, 'empirico-logical' thinking has to do with learning 'to do things correctly' on the basis of long experience. While 'incapable of formulating definitions of concepts, systematic classification of data, and deductive logic', Albright wrote, empirico-logical thinking nevertheless expresses 'concepts of concrete and abstract objects, actions, states and relations' and governs much everyday activity of 'primitive man' except for those forays into religion, magic, and imaginative creations, a zone of 'proto-logical thought...where the logical principles of identity and contradiction are flouted constantly'. For Albright, empirico-logic 'achieved a singular triumph in the Old Testament, where survivals from the early proto-logical stage are very few and far between' and where, Albright suggested, a need to reduce the confusing plurality of nature and deities led inexorably to the unifying idea of one world under the aegis of one God.[6]

Albright identified a third phase of mental accomplishment, 'formal logic,' with the rational achievements of Greek philosophers 'from Thales to Aristotle'.[7] Formal-rational logic is systematic, deductive,

---

5. *Religion of Israel*, pp. 25-26. Pagination refers to the Anchor Books edition (Garden City: Doubleday, 1969). The text is virtually unchanged from 1942, and Albright wrote in the preface to this fifth edition, p. xiv, that during the intervening years his approach to the 'ancient Near Eastern mind' had received 'practically no valid criticism'.

6. *Religion of Israel*, pp. 27-31. See 'The Human Mind in Action: Magic, Science and Religion', in *Christian Humanism*, pp. 70-71. By 1952, when he wrote the latter essay, Albright had become extravagantly dogmatic in claiming that 'under no conditions can the thinking of the Old Testament writers be termed pre-logical...' (p. 51). Furthermore, the 'logic born of experience, which had won great triumphs in the practical world of the Ancient Orient, became dominant in all Old Testament thinking. No matter where we turn in the extant literature of ancient Israel, we find sobriety and consistency beyond anything known in the older cultures. Israel discarded almost all proto-logical thinking' (p. 53).

7. *Stone Age*, pp. 2, 335-44. Pagination refers to the Anchor Books edition

'syllogistic reasoning'[8] which aims at demonstrating the truth of abstract propositions. By joining speculative reasoning with mathematics and empiricism, the Greeks worked out 'non-mythological cosmologies and cosmogonies', and laid the foundation for 'all scientific progress and technological achievement' of the modern Western world.[9]

Albright carried this threefold typology into the first century CE, and briefly described what he viewed as the still more advanced achievements of earliest Christianity. Against the background of Greek civilization, which had 'reached its climax', and the accomplishments of Hellenistic Jewish thinkers, who 'plumbed the depths of human relationship to God', Albright saw in the religion of Jesus and Paul an 'unrivalled fusion of proto-logical intuition, empirico-logical wisdom, and logical deduction'.[10] Jesus brought to the world a unique 'accumulation of lofty ethical injunctions', as well as an 'astonishing balance with regard to fundamentally non-religious and societal questions'. He, and the Gospels, spoke of a divine love that has 'far wider and deeper connotations' than anything in the Hebrew Bible. Although his ideas were suffused with the 'fine Hellenic sense of balance and of proportion', Jesus surpassed the universalistic tendencies of the Greeks (and by the way, the moves in this direction by the Pharisees) with a 'far wider and deeper' vision of universalism and philanthropy.[11]

The sweep of Albright's vision is breathtaking. It has a quaint ring about it some 50 years later—this attempt to tidy up the mess of human history with three stages of development (and inherent capacities), capped by a fourth integrative phase of reason. I am less interested in debating the truth of Albright's claims, which in any case would take me far beyond the limits of this presentation, than I am in reflecting on the implications of *believing* them to be true. What was at stake in this encompassing gesture of historical construction?

(Garden City: Doubleday, 1967) in which the original text was updated mainly in a new introduction and a few additional footnotes.

8. See 'The Place of the Old Testament in the History of Thought', in *Christian Humanism*, p. 97; also in the same volume, 'Toward a Theistic Humanism', pp. 54-55.

9. 'Human Mind in Action', in *Christian Humanism*, p. 72.

10. *Religion of Israel*, p. 31. See the fuller statement in *Stone Age*, pp. 334-403.

11. *Stone Age*, pp. 393-95, 403.

Ideological Critique

One of the first things to note about Albright's typology is that it functions as a first premise, a grid against which to organize and assess a mass of data. Albright spends little time justifying the rubric, preferring instead to appeal to the authority of anthropologists such as Lévy-Bruhl, who were similarly engaged in depicting the evolution of human culture. Indeed, the archaeological evidence he cites is extremely narrow in scope, and it is less evidential than illustrative of his concepts.[12]

A second feature to notice is the conflicting tone of Albright's language. On the one hand, objectivist description suggests disinterested detachment from that which Albright describes. On the other hand, adjective and innuendo conspire to give a strong impression of privileged place to empirical and rationalistic thought, as well as to new-born Christianity which is seen as triumphant over its predecessors and contemporary rivals.

Albright explicitly denies in a footnote to *Religion of Israel*, for example, that his use of 'proto-logical' is pejorative in any way. Pre-logical mentality is on a lower plane than logical, he wrote, only 'with reference to their relative positions in the scale of evolution'.[13] Yet, in the main text Albright asserts, without analysis or argument, that large segments of modern religion, literature, and art, such as 'astrology, spiritism and kindred divagations', were '*pronounced retrogressions*' when compared with the empirico-logic of the monotheistic Bible. Moreover he sweeps away much twentieth-century literature as a '*reversion* from classical and logical standards of morality and beauty into *primitive savagery or pathological abnormality*' and thus claims that modern authors lost all power to set standards for a generation that had '*deliberately tried to abandon* its entire heritage from the past'. Such willful rejection, Albright continues, was a retreat 'into the *jungle* from which man emerged through *long and painful millennia of disillusionment*' (emphases mine).[14]

If slightly horrified at the possibility of sliding back into a primordial jungle, Albright also is suspicious of formal logic unchecked by empirical experience. Thus he pronounces the Old Testament as more admirable

---

12. *Religion of Israel*, pp. 25-31.
13. *Religion of Israel*, p. 179 n. 64.
14. *Religion of Israel*, pp. 31-32.

than, even in some ways preferable to, the literary results of Greek philosophical rationalism. Why? Because the Bible's truths are rooted securely in empirico-logical reasoning, in 'experience and history', not in *a priori* 'undemonstrable premises' that lead to conclusions which may or may not be correct.[15] Indeed, in 1958, Albright was to confess in print his lifelong opposition to all systems of thought that were 'based on arbitrary postulates and [on] denying or disregarding the historical experience of mankind'. He dismisses on one side speculative philosophies that were removed from empirical verification and, on the other side, he opposes 'rigorously pragmatic and instrumental' philosophical systems, since they 'reject anything that cannot be determined experimentally or mathematically'.[16] Albright places himself in the middle: a champion of empiricism, shaped by rational thought, but suspicious of what he called 'exaggerated philosophical emphases' that would deny the need for religion or the nonmaterial realities of which it speaks.

What does this intricate system of privileged perspective and values come to?

First, recall that Albright's researches were burdened with the apologetic aims of many Christian scholars who began their careers in the late nineteenth and early twentieth centuries.[17] As an undergraduate, somewhat infatuated with scientific modernism, he had written of the necessity to embrace an 'enlightened faith' in place of reactionary orthodox dogmatism.[18] Upon entering The Johns Hopkins University, Albright described himself to his mother as a quiet crusader armed with historical acumen and a scientist's cold scrutiny, but zealously eager to scrape off false encrustations of tradition and refurbish the eternal, and original, truths of Christianity.[19]

---

15. 'Old Testament in the History of Thought', pp. 84, 91-92.

16. 'Return to Biblical Theology', in *Christian Humanism*, p. 289.

17. For the wider picture, see Winthrop Hudson, *Religion in America* (New York: Charles Scribner's Sons, 3rd edn, 1981), pp. 265-92; Sidney Ahlstrom, *A Religious History of the American People* (New Haven: Yale University Press, 1972), pp. 763-804; Stow Persons, 'Religion and Modernity', in James Smith *et al*, *The Shaping of American Religion* (Princeton, NJ: Princeton University Press, 1961), pp. 369-401; Martin Marty, *Pilgrims in Their Own Land: 500 Years of Religion in America* (Boston/Toronto: Little, Brown & Co., 1984), pp. 297-317.

18. W.F. Albright, 'Modernism', *Upper Iowa Academician* 1 (c. 1911), pp. 1-4. A copy is among the Albright papers housed at the American Philosophical Society, Philadelphia.

19. Letter, Albright to Zephine Albright, December 26, 1913. Albright Papers,

On graduating from Johns Hopkins some five years later, Albright explained to a close college friend that he was preparing a series of publications in which 'the prehistory of our Christology will be worked out as thoroly [*sic*] as possible'. He would be circumspect—polemics would be avoided, and no direct references would be made to the New Testament, he wrote, until 'all the train has been laid'. Then, reflecting on this astonishing ambition, the young Albright continued (he was only 27 years old at the time):

> For years, I have tried to find common ground, where scientific rationalism and evangelical faith can meet. Now I seem to find it. During the coming years I shall, if God wills that my eyesight be spared, devote myself quietly to my technical researches, incidentally building a structure too strong for the batteries of mistaken apologetics. When it is all over, orthodoxy will rub its eyes and say, wonderingly, 'What was I afraid of? It all seems so reasonable now!' Such are the laws of progress in our society.[20]

I believe that Albright realized his youthful ambition some 22 years later in publishing *Stone Age* and *Religion of Israel*.[21] The purpose of the former, he wrote, was to trace 'our Christian civilization of the West to its earliest sources'. In the translation into German, Albright added that he hoped to thereby 'deliver a small contribution to Christian theology of the future'.[22] Two years later Albright wrote that his purpose in writing *Religion of Israel* was 'nothing less than the ultimate reconstruction, as far as possible, of the route which our cultural ancestors traversed in order to reach Judeo-Christian heights of spiritual insight and ethical monotheism'. He was mainly concerned, he wrote, 'with the religion of the Old Testament, of which the religion of the New was only the extension and fulfillment'.[23]

One may read both of these works as projects to transpose traditional theological claims for the uniqueness and truth of biblical revelation into

American Philosophical Society, Philadelphia.

20. Albright to Samuel Geiser, October 8, 1918. Albright Papers. See a fuller treatment of these matters in Burke O. Long, 'Mythic Trope in the Autobiography of William Foxwell Albright', *BA* 56.1 (1993), pp. 36-45.

21. Many of the assumptions and themes of *Stone Age* may be found, although naturally less fully articulated, in an early article by Albright, 'Archaeological Discovery in the Holy Land', *BSac* 79 (1922), pp. 401-417.

22. *Stone Age*, p. 32. See *Von der Steinzeit zum Christentum* (Bern: Francke, 1949), p. 7.

23. *Religion of Israel*, p. 4.

the idiom of objectivist historical narrative. For example, ancient Israel, presumed rather uncritically to be a cultural and ethnic unity, is displayed over against the Canaanites who were morally and religiously deficient, if not depraved; Assyrian-Babylonian poetry had a 'curiously monotonous effect', but Israelite poets took inherited literary conventions, used them 'even more effectively' than their neighbors had, and preserved 'most of the beauties and few of the crudities of older national literature'. Even though parallels to the emotional heights of biblical poetry can be found in Mesopotamia, Albright wrote, as though he could measure such things, 'biblical literature maintains a much higher average level of feeling'.[24] Albright viewed the Bible more *against* its environment than *in* it. Or to paraphrase St. Paul, the Israelites lived *in* their world, but were not *of* it.

Indeed, an ancient, traditional structure of Christian historiography rules *Stone Age*: the Old Testament is preparation for the New. Headings for individual chapters, such as 'Praeparatio', or 'When Israel was a Child...', or 'In the Fullness of Time...', urge upon a reader inner biblical and traditional patristic hermeneutics. Moreover, various remarks leave no doubt that for Albright the purposive directionality in history was heavily weighted toward Christian self-characterization. Albright detected, for example, a 'certain movement in the direction of theological universalism' in Mesopotamian and Egyptian religion.[25] In the end— his rhetoric implies the full weight of the massive construction—Albright asserted that the 'Church Fathers saw truly when they represented these aspects of paganism [the pre-Christian elements of culture] as part of the divine preparation for Christianity'.[26]

Albright believed in short that the cultural and religious ideas of human beings in near Asia demonstrably evolved from primitive beginnings to the highest (and never-to-be-surpassed) truths of Christianity. Accordingly, he built a narrative of intellectual and cultural movement toward Christianity out of a theological position: a Jesus-centered, supersessionist reading of all that had gone before—Hebrew, Greek, and their ancient Near Eastern antecedents.

Within the framework provided by this apologetic purpose, Albright's typology of mental achievement was a powerful tool to assert the exclusive and exclusionary privilege of Christians and Jews, and finally

24. *Stone Age*, p. 281; *Religion of Israel*, pp. 14, 21.
25. *Stone Age*, p. 213.
26. *Stone Age*, p. 399.

Christians alone, to possess highest, truly universal, religious truth. Empirico-logical thought, already taken as an advance over proto-logical reasoning, reached its apex in the Hebrew Bible. Since empirico-logic is a matter of learning to do and understand things correctly, the Bible's supersessionist view of the Canaanites, for example, may be accepted; in turn, ancient Israel is endowed with romantic heroism, and the Canaanites with equally romantic demonism. The Israelites were a 'wild folk, endowed with primitive energy and ruthless will to exist', Albright wrote. And fortunately so, he continued, 'since the resulting decimation of the Canaanites prevented the complete fusion of the two kindred folk which would almost inevitably have depressed Yahwistic standards to a point where recovery was impossible'. And the Canaanites? They were people of far less empirico-logical achievement, a people given to 'orgiastic nature-worship', and 'gross mythology', a people whose

> cult of fertility in the form of serpent symbols and sensuous nudity... were replaced by Israel, with its pastoral simplicity and purity of life, its lofty monotheism [an almost inevitable logical development, Albright thought], and its severe code of ethics.[27]

These gestures of superiority and triumph come to their natural conclusion (or 'fulfillment') in Albright's typing of Jesus and early Christianity as a fusion of proto- and empirico-logic with Greek rationalism. Here, the superseded 'other' is Greek rationalism (logical thought) and Hellenistic Judaism, including that of the Pharisees, who were heirs to the earlier heights of empirico-logical thought expressed in the Old Testament. Again, typology of mental processes makes certain theological convictions invisible. It puts beyond question, for example, various polemical renderings of the Pharisees in the New Testament and their subsequent interpretation in Christian culture. While approving of their somewhat rehabilitated reputation among scholars, Albright nevertheless imagined the Pharisees as just deficient enough to allow for Christian triumph, or, in the idiom of Darwinian historical rhetoric, as something of an evolutionary dead-end. The Pharisees were 'not at all suited to become the vehicle of a great evangelistic movement', he wrote, because they were weighed down with a misguided 'mass of *secondary* regulations and *restrictions*'. The Pauline, and later generalized

27. *Stone Age*, p. 281. Albright accepted and transmitted rather uncritically a tradition of negative stereotyping of the Canaanites. See Delbert Hillers, 'Analyzing the Abominable: our Understanding of Canaanite Religion', *JQR* 75 (1985), pp. 253-69.

Protestant, contrast between letter and spirit, inner and outer, genuine piety and mere externals of religion, glimmer just beneath the surface of Albright's construction. Jesus's hostility toward the Pharisees, Albright wrote, was based mainly on a 'profound *sympathy* [note: interiority of spirit] for the poor and suffering', toward whom the Pharisees 'showed *charity* but scant sympathy [note: external action, devoid of heart]'.[28] It is not surprising, then, that when Albright chose to end his book with an anxious plea for revitalized faith, he bypassed altogether those forms of Judaism that were heirs to ancient Pharisaism: 'We need reawakening of faith in the God of the majestic theophany on Mount Sinai, in the God of Elijah's vision at Horeb, in the God of the Jewish exiles in Babylonia, in the God of the Agony at Gethsemane...'[29]

Besides supporting such religious apologetics, I suggest that Albright's typology of reasoning faculties helped him construct a Bible that was congenial to the values of a secular and scientific America. If one accepts the claim that the Hebrew Bible was a singular achievement of empirical logic, then Albright's emphasis on demonstrated-from-archaeology biblical history effectively effaces, or at least puts aside, most of the Bible's supernatural features. Hence, the Bible gains in appeal; it is less easily dismissed as outmoded or unreliable, especially under the tutelage of critical evaluation. Albright never tired of pointing out new discoveries that were presumed to confirm not so much all the historical details of the Bible as its emotional weight as a trustworthy text. The Bible was an ancient book thus made less alien from those in the modern world who gave high privilege to historical consciousness and historically defined knowledge. Hence Albright boldly asserted that Biblical thought evolved to the point where 'man's best judgements about his relation to God, his fellow men and the world were in most respects not appreciably inferior to ours'.[30]

Albright carried this theme even further in a 1961 lecture which concluded with a sweeping defense of Western democracies. Because all of the Bible's assumptions were implicit in empirical experience, he wrote, 'one simply cannot deduce ideological conclusions suitable to the purposes of demagogues'. And then the ringer: 'Neither Fascism nor Communism is imaginable in the thought-world of ancient Israel.'[31]

28. *Stone Age*, pp. 391-92. Emphases mine.
29. *Stone Age*, p. 403.
30. *Religion of Israel*, p. 31.
31. 'Old Testament in the History of Thought', pp. 83-100, esp. p. 100.

Such a remark is understandable in 1961, when so much public discourse in America was dominated by the ideological constructions of postwar East–West conflict. However, the sentiments derive from an earlier period of public anxiety. In 1922, probably reflecting the stress of America coming to terms with increased immigration from Eastern Europe, growing numbers of Socialists and Leninists, and the rise of labor unions, Albright used archaeology and the new constructions of the past it made possible to resist and contain the ideologies of revolutionary change. Thanks to the newly scientific archaeology, he wrote, 'educated men' are coming to grasp that social and religious institutions which have evolved over thousands of years 'possess an inherent stability and a permanent value'. Measured against such 'solidity', the 'hasty generalizations of modern speculative sociology' look quite ephemeral. Then, in a gesture of containment, Albright demanded checkmate:

> Our radical Socialist friends would do well to immerse themselves in the study of archaeology before attempting to repeat an experiment which failed a thousand times before the abortive communism of Mazdak, so like that of Lenine [*sic*], fifteen centuries later.[32]

The Bible, biblical archaeology, and an implicit Christian culture (Albright's article was addressed to evangelical Christian readers), are associated allies in this defense of nonsocialist (democratic) institutions. For while 'Palestinian archaeology' plays a role within this wider task of archaeology (Albright wrote 'task' but the sense seems to be more like 'beneficial result' of archaeology), it is of special interest insofar as it reinforces a commonsense notion of the biblical roots of Western (not Eastern, or Socialist) cultures. Thus 'Palestine is the land where the sacredest of possessions came into being, and hardly a mile of its surface is not hallowed by Biblical associations. In the illustration, elucidation, and, if need be, confirmation of this masterpiece of world-literature archaeology justifies itself finely'.[33]

Nearly 20 years later, in a 1941 lecture, unpublished as far as I can determine, Albright returned to the theme, this time in the context of arguing that science and Jewish/Christian religion not only complement one another without fundamental conflict, but that they naturally, inherently, oppose totalitarianism. 'There is no opposition between scientific thought and the historical religion of the Bible, the Judeo-Christian

---

32. 'Archaeological Discovery', pp. 402-403.
33. 'Archaeological Discovery', p. 403.

tradition,' Albright wrote. 'We cannot understand the latter as an historical phenomenon without the former; the former remains incomplete and futile without the latter.' Then, with the anxieties of world war rising to the surface, he continued:

> In these days when the tyranny of European dictators employs every means to eradicate Judaism and Christianity from their empires, it is incredibly [*sic*] folly to attack the Bible because it was written in a day when the sun was still believed to revolve around the earth... The religious insights of the Bible remain unsurpassed and have sustained our western civilization for nearly two thousand years since the collapse of pagan culture.[34]

What is important to see is the ease with which *apologia* for the historical reliability of the Bible addressed to its scientific skeptics slides into claims about the Bible's prime religious value, and then how both somehow support European-American democratic institutions. All is encoded, I believe, in the typology of reasoning faculties, which assigns extraordinary privilege to the biblical Israelites and their culture.

Albright's particular rendering of this theme cannot be isolated from similar stirrings among other academic and political leaders of the time. A year earlier, for example, Louis Finkelstein, Chancellor of the Jewish Theological Seminary, convened a conference on 'science, philosophy, and religion'. The purpose, as the official record of the proceedings put it, was to 'rally intellectual and spiritual forces' to meet the threat of totalitarianism and build 'more secure foundations for democracy...'[35] Each participant, Albright among them, spoke on specialized topics, and each addressed the Fascist and Marxist threats and how their disciplines were compatible with democratic, not totalitarian, values.

I think that this ideological bundle—the Bible as historically sound, the Bible as religiously true, the Bible as the foundation for democratic values, and the Bible as a masterpiece of 'empirico-logic'—when seen in relation to the events of the early and mid-twentieth century provides a social and political context in which to read Albright's typology of mental faculties. It seems hardly accidental that *Stone Age*, which was published the same year as the conference, concluded by sounding a

---

34. 'Science and Religion in a Changing World: Historical Religion and Scientific Thought'. A lecture delivered February 3, 1941. Typescript copy in Albright Papers.

35. *Science, Philosophy, and Religion. A Symposium.* (New York: Conference on Science, Philosophy, and Religion in their Relation to the Democratic Way of Life, Inc., 1941).

similar mix of claims. 'Yet today we see Occidental civilization totter-ing,' Albright wrote, referring to a broad recrudescence of tendencies that send us back to the 'jungle' of proto-logical reason. He continued, 'We see scientific methods and discoveries judged by Marxist and racist gauges instead of by independent scientific standards'. In such a world, Albright pleaded, we need a return to biblical (Christian) faith.[36] In *Religion of Israel*, Albright wrote that sound empirical logic, just that faculty which he attributed quintessentially to the Old Testament and its monotheism, that is, what Albright called the 'Judeo-Christian tradition', is the only defense against modern day catastrophe. Then, as though to imply a natural association with American democratic values, he asserted that sound empirical logic still was the rule of 'the ordinary man in his everyday dealings with his fellows, whatever aberrations may character-ize the doctrinaire fusion of prelogical concepts with logical deductions from them which we find in such contemporary movements as National Socialism and Communism'.[37]

Conclusion

In sum, what I suggest is the following: Albright's typology of mental faculties grew out of and served his religious apologetic purposes; the typology aided the attempt to assert cultural continuity between the Bible and contemporary Western values, including interested attachment to scientific historical knowledge and democracy. The endeavor took on a new urgency in the early days of Communist influence in America, and later during World War II, as Albright constructed a rhetoric of soli-darity against totalitarianism.

I believe—at least this is a matter for discussion—that the typology of mental faculties had less to do with what it purported to describe—stages of mental evolution and different types of mental function—than with what it masked, efforts to maintain social stability and ideological conformity in periods of challenge, conflict, and change.

36. *Stone Age*, p. 403.
37. *Religion of Israel*, p. 33.

PEOPLES AND CULTURES OF ANCIENT ISRAEL:
RECENT ARCHAEOLOGICAL DISCOVERIES

TEL MIQNE-EKRON:
AN IRON AGE I PHILISTINE SETTLEMENT IN CANAAN

Trude Dothan

At the beginning of the Iron Age, Canaan was undergoing significant changes. The Israelite tribes were settling in the hill country and the Philistines and the related Sea Peoples were settling the coastal areas. The longtime Egyptian presence, still maintained by the power of Ramses III, was in its last stages, and the once-mighty Canaanite city-states were definitely on the wane. The co-existence in Canaan of these diverse cultures was part of an even larger panorama of far-reaching social changes, population movements, and cultural transformation which characterized the transition from the Bronze to the Iron Age in this area of the world.

The Philistines arrived in Canaan from the Aegean as hostile invaders at the beginning of the twelfth century BCE, destroying the Canaanite cities that lay in their path. They settled on their ruins, or became mercenaries in Egyptian-controlled garrison towns. The finds at Ashdod, Tel Miqne, Tell el-Safi, Beth Shemesh, Ashkelon, Gezer, Beth Shean, and Megiddo validate this. But they also founded settlements on virgin soil, as in the case of Tell Qasile.

From thick layers of debris and ash found at most of the excavated sites, it is clear that the Philistine cities were destroyed around the beginning of the tenth century, either by King David or by the Egyptian pharaoh, Siamun. They were eventually rebuilt, sometimes on a smaller scale. Apparently, their wars with the Israelites were only temporary setbacks (or perhaps the Bible exaggerates their submission to David) and with the weakening of the Israelites after the division of the united monarchy into two kingdoms, the Philistines seem to have reasserted themselves as a commercial power.

From the middle of the eighth century, with the rise of Assyria as the controlling power over all of Palestine, some of the Philistine cities enjoyed a renaissance. Ekron, for example, reached the zenith of its economic growth and prosperity at the end of the eighth or beginning of the seventh century. Ashdod still had its own king and its own cultural distinction until the sixth century. But by the end of the seventh century, Babylonian ascendancy over the ancient Near East was taking its toll in Philistia. This was manifested in a wave of conquest and mass deportations, after which the political, economic, and social landscape of the country was changed forever. Although Gaza, Ashkelon, and Ashdod rose again to become flourishing cities in the Persian, Hellenistic, and Roman periods, their heritage was no longer even faintly Philistine.

Tel Miqne, which has been identified as Ekron and which lies on the border between ancient Judah and Philistia, is the northernmost and furthest inland city of the Philistine Pentapolis, which also includes Gaza, Ashdod, Ashkelon, and Gath. Ashdod has been extensively excavated and Ashkelon is still being excavated. The exact location of Gath has yet to be determined, while ancient Gaza sits beneath present Gaza, a densely populated city. The excavations at Tel Miqne-Ekron, which began in 1984 (after pilot excavations in 1981–82) and are still going on, are a joint American–Israeli project, headed by the author, from the Institute of Archaeology of the Hebrew University, and Seymour Gitin, Dorot director of the Albright Institute of Archaeological Research, Jerusalem. The findings from all of these places, as well as from Tell Qasile, a settlement on the northern border of Philistia, have made it possible for us to assess the initial appearance and development of the Sea People/Philistine culture in Canaan, with its patterns of settlement, urbanization, architecture, industry, cult, ceramic repertoire, metallurgy, glyptics, and other facets.

   Unlike Gaza, Ashkelon, and Ashdod, which kept their original names in one form or another over long periods of time, Ekron had disappeared as a geographical entity at the end of the Iron Age. Khirbet el-Muqanna, the Arabic name for Tel Miqne, lies on the western edge of the Inner Coastal Plain that in ancient times separated Philistia from Judah, overlooking the ancient network of highways leading from Ashdod to Gezer and inland, via Nahal Soreq, to the ancient city of Beth Shemesh. In 1924 William F. Albright noted the existence of the ten-acre upper tell there but because of its small size did not recognize it as Ekron. In 1957, Nathan Aidlin of nearby Kibbutz Revadim realized that the site included not only the upper tell but also a 40-acre lower tell.

Joseph Naveh of the Israel Department of Antiquities subsequently surveyed the area and his analysis of the archaeological evidence, including massive Late Iron Age fortifications, led him to identify the site as Ekron. Ten years of excavations have strengthened his assumption.

Biblical references would also seem to confirm it. Ekron is first mentioned in the book of Joshua (13.3), along with the other Philistine cities, as land that yet remained to be possessed by the people of Israel. There are some contradictory passages relating to the conquest of Ekron by Judah in Joshua since Judah is described as having taken 'Ekron and its territory'. But this passage is modified by another: 'Judah took possession of the hill country, but could not drive out the inhabitants of the plain [where Ekron is located] because they [the inhabitants] had chariots of iron' (Judg. 1.18-19). Most important, in 1 Samuel 5–6 when the Ark of the Covenant fell into the hands of the Philistines, it was taken to Ekron. The route by which the Ark traveled on its return to the Israelites at Beth Shemesh led along the Soreq Valley, near whose banks the mound of Tel Miqne lies.

Tel Miqne-Ekron is one of the largest Iron Age sites in Israel and is, as noted, composed of two parts: the upper city, or acropolis, which occupied an area of 10 acres, and a 40-acre lower city, flat and almost square in shape. During the first years of the excavation it became clear to us that Tel Miqne was just the tip of an archaeological iceberg: characteristic sherds from the lowest level of our stratigraphic trench revealed evidence of continuous occupation beginning in the Chalcolithic period in the fourth millennium BCE. The tell had, apparently, assumed its square shape from the original outline of the fortifications of the Middle Bronze Age Canaanite city, which was occupied in the period 1750–1550 BCE. This is the lowest level of nine extensively excavated strata, and spanned an area of 60 acres or more. It contained child burials in storage jars below the floors, which was a hallmark of the period. The Middle Bronze Age city was destroyed and abandoned in the mid-sixteenth century BCE. It was later resettled on a smaller scale of about ten acres on the upper tell, during the Late Bronze Age. The presence of the Late Bronze Age Canaanite settlement in this contracted area alone, first recognized by Dr Barry Gittlin, preceded the appearance of the Philistines.

Among the finds in the various Late Bronze Age strata were imported ware from Cyprus (monochrome and white-slip vessels); a burial which contained an Egyptian seal, a faience scarab from the nineteenth Dynasty, and an Egyptian-style alabaster goblet; local Canaanite and imported Mycenaean IIIB ware; an Egyptian-style large bowl and beer-bottle; and, of particular interest, copper slags and a bellows pipe, which testify to a bronze industry; and sherds of an Anatolian grey-slip krater. Like the Canaanite cities of Ashdod and Ashkelon, Canaanite Ekron was, apparently, part of an extensive Mediterranean commercial network.

The character of the city changed dramatically at the beginning of the twelfth century BCE. The destruction of the Canaanite city on the acropolis was total. On its ruins, the early Philistines established a large city, covering both the upper ten-acre tell and the larger lower city, which had lain empty for more than 400 years. The hallmark of the new settlement was the appearance of enormous quantities of locally made Mycenaean IIIC:1b ware.

The city developed and prospered in the twelfth century BCE and the first half of the eleventh. This period is characterized especially by Philistine bichrome pottery, different from the initial Mycenaean IIIC:1b ware although deriving from it. It is typified by red and black decoration on white slip, its division into decorative panels, and the widespread use of stylistic motifs such as birds, spirals, and loops.

In the second half of the eleventh century and the beginning of the tenth, the city continued to exist with minor changes, but its material culture began to reflect the influence of Phoenician culture, particularly in the dominance of burnished red slip on ceramic vessels.

If one examines the various aspects of the Iron Age I city, it is apparent that the fortifications of Ekron eventually encompassed an area of 50 acres in both the upper and lower cities. They were built of massive mudbrick walls 3.25m thick, and continued to serve the city until the seventh century BCE. In the course of time, adjoining tower rooms were built in the south and were repaired and strengthened from time to time.

The earliest inhabitants of this new city divided the city into different zones: a central area with monumental public buildings and shrines, domestic areas adjacent to them, and an industrial area adjacent to the fortifications. The expansion of Ekron was carried out according to a well-conceived master plan, based to some extent on an awareness of ecological factors. This basic idea has been confirmed and strengthened with every additional season of digging.

The industrial area of Ekron, built near the fortifications in the upper city, contained installations for pottery-making, bronze and iron work, and smelting. One of the first things made there were square and horseshoe-shaped kilns for the production of cooking and eating ware. There were large quantities of locally made Mycenaean IIIC:1b bell-shaped bowls and kraters with horizontal handles, jugs with strainer spouts, and stirrup jars, decorated in monochrome with a repertoire of Aegean motifs: variations of the spiral motif, suspended half circles, and the pictorial repertoire of birds and fish. In addition to this elegant tableware there was also coarse kitchen ware—kraters, cooking pots, and large undecorated *lekane*, also in the Aegean tradition. Nevertheless, there were examples of Canaanite ceramics as well, in the form of storage jars, juglets, bowls, lamps, and cooking pots. But the new/old Aegean style accounted for more than half of all the pottery. (A study of this pottery and its functions is being made by Ann Killebrew.) In addition to tableware, the Philistines also introduced dietary changes: according to the archaeozoologists Paula Wapnish and Brian Hesse, the Philistines introduced pork and beef in place of goat meat and mutton, which was, until their arrival, the main Canaanite fare.

Lumps of unbaked clay, biconical or rounded in shape, were also found near the pottery works and could be linked to another Aegean craft; they were used as loomweights in weaving. Loomweights of this type are also known from Ashdod and in Ashkelon in twelfth- and eleventh-century contexts and can be traced to Cyprus and the Mycenaean world.

Still other Aegean-linked finds in the area of the kilns were painted figurines of animals; a stylized head with a flat headdress and a bird face; and the earliest example of an 'Ashdoda'-type goddess figurine, so called because it was first discovered at Ashdod. The 'Ashdoda' is a stylized image of a woman whose body is shaped like a chair and derives from the goddess-mother of the Aegean world.

Also found in a huge installation lined with *hamra* in the industrial area was a crucible with traces of metal. The high technological and artistic level of bronze and iron metallurgy at Ekron was evident in a number of cult artifacts found there. Among the bronze objects were three wheels with eight spokes each, a frame fragment of a stand with a loop for the insertion of an axle, and a small pendant in the shape of a bud, all made of cast bronze. These finds were undoubtedly part of a square stand on wheels, known from Cyprus in the twelfth century BCE. A basin or laver, in which the offering was placed, would be set on top of the square stand, which provided a supporting frame. These stands were lavishly decorated with pictorial scenes deriving from Aegean art.

This was the first example of a wheeled cult stand found in Israel. The cult stand was reminiscent in shape, workmanship, and decoration of the biblical *mechanot*, or laver stands, made for Solomon's Temple in Jerusalem by Hiram, king of Tyre (see 1 Kgs 7.27-33).

Another unique find was a double-headed bronze linchpin, whose size may indicate that it was originally part of a wheel from a full-sized chariot. The upper part of the linchpin consisted of two faces looking out in opposite directions, closed above by a flat cap covering both heads. Stylistically, the double heads and flat cap strongly resemble the sphinxes that decorate wheeled ceremonial stands from Cyprus, and are clearly Aegean in origin.

The elaborate bronze objects are certainly an outgrowth of the bronze industry which flourished during this period in Cyprus, and which, in combining strong Aegean and obvious Oriental influences, was an example of the reciprocity between the East and the West.

The early iron objects found in Ekron were not utilitarian but rather cultic in character. Among them was a complete iron knife affixed by bronze rivets to an ivory handle with a ring-shaped pommel. Its cultic or ceremonial significance is indicated by its elegant craftsmanship and the context in which it was found—on the floor of one of the shrine rooms with a *bama*-dating to the first half of the eleventh century BCE. Three additional ivory knife handles of the same type were found in Ekron, also in cultic contexts. The insertion slot of one of them still bore traces of its iron blade and could be dated to the first half of the twelfth century BCE, thus linking it to the initial settlement of the Philistines at Ekron.

The most pertinent parallel for this type of knife handle from excavations in Israel was found in the northeast part of the courtyard relating to the earliest Philistine temple at Tell Qasile. Similar knives with ring-shaped handles have been found in Cyprus and the Aegean. They add to the quota of iron appearing in Philistine sites and raise anew the question of the role of the Philistines in the introduction of iron-working technology. From all the finds so far it is apparent that iron smelting and iron workshops were beginning to develop in Philistia but they focused not on objects of daily use but on the production of more precious and elaborate objects, predominantly relating to cult.

As we have seen in the knives, elephant tusk ivory was another precious material used in Tel Miqne-Ekron. The most important evidence of Aegean style in the craftsmanship of ivory objects could be seen in the elaborately incised ivory lid of a pyxis (found in the monumental shrine described below). It depicts animal combat among a griffin, a lion, and two bulls, and is executed in thirteenth- and twelfth-century Aegean style. This is an excellent example of the highly skilled Aegean-style craftsmanship in a twelfth-century Philistine context, both in the type of vessel and style of decoration. In one of the latest areas excavated a gold hair ring was found with parallels from the twelfth–eleventh centuries in the Aegean world.

At the heart of the city (work on which was supervised by Yosef Garfinkel from the Hebrew University), the initial phase of the settlement was represented by several architectural features. These include a one-story-high room—its walls were only one brick thick—with a rectangular, mudbrick hearth with a pebbled surface. Traces of firing and animal bones were found, along with a sunken storage jar. in the following phase a new hearth was built in the center of the room with two adjacent pillars, paved with pottery sherds—a feature well known in Cyprus as well as in the hearths in Tel Qasile (see below, Dikaios, Karageorghis, Mazar).

There was a dramatic change in the character of the superimposed building in the succeeding strata, but it was a peaceful development that continued the same cultural tradition, the outcome, no doubt, of economic stability and prosperity. The earlier building was leveled with fill, in order to prepare the terrain for the new building, whose massive stone foundations cut into the walls and enveloped the previous building. The heavy walls and stone foundations indicate an upper story.

This building is an impressive monumental temple or shrine, containing two superimposed hearths, well constructed with pebbled surfaces and plastered edges, 1.2m in diameter. Large amounts of burnt ashes and bones were on and around the hearth. More than an architectural element, however, the hearth represented a tradition that reflected the social structure and habits of everyday life in the Aegean (and Cypriot) palaces and shrines, as seen at the Mycenaean palaces of Pylos (Blegen 1966: 85-87), Mycenae (Mylonas 1966: 55-56, 60), and Tiryns (Kilian 1980). The Mycenaean megaton is a long building with an open front-entrance hall, a central hall with a hearth and side rooms. The hearth is the central feature of the main hall of the megaton. The hearths in these palaces and megara, though larger in diameter (ranging from 3.7 to 4m), are very similar to the Ekron hearth in a number of features: the modeled edge with a broad flat rim that encircles the center where the fire was kept burning, the white plaster-coated floor lipping up to it, and the stucco coating of the hearth.

A number of smaller hearths were also found in other places on the acropolis and in the lower city. At the top of the acropolis, for example, there was a surface area, 17m long and 3m wide, paved with wadi pebbles and pottery fragments. This was part of a large open area in which 25 hearths were found. They were about 50 to 70cm in diameter, in two superimposed layers. They indicate a special communal function of the area.

Only one other example of a hearth has ever been found in Canaan— at the Philistine temple at Tell Qasile. This was a small, freestanding keyhole-shaped hearth, and was assumed to have cultic connotations. It was found in the earliest stratum of this small Philistine harbor town, built on virgin soil. The Tell Qasile hearth had a central circular depression with a platform paved with storage jar fragments, for which parallels are known from Enkomi, Cyprus (Dikaios 1969: 175-206; Karageorghis 1997; Mazar 1986: 4).

By the second half of the eleventh century BCE, with their Aegean heritage fading into the past, the people of Ekron no longer used the hearth. In the last phase of the building the hearth itself had disappeared.

Another plastered public building with a monumental entrance is now in the process of being uncovered. The entranceway is about 5m wide and has a stone pillar base at its center. The entrance doorposts have a crenellated profile and rounded corners. The threshold is made of stones and stone steps lead up to it from the courtyard at the front. The courtyard is well paved and contains a drainage pit. There is a great deal of similarity between the architectural foundations of this structure and the building described above. Plastered mudbrick walls are characteristic of most of the buildings from the twelfth to the tenth centuries BCE.

Our knowledge of Philistine cult practices was considerably enhanced by finds in the large temple. On the north–south axis of the main hall, there were two pillar bases (and possibly a third), 2.5m apart, one located exactly in the center. This configuration resembled that in the Philistine temple at Tell Qasile, where support pillars stood about 2m apart. It also corresponds with the scene in the Bible (Judg. 16.29-30) in which the blind Samson brings down the Philistine temple on himself and his enemies by pushing the pillars apart.

There were three rooms on the eastern side opening onto the main hall. In the middle room, the focal point of cultic practice, was a

plastered mudbrick *bamah*, or offering platform, preserved to height of
c. 1m. The *bamah* was part of the local Canaanite tradition, but was also
well known from Cyprus and the Aegean.

On the periphery of the industrial belt and perhaps in what was part
of a residential area, we uncovered a smaller shrine which was, in fact,
one in a series of superimposed Iron Age shrines, each built on the
remains of the previous shrine. The Philistine tradition of sanctified areas
is known from the temple area at Tell Qasile. The shrine contained a
wide plastered floor, benches, and a platform. Outside, in a disposal area,
were found bichrome pottery and a number of animal and human
figurines, among them the fragment of a lion-headed vessel, similar to
one found at the Philistine temple at Tell Qasile.

On one of the earlier levels there was a miniature votive vessel, identical to the thousands found at the cult center at Athienou on Cyprus.
Four bovine shoulder blades, or scapulae, with incisions along their
edges provided another connection to Cyprus. The function of these
objects was either for oracular purposes or—as most scholars claim—as
musical instruments, and they were found in large quantities on the
benches in the temples of Enkomi and Kition. There were also crude
figurines in the Mycenaean tradition at one of the earlier levels. Their
spreading headdresses and birdlike faces prefigured the 'Ashdoda'-type
figurine found in large quantities at Ashdod, a conceptual and stylistic
continuation of the seated Aegean female goddess.

One of the domestic or residential areas of Ekron revealed three units
of large houses, each of which was composed of two rooms and a
courtyard. In one of the courtyards there were several baking ovens and
household installations, and in another a large stone bath. Next to the
bath was a monolith about 2m high. Inside, one of the small rooms had
plastered installations and an assemblage of ivory objects and ceramic
vessels, among which was a ring-like flask with an 'Ashdoda'-type
human face design. Another room contained an assemblage of complete
vessels, including a Mycenaean IIIC:1b stirrup vase, associated with the
earliest phase of the building.

In conclusion, it is evident that the ability to build this large new city
indicates a well-organized society with a firm economic structure which
fits our assumption of the Sea Peoples' military supremacy and technological abilities. The archaeological evidence shows that the material culture of this city was based on elements new to Canaan, elements which
reflected the Aegean background of the newcomers.

The evidence from Tel Miqne-Ekron, when joined to that of the other Philistine sites which have been excavated, enables us to reevaluate the first appearance of the Philistines/Sea Peoples in Canaan. It should be emphasized that the changes which took place in Canaan in the transitional period between the Late Bronze and Iron I Ages were not uniform and did not occur at one and the same time. Complex processes characterize this period, during which the indigenous Canaanite culture and the Egyptian, Philistine, and Israelite cultures often existed side by side, interacting and influencing one another. Philistine material culture lost its uniqueness when the Philistines reached the peak of their prosperity and their political and military power at the end of the eleventh century BCE. This period was one in which older Aegean traditions were abandoned, not only in Ekron but in the rest of Philistia as well, and new cultural influences, primarily Egyptian and Phoenician, took their place.

BIBLIOGRAPHY

Blegen, C.W.
   1966   *The Palace of Nestor at Pylos in Western Messenia*, I.1 (Princeton: Princeton University Press).

Dikaios, P.
   1969   *Enkomi Excavations 1948–1958* (Mainz am Rhein: von Zabern).

Dothan, T.
   1982   *The Philistines and their Material Culture* (New Haven, CT: American Oriental Society).
   1989   'The Arrival of the Sea People—Cultural Diversity in Early Iron Age Canaan', AASOR 49 (ed. S. Gitin and W. G. Dever): 1-14.
   1989   'Iron Knives from Tel Miqne-Ekron' (Hebrew), *Eretz Israel* 20: 154-63.
   1990   'Ekron of the Philistines, Part I: Where they Came from, How they Settled down and the Place they Worshipped in', *BARev* 16.1: 26-36.
   1992   'Bronze Wheels from Tel Miqne-Ekron' (Hebrew), *Eretz Israel* 23: 148-54.
   1992   'Social Dislocation and Cultural Change in the Twelfth Century BCE', in *The Crisis Years: The Twelfth Century BC* (ed. W.A. Ward and M. Joukowsky; Providence, RI: Brown University): 93-98.
   1993   'A Double-headed Bronze Linchpin from Tel Miqne-Ekron' (Hebrew), *Eretz Israel* 24: 62-67.
   1995   'An Early Phoenician Cache from Tel Miqne-Ekron' (Hebrew), *Eretz Israel* 25, in press.
   1995   'Tel Miqne-Ekron: the Aegean Affinities of the Sea Peoples (Philistines) Settlement in Canaan in Iron Age I', *AIA*, in press.

Dothan, T., and M. Dothan
    1992   *People of the Sea: The Search for the Philistines* (New York: Mac-
              millan, 1992).
Dothan, T., and S. Gitin
    1990   'Ekron of the Philistines', *BARev* 16.1: 26-36.
    1994   'Tel Miqne-Ekron: The Rise and Fall of a Philistine City' (Hebrew),
              Qadmoniot 105-106: 2-28.
Gitin, S.
    1989   'Tel Miqne-Ekron—A Type-Site for the Inner Coastal Plain in the
              Iron Age II Period', AASOR 66: 23-58.
    1992   'Last Days of the Philistines', *Archaeology* 54.3: 26-31.
    1995   'Tel Miqne-Ekron in the Seventh Century BCE: The Impact of
              Economic Innovation and Foreign Cultural Influence on a Neo-
              Assyrian Vassal City-State', *AIA*, in press.
Gittlen, B.
    1992   'The Late Bronze Age at Tel Miqne-Ekron', *Eretz Israel* 23: 50*-53*.
Gunneweg, J. *et. al.*
    1986   'On the Origin of Pottery from Tel Miqne-Ekron', *BASOR* 264: 17-
              27.
Karageorghis, V.
    1997   'Hearths and Bathtubs in Cyprus: A Sea People's Innovation?', in
              *Proceedings Volume of the International Symposium on Mediter-
              ranean Peoples in Transition, Thirteenth to Early Tenth Centuries BCE*
              (ed. S. Gitin, A. Mazar and E. Stern; Jerusalem: Israel Exploration
              Society, in press).
Kilian, K.
    1980   'Zum Ende der mykenischen Epoche in der Argolis', *Jahrbuch Des
              Romisch-Germanischen Zentralmuseums Mainz* 27: 166-95.
Mazar, A.
    1986   'Excavations at Tel Qasile 1982–1984', *IEJ* 36: 1-15.
Mylonas, G.E.
    1966   *Mycenae and the Mycenaean Age* (Princeton: Princeton University
              Press).

The Yigael Yadin Memorial Excavations at Hazor, 1990–93: Aims and Preliminary Results

Amnon Ben-Tor

Tel Hazor was excavated during the years 1955–58 and 1968–69 by a team headed by the late Yigael Yadin. The excavations were carried out on behalf of the Department of Archaeology of the Hebrew University and the Israel Exploration Society, with support from the Rothschild Fund.[1] The multiplicity of workers participating in the many seasons of excavations, as well as the vast dimensions of the site, classify Yadin's excavations as one of the largest conducted in Israel. The expedition team included several of the renowned pioneers of Israeli archaeology, such as Y. Aharoni, R. Amiran, and T. and M. Dothan. Excavation techniques and principles of surveying and stratification established at Hazor by I. Dunayevsky, the expedition architect, had a profound influence on contemporary Israeli archaeology. An entire generation of young Israeli archaeologists, who are today at the top of their field, received their initial training in field archaeology at Hazor.

The tell consists of two distinct parts: the upper city (acropolis), measuring approximately 25 acres, and the lower city, a vast rectangular plateau extending north of the upper city and covering a total area of about 200 acres (Figure 1). Consequently, Tel Hazor constitutes the largest mound in Israel and is appropriately named 'head of all those Kingdoms' (Josh. 11.10), and its king, Jabin, was also referred to as 'the King of Canaan' (Judg. 4.2).

Hazor's impressive dimensions, immense fortifications such as the vast earthen rampart protecting the lower city from the west (seen even

---

1. Y. Yadin et al., *Hazor I* (Jerusalem, 1958); *Hazor II* (Jerusalem, 1960); *Hazor III–IV* (plates) (Jerusalem, 1961); text (ed. A. Ben-Tor; Jerusalem, 1989 [henceforth *Hazor I, II, III–IV*]); Y. Yadin, *Hazor, the Head of all those Kingdoms*. The Schweich Lectures of the British Academy 1970 (London, 1972 [henceforth Yadin, 1972]).

prior to excavations), the numerous references to Hazor in both biblical
and external sources from the beginning of the second millennium to the
end of the eighth century BCE, its central role in the process of conquest
and settlement of the tribes of Israel in Canaan, as described in the
Bible—all combine to make Hazor a most remarkable site.

Figure 1. Aerial view of Hazor with main excavated areas
(acropolis in lower part of picture and lower city in background).

Yadin's excavations revealed the existence of 21 strata in the city,
spanning a period of approximately 3,000 years. Not all of Hazor was
settled throughout this period. During the Early Bronze Age (third millennium BCE) only the acropolis was settled. In the Middle Bronze Age
(the first half of the second millennium) the lower part of the city was
settled for the first time. Toward the end of the second millennium

Hazor was completely destroyed; both its upper and lower cities were engulfed in a huge fire, which Yadin associated with the destruction of Hazor by the tribes of Israel under Joshua's command (Josh. 11.10-14). From the fall of Canaanite Hazor until its final destruction and abandonment, only the upper city was inhabited.

The excavations conducted at Hazor in the fifties and sixties revealed an abundance of architectural, ceramic, artistic, and other finds, which have been discussed elsewhere in detail.[2] Mention will be made here of the impressive fortification installations comprising a wall, gates, ramparts, glacis, and fosse from the Middle Bronze Age, temples and cult objects from the Late Bronze Age, a gate and casemate wall from the Solomonic period, as well as a wall, fortress, and remarkable water-system from the time of Ahab's reign. Another group of finds deserving of particular attention consists of fragmentary cuneiform tablets. As previously mentioned, Hazor was referred to in textual sources, and according to the Mari archive, the city served as a prominent commercial center with trade links to the cities of Syria and Babylonia in the eighteenth century BCE. Presumably, archives containing economic, administrative, and other documents similar to those uncovered in the major cities of Syria and Mesopotamia also existed at Hazor. For unknown reasons, such archives have not yet been discovered in Israel. Yet, the Mari documents and those sent by the king of Hazor to Egypt, which were discovered at Tell el-Amarna, bear testimony to the notion that scribes resided at the court of the Canaanite monarchs of Hazor during the Middle and Late Bronze Ages. Fragments of documents revealed during the Yadin excavations, as well as a tablet discovered later by chance, reinforce this premise.[3] Most of the archives from the second millennium BCE, known to us in the ancient Near East, were uncovered in palaces or temples. If an archive indeed exists at Hazor, it will most likely be found at the Canaanite royal palace. A corner of a monumental building, which was identified as belonging to such a palace, was uncovered by Yadin's team in the fifties. Discovery of

2. *Hazor I, II, III–IV*; Yadin, 1972.

3. A. Malamat, *Mari and the Early Israelite Experience* (Oxford: Oxford University Press, 1989), pp. 55-57 (henceforth Malamat, 1989); M. Anbar and N. Naaman, 'An Account Tablet of Sheep from Ancient Hebron', *Tel Aviv* 13 (1986), pp. 8-10.

such an archive here would constitute a momentous archaeological achievement.

More than two decades have passed since the termination of Yadin's excavations at Hazor. The site and its finds, due to their great significance, have also raised controversial issues involving archaeology, history, biblical research, and art history. Over the years, dozens of articles have been written either supporting or contradicting Yadin's findings. Several important issues have been left unsolved even after the conclusion of the comprehensive dig.

In the summer of 1990, excavations, entitled 'Hazor Excavations in Memory of Yigael Yadin', were resumed at the tell. This is a joint project of the Philip and Muriel Berman Center for Biblical Archaeology of the Hebrew University, and Complutense University, Madrid.[4]

The renewed excavations focus on the following main objectives. 1) To examine the stratigraphy and chronology of Yadin's expedition by means of excavating several areas, primarily the area adjacent to the one excavated by Yadin at the center of the upper city, designated as area A. Nearly all of the strata determined by the Yadin expedition in the 1950s (except for stratum I from the Hellenistic period) were distinguished in this area. 2) To confront those problems left unsolved following the previous expedition. Although there are many, only a few will be recounted here, and these may be outlined as follows.

What is the layout of the public buildings of the Israelite period in the area of the 'Solomonic gate'? Is it possible to distinguish between the ceramic assemblages of the ninth and eighth centuries BCE, thus contributing to the refinement and precision of the ceramic typology of those centuries? What was the extent of the city attributed to the Solomonic period by the Yadin team? Did it consist only of the western half of the upper city? Is it possible precisely to date the construction of the different fortification systems erected at various stages during the Israelite period?

4.   The excavation at Hazor is a joint project of the Berman Center for Biblical Archaeology at the Hebrew University of Jerusalem and Complutense University, Madrid in co-operation with Ambassador University, Big-Sandy, Texas, and the Israel Exploration Society. The project is directed by Professor Amnon Ben-Tor of the Hebrew University. Professor Maria-Teresa Rubiato of Complutense University heads the Spanish team. The project is also supported by the Rothschild Foundation.

What are the reasons for distinguishing between strata XI and XII of the Iron Age I, and, by means of collecting additional data, can we more clearly define the character, chronology, and ethnic affiliation of the inhabitants of Hazor during the twelfth and eleventh centuries BCE? What can be gleaned by comparing the settlement at Hazor during this period to the nearby settlement at Tel Dan? What was the character of the last Canaanite settlement at Hazor?

Is it indeed possible to detect signs of the settlement's deterioration compared with the previous settlement? When exactly was it destroyed? What was the character of the settlement at Hazor during the fifteenth and fourteenth centuries and what was the extent of its foreign contacts? What was the nature of the transition from the Middle to the Late Bronze Age? What was the layout of the royal Canaanite palace at Hazor and its ancillary buildings during the second millennium? Will the city archive indeed be discovered?

Finally, when exactly was 'Greater Hazor'—encompassing the upper and lower cities—founded, and when was it initially fortified? Did this occur during the Mari period, or prior to it during the twentieth–nineteenth centuries BCE (Middle Bronze IIA)? What can be said about Hazor of the Middle Bronze I Age (= EB IV) and what were its ties to Syria? Finally, what can be said about Hazor of the Early Bronze Age— when was it founded and what were its foreign relations?

This is an ample list of questions and we anticipate that the renewed excavations will provide answers to at least most of them.

A further objective of the renewed excavations is to transform Hazor into an attractive site for visitors. The architectural remains, although a focal point for archaeologists, are of no particular interest to the average visitor in their present state. The expedition has transferred two buildings—a storehouse and a dwelling from the Israelite period—and relocated them in a neighboring area. In their original place, these two structures were deteriorating and, consequently, inaccessible to visitors. The intention is partially to reconstruct, and thereby to preserve, several additional monuments such as the cultic high place from the period of the Judges, the Solomonic gate and city wall, and the fortification and fortress facade from the time of Ahab's reign. It is hoped that upon completion of the restoration plan, the site will become a captivating attraction for visitors, deserving of its biblical title, 'head of all those Kingdoms'.

During the four seasons of excavations carried out thus far, between

1990 and 1993, research has primarily focused on the remains from the tenth–eighth centuries BCE, during which time Hazor was a prominent city in the kingdom of Israel. This period of time runs parallel to the reign of kings Solomon (tenth century BCE), Ahab (ninth century BCE), and Jeroboam II (eighth century BCE), until the days of King Pekah, at which time Hazor was destroyed (732 BCE) during the military campaigns of the Assyrian king Tiglath-Pileser III—a campaign which marked the beginning of the end of the independence of the Israelite kingdom (2 Kgs 15.29).

The Yadin expedition distinguished six strata consisting of ten phases (VA–B, VIA–B, VII, VIII, IXA–B, and XA–B) spanning the above-mentioned period of time. Three of the strata were destroyed in a conflagration apparently caused by enemy action, according to Yadin: IXA by Ben-Hadad king of Aram (c. 880 BCE), VII by another Aramaean campaign under the leadership of Hazal (c. 810 BCE), and VA by Tiglath-Pileser III in 732 BCE. The destruction of stratum VI was most likely wrought by an earthquake around 760 BCE.[5]

This situation, of an uninterrupted stratigraphic sequence consisting apparently of several chronological givens and spanning a time period of approximately 300 years, provided the opportunity for a thorough examination of the ceramic assemblages associated with each level. An important result of this examination was the suggested division of the Iron Age into three units: the first pertains to strata XII–XI, terminating c. 1000 BCE; the second pertains to strata X–IX–VIII, terminating c. 840 BCE; and the third pertains to strata VII–VI–V, terminating c. 730 BCE.[6]

Comparing this division, based on ceramic typology, to the layout of the architectural remains during the same time frame, it is evident that full symmetry does not exist between these remains and the ceramic division proposed by the excavators.

At the beginning of the stratigraphic sequence of the Iron Age, full symmetry exists between the architectural and ceramic profiles. Apparently, strata XII–XI constitute one unit from both the architectural

---

5. Yadin, 1972, pp. 143, 169, 187, 190. With regard to the destruction of stratum VI by an earthquake see also W.G. Dever, 'A Case Study in Biblical Archaeology: The Earthquake of Ca. 760 BCE', *Eretz-Israel* 23 (1992), pp. 27*-35*.

6. Y. Aharoni and R. Amiran, 'A New Scheme for the Subdivision of the Iron Age in Palestine', *IEJ* 8 (1958), pp. 171-84.

and ceramic standpoints. In the later sequence, two 'break points', that is, a radical change in the architectural layout, were detected: strata X–IX (construction of the gate and casemate wall, and some private dwellings) constitute one unit, terminating in total destruction, as previously noted.[7] Strata VIII and VII (doubling of the inhabited area; erection of the solid wall; construction of public buildings, such as the storage structure in area A, the citadel in area B, and the water system in area L) constitute a second unit, also terminating in complete destruction.[8] The third architectural unit comprises strata VI and V (characterized mainly by the erection of several private dwellings, building activity above the casemate wall [no longer in use in area A] and changes in the fortifications, evident mainly in the western extremity of the city).[9] The architectural differentiation between strata VI and VII on the one hand, and VIII and IX on the other, was emphasized in the following manner by Yadin:

> The city of Stratum VIII is entirely different from that of Stratum X–IX in layout, area, character, public buildings and installations... the destruction of Stratum VII in Area A had been total... new blocks of houses were built changing the nature of the area from public to residential... the center of the storage structures (which in Strata VIII–VII was in Area A) was at that time moved to Area G.[10]

Yadin's excavations have thus left us with three 'ceramic profiles' versus four 'architectural profiles'. Examination of this scheme is one of the challenges confronting the present expedition. It is, of course, possible that in the final analysis, Yadin's conclusion will be proven correct: a change in the layout of the city, even as a result of enemy destruction, does not necessitate a parallel change in the ceramic repertoire. Nonetheless, the previous expedition's conclusions definitely deserve further deliberation and research, which is what we are accomplishing today.

7. *Hazor II*, Pl. CXCIX; *Hazor III–IV* (Text), Plans VIII–X; Yadin, 1972, pp. 135-46.

8. *Hazor I*, Pl. CLXXII; *Hazor II*, Pls. CC–CCI; *Hazor III–IV* (Text) Plans XI–XII; Yadin, 1972, p. 179.

9. *Hazor I*, Pls. CCII-CCV; *Hazor II*, Pls. CLXXIII–CLXXIV; *Hazor III–IV* (Text), Plans XIII–XIV; Yadin, 1972, pp. 187-90.

10. Yadin, 1972, pp. 165, 179, 184.

Hazor Strata	Architectural Profile	Ceramic Profile
XII XI	1	1
X IX	2	
		2
VIII VII	3	
		3
VI V	4	

How do things stand in light of the renewed excavations? At this stage, excavations focus on two areas of the upper city (Figure 2): area A, comprising the western expanse of the main area excavated in the upper city by the Yadin team (we have uncovered an area of approximately 500m² at this spot), and area M, located in the center of the northern edge of the upper city. An area of 100m² was dug up at this spot by the Yadin team in 1968, with the aim of examining the relation between the two upper city fortification systems—the one associated with Solomon, the other with Ahab's reign.[11] At this location, the present team has widened the excavation area with the objective of: (A) examining Yadin's findings; (B) gathering additional information on the settlement, especially as pertains to the fortification systems from the Iron and Bronze Ages; and (C) excavating a stratigraphic section, 10m wide, that will connect the upper and lower cities and offer greater insight into the relationship between these two parts of the city and—as part of that objective—studying the character of the plateau located at the center of the northern slope of the upper city.

11. Yadin, 1972, pp. 118, 140-42, 165.

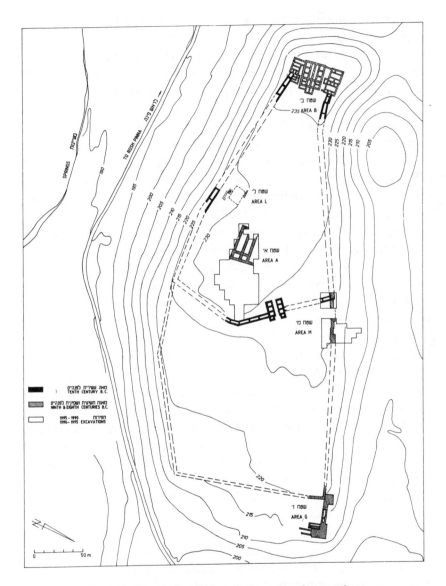

Figure 2. Plan of upper city and main areas of excavation
(prepared by Ms Ruhama Bonfil, Institute of Archaeology).

Numerous structures were uncovered throughout the four seasons of
the 1990–93 excavations, such as fortifications, public buildings, and
private dwellings, as well as industrial and agricultural installations with
their accompanying rich ceramic assemblages, mainly from the ninth
and eighth centuries BCE. It is still too early to draw comparisons

between the findings of the Yadin expedition and those of the new expedition team, since the ceramic assemblages from the ninth and eighth centuries that we uncovered are still in the initial stages of investigation. In addition, we have not yet uncovered the entire stratigraphic sequence of the Iron Age, nor have we researched the strata from the twelfth–eleventh centuries. Nonetheless, it has become evident, even at this early stage, that while several of Yadin's conclusions were proven correct (for example the dating of the six-chambered city gate and the casemate wall to the tenth century BCE, thus justifying the term 'Solomonic fortifications'), some amendments need to be made in the scheme set down by Yadin, particularly as regards the addition of phases in the stratigraphic sequence of the Iron Age. This will enable us to offer a more exact definition of the ceramic assemblages. Since it is appropriate at this early stage to refrain from drawing detailed comparisons between the present findings and those set down by Yadin, we will limit ourselves to a general description of our discoveries to date.

A considerable number of Arab sherds strewn throughout the area constitute the most recent evidence of human activity at Hazor. These sherds span several hundred years, beginning with the Early Islamic throughout the Mameluke period. Apparently, some of the sherds belonged to the inhabitants of a nearby village of Waggas, east of the tell, whose fields extended over the full area of Hazor. Up till now, these sherds have been exclusively found in area A with no known connection to any architectural remains; this is why no specific stratum number was assigned to that period in the stratigraphic sequence of Hazor. Mention should be made of the remains of an isolated building from the Mameluke period, visible, even today, at a distance of 100m east of area A.[12]

In our excavations of area A, no remains attributable to the Hellenistic and Persian periods were detected. The cemetery from the Persian period uncovered by the Yadin team[13] was apparently confined to the northern part of area A, west of the Solomonic gate.

The most recent architectural remains uncovered in area A are accompanied by Iron Age pottery. Yet only at certain isolated points was it possible to attribute floors that bear scant pottery remains to those latest Iron Age walls. The structures uncovered by us in area A during the four seasons of excavations are of a public as well as a residential

12. *Hazor I*, p. 21, Pl. LXVI: 1-5, Pl. CLXXV.
13. *Hazor III–IV* (Text), p. 49, Plan VII; (Plates) Pls. XIII, XXVII: 5-7, CXCI; Yadin 1972, p. 112.

nature. The large structures, with long halls and plastered floors (Figure 3), were apparently used as storage installations. A building of an administrative nature lies to the north. Numerous private dwellings were uncovered in the southern part of area A.

Figure 3. Ninth-century BCE storehouse in area A (photograph courtesy Stztulman-Kessel Photographic Services Ltd, Jerusalem).

In total, seven strata, and several floors pertaining to each one, were encountered by us. The sequence is characterized by its continuity of layout; walls built upon already existing walls, blocked passages, and new floors constitute the major changes between strata. Nonetheless, three 'break points' resulting in more significant changes can be discerned within the sequence at the following points: between the first and second strata; between the second and third; and between the fifth and sixth strata. In contrast, the change between the third and fourth strata is minimal and most likely represents two phases of the same stratum. The third stratum was destroyed in a conflagration whose traces are discernible in the north as well as in the southern part of the excavated area. This disaster is most probably to be associated with the Assyrian conquest of 732 BCE (Yadin's stratum V).

At present, the Iron Age I is represented by three isolated pits containing ashes, mill stones, and some Iron I pottery, uncovered near the pillared storehouse in the eastern part of the excavated area.

The remains of five strata were unearthed in area M and here, as well, several floors attributable to each stratum were discerned. During the cleaning of one of the rooms of the casemate wall excavated by the Yadin's expedition in the 1968 season in area M,[14] it became apparent that the excavation there had not reached the original floor level. The original floor was reached by us at a depth of about 50cm below the level at which the excavation of 1968 stopped, and the ceramic material found on the floor may clearly be attributed to the tenth century BCE. This confirms Yadin's assertion that the casemate wall and the six-chambered gate associated with it were built in the tenth century BCE, apparently in the reign of King Solomon. A 3-meter-thick solid fortification wall, extending along the northern edge of the site, and a cobbled street adjacent to it and separating it from the stretch of dwellings to its south constitute the main architectural features (Figure 4). During one of the phases—an exact date cannot be determined—the wall was strengthened at several points by a revetment wall externally attached to it and almost doubling its width. Two architectural 'break points' can be discerned: between the upper stratum and the second, and between the fourth and fifth strata. The second stratum has two phases, the latter of which was destroyed in a huge blaze—again probably attributable to the Assyrian conquest.

14. Yadin 1972, pp. 140-42, Pl. XXV: b, c.

Figure 4. General view of area M (note the solid city wall on the right
and the partially excavated storehouse in upper left corner; photograph courtesy
Stztulman-Kessel Photographic Services Ltd, Jerusalem).

In summing up the Iron II–III strata at Hazor, tenth-century Hazor, though hardly known, seems to be characterized mainly by the construction of the six-chambered gate and casemate wall, as well as a few isolated structures. Occupation during that period was confined to the western half of the upper city.

In the ninth century, Israelite Hazor reached its zenith, probably in the days of King Ahab. The extent of the city was doubled, and it comprised the entire area of the upper city. New fortifications (the 'solid wall') as well as a citadel were built, a huge water system was cut, and large storehouses, three of them in the so far excavated area, were constructed.

In the eighth century the public storehouses were replaced by private buildings, and Hazor shows signs of decline as time progresses. The fortifications were strengthened, probably in the second half of the eighth century, as a result of the growing Assyrian threat.

Remains of Bronze Age Hazor, including a building identified as the Canaanite palace of Hazor (or what appear to be two palaces), are concealed under Iron Age structures in area A. A considerable part of this Bronze Age complex is located under the pillared storehouse and the 'four-roomed house' (building 2a) uncovered by the Yadin expedition.[15] In order to unearth these earlier remains, it was necessary to remove the overlying Iron Age structures—already in a dilapidated state—from their original location, and to relocate them to a nearby area. Relocation of the structures was preferable for two additional reasons: a considerable amount of damage had already been inflicted upon these buildings due to the ravages of time and nature. As of late, the extent of damage is increasing and it is estimated that within several years, little will remain of these buildings. As for their location, especially that of the pillared storehouse, the escarpment created by the depth of the Yadin dig has made it impossible to keep the structure in its original place. Because of the precarious state of the walls, visitation at the two buildings has been prohibited. Relocation has enabled us not only to dig beneath the structures, but also to preserve them. With their restoration, partial reconstruction, and eventual opening to visitors, another key objective of the renewed excavation will have been met.

The area chosen as the new locus for the structures is 100m northwest of their present spot. The two buildings were relocated during the

---

15. *Hazor II*, Pls. CC–CCIII; *Hazor III–IV* (Text), p. 41, Plans XIII–XIV; Yadin, 1972, pp. 179-81, Pl. XXIII.

1992–93 seasons (Figure 5) and are a stone by stone duplication of the original buildings: all of the original stones were utilized with the greatest possible adherence to the ancient technique. This endeavor is the first of its kind in Israel: work was carried out by expert builders in co-ordination with the Antiquities Authority and the National Parks Authority with strict supervision by an observing architect and the archaeological expedition.[16]

Figure 5. Two Israelite structures, relocated and partially restored (photograph courtesy Stztulman-Kessel Photographic Services Ltd, Jerusalem).

It stands to reason that the main part of the work conducted in the first four seasons focused on Iron Age remains. According to the original plan, we were not slated to reach the Bronze Age remains much before the fifth season of excavations. As it happened, we encountered remains from the Bronze Age in area A as early as the second season of excavations. We attempted to avoid their excavation and concentrate on research of the Iron Age remains, which, according to our estimations,

16. Hazor staff member, Professor Maria Teresa Rubiato, from Complutense University in Madrid, plays a central role in the preparation of the plans of the buildings to be preserved and restored, as well as in the constant supervision of the actual field work.

would necessitate at least another season or two of work. It should, however, be made clear that there is no correlation between the scant amount of Bronze Age remains uncovered thus far and the likely overall volume and importance of those finds.

At a first glance at area A one immediately notices that it is located at the highest point in the center of the upper city. The area's terrain slopes in all directions with an especially sharp slant toward the east. This profile of the terrain was created, as we have discovered in the process of excavations, due to the fact that the Iron Age structures in area A were built upon the ruins of an extensive building complex consisting of what seems to be a palace or palaces (and perhaps also a temple) from the Middle and Late Bronze Ages. The northeast corner of this complex was uncovered by the Yadin expedition in the 1950s, and he identified these ruins then as the corner of the royal Canaanite palace of Middle Bronze Age Hazor.[17]

Remains of Bronze Age structures were uncovered just below the surface along the western edge of area A where these structures reach their maximum height. It has become evident that this area was devoid of buildings between the destruction of the Bronze Age structures and the final destruction of Iron Age Hazor. This would indicate that a wide-open space existed in the center of Israelite Hazor. At this stage, we do not have a definitive answer as to why this area was not utilized for building purposes during the Iron Age. Nonetheless, this fact affords direct contact with the well-preserved Bronze Age remains, undisturbed by later building activity. Hence, the brick walls of the Bronze Age complex were preserved (at this point) to an approximate height of 2m! The excavated wall sections are of a considerable width and are made of bricks, measuring $38 \times 38 \times 15$cm, placed upon a stone foundation, and a large amount of timber (cedar) was incorporated into the mudbrick. The lower part of the northern wall (so far the only outer wall of the building uncovered) is covered with orthostats of smoothed basalt, identical to those discovered in the temple in area H and in the temple entrance in area A by the Yadin expedition. In addition, a section of a large courtyard with two large pillar-bases, 1.7m in diameter, made of highly smoothed basalt, were uncovered (Figure 6). The building is clearly Syrian in character and shows a surprisingly close affinity in plan, as well as constructional details, to the palatial structures of Alalakh IV and VII.

17. *Hazor III–IV* (Text), pp. 6-23, Plans I–VI; Yadin, 1972, p. 124.

Figure 6. Forecourt of Late Bronze Age palace at Hazor (photograph courtesy
Stztulman-Kessel Photographic Services Ltd, Jerusalem).

The complex was destroyed in a violent fire leaving a layer of ashes
approximately 1m in height. The large amount of timber incorporated in
the walls added to the fire's intensity, and temperatures reached close to
1000°C, resulting in the partial melting of the mudbrick superstructure
of the walls. A group of pithoi was found on the floor of one of the
rooms. Similar pithoi dated to the fourteenth–thirteenth centuries were
also uncovered in the lower city by the Yadin expedition. In one of the
rooms, the following items were discovered: tens of simple and carinated
bowls, the remains of a wooden box covered in ivory, ten cylinder seals,
and several hundred beads of various types, apparently assembled in the
box and later scattered and broken into bits during the destruction of the
structure. The heads of two basalt statues, most likely portraying gods
(or rulers), which were found in the northwestern part of the excavated
area, imply that this part of the building may have served some cultic
purpose. The phenomenon of decapitation and disfigurement of the
statues of the gods (and kings?), which was most likely carried out by
the conquerors of Canaanite Hazor (the tribes of Israel?), was also perceived by the Yadin team during their excavations of the temples in the

lower city.[18] It should be noted that so far no trace of imported pottery has been uncovered in the debris, which can probably be explained by the fact that only a small portion of the buildings from the period under discussion have thus far been uncovered. Hence, the exact dating of the destruction of the complex—sometime during the end of the Late Bronze Age—must remain open. Certain questions concerning the destruction of Canaanite Hazor (such as When did it occur? What was the character of the last Canaanite city? Did it flourish or stagnate? What caused its ruin? Was there a time gap between the destruction of Canaanite Hazor and the beginnings of the first Israelite settlement there?) are central to our understanding of the period of transition from the Bronze Age to the Iron Age and of the settlement of the Israelites at Canaan. These questions induced Yadin to excavate Hazor and confounded many of his expedition colleagues. Scholarly opinion is still divided as to Yadin's findings. By gathering additional information, the present expedition hopes to contribute to this discussion of one of the major topics of biblical archaeology.

As previously cited, one of the objectives of the renewed excavations is completely to uncover the Canaanite royal palace. Moreover, one of our greatest hopes is that the archives of one or more of the Hazor monarchs will be found in the palace.[19] Indeed, this premise is reinforced by our discovery of two documents during the 1991 and 1992 seasons. Although excavations have not yet reached the strata ascribed to the period of the palace, and despite the fact that these documents have not been found in their original location, their importance should not be overlooked. The first document (Figure 7) deals with the distribution of quantities of silver[20] (on behalf of the palace at Hazor?) to a group of people: in the remaining section of the document a total of nine and a half shekels was distributed. Since only half of the original text remains, it is difficult to establish the purpose of the transaction, yet the list of names—19 in number—is of especially significant value. At least half

18. *Hazor I*, pp. 86-88, Pls. XXVII: 2, XXIX: 1, XXXI: 1; *Hazor III–IV* (Text): pp. 322-27, 335-37; *Hazor III–IV* (Plates) Pls. CCCXXIV–CCCXXVII, CCCXXX; Yadin, 1972, pp. 72, 84, 94-95.

19. See above; also nn. 3, 17.

20. W. Horowitz and A. Shaffer, 'An Administrative Tablet from Hazor: A Preliminary Edition', *IEJ* 42 (1992), pp. 21-33; for the archaeological context, see A. Ben-Tor, *Season of 1991: Introduction, IEJ* 42 (1992), pp. 17-20.

of the names are familiar to us from the Mari documents, including Abi-Erah, Abi-Rapi, and Hinni-El. The name of the storm-god Addu, a dominant component in names, appears nine times: Isput-Addu, Yanbi-Addu, Yahtuk-Addu, and others. The names imply that the population of Hazor was, in the main, of Amorite origin. The nature of the document, its writing style, and the selection of names clearly associate this document with the cultural milieu of Mari and Alalakh of the Old Babylonian period and, in turn, fixed the date of the Hazor document at the eighteenth or the seventeenth century at the latest.

Figure 7. Old Babylonian economic text from Hazor (photograph courtesy Stztulman-Kessel Photographic Services Ltd, Jerusalem).

Unlike the first document, the second one was evidently written by an expert scribe. There is no mention of either economic or administrative matters; rather it is a letter written to a man named Ibni ([[-Adad]? king of Hazor?) by one named Irpa. The letter concerns a woman or women being transferred from place to place. Since only a quarter of the document is intact, the context cannot be ascertained. Yet, as with the first document, its importance lies in the names cited within. A king of Hazor, referred to as Ibni-Adad, was mentioned several times in a document discovered in the Mari archive dealing with consignments of tin sent to Hazor.[21] This document, as well as the remainder of the documents from the Mari archive, is dated to the first half of the eighteenth century—the same time frame as the document discovered by us at Hazor, and it is likely that they both speak of the same person! The name Ibni-Adad is the Akkadian form of the West Semitic name Yabni-Hadad,[22] of which the name Jabin, king of Hazor (Josh. 11.1; Judg. 4.2), is a possible linguistic derivation. The Jabin referred to in the books of Joshua and Judges postdates Ibni-Adad of the Mari archive by more than 500 years, indicating that the name must have been a dynastic name, borne by more than one of the kings of Hazor.[23] It is likely that the sender of the new document from Hazor, the above-mentioned Irpa, is familiar to us from a legal document accidentally discovered several years ago at Hazor.[24] In that particular document, the name Irpa-Addu (maybe the name Irpa in our new document should be completed accordingly, i.e., Irpa-Addu) is mentioned as one of the persons who appeared before the king of Hazor; is it possible that it is the same person who is referred to in both documents?! It should be noted that in the above-mentioned legal document as well, Irpa-Adad is mentioned in connection with a woman (Shumu-la-ilu) who was judged by the king of Hazor. It is disappointing that the new document is so fragmentary, yet it feels as though we are already well acquainted with the acting figures!

This is just an initial progress report on the Hazor excavations. What has been uncovered thus far is negligible in comparison to what still

21. G. Dossin, 'La route de l'étain en Mésopotamie au temps de Zimri-Lim', *RA* 64 (1970), pp. 97ff.; A. Malamat, 'Syro Palestinian Destinations in a Mari Tin Inventory', *IEJ* 21 (1971), pp. 31-38. For a recent summary of the relations between Hazor and Mari and additional mentionings of the King of Hazor by name (document M8140 and M13041), see M. Bonechi, 'Relations Amicales Syro-Palestiniennes: Mari et Hasor au XVIIIe Siècle av. J.C.', in D. Charpin *et al.*, *Memoires de N.A.B.U.*, I (Paris, 1992), pp. 9-22.

22. W.F. Albright, *The Biblical Period from Abraham to Ezra* (New York, 1963), p. 102 n. 83: Malamat, 1989, pp. 55, 58.

23. Malamat, 1989, p. 58 (n. 111); Yadin 1972, p. 5

24. W.W. Hallo and M. Tadmor, *A Lawsuit from Hazor*, *IEJ* 27 (1977), pp. 1-11.

awaits us. Yet even the little that we have uncovered sheds light on the magnitude, richness, and significance of those finds still buried under our feet, which will, undoubtedly, occupy and amaze us for years to come.

(Manuscript completed October 1994.)

DISCOVERIES AT TEL DOR

Ephraim Stern

Identification and History

Biblical Dor, known as Dora in most Hellenistic sources, is identified with Khirbet el-Burj on the Carmel coast, c. 21 km south of Haifa. According to Greek and Latin sources, Dor was situated between the Carmel range and Straton's Tower (Caesarea). The Tabula Peutingeriana places Dor 8 Roman miles north of Caesarea, while Eusebius gives the distance as 9 Roman miles (*Onom.* 9.78; 16.136). On the basis of these two sources, the location of ancient Dor can almost certainly be established at the site of Khirbet el-Burj.

The city is apparently mentioned in an inscription dating to the reign of Ramses II (thirteenth century BCE) found in Nubia. Dor is first mentioned in the Bible in connection with the Israelite conquest of Canaan. Joshua defeated the king of Dor (Josh. 12.23), one of the allies of Jabin, king of Hazor (Josh. 11.1-2). Canaanite Dor, located in the territory of the tribe of Manasseh, was not conquered by the Israelites until the reign of King David (tenth century BCE).

In Wen-Amon's account of his journey to Byblos (c. 1100 BCE), he mentions Dor and its ruler, Beder, king of the Sikils, one of the tribes of Sea Peoples who invaded the eastern Mediterranean in the twelfth century BCE. During Solomon's reign, Dor was the capital of the fourth administrative district, whose governor was Ben-Abinadab, Solomon's son-in-law (1 Kgs 4.11).

The city was conquered by Tiglath-pileser III in 732 BCE, along with the entire coastal region of the Israelite kingdom. It became the capital of an Assyrian province extending from the Carmel range to Jaffa. According to the inscription on the coffin of Eshmunazar, king of Sidon, Dor was ruled by the Sidonians in the Persian period. In the Hellenistic period, it was a particularly powerful fortress. Josephus described Dor as 'a fortress hard to be taken' (*Ant.* 13.7, 20), and Polybius (*Hist.* 5.66) related that Antiochus III Megas laid siege to it in 219 BCE but was unable to conquer it. Some 80 years later, history repeated itself. Literary sources (1 Macc. 9–14, 25–27; Josephus, *Ant.* 13.7, 2 and *War* 1.2, 2) record that the Seleucid commander Tryphon (142–139 BCE) took refuge at Dor when fleeing from Antiochus VII Sidetes. Antiochus laid siege unsuccessfully to the city both from the land and the sea. Thus, neither Antiochus III nor Antiochus VII was able to breach its walls.

Both Dor and Straton's Tower (later Caesarea) were ruled by the tyrant Zoilus up to the late second century BCE when Alexander Jannaeus conquered these two fortified cities. The Hasmoneans ruled Dor until it was taken in 63 BCE, by Pompey, who granted the city autonomy and the right to mint coins; this event also marks the beginning of the era of Dor from which it dated its history.

The coins of Dor indicate that its inhabitants worshiped Zeus (or Dorus) and Astarte. The existence of a Jewish community and synagogue during the reign of Agrippa I is mentioned in literary sources. Hieronymus (late fourth century CE) described the city as being in ruins and abandoned. On the other hand, it is known that bishops resided in the city until the seventh century CE. Dor remained desolate from that time until the Crusaders built the fortress of Merle there.

In 1923–24, the first excavations at Dor were undertaken by the British School in Jerusalem, headed by J. Garstang, at a time when archaeology was still in its infancy. The trenches revealed settlement strata dating from the Late Bronze Age to the Roman period. In 1924, remains of large structures were uncovered on the southwest side of the mound. The archaeologists interpreted them as temples erected on a podium surrounded by a temenos. They dated the entire complex to the Hellenistic period.

Excavations were resumed on a large scale in 1980 under the auspices of the Philip and Muriel Berman Center at the Institute of Archaeology at the Hebrew University of Jerusalem, and the Israel Exploration Society, led by E. Stern, in co-operation with groups of archaeologists from overseas universities. By 1993, seven main areas had been excavated in the course of 13 seasons. Three areas—C, A, and B, running north to south—are at the eastern fringe of the mound; area D is on the southern slope above the south bay and flanking Garstang's trench; areas F and E are on the western slope of the mound; and area G is in the center. The excavations indicate that the site was first inhabited at the beginning of the Middle Bronze Age IIA and that the city continued to exist almost continuously until the third century CE. Dor began to decline and was gradually abandoned after Herod built the harbor at Caesarea. The following is a survey of the excavation results by period, from the beginning of settlement at Dor up to the Hellenistic Age.

The Middle and Late Bronze Ages

Remains from the Middle Bronze Age have so far been found in the western part of the mound where the sea's incursions have eroded the mound to bedrock, partially destroying the western section of the city. In the excavation square closest to the shore, a level with some building remains, probably dating from the Middle Bronze Age IIB to IIC, was uncovered. Soundings next to the shore close to the bedrock have shown that Middle Bronze Age IIA remains reached the water's edge. Numerous fragments of local and imported pottery from this period have been recovered. The latter includes Cypriot pottery of all types known in Israel. Fragments of Egyptian faience vessels, scarabs, and fibulae were also uncovered. The exact location of the eastern boundary in the Middle Bronze Age city is as yet unknown. No building remains from the Late Bronze Age have been identified yet either, but the excavations yielded scarabs and pottery from this period.

In other places we reached layers of sand that originally belonged to the Late Bronze strata and were used as a fill for later constructions. It is already clear that the number of vases found in these strata was large, and that statistically the number of imported vases of the period is larger than that of local ones. We uncovered examples of virtually every known type of imported vessel: Minoan and Mycenaean, and all known imported Cypriot types recognized in Palestinian assemblages, including white painted I–II, bichrome, white-slip I–II, and white shaved. This phenomenon repeated itself whenever we encountered even the smallest deposit belonging to this period. We can therefore conclude that already in this early age Dor was an important harbor town for imports from the West.

Iron Age

To the best of our knowledge, the Canaanite city of Dor was destroyed by the Sikils (a tribe of Sea Peoples) at the beginning of the twelfth century BCE. The Sikils built the city and fortified it during this same century (though we have as yet to uncover any Mycenaean IIIC sherds). We have no evidence of any import from 'the dark age', as this period is commonly called. At Dor, this stratum is number XII and was uncovered mainly in area B1 (east side) and area G (central part of the mound (cf. Figure 1). It was composed of a thick layer of heavy destruction debris and ashes. The conflagration burned clay bricks to a fiery red and reduced residential constructions to piles of calcified limestone. This accumulation of debris, more than 2m deep, was sealed by the floors on which we found Cypriot and Phoenician vessels of the second half of the eleventh century BCE.

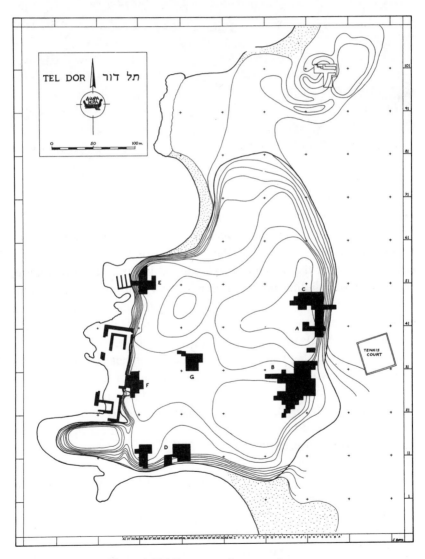

Figure 1. Tel Dor, map of excavated areas.

Figure 2. Aerial view of area B at Tel Dor looking west.

We also encountered this same destruction layer in a deep pit in area F, on the western side of the mound, but here we have yet to reach the bottom of the debris. Also to this stratum belong the sections of two rooms uncovered in area E on the western side of the mound. These discoveries demonstrate that the town must have covered the entire area of the mound. Furthermore, we should note that during A. Raban's undersea survey of the town's southern harbor (south of area D), the team uncovered remains of this period, which leads us to conclude that the Dor of the Sikils occupied the entire area of the present mound.

Even though the Egyptian historical records indicate that Dor was a vital harbor town in this brief period, no import of any certainty has come to light from this 'dark age' stratum. Up to now, we have only found local pottery in this stratum, namely some sherds of the typical bichrome decorated ware that we consider to be of local manufacture, though elsewhere it is attributed to the Philistines. We also uncovered a decorated lion's head rhyton of the type known from other Philistine sites. To this short list of possible imports, we should perhaps add a cow scapula, a shoulder blade incised with parallel lines along the upper edge of a type which was found elsewhere in Philistine contexts: one in the Philistine sanctuary uncovered recently at Ekron, and another from Cyprus. We could concur with the Ekron excavators' assumption that the scapula was used by the Philistines, or the Sikils in our case, to divine a message from a god. Although the purpose of the notches is uncertain, they may have been cut to produce a musical sound. According to the Ekron excavators, these instruments were brought by the Sea Peoples from Cyprus after their journey across the Mediterranean to Palestine. Further evidence of the Sikil city was uncovered in recent seasons in area G. A small cult place was discovered containing about one dozen clay vases. Two of these vessels clearly belong to the Sea Peoples' repertoire. We should also mention the appearance of an iron knife, typical of Philistine types.

Above this stratum, remains of several settlement phases, dating from the second half of the eleventh century BCE, have been uncovered. The settlement's Phoenician character is affirmed by the Phoenician bichrome pottery prominent in the ceramic assemblage from the first phase onward. Area B1, which extends to the north of the city gate, apparently was a residential district at this time. A row of rooms that may have abutted the city wall (which has not yet been uncovered) was excavated on the east side of the area. The rooms opened onto a north–south street, running parallel to the conjectured line of the city wall. On the other side of the street, remains of mudbrick structures built on stone foundations were exposed. A large structure extends over most of the area west of the street, but only part of it was within the excavated area. A number of superimposed floors were identified in this structure. Building remains dating to the late eleventh century BCE were also found in area G, in the center of the mound, and in area E, to the west. It is in one of these area G structures that the skeletal remains of a young woman crushed by a collapsed wall were found.

The floors of these phases yielded a considerable quantity of Phoenician bichrome ware. Especially noteworthy is a group of Cypriot potsherds of extremely rare types that we retrieved from the floors of the large buildings. The sherds belong to two main groups—white painted I and white painted/bichrome I. Very few of these types appear among the wares imported into Palestine. Only isolated examples have been found in the area, mostly from sites along the Phoenician coast. Parallels to the Dor vessels in Cyprus are mainly found in Cypro-Geometric I contexts from the second half of the eleventh century BCE or slightly later. Thus, these vessels confirm the date we had previously assigned to this phase (c. 1000 BCE), a date deduced independently from the local pottery. More significantly, however, is their indication of the renewal of Cypriot imports to Palestine in the Late Iron Age I after the cessation of imports at the end of the Late Bronze Age, a gap of approximately 100 years. We have attributed this town, which was built on the ruins of the Sikil settlement, to the Phoenicians who at the same time also settled in Cyprus and were responsible for the reurbanization there.

The next stratum should probably be dated to the tenth century BCE. Its main feature is a broad mudbrick city wall, sections of which have been found in all areas of the eastern part of the mound. In area B1, two rows of buildings have been exposed on both sides of a north–south street running parallel to the wall. Some of these structures were built of mudbrick on stone foundations, while others were built of stone. Remains of this stratum were also uncovered under the four-chambered city gate in areas B, E, and G. Of special interest among the finds in this stratum are the numerous early Cypriot pottery vessels, including Phoenician bichrome ware, black-on-red vessels and local pottery. Some seals were also recovered, the most interesting of which is made of animal horn and depicts a finely incised scene of two deer or ibexes standing on mountain peaks. The workmanship is of the highest quality.

This city was destroyed at the end of the tenth century BCE, most likely by the Egyptian Pharoah Shishaq. The Iron Age town was again fortified during the ninth century BCE, at the time of the Israelite divided monarchy, by an offset–inset wall and by a four-roomed gate. Later, after its destruction at the end of the eighth century BCE, the Assyrians rebuilt the wall adding to it this time a two-roomed gate. This system continued to exist until the mid-fourth century BCE.

The import of Cypriot material to Dor continued through the period of the divided kingdom (ninth–eighth centuries BCE). These imports also continued during the late Iron and Persian Ages, but their number and prominence decreased. During the Iron Age II, the flow of imports from the mainland of Greece was renewed, too. The first Greek sherd found in stratigraphy at Dor was a bowl belonging to the late Geometric period (late eighth century BCE). The sherd was uncovered on the floor of the city gate of the Israelite period which was destroyed by the Assyrian armies in 733 BCE. In addition to the fact that this find confirms the date of the destruction of the Israelite town, it moves up the date for the beginning of Greek imports to Dor (even though at some other coastal sites, such as Tyre and Tel Abu Hawam, there are earlier sherds). From this time on, more Greek imports began to stream into Dor. We should mention here that during the seventh century BCE and later, proto-Corinthian imports started to arrive; however, the majority of imports came from the east Greek Islands.

Of the upper Iron Age strata (the Assryian and Babylonian periods), all that remains are a number of installations, pits (some of which have damaged the four-chambered gate; see below), and sections of pavement that do not form a coherent plan. Delicate Samaria ware was found, which continued to be made up to the last days of the Iron Age. Some of the finds can be attributed directly to the period of Assyrian rule, such as the numerous Assyrian-type bowls, an amphoriskos that is an obvious imitation of an Assyrian prototype, and an Assyrian cylinder seal which may have belonged to one of the officials in the province. An Assyrian seal stamp was discovered in area B. Another Assyrian find of interest is a limestone 'shekel' weight from Judah, uncovered in one of the pits. We should also mention a particular seal found near Samaria and published by N. Avigad. The inscription on the seal mentions a person referred to as 'the priest of Dor.' According to Avigad, this was a priest who served at Dor in the Israelite period, in a sanctuary similar to those at Dan, Shiloh, and Beersheba.

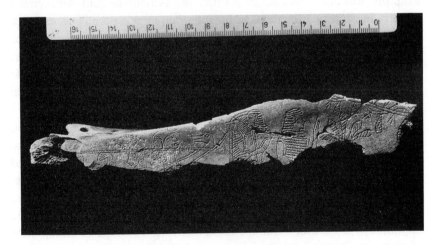

Figure 3. Bone *scapula* decorated with a maritime scene:
a Phoenician boat leaving a harbor (Late Iron-Persian period).

In this period, from the seventh century BCE and onward, two types of Greek pottery became the most common import to Dor: one originates at Corinth and the other in east Greece. Though the number of Corinthian sherds found is meager, this is not the case with the east Greek material, of which we believe we have the largest and most complete assemblage from all the settlements lining the eastern coast of the Mediterranean Sea (including Al Mina, Sarepta, Mezad Hashavyahu and even Tel Sukas). These vessels come from the many sites in the east Greek Islands, such as Lesbos, Samos, Kos, Chios, Knidos, and Rhodes, as well as from the sites along the Anatolian and Cilician Coast. While this assemblage remains presently in the hands of experts for further study, it is already clear that despite their abundance at Dor in the seventh–sixth centuries BCE, they continued to be imported to the region during the fifth century BCE as well.

The picture found at Dor is by no means unique to the site, but parallels that of all sites along the eastern coast of the Mediterranean Sea and on Cyprus. Though they continued into the fifth century BCE, by the latter part of the sixth century BCE the east Greek imports had already become an insignificant part of the assemblage in comparison to the Attic ware which began to flow into Dor during the fifth–fourth centuries BCE. The east Greek imports decreased in number until they were superseded at Dor by an almost total Attic monopoly. Aside from the occasional Greek sherd which can be found from other sources, for example Boeotian and south Italian, the Athenians had succeeded entirely in capturing the demand for imported Greek ware. This change in source of imported Greek ware and the absolute dominance of Attic pottery throughout the late sixth–early fifth centuries BCE are not unique to Dor, but were recognized elsewhere along the Phoenician and Palestinian coasts and in Cyprus.

The Persian Period

Remains from the Persian period were discovered in two main strata. During this period, the entire eastern part of the mound was a residential district, laid out meticulously according to the Hippodamian plan. The closest parallels to the town plan of Dor in the Persian period are Olynthus in Greece and Monte Sirai in Sardinia. This type of orthogonal planning probably originated in the sixth century BCE and continued almost unchanged until the Early Roman period. In it, residential quarters are divided into long narrow blocks (*insulae*), approximately 15m wide, separated by streets intersecting at right angles. The city's two eastern blocks and its two easternmost streets, running from north to south parallel to the city wall, were excavated in area C.

Figure 4. Tel Dor, limestone Cypriote goddess head, Persian period.

In the Persian period strata, large quantities of both local and imported pottery were found, especially Attic ware, including many fragments of painted vessels and east Greek and Corinthian pottery. The hundreds of vessels recorded, some of rare types, comprise perhaps the largest assemblage of Greek pottery found to date on any site in Israel. Of special interest are types of large wine amphorae not previously found in Israel's coastal region. In addition to the many ceramic vessels, there were scores of figurines and statuettes uncovered and a relatively large number of seals, some recovered *in situ*. The majority of the seals are scarab-shaped. Of particular interest is a conical glass seal carved with the figure of a Phoenician sphinx. Two glass scaraboids are outstanding: on one, the king of Persia is depicted in his chariot; on the other, the king of Persia fights two griffins or lions. Undoubtedly these seals, whose motifs often appear on Sidonian and Tyrian coins, belonged to local officials. In addition, many coins of all the known types—Greek, Phoenician, and local—have been recovered from the Persian period strata.

Several ostraca found in recent excavations were written in Phoenician, in ink (one was incised). They have been deciphered by J. Naveh. Other ostraca bear incised inscriptions in Greek, and are the first Greek inscriptions found in Israel in strata from the Persian period.

Many cult objects from the Persian period have been recovered. These primarily include clay figurines, stone statuettes and faience amulets, reflecting both official and popular Phoenician cult and the various foreign influences absorbed by it. Two bronze censers, also used in cult and ritual, were found. Some of the seals mentioned above may have had a cultic function as well. Most of the figurines were discovered in two large groups in *favissae* (pits in which broken figurines were intentionally buried), one in area B and the other in area C. These pits were probably situated close to temples, of which no trace has survived. Objects of a similar nature were scattered throughout the other excavated areas.

Four kinds of cult objects were found in the area B *favissa*: (1) clay figurines in the Eastern style; (2) clay figurines in the Western, mainly Greek, style; (3) limestone statuettes originating from Cyprus; and (4) a necklace of faience beads. The first three categories represent the official Phoenician cult of Baal, Astarte, and their son.

Figure 5. Tel Dor, bronze plaque depicting a Greek dancer, late Persian period.

The nature of the objects found in the *favissa* excavated in area C differs considerably from that of the objects in the area B *favissa*. In fact, the assemblage in this *favissa* differs from that of the *favissae* known so far in Israel. All the figurines recovered were fashioned in an unmistakable archaic Greek style, and so far constitute the only example of this style found in Israel. Most of the sherds found also are Greek, either Attic or east Greek. These are probably the remains of a Greek temple that can be dated precisely to the second half of the fourth century BCE. It may well be that this was the temple used by the Greek inhabitants of this Phoenician city who may have resided in their own quarter. This evidence corresponds with the many discoveries, both past and recent, at sites along the Mediterranean coast.

A unique find of the period that should be mentioned here is a Cypro-Phoenician bone scapula decorated with a rare maritime scene.

The Hellenistic Period

The walls of the houses built in the Hellenistic period rested directly on the residential *insulae* of the Persian period. The facades of the houses followed the same alignment; only the partitions within were changed. The building style remained Phoenician—ashlar piers with rubble fill. Some of the facades lining the street were built of ashlars only. It can be assumed that the walls exposed in the excavations belong to the ground floors and that the buildings were at least two stories high. In some of the houses, there was evidence of cellars.

The houses from the Hellenistic period existed from the fourth to the first centuries BCE. In the course of those centuries, they underwent repairs and changes: entrances were blocked, floors were raised, and the internal division of the rooms was changed. At times, the function of the various auxiliary units also changed. In area C, for example, two plastered pools were added in one of the phases. Despite this activity, the location of the buildings' facades remained unchanged.

Urban planning is especially evident at the eastern margin of the mound. Adjacent to the city wall, where previously the 'casemates' associated with the intermediate Persian/Hellenistic phase were located, a long row of shops and workshops was erected facing the eastern lengthwise street. In one of the workshops, a deep layer of crushed murex shells was found. Excavation has revealed a well-planned city, built on an orthogonal plan—that is, a city whose streets intersect at right angles and whose lengthwise streets run parallel to the city wall. A row of shops and workshops abutted the city wall line of the easternmost north–south street. The city's main transverse street, running from east to west, led (as in the previous period) from the eastern gate in area B (see below) to the public buildings on the west of the mound. Long, well-built, Phoenician-style walls were uncovered on both sides of this street.

Hellenistic buildings and streets were also exposed in area D in the southern part of the mound. Here, too, the intersection of a lengthwise and a transverse street was discovered. The town plan in this area resembles that of the eastern part of the mound.

Figure 6. Tel Dor, clay decoration depicting a satyr head, Hellenistic period.

On the western part of the mound (area F), remains were uncovered of some of the largest temples known in the country so far; they were probably built in the Hellenistic period but were used into the Roman period as well. These buildings, which are located near the seashore, were excavated in the 1920s by Garstang, as discussed above. During the Hebrew University excavations, the outer east side of these monumental structures was excavated and a row of rooms, built in the Phoenician style and extending north–south, east of the temples, was exposed. The rooms apparently lined a street (as yet unexcavated) that in the period ran along the western margin of the mound and was the main access road to the temples.

In area G at the center of the mound, excavations of a large ashlar-built public building have begun. Although its plan and function have not yet been identified, it seems to have been connected to some sort of administrative-commercial activity in the area where the Roman forum was later built.

The Hellenistic strata yielded an abundance of finds. There were numerous coins—hoards of silver coins from the reigns of Ptolemy I and Ptolemy II and coins of several Seleucid rulers, as well as of Tryphon, who was besieged in Dor. There were also stamped amphora handles, mainly from Rhodes and Cnidus, which make it possible to date the various Hellenistic strata.

The large and varied assemblage of local pottery—storage jars, bottles, jugs, juglets, pilgrim flasks, and censers—is a window to the ceramic typology of the Hellenistic period in Palestine. We have uncovered a rich collection of lamps that not only includes nearly all the known types found in Israel, but some that are rare and even unique. Large quantities of imported vessels have also been recovered: wine *amphorae* from the Greek islands and domestic ware of almost all the types from the period in the eastern Mediterranean—West Slope ware, 'Megarian' bowls, and Terra Sigillata ware.

During the Hellenistic and Roman periods, Dor was already a completely pagan Greek city. Among the figurines and statues from these periods are a marble head of Hermes, the head of a ceramic figurine (probably of Aphrodite), and a 'temple-boy' pottery figurine; the latter was recovered from the Hellenistic fill in area D. A number of marble fragments found west of the east gate bear large carved Greek letters and a few words. Also worthy of mention is the large collection of ballista stones of various sizes, of which five bear incised letters indicating their theoretical weight. This area may have been the city arsenal.

Even though the Tel Dor project has completed its thirteenth season, the work conducted thus far represents only the beginning. We intend to continue excavations throughout the coming years in the hope of revealing Dor's ancient harbor as well as unearthing further material of the various cultures that once existed at this ancient port city.

BIBLIOGRAPHY

Avigad, N.
  1975   'The Priest of Dor', *IEJ* 25: 101-105.
Dahl, G.
  1915   'The Materials for the History of Dor', *Transactions of the Connecticut Academy of Arts and Sciences* 20: 1-181.
Garstang, J.
  1924   'Tanturah (Dora)', *Bulletin of the British School of Jerusalem* 4: 35-47; 6: 65-75.
Raban, A.
  1987   'The Harbor of the Sea People at Dor', *BA* 50: 118-26.
Sharon, I.
  1987   'Phoenician and Greek Ashlar Construction Techniques at Tel Dor, Israel', *BASOR* 267: 21-42.
Stern, E.
  1994   *Dor: Ruler of the Seas* (Jerusalem: Israel Exploration Society).

THE EXCAVATIONS AT TEL BETH SHEAN
DURING THE YEARS 1989–94

Amihai Mazar

Introduction

The Talmudic sage Reish Lakish is quoted as saying: 'Paradise: if it is in the Land of Israel, Beth Shean is its gate' (*'Erub.* 19.2). When digging at Beth Shean in the sweltering summer heat of more than 100°F, it is difficult to concur with this Talmudic optimism. Yet there is no doubt that Beth Shean is superbly located, in the midst of the fertile and amply watered Beth Shean Valley, as well as at the intersection of two important highways: a latitudinal road running along the Jezreel and Harod Valleys, in the direction of the Jordan River fords facing Pehal (Pella); and a longitudinal road, passing through the Jordan Valley.

The mound is situated on a naturally prominent hill, sloping toward the northwest, encompassed by two ravines. This strategic location, and the abundance of water and fertile land in the surrounding valley, made Beth Shean an ideal site for human habitation.

The expedition of the University of Pennsylvania conducted ten excavation seasons at Tel Beth Shean between 1921 and 1933. Working for several months every year with hundreds of local workers and Egyptian experts in the remote and malaria-stricken region of Beth Shean, the three successive directors, C. Fisher, A. Rowe, and G.M. FitzGerald, revealed 18 successive occupation strata. Their methods were similar to those used throughout the Middle East at that time: large areas of upper occupation layers of the mound were exposed and removed. As the excavation proceeded, the areas of excavation were reduced, until finally, in 1933, a mere 16 × 24 m shaft was sunk down to bedrock. This was one of the most important archaeological enterprises in the country during the years following World War I, producing the first continuous stratigraphic sequence covering most of the periods from the Late Neolithic to the Early Arab period. Particularly important were the

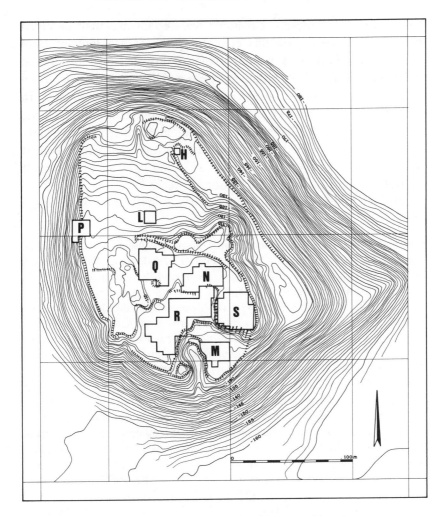

Figure 1. Tel Beth Shean, topographic map and location
of excavation areas (drawing: M. Caplan).

rich discoveries relating to the second half of the second millennium
BCE, which included the famed series of temples and the abundant finds
relating to the Egyptian governmental stronghold at Beth Shean.[1]

1.   The following are the final reports published on the excavations: A. Rowe,
The Topography and History of Beth-shan (Beth-shan I), (Philadelphia: University
Museum, 1930); G.M. FitzGerald, *The Four Canaanite Temples of Beth-shan, The
Pottery* (Beth Shan II:2), (Philadelphia: University Museum, 1930); G.M. FitzGerald,
Beth-shan Excavations 1921–23, The Arab and Byzantine Levels, (Beth-shan III),
(Philadelphia: University Museum, 1931); A. Rowe, *The Four Canaanite Temples of*

However, since these excavations were conducted with outdated methods, numerous problems concerning the archaeology of Beth Shean remained open, and the importance of this site called for renewal of the excavations. In 1983 Shulamit Geva and the late Professor Yigael Yadin carried out a lone 3-week excavation season on the mound.[2] In 1989 the possibility materialized to integrate the excavations on the mound as part of the large-scale archaeological enterprise presently being carried out at Beth Shean on behalf of the Beth Shean Tourist Development Administration. Between 1989 and 1994, seven seasons of excavations were conducted, each lasting 6 weeks.[3]

The University of Pennsylvania excavations created three huge

Beth-shan (Beth-shan II:1), (Philadelphia: University Museum, 1940); F. James, *The Iron Age at Beth Shan: A Study of Levels VI–IV* (Philadelphia: University Museum, 1966); E.D. Oren, *The Northern Cemetery of Beth-Shean,* (Leiden: Brill, 1973); F.W. James and P.E. McGovern, *The Late Bronze Egyptian Garrison at Beth Shan: A Study of Levels VII and VIII* (II Volumes), (Philadelphia:University Museum, 1993). For a summary and additional literature see A. Mazar, 'Beth Shean, Tel', in: *The New Encyclopedia of Archaeological Excavations in the Holy Land* (rev. edn, ed. E. Stern; New York: Simon and Schuster, 1993); P.E. McGovern, 'Beth-Shan', in AB (New York: Doubleday, 1992), vol. 1, pp. 693-96.

2.   Y. Yadin and S. Geva, *Investigations at Beth Shean: The Early Iron Age Strata* (Qedem 23), (Jerusalem: Hebrew University, 1986).

3.   The excavations at Tel Beth Shean are directed by the author on behalf of the Institute of Archaeology of the Hebrew University of Jerusalem in the framework of the Beth Shean Archaeological Expedition, which is sponsored by the Israel Antiquities Authority and the Beth Shean Tourist Development Authority. The directors of the united expedition are Y. Tzafrir, G. Foerster, and G. Mazor. Part of the research is sponsored by the Philip and Muriel Berman Center of Biblical Archaeology at the Hebrew University. The main staff members of the expedition during the seven seasons were N. Appelbaum (1993–94), M. Arazi (1991–94), R. Belamy (1990), A. Cohen (1992–94), G. Gilmour (1990), N. Ginzburg (1991–92), A. Harash (1989–90), A. Killebrew (1991–94), S. Kim (1990–93), A. Maier (1991–92), R. Mullins (1989–94), N. Panitz-Cohen (1989, 1991–94), Y. Rand (1991–93), O. Shamir (1989), D. Stacey (1989–90), G. Stiebel (1993–94), R. Voss (1991–92), D. Weinblatt (1992–94), A. Ziv (1992–94). The plans were prepared by B. Arubas and M. Caplan. Archeozoology: L. Kulska-Horowitz; Archeobotany: U. Baruch. For a preliminary report see: A. Mazar, 'The Excavations at Tel Beth Shean in 1989–90', in A. Biran and J. Aviram (eds.), *Biblical Archaeology Today 1990, Proceedings of the Second International Congress on Biblical Archaeology* (Jerusalem: Israel Exploration Society, 1993), pp. 606-619; *idem*, 'Beth Shean in the Iron Age: Preliminary Report and Conclusions of the 1990–91 Excavations', *IEJ* 43, (1993), pp. 201-29.

terraces in the southern part of the mound. On the highest terrace, the excavation stopped at Iron Age I levels (stratum V), on the middle terrace at a fourteenth century BCE level (stratum IX), and on the third terrace at an Early Bronze Age III level (stratum XIII). The renewed excavations continued digging all three terraces, as well as opening new areas in other parts of the mound. Our goal was to clarify various problems left unsolved by the previous excavations, and to reconstruct the entire history of the site with the aid of modern research methods.

Figure 2. Tel Beth Shean, view to the northeast. At the front:
remains of the Roman–Byzantine city (photo: A Mazar).

The mound of Beth Shean is one of a considerable number of sites located throughout the Beth Shean Valley, which appears to have been one of the most densely populated regions in the land. Thus, it is imperative to investigate the occupational history of Tel Beth Shean against the broader regional background.[4]

This paper is intended to provide an overall summary of the main results of our excavations, relating to each of the periods under investigation.

4.   Such a regional approach is the guideline of a PhD thesis which is being prepared by A. Maier on the Beth Shean Valley during the Middle Bronze Age. The results of the excavations on the tell are integrated in this research with a spatial view of the entire valley and its natural resources.

The Early Bronze Age

Several occupation levels from this period were discovered at Beth Shean by our predecessors. Strata XVII–XVI are characterized by gray burnished ware, while in stratum XV this pottery becomes rare and in stratum XIV, most likely to be dated to the late Early Bronze I, it disappears. Stratum XIII may tentatively be dated to Early Bronze II while strata XII–XI represent the Early Bronze III period. However, this division is schematic and tentative.[5]

In our area M, on the southeastern part of the mound, the present excavation continued where the University of Pennsylvania stopped at the Early Bronze III level (stratum XIII). Three occupation levels were explored. Phase M3 (late Early Bronze I) probably corresponds to stratum XV.[6] In this level, an impressive building was discovered, constructed of mudbrick walls over 1 m wide, preserved to a height of over 1 m. The building was destroyed by heavy fire, and the large amount of collapsed mudbricks indicate that there was a second floor. An expansive hall excavated in this building is 7 m wide and at least 6 m long. In it, large quantities of carbonized grain and lentils, as well as many broken large jars (pithoi), are evidence for food storage.

During this period (late Early Bronze I, late fourth millennium BCE), the valley of Beth Shean was densely settled, as revealed in systematic surveys and occasional discoveries made in the region. Major sites known from this period include Tel Yaqush, Tel Kitan, Tel Shalem, and Tel ed-Diabe. It appears that for the first time, the settlers of the valley employed irrigation agriculture; this perhaps was associated with the emergence of a centralized authority which controlled the economy in the entire valley. The building at Beth Shean, located on the highest point of the mound during that time, may have been related to an innovative socioeconomic system, where a central authority regulated the storage and redistribution of food.

Following the destruction by fire of this building, new buildings were erected along a curvilinear street. Two building phases were defined

5.   See G.M. FitzGerald, 'The Earliest Pottery of Beth-shan', *The Museum Journal* 24 (1935), pp. 5-22. The pottery plates show some degree of mixture, particularly in strata XI–XII, where Middle Bronze pottery is mixed with Early Bronze pottery.

6.   Separate stratigraphic phases are counted for each excavation area. Thus, in Area M we numbered Phases M1, M2, M3 etc., with M1 the uppermost phase.

(M2A and M2B). In the lower one (M2B), a hoard of three copper axes and a spearhead, as well as an alabaster macehead, are luxury items which indicate the importance of these buildings. These two phases may be dated to the end of the Early Bronze I or beginning of the Early Bronze II.

During the Early Bronze III, the Beth Shean region was settled by people who produced 'Khirbet Kerak' ware. This Trans-Caucasian–Anatolian pottery style was probably made by immigrants who continued to produce it for a long time following their emigration, with Beth Shean their southernmost settlement site.[7] Three points should be stressed in relation to this period: 1) Tel Beth Shean was only part of a much broader settlement of the Khirbet Kerak people in the same vicinity. Extensive occupation dating to this period was also found at Tel Istaba, opposite Tel Beth Shean on the northern bank of the Harod (Jalud) river.[8] 2) Though quantitative data from our excavations are unavailable as of yet, it appears that the Khirbet Kerak pottery comprises the bulk of the fine 'tableware' of the period. 3) Khirbet Kerak pottery appears in several occupational phases at Tel Beth Shean. At least four successive floors from this period were found in area R, where there is no indication for a deterioration of the quality of the Khirbet Kerak pottery during these phases. 4) Khirbet Kerak pottery appears at Beth Shean almost until the end of the period. It appears that the end of the Early Bronze III city was abrupt; there is no evidence for any gradual decline before it terminated.

In the following period (Middle Bronze I, Early Bronze IV, or Intermediate Bronze Age, according to the various terminologies), there was a poor, probably seasonal, settlement on the site. Patches of floor surfaces were found in several sporadic places with no architectural remains whatsoever. The pottery and some copper objects found on these floors are typical of the Beth Shean region during this period, and are similar to those found in the contemporary Northern Cemetery of Beth Shean. The material culture in this transitional phase differs to a large extent from that of the last Early Bronze III phase at the site.

---

7. C. Burney, 'The Khirbet Kerak Question and the Early Trans-Caucasian Background', in P. de Miroschedji (ed.), *L'urbanisation de la Palestine a l'Age du Bronze ancien: Bilan et perspectives des recherches actuelles, Actes du Colloque d'Emmaus (20–24 octobre, 1986)* (BAR International Series, 527.2; Oxford: Biblical Archaeology Reports, 1989), pp. 331-39.

8. My thanks to G. Mazor and R. Bar-Natan for this information.

There must have been either a chronological gap between these two phases, or a distinct cultural shift.

The Middle Bronze Age

Following the EBIV/MBI transitional phase, there was an occupational gap at Beth Shean which lasted for about two to three centuries. The site was settled again in an advanced phase of the Middle Bronze IIB period, perhaps some time in the eighteenth or early seventeenth century BCE. An extensive area containing remains from this period was uncovered by the present excavations below the Late Bronze Age stratum IX sanctuary discovered by the University of Pennsylvania. The Middle Bronze remains in this area can be divided into three parts. In the western part, a dwelling quarter was uncovered. Three successive building phases were detected (R5, R4, R3), all comprising of houses constructed on both sides of a street which runs parallel to the southern edge of the mound. Several infant jar burials, typical of this period, were found below the floors of the houses. A complete human skeleton found in phase R4 may indicate a destruction by earthquake of this particular phase. The pottery found on the various floors is virtually homogeneous, yet during the last phase (R3), the pottery style known as 'chocolate on white' became common. No bichrome ware or Cypriot imports were found. The various finds from the buildings include 'Hyksos' scarabs, one cylinder seal which is a local version of the Syrian Style, bone inlays, alabaster vessels, jewelry, and clay model wheels.

In the central part of the area a singular phenomenon was discovered: a huge pit, oval in shape, 24 m long, 18 m wide, and at least 6 m deep was cut here through the Early Bronze strata. This pit or 'pool' was filled with layers of disposal composed of soft earth and ash, containing Middle Bronze pottery of phases R5–R4 (prior to the appearance of the 'chocolate on white' ware). The earth layers were dumped into the depression from all sides into its center. The date and purpose of this large sunken area remain enigmatic. Was it a water reservoir of the Early Bronze Age which was filled by refuse during the Middle Bronze Age, or was it cut during this latter period? These questions remain unanswered at this stage of research.

In any case, this pit or 'pool' comprises formidable earthworks. By phase R3 of the sixteenth century BCE, this depression was already filled with refuse, and structures were built on this fill. These included a large open space with several installations, bordered on the north and south by rows of rooms. 'Chocolate on white' pottery, typical of the sixteenth century BCE, was found in this level.

An open space at least 15 m long was uncovered in the eastern part of the area. It was paved with a thick layer of lime, on which several ovens and circular fireplaces paved with small stones were found. This appears to have been a public piazza with cooking facilities; it may have been related to a still undiscovered temple which stood nearby.

The nature of the end of the period is contradictory. While one architectural complex of phase R3 was found destroyed by fire in an abrupt destruction, no evidence for such a violent end was found in other areas of the excavation, and the town appears to have been partly rebuilt soon after its end. It should be stressed that no fortifications of the period were found in any of the excavations at the site. Such fortifications either did not exist or were completely eroded on the southern side of the mound. Thus, it appears that no glacis or rampart, so typical of the period, existed at Tel Beth Shean.

The results of a probe in area L indicate that the Middle Bronze and Late Bronze occupation did not expand to the northern part of the mound, so that the town during these periods probably did not exceed 4 acres. Thus, the Middle Bronze town appears to have been a rather small urban center, probably not a central city-state. Such a center probably was located at nearby Tel Rehov.

A Late Bronze I Temple

Above the large 'pool' described above and above the building remains of phase R3, a small temple of the Late Bronze I Age (phase R2) was discovered, the first in a series of temples which were built at this same location during the following centuries. It appears that this earliest temple preceded the Egyptian occupation of Beth Shean, and thus pre-dates the reign of Tuthmosis III, though this is not definitive. The temple is a modest building of unique plan. Its dimensions are 11.70 × 14.60 m, with a tripartite plan which includes an entrance hall, a central hall with benches and raised platforms, and an inner room (sanctuary) whose walls were lined with benches. All the walls, benches, and floors were coated with white plaster. Yet, contrary to the case in other tripartite temples, the passage from the entrance hall into the main hall was at the side of the dividing wall between the two. The building had two side chambers in its western wing; in one, a number of cylindrical pottery cult stands were found, while the other appears to have been a bath (perhaps for ritual purposes) or a lavatory. In the courtyard in front of the temple there were various installations; a deep stone-lined pit found here perhaps was used for water or grain storage.

Architecturally, this temple can be defined as the earliest example of a group of temples which we defined elsewhere as 'non-monumental, irregular temples'.[9] This group includes the Fosse Temples at Lachish, the temples of Tel Mevorakh, and the temples of Tell Qasile strata XI–X. In the discussion of these temples, the author has claimed that they differed from the mainstream of Canaanite temples, which in most cases are symmetrical buildings with a direct approach to the Holy of Holies. Since the sixteenth century BCE was a time when northern population groups such as Hurrians and Indo-Europeans settled in Canaan, it may be suggested that this new type of temple was introduced by such groups, though it could also have been a local indigenous development.

The discovery of the Late Bronze I temple at Beth Shean demonstrates once again the principle of continuity in the location of cult places in ancient towns of the Near East. Furthermore, it appears that the location of the sacred precinct at Beth Shean preceded the establishment of the Egyptian stronghold at this town.[10] The temple was found empty of any finds; it appears that the building went out of use due to deterioration or damage caused by an earthquake: the walls were found sunken toward the center of the earlier 'pool', on which the building was constructed. It appears that the temple was cleaned of any objects before it was abandoned, and was filled with an artificial fill up to the top of the wall stumps.

The Egyptian Garrison Town at Beth Shean

From the fifteenth century BCE until the late twelfth century BCE, Beth Shean was a stronghold of Egyptian administration in Canaan. Four main strata related to this period (strata IX–VI) were defined by the

9. A. Mazar, *Excavations at Tell Qasile Part 1* (Qedem 2) (Jerusalem: The Hebrew University, 1980), pp. 62-68; A. Mazar in A. Kempinski and R. Reich (eds.), *The Architecture of Ancient Israel* (Jerusalem: The Israel Exploration Society, 1992), pp. 177-83.

10. For a more detailed description and discussion of this temple see Mazar, *Biblical Archaeology Today*.

University of Pennsylvania. In broad terms, these strata correspond to the Egyptian dynasties as following:

Stratum IX: Eighteenth Dynasty
Strata VIII–VII: Nineteenth Dynasty
Stratum VI: Twentieth Dynasty

Our large-scale excavations in areas R, S, N, and Q enabled us to define additional building phases from this period. Stratum IX can now be divided into two phases in certain areas. A new stratum between stratum VII and VI was discovered; this new stratum seems to be identical to stratum 'Late VII' which was identified in several places in the previous excavations.[11]

Stratum IX: The Time of the Eighteenth Dynasty
In area R, below the western part of the large sanctuary of stratum IX (phase R1a, fourteenth century BCE), several rooms of an earlier phase of this sanctuary were discovered (phase R1b, probably of the late fifteenth century BCE). Some of the walls of this phase were constructed above the remains of the earlier temple of phase R2, with no architectural continuity. In several rooms of phase R1b a rich collection of pottery vessels was found, consisting mainly of bowls, kraters, and Egyptian 'beer bottles'; these probably served as offering vessels in the sanctuary. Two bronze daggers, typical of this period, were also found. The present excavations have shown that what was defined by some as a 'casemate wall'[12] in the southern part of the area was probably part of a larger structure which extended further to the south, now severely destroyed by erosion. One of the 'casemate' rooms was found to be a large bath, with wide plastered steps, a supplying water channel and a drainage channel. This bath is a unique feature in this period. In the northeastern edge of the area, part of phase R1a (the original stratum IX) was found destroyed by heavy fire. Several intriguing installations were found here, as well as a fine group of pottery vessels. Among the finds was a painted pottery sherd showing a human figure (only the body was preserved) in a unique style, perhaps a product of the same artist who painted two human portraits on pottery sherds found by the University of Pennsylvania.

11. See James and McGovern, *The Late Bronze Egyptian Garrison at Beth Shan*, pp. 1-67.
12. A. Kempinski in A. Kempinski and R. Reich (eds.), *The Architecture of Ancient Israel* (Jerusalem: The Israel Exploration Society, 1992), p. 140 and Fig. 25.

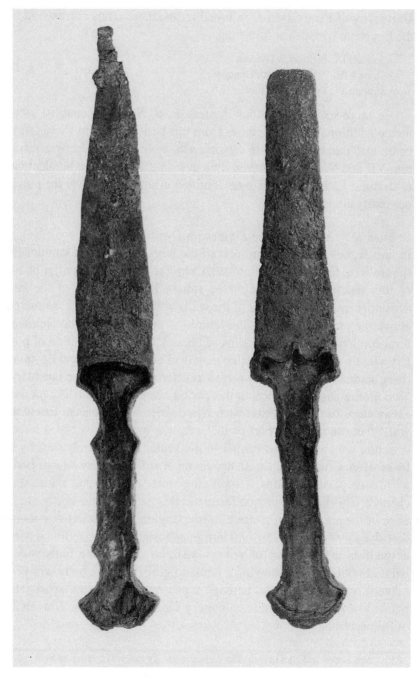

Figure 3. Two bronze daggers of the Late Bronze Age
(Stratum IX) (photo: G. Laron).

Figure 4. A group of pottery vessels from Stratum IX (fourteenth
century BCE) including (left) an Egyptian bottle (photo: G. Laron).

The pottery assemblages of both phases R1a and R1b contained vessels that are Egyptian in form and technique, yet were produced locally
at Beth Shean, most probably by Egyptian potters brought with the
Egyptian garrison to the town.

The heavy destruction of phase R1a (stratum IX) is evidence of a
crisis in the history of the garrison city at Beth Shean, perhaps during
the period of turmoil that characterized the final days of the Eighteenth
Dynasty, some time following the Amarna period.

Strata VIII-VII: The Time of the Nineteenth Dynasty
Structures dating to the thirteenth century BCE were excavated by us in
area N, which is located north of area R. Here the University of
Pennsylvania expedition reached stratum lower VI of the twelfth century
BCE. The present excavations revealed that the rooms attributed to this
stratum in fact represent a rebuild of a much larger building dating to
the thirteenth century (stratum VII). This earlier building is one of the
most massive on the entire mound. Its size and the thickness of the walls
recall the so-called 'Migdol' building of stratum VII, excavated by the

University of Pennsylvania.[13] Two of its mudbrick walls are over 2.60 m
wide, and its western wall, which faces a north–south street, is 1.20 m
wide. A large hall in this building, measuring 6 × 3.7 m (inner dimensions), contained a square bin and a bench, on which a basalt grinder
with quern and pestle was found. An entrance led from this large hall to
a small, narrow elongated chamber in which large quantities of grain
were found. The building was destroyed by heavy fire. Restorable pottery vessels found in the destruction level included imported Egyptian
jars, Cypriot pottery, and local Canaanite pottery. A complete 'collared
rim' pithos, one of the earliest of its type, was found as well.[14] This
formidable building, located close to the northern end of the town, was
perhaps one of the Egyptian administrative buildings. Its fatal destruction
by fire marks another crisis in the history of the Egyptian garrison town,
perhaps at the end of the Nineteenth Dynasty.

Strata 'Late VII' and 'Level VI': The Time of the Twentieth Dynasty
The terms employed here are those used in the final publications of Beth
Shean for two strata which relate to the time of the twentieth Dynasty–
the twelfth century BCE. Stratum 'Late VII' was defined in only few loci
in the previous excavations.[15]

In area S, a clear distinction was made between the two strata, which
were termed S4 and S3, yet both can be attributed to the time of the
Twentieth Dynasty. Moreover, in both strata, and particularly in stratum
S3, subphases of reconstruction could be defined. Extensive activity
from this period is demonstrated by both the thickness of the accumulation (up to 3 m for the two strata) and the many floor layers in both
strata. An area of dwellings dating to this period which had been partly
exposed by Yadin and Geva was expanded in the present excavations.[16]
The area included two intersecting streets, flanked by segments of

13. See James and McGovern, *The Late Bronze Egyptian Garrison at Beth Shan*
(1993), pp. 55-60.

14. This type of pithos was widely discussed in relation to the Israelite
settlement. Today it is known from thirteenth century contexts at Aphek, Tel Nami,
and Beth Shean. For the most current discussion with previous bibliography see
D.L. Esse, *The Collared Pithos at Megiddo: Ceramic Distribution and Ethnicity*,
JNES, 51 (1992), pp. 81-104.

15. James and McGovern, *The Late Bronze Egyptian Garrison at Beth Shan*
(1993), pp. 1-67.

16. See Yadin and Geva, *Investigations at Beth Shan*, and my detailed report,
'Beth Shean'.

houses. The houses were ordinary dwellings, probably serving the officials of the Egyptian garrison and their families. They were built of mudbrick walls with or without stone foundations; floors were made of beaten earth, sometimes laid on a flagstone bedding. Each house contained a large space with square bins and clay ovens. Fragments of an Egyptian-style lintel and a small fragment of a relief showing an Egyptian official sitting on a folded stool indicate that there had been monumental Egyptian decorations in this area.

Figure 5. Building remains of the Egyptian garrison city
of the twelfth century BCE (photo: A. Mazar).

The pottery assemblage found in both strata is similar, containing typical twelfth century BCE local pottery, as well as abundant Egyptian forms. Most of the Egyptian pottery was made locally, though several vessels were imported from Egypt.[17]

Various finds provide evidence for the high rank of the inhabitants; these include gold objects (jewelry, gold foils, and a gold sheet worked in the form of a ram's head), a hoard of silver scrap metal and broken jewelry wrapped in Egyptian linen, scarabs, faience pendants of Egyptian deities, and clay bird figurines. Seal impressions on clay bullae are evidence for administrative activity in this area.

17. Based on results of petrographic research carried out by A. Cohen.

Figure 6. A group of of pottery vessels of Egyptian form, produced locally
at Beth Shean (twelfth century BCE) (photo: G. Laron).

More than a dozen sherds of Mycenaean IIIC vessels were found,
mostly in phase S4, and thus can be dated to the earlier part of the
Twentieth Dynasty. This Mycenaean pottery is of high quality, and
probably was imported either directly from Greece or Cyprus. It was
either brought by Aegean mercenaries (such as the Sherden) who
served in the Egyptian troops, or arrived through trade. In any case, the
stratigraphic context of this pottery at Beth Shean is most important for
establishing the date of similar pottery in the Aegean and the Levant.[18]

The earlier of the two Twentieth-Dynasty strata (S4) appears to have
come to a peaceful end, as no evidence for violent destruction was
found. The later stratum (S3 = 'Level VI') was destroyed by heavy fire,
with thick debris of fallen bricks, burnt beams, and smashed pottery vessels. The destruction was so severe that some of the pottery vessels were
totally distorted in the fire.

In area N, the massive building of stratum VII (phase N5) was rebuilt
on a somewhat different plan in two successive phases (N4 and N3),
which correspond to phases S4 and S3 in area S. The larger spaces of

18. On similar Mycenaean IIIC pottery from Tell Keisan see J. Balensi, 'Tell
Keisan, temoin original de l'apparition du "Mycénien IIIC 1a" au Proche-Orient', *RB*
88 (1981), pp. 399-401.

the previous building were divided into smaller spaces. These rooms were excavated by the University of Pennsylvania.

Figure 7. A bronze bull figurine (twelfth century BCE) (photo: G. Laron).

Area Q, in the northwestern part of the acropolis, was opened in order to study the history of Building 1500, a monumental governor's residence excavated by the University of Pennsylvania.[19] This building measured 20 × 20 m, with a central hypostyle hall surrounded by rooms. T-shaped doorsills and doorjambs with hieroglyphic inscriptions are evidence for the importance of this structure. The present excavation went below the floors of this building, and it soon became clear that the building had stone foundations which were constructed above the stumps of an earlier building of similar dimensions. This earlier building (phase Q2), preserved to only one or two courses, had mudbrick walls

19. R. James, *The Iron Age at Beth Shan* (1966), pp. 9-11.

with no stone foundation, as well as mudbrick floors—two typical Egyptian building techniques. Though the outer layout of the earlier building is similar to that of its successor, its inner plan was distinctly different; it was divided into small chambers and corridors. Its plan, size, and building technique recall that of the Egyptian fortress of the Nineteenth Dynasty uncovered at Deir el Balah.[20] Though the floors of the earlier building were found empty of finds, stratigraphically it appears that this building corresponds to phases S4 and N4 and thus should be dated to the earlier part of the Twentieth Dynasty.

The violent destruction at the end of Level VI (phases S3, N3 and Q1) marks the end of the Egyptian presence at Beth Shean. It is difficult to determine the circumstances of this destruction. It could have occurred as a result of an attack on the city related to the collapse of the Egyptian domination of Canaan. The Midianite invasion and Gideon's response related in the Bible, which occurred in the region of Beth Shean, is one possibility for the identification of the attackers, though a local Canaanite revolt against the Egyptian garrison may also be considered.

The Eleventh Century BCE

The University of Pennsylvania excavations failed to clarify the fate of Beth Shean during the eleventh century BCE. Stratum 'upper VI' belongs to this period, though only a few structures were attributed to it. Yadin and Geva's conclusions concerning this period were based on insufficient data, and added confusion to this issue.[21] This period sparks particular interest due to the biblical account of Beth Shean as the place where the Philistines hung the bodies of Saul and his sons after the battle of Gilboa (1 Sam. 31.10). The excavation results in area S have shown that during the eleventh century (phase S2) the town was rebuilt according to the same layout as that of its twelfth-century predecessor. The material culture of this level is basically Canaanite, with no Egyptian or Philistine pottery forms or objects, and it appears that local people rehabilitated the town after the Egyptians were expelled.

20. T. Dothan, 'Deir el-Balah', in *The New Encyclopedia of Archaeological Excavations in the Holy Land* (rev. edn, ed. E. Stern; New York: Simon and Schuster, 1993), pp. 343-47.

21. See my comments (above n. 3, 1993).

Figure 8. A clay figurine showing a male head
(eleventh century BCE) (photo: G. Laron).

Two architectural complexes uncovered by the University of Pennsylvania may be attributed to this period. It is the author's opinion that the double temple complex (the Northern and Southern Temples) excavated by the University of Pennsylvania and attributed to Stratum V should be dated to this period rather than to the tenth century BCE as suggested by F. James and others. The eleventh century date is supported by the painted pottery cult objects and the pottery vessels found in relation to these temples. The collection of Egyptian monuments found in the courtyard of these temples is more suited to the period directly following the end of the Egyptian presence in the town. They were probably saved as heirlooms from the time of the zenith of the Egyptian garrison at Beth Shean.[22] The second complex is Building 1700, a monumental structure with a 15 m long northern wall constructed of a foundation of large basalt stones and additional wide mudbrick walls. The building was attributed by its excavators to Level VI, though the present excavations revealed that it was constructed later than structures of phase N3 (= Level VI) in area N, and thus probably belongs to the eleventh century. Thus, the eleventh-century town at Beth Shean appears to have been well planned; some of its layout continued that of the preceding period, while several new massive structures constructed during that time are evidence of a vigorous urban revival.

In area S evidence was found for the destruction of the eleventh-century city by fire only in two loci, and thus may be coincidental. The pottery in the burnt loci recalls that of Megiddo stratum VIA; both these cities may have been destroyed in the early tenth century BCE, perhaps when David annexed the region to his kingdom.

The Iron Age II Period

Beth Shean is mentioned in the biblical texts relating to the time of the monarchy only once, as a city in the fifth district of King Solomon (1 Kgs 4.12); it later appears in Shishak's list at Karnak as one of the cities conquered during his campaign shortly after the division of the monarchy.

22. F. James, *The Iron Age at Beth Shan* (1966), pp. 32-40, 133-36; F.W. James and P.E. McGovern, *The Late Bronze Egyptian Garrison at Beth Shan* (1993) p. 695. James' interpretation was based on pottery which probably did not belong to the original double temple complex. It appears that her stratum 'lower V' contains a mixture of two different periods: a northern block of well-planned buildings which was in use during the tenth century BCE, and the double temple complex which is earlier, though reused to some extent in the tenth century BCE as shown by the upper floor in the Northern Temple.

Though most of the Iron Age II remains in the upper part of the mound were removed by the University of Pennsylvania excavations, important remains of the Solomonic era were found during the present excavations in the southeast corner of area S, where part of a massive building was uncovered. The excavated remains include massive walls, 1.60–2.5 m wide, with foundations made of large basalt stones. Wooden beams were laid between the stone foundations and the brick super-structure. It appears that these remains are part of a citadel, located at the uppermost point of the mound, overlooking the valleys to the east and south. The building was destroyed by a violent conflagration; the brick superstructure was burnt at such a high temperature that the bricks fired to the hardness of pottery. In one of the rooms, fallen debris buried a collection of broken storage jars and other pottery vessels typical of the tenth century BCE. The violent destruction may be attributed to the invasion of the region by Shishak, 5 years after the death of Solomon. Destructions which can be attributed to the same event were detected at other sites in the region as well, such as Tell el-Hama and Tel Amal. It thus appears that on his route from the Jordan Valley to Megiddo, Shishak's invasion wreaked considerable havoc.

In area S, no remains later than the tenth century BCE were left for investigation. Thus, the study of the later Iron Age II period was located in a new area near the western slope of the mound, area P, where the excavation started from topsoil. A large architectural complex of the eighth century BCE was revealed here. Its massive mudbrick walls, 1.20 m wide, preserved to a height of over 1 m, were covered with mud plaster. Though this complex is still in the initial stages of investigation, it appears to have been integrated into a city wall. It was destroyed by heavy conflagration, most probably the result of the conquest of the northern part of the kingdom of Israel by Tiglath Pilesser III in 732 BCE.

Several ink inscriptions on fragments of a storage jar from this period were found at the bottom of a pit, representing lists of names and quantities of some commodities; the rare name *zm'a* appears three times in these inscriptions.

Following the destruction of the Iron Age city by the Assyrians, some squatters settled on top of the ruined city. In area P, one thin wall from this period was discovered. Following this short occupational phase, the mound was abandoned for several centuries.

The Late Periods

Tel Beth Shean was settled again from the Hellenistic period onwards. In three excavation areas—H, L, and P—remains of these later periods were investigated.

In area P, two phases of occupational levels from the Hellenistic period contained the remains of private dwellings with thin stone walls, large courtyards, and several ovens. The rich assemblage of pottery includes imports from Greece and the eastern Mediterranean. The end of the period is marked by silver coins of Tyre, dated to the middle of the first century BCE.

During the Roman period, a monumental temple stood at the top of the mound (revealed by the University of Pennsylvania). However, this was an isolated building, overlooking the Roman city at the bottom of the mound, while the rest of the mound remained unsettled. During the Byzantine period a flourishing dwelling quarter was constructed on the mound, dominated by a circular church at the top of the mound. In areas H, L, and P remains of well-constructed houses of this period were found, and it appears that the mound served as an elite zone in the large Byzantine city of Beth Shean.

During the early Arab period (eighth century CE) many of the Byzantine structures were replaced by new buildings. The entire mound was settled during this period, perhaps until the destruction of Beth Shean by the earthquake of 749 CE.

During the Medieval period, the mound probably served as an estate. A wall that surrounded the entire mound, as well as a fortified gate at the northwestern corner of the mound, was constructed during that period, probably in the twelfth century CE. Yet most of the mound remained unbuilt, except for a few structures along the city wall and perhaps on the summit.

Thus, the seven seasons of renewed excavations enabled investigation of almost all the periods of occupation at Tel Beth Shean. The detailed stratigraphic work and the abundance of finds have allowed for a more detailed study of the cultural history of this important site.

(This paper went to press in 1995 and does not include the results of the 1995–96 seasons.)

All photos copyright Beth Shean Expedition, Institute of Archaeology, Hebrew University.

ARCHAEOLOGY AND SOCIAL HISTORY
OF THE SECOND TEMPLE
AND RABBINIC PERIODS

The Revolutionary Effects of Archaeology on the Study of Jewish History: The Case of the Ancient Synagogue

Lee I. Levine

Studies of the ancient synagogue have proliferated dramatically over the last decades. Archaeological finds and the information gained from their study are producing a sizable corpus of material. Never a year passes without a new synagogue being discovered or a known one being re-excavated, adding new facts and new theories to what is already known.[1]

The pioneering work on ancient synagogues was done by H. Kohl and C. Watzinger in 1905–1907 when they surveyed 11 known Galilean buildings; their findings were published a decade later, in 1916. In their report, which to this day remains indispensable for the study of these edifices, Kohl and Watzinger carefully recorded all the known architectural and artistic remains, drew up plans, and proposed possible reconstructions of the buildings. With the help of limited probes, they also related to the larger Roman context in the dating of the buildings and in accounting for the source of their architectural and artistic motifs.[2]

The next few decades (1920–48) witnessed a slow and gradual accumulation of data. Synagogues at Naʻaran and Ḥammath Tiberias were excavated in 1920–21, Beth Alpha in 1929, followed by Ḥuseifa, Eshtemoa, Jericho, Gerasa, Ḥammat Gader, and Beth Sheʻarim in the 1930s.[3] With the founding of the State of Israel in 1948 and its newly

---

1. See the most recent listing of known synagogues by Zvi Ilan, *Ancient Synagogues in Israel* (Tel-Aviv: Israel Ministry of Defense, 1991) (Hebrew), although one should use some of these identifications with caution. The author has a tendency to include sites which are doubtful.

2. Heinrich Kohl and Carl Watzinger, *Antike Synagogen in Galilaea* (Leipzig, 1916; reprint Jerusalem: Kedem, 1973).

3. On these and other specific sites noted below, see the up-to-date summaries

constituted Department of Antiquities (from 1990 called the Antiquities Authority), efforts continued to uncover and preserve archaeological finds. Over the next several decades synagogues were excavated at Caesarea, Ḥammath Tiberias, Beth Shean, Yafia, and Maʻon (Judea).

The post-1967 era witnessed a dramatic increase in archaeological initiatives; the new political reality opened up regions heretofore unexplored by Israeli archaeologists, producing not a few surprises. The remains of five synagogues were discovered in the eastern, southern, and western extremities of Judea ('En Gedi, Susiya, Maʻon, 'Anim, and Ramon), and in Gaza along the coast. Before the 1967 war three synagogues were known to have existed on the Golan; today, fifteen additional buildings (including one at Gamla) have been located and traces of another eight sites have been identified. A second factor responsible for the increased activity in synagogue studies was the initiative taken by the Ministry of Tourism to support archaeological excavations for the purpose of developing ancient sites.

A further factor in stimulating this interest was the initiative of the American archaeologist E. Meyers, who excavated four Galilean synagogues over the last two decades (Khirbet Shemaʻ, Gush Ḥalav, Meiron, and Nabratein). Additional synagogues have been found in the Galilee (Meroth, Sepphoris) and the Beth Shean area (Reḥov, Maʻoz Ḥayyim, Beth Shean B), while a number that had already been excavated underwent further study (Capernaum, Ḥorvat ʻAmmudim, Chorazim). Today we have solid evidence for well over 100 synagogue sites in Israel, although by some counts the number runs much higher.[4]

If only for the sheer quantity of sites, the field of synagogue studies over these last decades is noteworthy. What makes these finds indeed revolutionary is the range, diversity, and type of material brought to light and its far-reaching implications. The field of ancient Jewish art rests heavily on synagogue finds. The synagogue material unearthed— from mosaic floors to carved stone moldings—has not only modified our perception of the Jews' attitude towards this medium but, as we

offered in Ephraim Stern (ed.), *The New Encyclopedia of Archaeological Excavations in the Holy Land* (= *NEAEHL*) (4 vols.; Jerusalem: Israel Exploration Society, 1993). Cf. also Eleazar L. Sukenik, 'The Present State of Ancient Synagogue Studies', *Bulletin I—Louis Rabinowitz Fund for the Exploration of Ancient Synagogues* (Jerusalem: Museum of Jewish Antiquities and Hebrew University of Jerusalem, 1949), pp. 7-23.

4. See above, n. 1.

shall see below, has also presented us with a host of new issues regarding its religious and cultural implications.[5] The discovery of ancient synagogues has also enriched the field of Jewish epigraphy. Beth She'arim excepted, the overwhelming majority of inscriptions from Palestine of late antiquity has come from synagogues. To date, we know of over 150 such inscriptions in Greek, Aramaic, and Hebrew. Most are dedicatory in nature, and the information they provide on Jewish prosopography, official titles, professions, architectural elements of the synagogue building itself, etc., is invaluable for our knowledge of the period.[6]

The significance of synagogue finds becomes even more apparent when we realize that they are the singlemost important nonrabbinic source of information for the period. The scores of works comprising rabbinic literature are, of course, our principal source of information for late antiquity. There are few areas of Jewish life in Israel that are not reflected in some form or fashion in this corpus. However, for all its value, this material is also limited, for when all is said and done rabbinic sources are tendentious, reflecting the interests, prejudices, and views of the rabbis, who constituted but one—albeit important—sector of Jewish society at the time. Therefore, extrarabbinic testimony for this period is most welcome. Not only does it offer us additional information and vastly differing perspectives, but it also allows us to evaluate more accurately the strengths and weaknesses of the rabbinic corpus itself.[7] In contrast to the pre-70 era, for which we have at our disposal a wide variety of sources (Josephus, Philo, the New Testament, the Apocrypha, Pseudepigrapha, Qumran scrolls, pagan writings, archaeology, and rabbinic material), the evidence available for the post-70 period is far more meager in its range of sources. Archaeological material, and especially synagogal remains, thus become a crucial component in the study of late antiquity.

We propose to examine five areas of Jewish life in Palestine of late

---

5.   Monumental, of course, is the work of Erwin R. Goodenough, *Jewish Symbols in the Greco-Roman Period* (13 vols.; New York: Pantheon, 1953–68), and the more recent Rachel Hachlili, *Ancient Jewish Art and Archeology in the Land of Israel* (Leiden: Brill, 1988).

6.   Relatively up-to-date corpora of the inscriptions found in Israel are to be found in Joseph Naveh, *On Stone and Mosaic* (Jerusalem: Israel Exploration Society, 1978) (Hebrew); Leah Roth-Gerson, *The Greek Inscriptions from the Synagogues in Eretz-Israel* (Jerusalem: Yad Izhak Ben Zvi Press, 1987) (Hebrew).

7.   See my comments in *The Rabbinic Class of Roman Palestine in Late Antiquity* (Jerusalem: Yad Izhak Ben Zvi Press, 1989), pp. 16-22.

antiquity which have been significantly impacted by the archaeological finds of the past decades.

Geography—Where Jews Lived. Given the disruptions caused by the unsuccessful revolts of the first two centuries, what were the centers of Jewish settlement in their aftermath? Rabbinic literature leaves us with a very clear impression of Jewish settlement patterns. From the second century onward Jewish life concentrated in the Galilee; only scattered remains of Jewish communities are in evidence in Judea and along the coast. Archaeological material confirms this impression and elaborates upon it.[8] About half the synagogues discovered in Israel to date are located in the Galilee (Figure 1); the scattered nature of Jewish settlement along the coast is likewise verified by some material remains attesting to Jews living in the major urban centers such as Caesarea, Ashdod, Ascalon, and Gaza. Moreover, the total absence of Jewish presence in Samaria is evident in the archaeological remains and corresponds to the situation reflected in rabbinic literature as well.

With respect to Judea, however, the material finds have altered our impressions considerably. The number of Jewish settlements in the area was far greater than might have been imagined on the basis of the rabbinic evidence alone. This region was practically ignored by the rabbis, simply because very few sages in late antiquity came from or lived there (Lydda excepted). Today we know that many Jews who were banned from the Judean highlands, following the Bar Kokhba Revolt, established communities on the eastern, southern, and western fringes of the Judean hinterland.

By far the most dramatic revision of our knowledge regarding Jewish settlement in late antiquity relates to the Golan. Mentioned only a few times in rabbinic sources, the Golan should appear to have been bereft of any sizable Jewish community. Today, however, this rather limited area has yielded 25 sites containing synagogal remains from late antiquity (excluding Gamla). Clearly, the Golan was a region intensively settled by Jews.

Thus, archaeology plays a significant role in attesting to the geographical distribution of the Jewish population in late antiquity, at times confirming, at times correcting, and at times totally revising what we know from literary sources.

---

8. See the map in *NEAEHL*, IV, p. 1421, which also includes Samaritan synagogues.

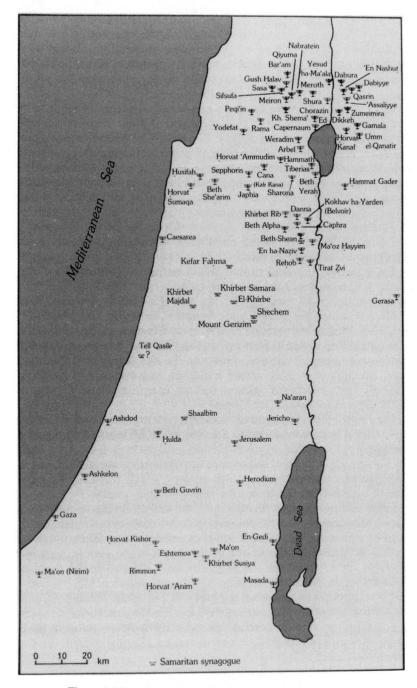

Figure 1. Map of ancient synagogues of Palestine in late antiquity
(photograph: Israel Exploration Society).

Chronology—Patterns of Synagogal Remains. Of the more than one hundred sites in Palestine containing synagogue remains, all but four can be securely dated from the third to the seventh centuries. Only Gamla, Masada, Herodium, and the synagogue in Jerusalem referred to in the Theodotos inscription are pre-70, and the earliest stage of the Nabratein synagogue may perhaps be dated to the second century CE. Other than these, all the other synagogue buildings are dated to late antiquity, especially the fifth to seventh centuries.

This dating raises not a few intriguing questions. For one, why are there only negligible synagogal remains from the Second Temple period? If, indeed, there were some one to two million Jews living in Judea in the first century CE, and given the fact that the synagogue had already become a central communal institution by that time, how is it possible that there are so few remains? The question becomes even more poignant if we recall that of the four Second Temple synagogues mentioned above, two date from the first revolt against Rome (66–74 CE), i.e., the very last years of the period. In other words, we know of only two sites containing synagogal remains from the pre-66 era.

The most obvious answer to this dilemma seems to lie in the fact that this situation with respect to the synagogue is far from being *sui generis* in Palestinian archaeology. Pre-70 physical remains in general are woefully limited. With the exception of Jerusalem, where Herodian construction was uniquely monumental, and the remote desert areas, where palaces and fortresses were well preserved owing to their isolation (e.g., Masada, Jericho, Herodium), there is very little in the way of material remains from this period. With the exception of Jerusalem and Jericho, burial sites, for example, are almost nonexistent, and the same holds true for remains of the many cities that flourished at the time, e.g., Caesarea, Tiberias, Sepphoris, and Jericho.

This dearth of earlier material may also account for the absence of synagogal remains (once again, with the possible exception of Nabratein) for several centuries after 70. Only during the course of the third century do synagogues appear in significant numbers throughout most areas of Palestine, and especially in the Galilee. As we have noted with respect to the pre-70 period, it is possible that the intensive and extensive construction of subsequent centuries largely obliterated these earlier, pre-third century remains.

No less surprising is the fact that synagogue construction commenced vigorously in the mid to late third century CE, a period traditionally viewed as fraught with anarchy and invasions, runaway inflation, recurring droughts, and plagues. In such a setting of perpetual crisis, one would not expect there to have been large-scale public building. Nevertheless, the fact remains that synagogues were being constructed, sometimes in rather monumental proportions.

How can this be reconciled? In the first place, our impression of the third century as an age of turmoil and anarchy may be overstated. In general, the perception of crisis reflected in certain sources is much greater than seems warranted.[9] Although this period has been so characterized because of the preponderance of catastrophes that swept the empire at the time, and because certain key areas in particular were adversely affected, it may very well be that other regions of the empire suffered to a lesser extent and that daily life, including building activity, proceeded unhampered. Secondly, it is not at all certain that monumental building would be an unlikely occurrence in times of economic or political adversity. It is precisely in times of crisis that major edifices may have been erected to reassert the authority, presence, and continuity of a community and its leadership.

However, the most far-reaching chronological implications of synagogal finds have to do with the end of the period under consideration, i.e., the latter part of the Byzantine era. This period has always been considered a 'dark ages' for the Jews of Palestine. A process of decline—beginning with the two revolts against Rome in the first and second centuries, continuing with the anarchy of the third century, and the rise of Christianity in the fourth—reached its nadir in the fifth century with the hasty compilation of the Jerusalem Talmud (c. 400) and the disappearance of the Patriarchate (c. 425).

However, archaeological finds, particularly those of ancient synagogues, have demonstrated that this scenario of decline and persecution was in reality one of relative prosperity, expansion, and vitality for the Jewish people. The many synagogues flourishing at the time testify to the continued vigor of Jewish life in the country right down to the Arab conquest in the seventh century and beyond. What is impressive, however, is not only the number of synagogues and their dispersal throughout all areas of the country, but also the size, ornamentation, and overall physical presence of many—thereby reflecting a community with considerable political clout and economic means at its disposal, as well as

9. Cf. Ramsay MacMullen, *Roman Government's Response to Crisis—AD 235–337* (New Haven: Yale University Press, 1976).

religious pride and communal stature. Recalling how the Capernaum synagogue dwarfs the neighboring Christian church in the fifth and sixth centuries, one can imagine the status and prominence such a Jewish community must have enjoyed at the time. Moreover, the construction and repair of their synagogues defied a series of laws forbidding such activity at this time.[10]

The synagogal remains are reinforced and corroborated by evidence found in the Cairo Genizah. Material published from that trove of texts has clearly established the heretofore unimaginable extent to which the Jews of Byzantine Palestine enjoyed a cultural heyday. True, the compilation of the Talmud had come to a close; but in its stead Jewish religious figures—rabbis and others—were creating a diverse and rich alternative culture, one which found expression in liturgical poetry (*piyyut*), midrashic compilations, *targumim*, mystical, magical and apocalyptic literature, as well as new genres of halakhic works.[11] The case of the Jews of Palestine was not unique. In fact, large parts of Syria, as well as other provinces of this period, were enjoying a period of relative prosperity and vigor.

Heterogeneity. Were one to open any standard text or introductory book on synagogue architecture written up to just a few years ago, one would find one standard description of the Palestinian synagogue's physical development in antiquity. The classic tripartite division of the architectural development of the synagogue was first conceived by E.L. Sukenik, later embellished and refined by M. Avi-Yonah, and then adopted by E.R. Goodenough and others.[12] This reconstruction posits that there were three types of synagogue buildings: an early Galilean-type, a transitional broadhouse-type, and a late basilical- (or apsidal-) type. The early type was dated to the second or third centuries, the transitional type to the fourth century, and the late type to the fifth–seventh

10. Amnon Linder, *The Jews in Roman Imperial Legislation* (Detroit: Wayne State University Press, 1987), pp. 41, 47.

11. This phenomenon has not yet received the full treatment it deserves, particularly in English. For surveys of this phenomenon, see Yaron Dan, 'Byzantine Rule,' in M.D. Herr (ed.), *The History of Eretz Israel*, V (Jerusalem: Keter Press, 1985), pp. 338-48 (Hebrew).

12. Eleazar L. Sukenik, *Ancient Synagogues in Palestine and Greece* (London: Milford, 1934), p. 27; Michael Avi-Yonah, 'Synagogues', in Michael Avi-Yonah and Ephraim Stern (eds.), *Encyclopedia of Archaeological Excavations in the Holy Land* (4 vols.; Jerusalem: Israel Exploration Society and Massada Press, 1975–78), IV, pp. 1129-32; Goodenough, *Jewish Symbols*, I, pp. 178-267.

centuries. Thus, according to this approach chronological developments dovetail quite neatly with typological distinctions.

What has become of this theory over these last decades? Put very simply, new archeological finds have completely undermined the validity of such a rigid typology. Let us briefly review some of the major finds which challenge this theory (the presentation is organized in the chronological order of discovery).

1. *Capernaum*

Fathers V. Corbo and S. Loffreda of the Franciscan Order were the first to excavate extensively this large synagogue in the late 60s and early 70s of this century (Figure 2). Their efforts yielded coins and pottery from under the floor and benches, and in the foundation-trenches of the building dating as late as the mid-fifth century. Thus, from a strictly archaeological point of view, this monumental Galilean-type synagogue could not have been built before the latter part of the fifth century.

Figure 2. Proposed reconstruction of Capernaum synagogue (photograph: Israel Exploration Society).

Those who attempt to refute these findings contend that this building had already been standing since the second or third century and had undergone extensive repairs. However, given the fact that many of these late remains were found in numerous places under the synagogue's foundations or embedded in its mortar substratum, most scholars today reject this explanation and agree with the excavators that we are dealing with the construction of the entire building. Interestingly, in one of the early responses to the excavation findings, Avi-Yonah remarked that were Capernaum a later edifice, then we would be confronted with the 'strange' situation of Jews building synagogues in radically contrasting ways at the same approximate time and in the same locale. Avi-Yonah was then referring to the contrast between the synagogues at Hammath Tiberias and Capernaum. What was difficult for him to conceive some 20 years ago has now become well accepted in the study of synagogue development.[13]

2. *Khirbet Shema'*

Excavated in the early 1970s, this broadhouse-synagogue is located in the heart of the Galilee, next to Mt Meiron. In terms of the older division, this building should have been categorized as a transitional-type synagogue and thus dated to the fourth or perhaps fifth century. However, excavation results have demonstrated that this building was erected in the mid-third century, at almost the same time as the nearby Galilean-type synagogue of Meiron.[14] In light of its dating and the fact that Khirbet Shema' is situated in the very heart of Jewish Upper Galilee, in the midst of numerous Galilean-type buildings, the claim to a neat periodization of synagogue types was once again seriously challenged.

3. *Excavations of Other Galilean-type Synagogues*

During the last several decades a series of previously identified Galilean synagogues was further explored. In no instance were these buildings dated to the second or even early third century, as postulated earlier. Each of these synagogues was stratigraphically dated to the last half of the third century—Gush Halav to the mid-third century, Meiron to the

13. For some of these early views and reactions, see the articles of Stanislao Loffreda, Michael Avi-Yonah, and Gideon Foerster, in Lee Levine (ed.), *Ancient Synagogues Revealed* (Jerusalem: Israel Exploration Society, 1981), pp. 52-62.
14. Eric M. Meyers *et al.*, *Ancient Synagogue Excavations at Khirbet Shema', Upper Galilee, Israel 1970–1972* (Durham: Duke University Press, 1976), pp. 33-102.

last quarter of the third, and Horvat 'Ammudim to the turn of the fourth century. Similarly, the first (or perhaps second) stage of the Nabratein synagogue building belongs to the mid-third century.[15] Moreover, not only was the chronology of these buildings different from that posited by the classical theory, but so were a number of their salient characteristics. Accordingly, early Galilean synagogues were not 'supposed' to have had permanent Torah shrines or *bimot*, yet such installations were found at Gush Halav and Nabratein (although not at Horvat 'Ammudim or Meiron); only later synagogue-types were 'supposed' originally to have had mosaic floors, yet it appears that the one at Horvat 'Ammudim had a mosaic floor from its very inception, around the turn of the fourth century.

4. *The Golan*

As noted above, the most dramatic finds of the last decades have come from the Golan region. The number of sites there that has been identified as synagogues has grown from three to twenty-six. They bear some resemblance to Galilean ones, yet also reflect many local characteristics.[16] All the Golan buildings (again, with the exception of first-century Gamla) can now be dated to the fifth–seventh centuries CE. Moreover, they were primarily decorated with stone moldings, a characteristic that, according to the older theory, was not associated with Byzantine synagogues. Their orientation is likewise quite unique, facing either south or west. One intriguing solution which has been suggested is that this variation in orientation stems from the different origins of the Byzantine settlers in the area. Assuming that there was a marked increase in Jewish settlement in the fourth and fifth centuries, as is reflected in the large number of synagogue buildings in the region, some of the new residents may have come from Transjordan to the south, an area that was heavily populated by Jews in the Second Temple period. Others moved to the Golan from the Galilee, perhaps as a result of economic or political hardships. Each group, then, preserved its former local traditions regarding synagogue orientation; those from Transjordan continued to build their synagogues facing west, and those from the Galilee constructed their synagogues facing south. As interesting as this suggestion may be, there is—as yet—simply no evidence to substantiate it.

15. Cf. the relevant articles in *NEAEHL*, passim.
16. See *NEAEHL*, II, pp. 539-45.

5. Meroth

This synagogue, located in the eastern part of the Upper Galilee, was discovered in the early 1980s.[17] It shares many features with the dominant Galilean-type building—a tripartite entrance oriented towards Jerusalem, stone moldings, and a heavy influence of Roman-Syrian architectural forms (Figure 3). Yet this synagogue was built only in the fourth century and continued to exist well into the Middle Ages! Some of the changes introduced in the late Byzantine period are also of interest. The earlier synagogue was decorated with a mosaic floor, the later one with flagstones. This is the very opposite of the earlier theory, which posited flagstone floors for the earlier type and mosaic floors for the later one.

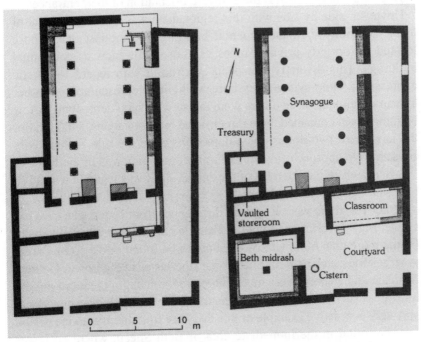

Figure 3. Plan of Meroth synagogue: stage 1, fourth century (photograph: Israel Exploration Society).

17. Zvi Ilan, 'The Synagogue and *Beth Midrash* of Meroth', in Rachel Hachlili (ed.), *Ancient Synagogues in Israel, Third–Seventh Century CE* (BAR International Series, 499; Oxford: British Archaeological Reports, 1989), pp. 21-41.

In light of all these discrepancies, it is clear that we should now view synagogue development in Palestine quite differently. No longer can we assume a linear, monolithic development in architectural forms and artistic modes among local Jewish communities. Rather, diversity was very much in evidence. At times one can discern certain salient regional characteristics, the most striking example, of course, being the Galilean buildings, with their monumental facades, Roman-Syrian-inspired ornamentation, three entrances facing Jerusalem (and, in the case of small structures, one entrance), stone-paved floors, three rows of columns, and stone benches. The Golan buildings constitute a second regional type that shares a number of common characteristics, particularly regarding the use of certain artistic motifs. Moreover, a cluster of four synagogues from southern Judea (Eshtemoa, Susiya, Ma'on, 'Anim) has recently been identified as having a number of features in common, the most prominent of which is the eastward orientation of their entrances.

However, side by side with this regionalism was also a great deal of local variation—e.g., monumental buildings vs. modest ones, those located in formerly private homes vs. those built anew as communal buildings. This diversity is especially striking with regard to artistic expression; some synagogues bore no figural representations, either human or animal, while others were lavish with such depictions. A few buildings even contained three-dimensional representations, although, for the most part, two-dimensional depictions were the rule. A markedly conservative approach towards figural representation is in evidence at 'En Gedi, where a written list of the zodiac signs was featured instead of the usual figural representations.[18]

Moreover, there were linguistic differences from synagogue to synagogue. Most inscriptions found in Palestine are in Hebrew or Aramaic. Of the more than 60 in Greek, most are to be found in the coastal area, in large cities such as Beth Shean and Tiberias or in the Lower Galilee. Aramaic and Hebrew were much more predominant in the more remote rural areas such as the Upper Galilee, the Golan, or the Judean hinterland.

A very instructive example of this diversity from the Byzantine period may be found in the immediate area of Beth Shean, where no fewer than six synagogues are known to have existed in the sixth century.[19]

18. Dan Barag *et al.*, 'The Synagogue at 'En-Gedi', in *Ancient Synagogues Revealed*, pp. 116-19.

19. See Marilyn J. Chiat, 'Synagogues and Christian Architecture in Byzantine Beit She'an', *Journal of Jewish Art* 8 (1980), pp. 6-24.

The differences between some of these structures are enormous. Reḥov, to the south, contained what was apparently an extremely conservative community (Figure 4). No figural representations graced its walls or floors, all inscriptions were in Hebrew, and the one halakhic inscription

Figure 4. Halakhic inscription from Reḥov synagogue, sixth–seventh centuries (photograph: Israel Exploration Society).

ever to be found in a synagogue setting was discovered here. In contrast, the synagogue of Beth Alpha, to the west of the city, is replete with figural representations (Figure 5), including zodiac signs and the figure of Helios; it contains two prominent inscriptions, one in Greek, the other in Aramaic; the building was apsidal in contrast to Reḥov, which had a *bimah* and adjoining side rooms. In the city of Beth Shean itself, a prayer room containing rich mosaic decorations of the amphora and vine tendrils pattern, quite common in the Byzantine world, was discovered. The inscriptions found there are in Greek and Aramaic. Near this room, and presumably associated with it in some way (a large private home? a community-center complex?—known today as Beth Leontis), was a large mosaic pavement containing scenes from Homer's *Odyssey* as well as depictions of the Nile, its god, the city of Alexandria, and a dedicatory inscription in Greek. Just to the north of the Beth Shean city wall a relatively large synagogue facing northwest (!) was discovered. In one of its rooms is an inscription in paleo-Hebrew script, normally associated with the Samaritans in this period. Whether the building as a whole belonged to the Samaritans or whether it was a Jewish synagogue is still debatable. Thus, just from the area of sixth-century Beth Shean we see that each of the synagogues in the area was unique, reflecting the values and cultural proclivities, as well as the economic means, of its members.

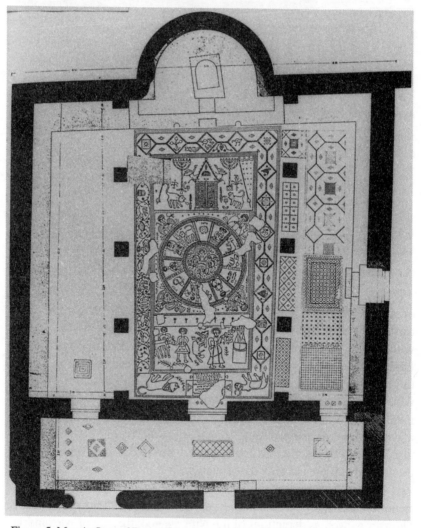

Figure 5. Mosaic floor of Beth Alpha synagogue, sixth century (photograph: Israel Exploration Society).

Interestingly, this diversity among synagogues is reflected in the realm of liturgy as well. Over the past few decades we have become increasingly aware of the significant fluidity which marked various liturgical forms at this time. The most salient example in this regard relates to the various practices of reading the Torah.[20] We know of at least five ways in which the readings were divided from week to week. Some communities at the time divided the Torah-reading over 141 weeks, others over 154, 167, and even 175 weeks. For all of these congregations it took between 3 and $3\frac{1}{2}$ years to complete the reading. In addition, the practice of concluding the reading of the entire Torah in 1 year—as is customary today—was also in evidence at this time. Thus, different synagogues, presumably even those in the same city, were reading different parts of the Torah at any given time. The same holds true with the newly introduced practice of reciting *piyyutim* (liturgical poems) in the synagogue. Communities that were fortunate to have *paytanim* (liturgical poets) were able to introduce their compositions on a given Shabbat, although here, too, there was no one fixed practice. In some synagogues the *piyyut* may have replaced many of the regular prayers, in others these *piyyutim* may have been appended to the regular service.[21] Similarly, differences were evident in the form of prayer itself. As J. Heinemann has demonstrated, much of the prayer service remained fluid throughout antiquity, with only certain basic elements clearly fixed for public or private recitation; the remainder was open to individual or congregational adaptation and variation.[22]

Thus, the picture of the ancient synagogue in Palestine, both from within and without, liturgically and architecturally, was quite different from that projected in the past. Diversity and heterogeneity were no less in evidence than were conformity and standardization.

Hellenization
There is probably no area in the study of ancient Judaism which has merited more attention over the past 50 years than the question of

20. Cf. Joseph Heinemann, 'The Triennial Lectionary Cycle', *JJS* 19 (1968), pp. 41-48.

21. Jakob Petuchowski, *Theology and Poetry* (London: Routledge & Kegan Paul, 1978), pp. 11-15.

22. Joseph Heinemann, *Prayer in the Talmud: Forms and Patterns* (Berlin: de Gruyter, 1977); cf. also Lawrence Hoffman, *The Canonization of the Synagogue Service* (Notre Dame: University of Notre Dame Press, 1977), pp. 1-9.

external influences on the Jews and Judaism. The factors accounting for this intense interest are not difficult to understand. The publication of a wealth of new documents, the awareness of cross-cultural influences in the modern world, and the discovery of large quantities of archaeological material reflecting its contemporary context have all contributed to the ever-growing popularity of this area of study.

All of the above considerations have played a role in the study of Jewish history in late antiquity; however, the finds at the large Jewish necropolis of Beth She'arim in the Galilee in particular have proven to be a powerful catalyst. The first discoveries were made in the late 1930s by B. Mazar of the Hebrew University of Jerusalem. The evidence of Greco-Roman influence there is overwhelming—the architecture of many catacomb facades, the impressive funerary monuments, the extensive art remains, and especially the inscriptions, almost 80% of which are in Greek.[23] Soon after these discoveries, and at least in part because of them, S. Lieberman published his seminal and monumental *Greek in Jewish Palestine*, a pioneering work demonstrating the degree of penetration of Greek language and culture into Jewish life generally and among the rabbis in particular.[24] Thereafter studies abounded regarding almost every conceivable area of Jewish life in antiquity, and, as a result, a fascinating picture of the complex relationship between the Jews and their surrounding cultures has emerged.

The large quantity of archaeological finds relating to ancient synagogues is an important factor in any discussion of Hellenization and its effects in late antiquity. There is no aspect of the material remains of this institution which does not reflect some form or degree of interaction with the surrounding world. The very shapes and forms of most synagogue buildings were clearly borrowed from Roman models. The Galilean-type synagogue seems to have been adapted either from nearby Nabatean temple courtyards (theaters) or Roman basilicas. The large facades of these Galilean buildings which faced Jerusalem were typical of Roman facades on buildings, funerary monuments, or triumphal arches.[25] The degree to which synagogues resembled Roman buildings is

23. Benjamin Mazar, Moshe Schwabe, Baruch Lifshitz, and Nahman Avigad, *Beth She'arim* (3 vols.; New Brunswick, NJ: Rutgers University Press, 1973–76).

24. Saul Lieberman, *Greek in Jewish Palestine* (New York: Jewish Theological Seminary, 1942), followed by his *Hellenism in Jewish Palestine* (New York: Jewish Theological Seminary, 1950; reprint, 1962).

25. Kohl and Watzinger, *Antike Synagogen*, pp. 147ff.; Gideon Foerster, 'The

vividly reflected in a rabbinic discussion of a person who passed a pagan temple and, thinking it was a synagogue, proceeded to bow down before it.[26] The very fact that the rabbis would invoke such an instance as a basis for a halakhic discussion indicates that such a reality was indeed a familiar phenomenon. Moreover, the basilica-like synagogues of the later Byzantine period likewise reflected the surrounding culture; in this case the model seems to have been contemporary churches. An architectural plan, which included an atrium, narthex, and sanctuary consisting of a nave and side aisles separated by two rows of columns, in addition to a chancel screen, seems to have been adopted by the Jews from Christian models.[27]

The same holds true with respect to the artistic depictions in these synagogues. Influence seems to have been a constant with the only variables being its extent and nature.[28] On the one hand, depictions such as the zodiac and Helios, or a mosaic pattern of vine tendrils flowing from an amphora and forming medallions or representations of animals, fish, baskets, and assorted geometric shapes, are frequently used patterns borrowed directly from the surrounding Byzantine world. Even distinctly Jewish symbols, such as the Torah shrine, menorah, and shofar, were influenced by contemporary models and patterns. Stone moldings, which predominate in the art of the Galilean and Golan buildings, were clearly borrowed from traditions of Roman art in evidence throughout the eastern Mediterranean in late antiquity.[29]

Finally, the use of Aramaic and Greek, both *lingua franca* in the Roman East, in over 90% of the synagogue inscriptions in Palestine, bears testimony to the impact of the surrounding world. Many of the names of donors, particularly those in Greek, as well as the formulae invoked in many Greek inscriptions, were likewise borrowed from outside usage.

There is certainly justification in assuming that this influence was not confined only to externalities. The introduction of *piyyut* into the liturgy

Art and Architecture of the Synagogue in its Late Roman Setting in Palestine', in Lee I. Levine (ed.), *The Synagogue in Late Antiquity* (Philadelphia: American Schools of Oriental Research, 1987), pp. 139-46.

26. *b. Šab.* 72b.

27. Yoram Tsafrir, 'The Byzantine Setting and its Influence on Ancient Synagogues', in *The Synagogue in Late Antiquity*, pp. 147-57.

28. See above, n. 5.

29. See above, n. 25.

was parallel to and perhaps even influenced by similar developments in the Byzantine church. One rabbinic tradition reports that in at least one fourth-century synagogue of Caesarea Jews did not know enough Hebrew to recite the basic *Shema'* prayer in the original Hebrew, but rather did so in Greek.[30] One can assume that most, it not all, of the prayer service in that particular synagogue was in Greek, and this would have undoubtedly included the Torah-reading and sermon. Even the gradual transformation throughout late antiquity of the synagogue into a primarily religious institution with a very distinct holy dimension parallels more general lines of development in that society. By the late Byzantine period, synagogue orientation towards Jerusalem was much more definitive, Jewish religious symbols were far more prominent, inscriptions bore the words 'holy place', and the building was referred to as a 'miniature temple' or viewed as a modest substitute for the Jerusalem Temple.[31]

Given the pervasive influence of the surrounding environs, each community responded in its own way. Synagogues located in large cities were often largely influenced by their neighbors' cultures. In Caesarea, for instance, all the inscriptions found in the one known synagogue building were in Greek (with the exception of one word, 'Shalom'),[32] and the biblical quotations were taken from the Septuagint. (This conforms with the above-mentioned tradition discussing that community's recitation of the *Shema'* prayer in Greek.) In more rural areas of the Galilee, Judea, and the Golan Greek influence was significantly restricted.

Nevertheless, it appears that most Jewish communities, and certainly the largest and most influential among them, were significantly influenced in one way or another by the world in which they found themselves. These communities incorporated many of these influences, utilizing them for the enhancement of their synagogues, both externally and internally.

---

30. *y. Soṭ.* 7, 1, 21b.

31. See Shaye J.D. Cohen, 'Pagan and Christian Evidence in the Ancient Synagogue', in *The Synagogue in Late Antiquity*, pp. 161-65; Lee I. Levine, 'From Community Center to "Lesser Sanctuary": The Furnishings and Interior of the Ancient Synagogue', *Cathedra* 60 (1991), pp. 79-84; *idem*, 'Caesarea's Synagogues and Some Historical Implications', in *Biblical Archeology Today—1990: Proceedings of the Second International Congress on Biblical Archeology* (Jerusalem: Israel Exploration Society, 1993), p. 673.

32. Roth-Gerson, *Greek Inscriptions*, pp. 111-24.

The Judaism of the Synagogue

What was the religious orientation of the people who built and attended these synagogues? What did they believe in and what kind of Judaism did they espouse? These questions are tantalizing in nature, but almost impossible to respond to with certitude. In the past, the answers offered were often oversimplified and extreme. For example, it has usually been assumed that these synagogues, like everything else in Jewish life at the time, were under the aegis and authority of the sages, and that the Judaism reflected therein was that of the rabbis. Although speaking of the Pharisees, G. Alon's classical formulation could have applied even more to the rabbis:

> It is a known fact that from the days of the Hasmoneans and onwards the Pharisees constituted the vast majority of the nation, and hence, generally speaking, we have to regard the history of Jewry in our period, in all spheres, as also reflecting the history of the Pharisees... At all events, 'the Sages of Israel' gave expression to the spirit and life of the nation, whose history mirrored the thoughts and deeds of the majority of the Pharisees.[33]

At the other end of the scale stood E.R. Goodenough, who saw in the archaeological remains vestiges of a popular mystically oriented religion that was fundamentally non- and even antirabbinic.[34]

Neither of these extremes does justice to the historical reality, although both contain some element of truth. The sages were undoubtedly a factor in synagogue life that probably tended to increase in the course of late antiquity. Nevertheless, they certainly were not in control of the affairs of that institution, neither in its administrative-political realm nor in its religious-liturgical dimension. To put it very simply, on the basis of rabbinic sources alone there is no way we could have imagined the synagogues as archaeology has uncovered them. At times, it appears that these discoveries have exposed us to different types of Jews and a differently nuanced Judaism, not necessarily antithetical to the rabbis as Goodenough would have it, but certainly not cut from the

33. Gedaliah Alon, *Jews, Judaism and the Classical World* (Jerusalem: Magnes Press, 1977), p. 22 and n. 11.
34. Above, n. 5.

same cloth as the rabbis, as Alon had assumed.[35] The following source aptly reflects this last point:

> All images are forbidden, because they are worshipped at least once a year; these are the words of R. Meir. The sages say: Nothing is forbidden unless it holds in its hand a staff [i.e., a sceptre], a bird, or a sphere [i.e., the earth]. R. Simeon b. Gamliel says: Anything which holds any object [is forbidden].[36]

This source makes it very clear that the sages drew a clear line with regard to certain forms of pictorial representation which they did not hesitate to forbid, i.e., that which smacked of idolatry. E.E. Urbach, in commenting on this passage, interpreted the symbols mentioned as referring to the emperor cult widespread in the second and third centuries.[37] It was this cult to which the rabbis vigorously objected. Yet, just 3 years after Urbach's article appeared, the synagogue of Ḥammath Tiberias was discovered (Figure 6), wherein a depiction of Helios holding a number of the above-mentioned symbols was found in the very center of the mosaic floor. Clearly, those who built and frequented this synagogue were either unaware of this rabbinic prohibition or simply chose to ignore it. It should be remembered that we are not dealing here with some remote community, but rather with an important synagogue in the major Jewish city of the time. The principal donors to this building all bore Greek or Latin names, and the central figure was one Severos, who was associated with the Patriarchal house.[38]

Moreover, rabbis undoubtedly would have been quite uncomfortable with many of the depictions which appeared in the synagogues of the time. The Jerusalem Talmud reports that R. Yoḥanan (third century) and R. Abun (fourth century) noted the introduction of figural images on the walls and mosaic floors of buildings, and neither objected.[39] Clearly, these changes were not being introduced under rabbinic auspices, much

35. For a more detailed exposition of this point, see my 'The Sages and the Synagogue in Late Antiquity: The Evidence of the Galilee', in Lee I. Levine (ed.), *The Galilee in Late Antiquity* (New York: Jewish Theological Seminary, 1992), pp. 201-22.

36. *m. 'Abod. Zar.* 3.1.

37. Ephraim E. Urbach, 'The Rabbinical Laws of Idolatry in the Second and Third Centuries in the Light of Archaeological and Historical Facts', *IEJ* 9 (1959), pp. 235ff.

38. Moshe Dothan, *Hammath Tiberias* (Jerusalem: Israel Exploration Society, 1983), pp. 54-62.

39. *y. 'Abod. Zaro* 3, 42d.

less with their blessing. The forces for change were originating elsewhere. These two sages chose to acquiesce to public will rather than make an issue of these developments.

Figure 6. Depiction of Helios: Ḥammath Tiberias B synagogue, fourth century
(photograph: Israel Exploration Society).

The most intriguing representation within the art of the synagogue is undoubtedly that of the zodiac, a symbol which appears in at least 5 synagogues found in quite different parts of the country and dating from the fourth to the sixth–seventh centuries.[40] The zodiac was a blatantly

40. Goodenough, *Jewish Symbols*, VIII, pp. 167-218; Rachel Hachlili, 'The Zodiac in Ancient Jewish Art: Representation and Significance', *BASOR* 228

pagan symbol, and one very much in vogue in the Roman world of the third and fourth centuries. The question arises as to its significance and meaning within the synagogal context. Opinions have ranged far and wide, from the very minimalist to the extremely maximalist view. Among the former are those who have interpreted the zodiac as purely ornamental in character or perhaps representative of the centrality of the calendar in Jewish life. Among the latter are those who attribute more profound meaning to this depiction, possibly indicating religious beliefs not fully articulated—or even found—in rabbinic sources. Goodenough was the most extreme in this regard, suggesting that Helios was a Jewish attempt at representing the deity. M. Smith, however, has more plausibly linked these depictions with the text of *Sepher Ha-Razim*, a fourth-century Palestinian work about magic which accorded especial prominence to Helios among the angels:[41]

> Holy Helios who rises in the east, good mariner, trustworthy leader of the sun's rays, reliable [witness] who of old established the mighty wheel [of the heavens], holy orderer, ruler of the axis [of the heaven], Lord, Brilliant Leader, King, Soldier...[42]

The question naturally arises as to whether such beliefs as expressed in *Sepher Ha-Razim* were representative of only a small coterie of Jews or rather reflected much wider circles, as attested by the synagogues' zodiac designs. If the latter, one could then assume widespread beliefs in the presence and power of angels shared by many circles and communities within the Byzantine Jewish community. Thus, our understanding of the diverse nature of Judaism and its nonrabbinic dimension at this time would require some sort of redefinition on the basis of these archaeological data.

In summary, what should be clear is the incredible extent to which our perception of Jews and Judaism of antiquity has been enhanced by the archaeological discoveries of the last century. The material brought

---

(1977), pp. 61-77; *idem, Ancient Jewish Art and Archeology*, pp. 301-309. These sites include Beth Alpha, Ḥammath Tiberias, Ḥuseifa (Carmel), Naʿaran, and the one recently discovered in Sepphoris. Some would include Susiya and perhaps Yafia as well.

41. Morton Smith, 'Observations on *Hekhalot Rabbati*', in Alexander Altmann (ed.), *Biblical and Other Studies* (Cambridge: Harvard University Press, 1963), pp. 159-60.

42. Michael A. Morgan, *Sepher Ha-Razim (The Book of the Mysteries)* (Chico, CA: Scholars Press, 1983), p. 71.

to light is extensive and has implications for a wide range of topics in Jewish history. Although archaeological material is, almost by definition, fragmentary and fortuitous, and by itself cannot offer a comprehensive picture of Jewish life, it still has the potential to illuminate many dimensions of contemporary society by corroborating information known from other sources as well as by standing alone. Thus, while no history of the Jews can be written on the basis of archaeological material alone, it is also clear that no such history can be complete without taking into account the information and insights accorded by this evidence.

JEWISH RITUAL BATHS—INTERPRETING THE DIGS AND THE TEXTS: SOME ISSUES IN THE SOCIAL HISTORY OF SECOND TEMPLE JUDAISM

Benjamin G. Wright III

1. *Introduction*

Scholars who are interested in the reconstruction of the history of Second Temple Judaism must synthesize the results of different sorts of investigations. Those of us who are concerned primarily with the textual remains of Jews in this period cannot neglect the results of the archaeological excavations of Second Temple sites. And, conversely, archaeologists often must rely on written texts in order to interpret what they find in the ground. The textual scholar and the archaeologist are, then, engaged in a similar exercise—the interpretation of the textual evidence together with the archaeological evidence in order to reconstruct what went on in antiquity. It is precisely this interpretive interplay between the texts and the physical remains that is at the heart of several important discussions among scholars of Second Temple Judaism today. One well-known example is the beginnings and development of the synagogue.[1]

In this essay, I want to look at another such problem, the discovery and identification of numerous stepped baths in Israel that date from the Second Temple period, many of which have been identified as *miqva'ot* or Jewish ritual baths. If one can show that Jews used these stepped baths for the purpose of removing states of ritual impurity, then the presence of a large number of them could indicate a generally high concern among Jews in this period with keeping those purity laws of Leviticus that enjoin bathing/washing for certain kinds of impurity.[2] On the other hand, if the number of these baths that can be demonstrated to

1. See especially Lee I. Levine (ed.), *The Synagogue in Late Antiquity* (Philadelphia: The American Schools of Oriental Research, 1987).
2. See Nahman Avigad, *Discovering Jerusalem* (Nashville, TN: Nelson, 1980), p. 139, who draws such a conclusion about the Upper City of Jerusalem.

be for ritual use is relatively small, this too needs to be taken into account in any reconstruction of Second Temple Jewish religiosity. The interpretive consequences of these different positions are important. E.P. Sanders, for example, following the conclusions of Ronny Reich,[3] has accepted that almost all of these baths, even those that do not accord with mishnaic halakha, are *miqva'ot*. This position leads him to argue that although Jews were generally very concerned with ritual purity, they were not necessarily worried about maintaining that purity through the same rules as the Mishnah requires.[4] I originally began to think about these stepped baths because of the large number of them discovered in different contexts: in the isolated community of the *yaḥad* at Qumran, in the houses of the aristocratic residents of the Upper City of Jerusalem, and in the apparently more plebeian residences of Sepphoris.[5] I initially accepted the notion that all these baths were built for ritual use, but consequently began to wonder why there was such a corresponding dearth of evidence concerning ritual bathing in Second Temple texts (the notable exception being the Qumran sect's writings). As I began to think about the relationship between the texts and the archaeological remains, I started to question how one would be able to tell if something ritual was going on in these stepped pools. Were they all ritual baths to begin with? And, if all these baths were not for ritual use, would that argue for

3.   Reich's position is set out most fully in his PhD dissertation, '*Miqva'ot* (Jewish Ritual Baths) in the Second Temple Period and the Period of the Mishnah and Talmud' (Hebrew University of Jerusalem, 1990) (in Hebrew). His conclusions are accessible to English speakers in several English language articles. 'Domestic Water Installations in Jerusalem of the Second Temple (= Early Roman) Period', in *Papers at the Symposium of Historical Development Project in the Eastern Mediterranean, Jerusalem, 1983*, Mitteilungen des Leichtweiss Institut für Wasserbau der Technischen Universität Braunschweig 82 (1984); 'More on Miqwa'ot', *BARev* 13 (1987), pp. 59-60; 'Four Notes on Jerusalem', *IEJ* 37 (1987), pp. 158-67; 'The Bath-House (Balneum), the Miqweh and the Jewish Community in the Second Temple Period', *JJS* 39 (1988), pp. 102-107; 'The Great Mikveh Debate', *BARev* 19 (1993), pp. 52-53.

4.   See the various discussions concerning purity in E.P. Sanders, *Jewish Law from Jesus to the Mishnah* (Philadelphia: Trinity Press International, 1990).

5.   The baths at Sepphoris have not yet been published, although several are commented on in *IEJ* reports. I thank James F. Strange, one of the principal excavators, for making his team's field notes available to me for consultation. Not all the residences at Sepphoris can be characterized as 'plebeian', however. A large villa is under excavation by Strange's team that seems to have been the residence of someone of means.

a corresponding deemphasis on keeping the laws of ritual purity in this period? The results of my initial musings on these topics are a paper which is essentially an exercise in question-asking. With regard to these stepped pools, how have the physical remains and the textual evidence been interpreted? Can they be interpreted differently, and with what consequences to reconstructions of Jewish life in this period?

I want to distinguish, however, between an overall concern for purity and the details of who or what is impure and the practice of immersion as a means of removing states of ritual impurity. That Jews were generally concerned about purity is not at issue. The Hebrew scriptures discuss states of purity and impurity, and the later rabbinic literature is very concerned with these problems as well. It is impossible to believe that these same issues were not also a concern for Jews in the Second Temple period. The problem I propose to inquire about here is the actual practice of ritual bathing. What is the evidence for where and how Jews performed this ritual activity?

One initial and very critical problem is the extent to which rabbinic literature, primarily the Mishnah, can be used as evidence for pre-70 CE Jewish practice. Although it is almost obligatory to note the difficulties connected with using the Mishnah as a witness to pre-70 CE Judaism, at some point the rabbinic requirements contained in it are almost always invoked in discussions of the stepped baths discovered in Israel. And yet recent discussions have suggested that even in their own periods the sages were (a) probably not very numerous and (b) probably not able to compel significant numbers outside of their own circles to comply with their interpretations of Jewish Law. For the pre-70 period the legal regulations of the Pharisees pose a similar problem, and there is much disagreement over their particular interpretations, their influence among other groups of Jews, and their continuity with the rabbinic sages.[6] But

6.   On these issues see Lee I. Levine, *The Rabbinic Class of Roman Palestine in Late Antiquity* (Jerusalem/New York: Yad Izhak Ben-Zvi/The Jewish Theological Seminary of America, 1989), pp. 66-69. Levine's argument is about the generations of the amoraim, but probably applies to the tannaim as well. On the tannaim see Shaye J.D. Cohen, 'The Place of the Rabbi in Jewish Society of the Second Century', in Lee I. Levine (ed.), *The Galilee in Late Antiquity* (New York: The Jewish Theological Seminary of America, 1992), pp. 157-73 and 'Epigraphical Rabbis', *JQR* 72 (1981), pp. 1-17. See also, J. Neusner, *From Politics to Piety: The Emergence of Pharisaic Judaism* (Jerusalem: Ktav, 1979), *Rabbinic Traditions about the Pharisees before 70 AD* (Leiden: Brill, 1971) and the arguments in Sanders,

even if one could securely date certain rabbinic regulations to the pre-70 period, it is not likely that they would have been any more influential at that time than during the flourishing of the rabbinic sages who compiled them. Nevertheless, in some quarters these rabbinic rules seem to be given a sort of interpretive hegemony over the physical remains.

Of course, I do not mean to imply the contrary position, that no rabbinic regulations predate 70 CE. Some of the stepped pools at issue here provide evidence that some most likely did. They were not, however, universally followed or perhaps even known in many quarters. In fact, the evidence may be read to support the notion that the sages were normatizing traditions that were already in use among some people, most likely the Pharisees, in the period before their greatest influence.

With these remarks in mind, I intend to take a bit of a different tack in the following analysis. The rabbinic regulations about valid/invalid water or the physical requirements of ritual baths will turn up very infrequently. This approach is not meant to deny the regulations of the sages a place in the interpretive framework, but it is intended as a look at the evidence from a different starting point. If we take away the interpretive hegemony of the rabbinic literature, how might one interpret the data or draw the picture differently? Consequently, in what follows I will look both at the archaeology of these stepped pools and at the textual evidence of Second Temple Jewish sources. Finally, I will make some concluding remarks about what people may have been doing about ritual bathing in the period before the rise of the sages.

2. *The Archaeology of* Miqva'ot

Archaeologists have identified several different types of water installations from the Second Temple period: 1) cisterns, 2) bathtubs, 3) bathhouses, 4) swimming pools, 5) immersion or stepped pools, 6) secondary storage pools or *otzarot*.[7] At times, more than one of these types may be found in the same installation as, for example, in the Upper City of Jerusalem where one house has a bathtub, stepped pool, and secondary storage pool (with steps) as parts of the same larger installation.[8] According to Ronny Reich, whose Hebrew University of Jerusalem

Jewish Law, pp. 35ff. and *Judaism Practice & Belief 63 BCE–66 CE* (Philadelphia: Trinity Press Inernational, 1992).
7.   This list is taken from Sanders, *Jewish Law*, pp. 216-17.
8.   This is the house in Area T-4. Avigad, *Discovering Jerusalem*, p. 140.

dissertation is the most complete study of *miqva'ot* to date, more than 300 stepped or immersion pools have been excavated in Israel.[9] These baths vary according to a number of features. The sizes of these pools range from small stepped pools like some of those in Jericho or Sepphoris to very large ones like several excavated at Qumran. The number of steps leading down into the pools varies widely. Some have dividers or partitions on the steps; some do not. Some pools are adjoined by a second pool, either a storage pool or a cistern; some are not. Some pools stand independently; some are part of larger water installations that may include other pools (Jericho), a bathtub room (some houses in the Upper City of Jerusalem), or even a hot room with hypocaust (Masada, houses in Jerusalem's Upper City).[10]

The varied morphology of these stepped pools has caused some to argue that very few of them were used as ritual baths (those whom Sanders calls 'minimalists'[11]) because they were not constructed according to rabbinic standards, and has led others, like Reich and Sanders, to claim the 'maximalist' position that nearly all of these installations were used for ritual purposes.[12] Since they are clearly not cisterns, bathtubs, or swimming pools, so the argument goes, then, as Reich asks, 'If these installations are not the *miqva'ot* mentioned so frequently in rabbinic literature, what are they?'[13] This is surely a question that deserves discussion, and if the alternatives were simply all or none as they are set out here, I would probably have to side with the maximalists. But an examination of baths at several Second Temple period sites reveals other plausible ways of construing the evidence besides these two.

In his study Reich surveys all of the stepped pools excavated up until the late 1980s.[14] His general conclusion is that 'a water installation which is cut or built into the ground, into which rainwater, spring waters or runoff could be led, which had a staircase offering convenient access

9.   Reich, '*Miqva'ot* (Jewish Ritual Baths) in the Second Temple Period', p. 80; 'The Great Mikveh Debate', p. 52. In the baths that Reich treats here, those excavated at Sepphoris and more recently at Pisgat Ze'ev and several other sites in the hills surrounding Jerusalem have not been included (these latter were discussed by Reich at the 1993 Society of Biblical Literature annual meetings in Washington, DC).

10.   See further on these characteristics below in section 3.

11.   Sanders, *Jewish Law*, p. 216.

12.   Sanders, *Jewish Law*, p. 216.

13.   Reich, 'The Great Mikveh Debate', p. 52.

14.   Except for those at Sepphoris, which do not seem to have been generally accessible to him.

into the water, and which could be plastered to prevent leakage—any installation which met these requirements, could have been used in the Second Temple Period, as a *Miqweh*'.[15]

Such a definition is the quintessential statement of the 'maximalist' position described by Sanders, which identifies almost all of the stepped baths discovered in Israel as potential *miqva'ot*. According to Reich, these criteria meet the fundamental requirements of a ritual bath, and no other features were compulsory. My own view is that this definition is too broad, and thus overestimates the number of pools that should be considered to be *miqva'ot*. I do not want, however, to retreat into a minimalist assessment of the problem, that only those pools that fit mishnaic halakha should be considered *miqva'ot*. The issue, it seems to me, is the extent to which one can determine whether any particular pool was used for ritual or secular purposes.

When speaking of bathing, in any context in the Second Temple period, its widespread cultural importance in the Greco-Roman world must be considered. Baths and bathing were a fundamental part of ancient life, and for people of both genders throughout the Mediterranean world, both public and private baths were a feature of everyday activity.[16] Bathing was recommended for bodily cleanliness, for relaxation, and frequently for medical reasons.[17] Although Greco-Roman bathing usually combined hot, warm, and cold baths, baths of any temperature might be taken depending on one's purpose.[18] Ancient Palestine was not exempt from the cultural ideals of the larger Mediterranean world, and the indispensable nature of bathing was certainly appreciated by at least the upper class Jews in Palestine (and perhaps the lower classes as well), as the existence of the large bathhouse at

15. Reich, *'Miqva'ot* (Jewish Ritual Baths) in the Second Temple Period', English Abstract, p. 5.

16. For Roman bathing practices, see Jerome Carcupino, *Daily Life in Ancient Rome* (New Haven: Yale University Press, 1940), pp. 254-63, and in much greater detail Fikret Yegül, *Baths and Bathing in Classical Antiquity* (Cambridge: MIT Press, 1992). Inge Nielsen, *Thermae et Balneae: The Architecture and Cultural History of Roman Public Baths*, 2 vols. (Aarhus: Aarhus University Press, 1990) was unavailable to me at the writing of this paper.

17. On the latter see especially the writings of Aelius Aristides.

18. Carcupino, *Daily Life in Ancient Rome*, p. 261. Aristides' baths are most often cold plunges into rivers or streams. Sometimes Roman adolescent boys were encouraged to take only cold baths in order not to stunt their growth. See Aline Rousselle, *Porneia* (Oxford: Basil Blackwell, 1988), pp. 59-60.

Masada, the Hasmonean and Herodian baths at Jericho, and the hypocaust systems of the aristocratic houses of the Upper City of Jerusalem
demonstrate. The high value attached to bathing must have affected all
aspects of its practice in ancient Palestine including the way baths, both
public and private, were built.

Stepped Pools in Bathhouses: The Large and Lower Terrace Bathhouses at Masada

The Large Bathhouse near the Northern Palace of Masada underwent
two initial building stages. According to Ehud Netzer, the bathhouse and
courtyard were built together originally, but in a later modification to
the courtyard, a stepped pool was added.[19] From the courtyard the
entrance to the bathhouse leads into an apodyterium, or changing room.
From the changing room, one enters a warm room (tepidarium). Once
in the tepidarium the bather could choose to enter either the hot room
(caldarium) or a cold stepped pool (frigidarium). This pool is connected
via a pipe to a cistern on the outside of the building.[20] Netzer remarks
that the arrangement of a stepped pool with adjoining pool outside
'could have been devised to permit the use of the stepped pool as a
ritual immersion pool'.[21] Reich seems more certain that this pool would
have been used for ritual purposes. As part of his study he gives a list of
all the stepped pools and provides his estimation of whether each pool
would likely have been used as a *miqveh* or not. In the case of the
stepped pool in this bathhouse, Reich notes its size (definitely large
enough for a person to immerse) and connection to the outside pool
(which he hesitantly identifies as an *otzar*). He assigns it a high probability for use as a *miqveh*. He also notes more generally that those stepped
pools that have been identified in bathhouses in Israel as cold rooms are,
in fact, ritual baths.[22]

A similar situation can be seen in the bathhouse on the Lower Terrace
of the Northern Palace.[23] Although it is much smaller in size, this

19. For a complete discussion of the archaeological aspects of this building, see
Ehud Netzer, *Masada III* (Jerusalem: Israel Exporation Society, 1991), pp. 76-101.

20. The pool measures 4.3 m × 2.05 m and has watermarks to a depth of 2.0 m
on the plaster which lined it. Netzer, *Masada III*, p. 86.

21. Netzer, *Masada III*, p. 94.

22. Reich, '*Miqva'ot* (Jewish Ritual Baths) in the Second Temple Period',
p. 112.

23. See Netzer, *Masada III*, pp. 164-69.

bathhouse is arranged like the Large Bathhouse; one enters a tepidarium from which one can enter either a stepped pool (frigidarium) or the caldarium. Reich assigns to this stepped pool as well a high degree of probability for use as a *miqveh*.

To argue that these pools were used for ritual purposes is not necessary, however. They can just as easily be seen as adaptations of the Roman bathhouse to the Masada fortress. Roman bathhouses contained several consistent features, although their form and arrangement differed according to the locale. When one compares the two bath complexes at Masada with other Roman bathhouses, three characteristics (a pool as opposed to *labrum* in the frigidarium, the pool's shape and size, access to the pool) suggest that the stepped pools at Masada may be simply frigidaria. Although many Roman bathhouses did not have a pool in the cold room, but only a large basin filled with cold water (*labrum*), this was not a standard feature, and numerous bathhouses, in fact, have a pool or pools in the cold room. Many of these pools, although not as deep as the stepped pools at Masada, were certainly large enough to plunge into. Further, these pools varied widely in size and shape. In the Forum Baths at Pompeii and Herculaneum, these pools are circular (a model copied by Herod in one of his Jericho palaces).[24] In the large North African baths of the second century CE the pools in the frigidaria tend to be rectangular, and in the baths from Asia Minor one frequently sees rectangular pools or very large swimming pools.[25] Finally, access to the frigidarium varies. In some cases the three bathing rooms are arranged in a line, the so-called single-axis row type, with initial entry from the apodyterium to the frigidarium, tepidarium, caldarium in that order.[26] In other baths the frigidarium may be accessed separately, as in the two bathhouses at Masada. At Pompeii and Herculaneum, for instance, the Forum Baths have the frigidarium in a separate room accessed only through the apodyterium.

Sanders places great weight on the separate entrances to the different baths. The idea that someone could go into either the frigidarium or the caldarium indicates to him its religious function. For this he relies mostly on the analysis of David Small who gives a spatial analysis of the two

24. For plans of these baths, see Yegül, *Baths and Bathing*, p. 65.

25. For plans of both North African and Asia Minor baths, see Yegül, *Baths and Bathing*, Appendices C and D. The large size of many of these pools should be attributed to their general public use.

26. Yegül, *Baths and Bathing*, p. 61.

Masada bathhouses along with several others. Small notes that the stepped pool areas and bathroom areas of the bathhouses that he examines operated independently because the bather could choose which area to enter. He accepts that these pools are *miqva'ot* and concludes that 'this [arrangement] left the *miqveh* open for ritual bathing without having to involve oneself in a larger bathing regime'.[27] But in the baths at Pompeii and Herculaneum, the frigidaria could also operate independently since they are in separate rooms accessed through the apodyterium only. They are not *miqva'ot*, however.

Admittedly, there are many differences between the Italian, North African, and Asia Minor baths and the Masada complexes, but the location and apparent function of the Masada stepped pools appear comparable to those in other Roman bathhouses. In addition, Herod's familiarity with Rome and Roman ways also suggests that the Masada bathhouses would have been built in line with Roman archetypes.[28]

The primary differences between the stepped pools in the bathhouses at Masada and bathhouses elsewhere are their depth and shape and, at least in the Large Bathhouse, the presence of an adjoining pool. If the stepped pools are to be interpreted simply as frigidaria, normal features of bathhouses, then the depth might be explained as an accommodation to the smaller space and the need to accommodate fewer people than the large swimming pools or plunge baths of public Roman bathhouses, as a way of compensating for evaporation in a dry environment, or simply as the adoption of a locally popular form.[29] The adjoining pool of the Large Bathhouse almost certainly was for gathering rainwater from the roof of the bathhouse in order to fill the frigidarium inside. Considering the scarcity of water in that environment, the pool could

27. See, Sanders, *Jewish Law*, p. 220 and David Small, 'Late Hellenistic Baths in Palestine', *BASOR* 266 (1987), pp. 59-74. Besides the Masada bathhouse, Small includes the palaces at Jericho and the baths at Kypros and Machaerus.

28. In his more popular publication of the Masada excavations, Yigael Yadin notes the similarity of the Large Bathhouse to those at Pompeii and Herculaneum, and he calls the stepped pool (frigidarium) one of the 'customary additional rooms of the standard Roman bath-house'. Yigael Yadin, *Masada: Herod's Fortress and the Zealots' Last Stand* (Jerusalem: Steimatzky, 1966), pp. 80-81.

29. In the larger and more sumptuous surroundings of one of the Jericho winter palaces, the frigidarium in the bathing complex is circular. This bathhouse is also connected with a palaestra, common as an adjunct to many Roman bathhouses, but the Masada bathhouses have no palaestra presumably because space restrictions made such a feature impractical.

capture a large amount which would fill the stepped pool from which water would undoubtedly have evaporated during the dry season.[30]

The Private Houses of the Upper City of Jerusalem

On a smaller scale, the same situation can be found in the Upper City of Jerusalem. Nahman Avigad's excavations in the Jewish Quarter of Jerusalem's Old City brought to light a number of dwellings from the Second Temple period. In most cases the owners were apparently well to do and appointed their houses in lavish style. Quite a number of stepped baths were discovered in these dwellings. According to Reich at least three and possibly four dwellings contained water installations with a caldarium with hypocaust and at least one stepped pool.[31] These installations make it apparent that the residents of these houses were adapting the Roman bathhouse model to the private residential dwelling. Having a private bathing installation, rather than attending public baths, most likely enabled the owners to avoid contact with strangers or lower class citizens, to provide an opportunity for a display of wealth,[32] and/or to maintain appropriate standards of modesty. Additionally, as Avigad notes, some of the Upper City dwellings contain several stepped baths.[33] Some may have served ritual purposes while others fulfilled secular ones.

As in the cases of the more public bathhouses of Masada and the Northern Wing at Herodium, which is built similarly to those at Masada,[34] the caldarium is accompanied by a cold pool, an element that

---

30. At some point the pipe between the two pools was blocked up, but it is uncertain when that occurred, Netzer, *Masada III*, p. 87. It is not clear how the frigidarium in the Lower Terrace bathhouse was supplied with water, Netzer, *Masada III*, p. 167.

31. Areas P-3, T-1 and the border between Areas T-2 and T-7. Unfortunately, detailed site plans were not available to me. Neither of the two major sources for this excavation, Avigad, *Discovering Jerusalem*, and Reich, '*Miqva'ot* (Jewish Ritual Baths) in the Second Temple Period', contain drawings of the caldaria with hypocausts, although both speak of them.

32. Reich, '*Miqva'ot* (Jewish Ritual Baths) in the Second Temple Period', p. 111. Avigad, *Discovering Jerusalem*, p. 142, simply notes that such wealthy people would not have resorted to the 'plebeian means' of attending a public bath.

33. Avigad, *Discovering Jerusalem*, p. 139.

34. For discussion and plans see Ehud Netzer, *Greater Herodium* (Qedem, 13; Jerusalem: Institute of Archaeology, 1981), pp. 46-49.

would be expected in a bathing complex. These stepped pools may be interpreted simply as bathhouse frigidaria.

The methodological point here is an important one. Although it is true that these baths resemble others that might be more securely interpreted as ritual baths, I do not find compelling the argument that these particular baths must have served ritual purposes. Part of the problem here is of approach. Reich asks,

> If these are not the *Miqva'ot*, what are they? Over 300 items—out of which c. 150 alone are in Jerusalem—deserve a comprehensive explanation. If these [all the stepped baths in his study] are not *Miqva'ot*, then where are the *Miqva'ot* of the scriptures? It seems impossible to provide different positive answers to these questions.[35]

But why do they deserve a 'comprehensive' explanation, which seems to presume that all of these baths must have served the same function? They are baths, of course, built in a way unique to baths in this part of the Mediterranean world, but similarity in form may not necessarily indicate identity of function. Other factors, like their context, would *prima facie* also be important for understanding their use. Therefore, if one interprets these bathhouse pools as frigidaria, to be expected within the confines of a Roman-style bathhouse, then other, specific features can be explained as local adaptations to particular needs.[36] If the presence of an adjoining pool and size large enough for immersion *must* indicate a *miqveh*, then these stepped pools will be seen as *miqva'ot* regardless of their context. *Could* these pools have functioned as miqva'ot? I imagine that they could have, but even as a cigar is sometimes just a cigar, so a frigidarium might sometimes be just a frigidarium.[37]

35. Reich, '*Miqva'ot* (Jewish Ritual Baths) in the Second Temple Period', English abstract, p. 6.

36. Sanders, *Jewish Law*, p. 220, says, 'Herod knew about Roman or Hellenistic baths, as well as about immersion pools, and he incorporated the latter into the former'. What I find problematic here is the implication that the incoporation of the stepped pool into Herod's baths necessarily includes the notion of their ritual function.

37. I think that the same explanation applies to the bathing complex in the Northern Wing at Herodium. The caldarium with hypocaust is accompanied by a stepped bath that functioned as the frigidarium.

The Identification of Miqva'ot by Their Characteristic Features

The presence of stepped pools in bathhouses and aristocratic residences does not by any means exhaust the large number of them that have been identified as *miqva'ot*. Reich notes that several features of these pools recur often enough for them to be considered characteristic of the *miqveh* although no single pool has all of these features at once. In his list of the stepped pools that have been discovered in Israel, he uses the presence or absence of these characteristics to indicate how certain he is of each pool's use as a *miqveh*.[38] He ranks each pool according to five probabilities: 1, the highest probability; 2, a 'middle probability'; 3, a low probability, but these pools, he says, could have been used as *miqva'ot* 'at a time of dire need'; 0, no possibility of use as a miqveh; ?, the lack of archaeological data precludes any judgment.[39] He then uses the following features in his analysis. (1) The size of the pool. Reich denotes each pool's size. 1 indicates a large pool whose volume is 8-10 m^3; 2 is a middle designation (he does not give a volume); and 3 is a small pool whose volume is 1-2 m^3. (2) The location of the pool. In a private house a pool might be found on the residential floors or in the basement. Public pools are also denoted (i.e., the Temple area, a synagogue, a bathhouse). (3) The presence of a double opening/entrance or partitioned steps. (4) The pool as one of a pair of stepped water installations. (5) The presence of an *otzar* (here defined as a pool somehow joined to the one under consideration). (6) The presence of a cistern. (7) The type of staircase (alternating broad and narrow steps). (8) The presence of an adjacent water installation.

The difficulty of determining a pool's use for ritual purposes is highlighted by looking at several examples from Reich's list. Perhaps the biggest obstacle to a pool being considered a *miqveh* is its size. Of the 59 pools from the Second Temple period listed by Reich whose sizes are denoted as 3 (1-2 m^3 in volume), only 8 are listed by him as the highest probability for use as a *miqveh*.[40] In seven of these eight, other features

38. For the discussion of these characteristics and the list of pools, see Reich, '*Miqva'ot* (Jewish Ritual Baths) in the Second Temple Period', pp. 72-81.

39. Reich, '*Miqva'ot* (Jewish Ritual Baths) in the Second Temple Period', p. 74. For category '3' Reich writes ניתן היה בשעת הדחק להשתמש במתקן לטבילה. For בשעת הדחק the various Modern Hebrew dictionaries give such English equivalents as 'in an emergency', 'in time of stress', 'in time of duress' 'at a time of dire necessity or need'.

40. Many of the unpublished stepped pools from Sepphoris may fit into the category of small pools. For example, according to James F. Strange, the stepped pool

such as location near a 'synagogue' or the presence of a connected pool, appear to determine the judgment. For one pool listed as the highest probability (the small stepped pool in Building 11 at Masada), the only features listed by Reich are its presence in a residential building and its small size.[41] It is not immediately apparent why he is certain about the pool's use, but perhaps the judgment was made because the structure was built in the Zealot period,[42] and it is central to the courtyard in which it is located. In any event, it has no other common features of a *miqveh*.

In other cases, most of the smallest pools are judged to be the lowest probability, even when they have other characterizing features and would appear to be located in a context where *miqva'ot* might be expected. One pool in a public area near the Temple Mount[43] is identified as perhaps being one of a pair of stepped installations and also as possibly having an *otzar*, but it is assigned a probability 3 by Reich. Another pool in one of the Upper City residences[44] is one of a pair of stepped pools, one which may be an *otzar* according to Reich, and has a cistern nearby. Reich considers it too to have a low probability of being a *miqveh*. In contrast, a small pool at Qumran[45] having the same

(C238) in Field I (the 'Field Villa') would only accommodate a human person with difficulty. It had a vaulted ceiling with no apparent source of light (no lamp niches or obvious route for sunlight). According to Eric Meyers, Ehud Netzer, and Carol Meyers, *Sepphoris* (Winona Lake, IN: Eisenbrauns, 1992), pp. 28-29, the western residential quarter contains a number of stepped pools that resemble the photograph on p. 28, which looks as if it is fairly small. The dating of the Sepphoris pools is very difficult because the pools are dug into bedrock and stratigraphic analysis of the site is very difficult. In various *Israel Exploration Journal* reports, dates in the 'Early Roman period' are given. Such a date is fuzzy, however, in that it includes most of the second century CE. For reports on the Sepphoris excavations see *IEJ* 35 (1985), pp. 295-97; 37 (1987), pp. 275-78; 38 (1988), pp. 188-90; 39 (1989), pp. 104-106; 40 (1990), pp. 219-22; 43 (1993), pp. 190-96.

41. Reich, '*Miqva'ot* (Jewish Ritual Baths) in the Second Temple Period', p. 79. Reich's designation is Masada 18.

42. Netzer, *Masada III*, p. 319.

43. Temple Mount Number 16 in Reich's list.

44. Upper City Number 15.

45. Reich's Qumran Number 5, #83 in the drawing in Roland de Vaux, *Archaeology and the Dead Sea Scrolls* (London: Oxford University Press, 1973), Plate xxxix. The problem of which Qumran pools were actually for ritual puposes is longstanding. De Vaux argued that most were simply for water storage and few were for actual ritual bathing. Bryant G. Wood, 'To Dip or to Sprinkle? The Qumran

features—it is one of a pair of stepped installations, perhaps with an *otzar*—is assigned the highest probability, presumably because it is located in the ruins of a community known from their texts to be very concerned with aspects of ritual purity.

The existence of a significant number of these small stepped pools to which Reich assigns a low probability for use as *miqva'ot* raises the question of *their* use. What are they for, if not primarily for ritual use? Reich can only propose an answer for some specific pools. 'Those [the small pools given a 3 probability] that are located in residential houses on residential floors (in contrast to the pools that are located in the basement), these were constructed for use as partial washing installations (feet?) in connection with entry rooms to the house, with entry to guest rooms and meal rooms, in connection with courtyards in which the daily work of the house was carried out, etc.'[46] What use the others have he does not make clear.

A contrasting situation pertains to the largest of these stepped pools. In no case is a pool whose volume is at the high end of the scale (8–10 m³) given anything less than a middle probability, regardless of the presence or absence of any of the features thought by Reich to be characteristic of *miqva'ot*. He assigns the highest probability for use as a *miqveh* to stepped baths in various locations, including four of the five stepped pools in the bathhouse at Kypros even though they have none of the other characteristic features in his list.[47] It appears that if a stepped pool is large enough to immerse a human body, then it is to be considered a potential *miqveh*.[48]

By tabulating the probability judgments that Reich assigns to each stepped pool in his list, he finds 163 installations that almost certainly

---

Cisterns in Perspective', *BASOR* 256 (1984), pp. 45-60, argues that all the stepped pools were ritual baths.

46. Reich, '*Miqva'ot* (Jewish Ritual Baths) in the Second Temple Period', p. 81. Translation from the Hebrew is mine.

47. Others noted as highest probability include Temple Mount 1, 2, and 9, Upper City 59, 61, Jerusalem, Citadel, 4. Those of the largest size assigned a middle probability include Tombs of the Kings, Northern Jerusalem 2, Ramat Rachel 4. Several others with the highest probability rating have only one feature.

48. In several cases pools that are of the middle size are rated as a low probability for use as a *miqveh*. They have none of the major identifying features of the *miqveh*, that is, they lack an *otzar* or accompanying stepped pool; they are not part of a larger installation; and they are all in basements.

functioned as ritual baths (probability 1), 50 whose function is 'probable' (probability 2), 45 whose use as ritual baths is 'possible' (probability 3), and 22 that either were not *miqva'ot* or for which there were not enough data to judge.[49] Thus, 53.3% of the stepped water installations in question, in Reich's judgment, almost certainly were used for ritual purposes, provided one agrees with Reich's assigned probabilities. In the foregoing analysis, however, I argued that several pools that were assigned the highest probability do not have to be identified as ritual baths. This would lower the percentage given above.

What the above analysis suggests is that there is a certain presumption given to a pool's size. The small size of a pool, because of the difficulty of immersing in it, generally can rule it out as a likely candidate for a *miqveh*, but a pool's large size, because of the ease of immersion, always includes it.

In making the arguments I do here, I do not want to give the impression that I think Jews in the Second Temple period were not interested in ritual purity and never used ritual baths. As I said above, I am sure that ritual purity did concern them and that some did use *miqva'ot*. Many of the baths identified by Reich and others as *miqva'ot* probably were just that. For example, the need for both priests and ordinary Jews to enter the Temple precincts in a state of ritual purity does seem to warrant the identification of so many stepped baths near the Temple Mount area as ritual baths. The same reasoning may be applied to some of the baths in the houses in the Upper City of Jerusalem where it is reasonable to expect that priests lived.

I also am not objecting here to certain pools being identified as *miqva'ot*, but as a methodological point of departure I do not accept that similarity of form requires us to interpret an identity of function. I do not see these lines drawn as firmly as do those who see the great majority of these pools as baths having ritual uses. Ultimately we return to the issue of how we know that something religious or ritual was going on in these baths. We think we know not simply because of the form and features of these pools, but because the textual materials tell us that the religious issues of purity and how to maintain it were important to Jews in antiquity. But even if all these baths were not ritual baths, would that lead to the conclusion that Jews were less concerned about ritual purity than if all these baths were *miqva'ot*? I do not think that

49. Reich, '*Miqva'ot* (Jewish Ritual Baths) in the Second Temple Period', p. 81.

necessarily to be the case. *Miqva'ot* were not the only option available for ritual bathing. As we will see, rivers, streams, and the sea could also be used, and people almost certainly resorted to them along with the developing use of *miqva'ot*.

3. *The Witness of Second Temple Literature to the Practice of Ritual Bathing*

When one turns to the evidence of Second Temple period literature for ritual bathing as a way of removing states of impurity, except for the literature extant from the Qumran community, little will be discovered from which to build a detailed picture. The several texts that talk about washing hands before praying or meals speak to a purity issue particular to this period, but not to ritual immersion per se, although some of these texts may be helpful in identifying contexts for immersion/bathing.[50] The literature does provide some evidence for the questions of how and where people immersed and what conditions called for immersion. I will focus in this section primarily on the former question of how and where people ritually bathed. The subsequent discussion will focus on Second Temple literature and be followed by a short discussion of the literature from Qumran.[51]

Jewish Literature from the Second Temple Period[52]
Those Second Temple texts that do talk about bathing make it clear that, on the whole, immersion was practised to remove the states of impurity spoken of in the Jewish scriptures, although the practice was extended to

50. The texts are *Aristeas* 305-306; *Jos. Asen.* 14.12, 15; 18.8-10; Mk 7.5 and several Qumran texts. *Sib. Or.* 3.591-93 may fit here as well. The text speaks of Jews 'always sanctifying their flesh', but an important textual variant reads 'hands' for 'flesh'. See the discussion on washing hands in Sanders, *Jewish Law*, pp. 30ff. He appears, however, to elevate the practice from a Jewish custom, which is what Aristeas 305-306 says, to a requirement to wash in the sea.

51. I do not intend a full discussion of the problem of purity issues in Second Temple Judaism, but rather to give a summary of some basic problems. The issues are discussed in full in Sanders, *Jewish Law* and *Judaism: Practice & Belief* and the bibliography that he cites.

52. In this section I cite that literature in which the practice is clearly bathing for the purpose of ritual purity. The question of bathing or baptizing for repentence and its connection to ritual bathing is fascinating, but beyond my purposes here. Examples of this sort of bathing can be found in the Apocryphal Adam and Eve

some nonbiblical problems as well. Almost all of the texts discussed in this section come from Disapora communities and so may only be indicative of practice outside Palestine. One possible, but difficult, example would be Philo's sometimes cryptic discussions of lustration rites, which led Sanders to argue for a particularly Alexandrian Jewish rite for removing corpse impurity and the impurity of sexual intercourse.[53] The presence of many stepped pools in Palestine and none in the Diaspora is problematic, although Justin Martyr in the middle of the second century may be referring to such pools when he says to Trypho that the cisterns (λάκκοι) that the Jews have built 'are broken and useless' (*Dialogue* 46.2). On the other hand, the main lines of thought of Diaspora texts do not appear to diverge greatly from Palestinian texts, and the distinction may not be all that meaningful.[54] Consequently, I will treat the evidence from the Diaspora and Palestine together here.

In this literature, no one word consistently designates the performance of ritual bathing. In general two types of words are used to indicate this activity. The first type is characterized by words whose meaning primarily concerns washing, bathing, or sprinkling and which describe the action taken by the individual. All occur elsewhere in Greek literature in religious and nonreligious contexts.[55] The washing/bathing words are the

literature, the figure of John the Baptist, and Early Christianity along with other Jewish baptizing groups. On Jewish baptismal groups see J. Thomas, *Le Mouvement baptiste en Palestine et Syrie (150 avec J.-C.—300 après J.-C.)*, Diss. Theol. Lovanensis, Ser. II, 28 (Gembloux, 1935) and more recently Kurt Rudolph, *Antike Baptisten: Zu den Überlieferungen über frühjüdische und -christliche Taufsekte*, Sitzungsberichte der sächsischen Akademie der Wissenschaften zu Leipzig, phil.-hist. Klasse 121.4 (Berlin: Akademie-Verlag, 1981). In his article 'The Purification Rituals in *DJD* 7' (in D. Dimant and U. Rappaport [eds.], *The Dead Sea Scrolls: Forty Years of Research* [Leiden/Jerusalem: Brill/Magnes/Yad Izhak Ben-Zvi, 1992], pp. 199-209), Joseph M. Baumgarten argues for a connection between purity and penitence in the rituals at Qumran.

53. Sanders, *Jewish Law*, pp. 263-70 gives a long, and largely convincing argument, that the use of περιρραντήριον to mean 'sprinkling from a basin' indicates a special Alexandrian rite of sprinkling in connection with corpse impurity.

54. Sanders, *Jewish Law*, pp. 258-71 contains a detailed argument about Diaspora practices of purity. His distinction between the Diaspora and Palestine is in reaction to the idea that Pharisaic discussions can be transferred to Diaspora situations. In arguing against such a position he is probably right.

55. Meanings and usages have been taken from H.G. Liddell, Robert Scott, Henry Stuart Jones, and Roderick McKenzie (eds.), *A Greek-English Lexicon* (9th edn; Oxford: Clarendon Press, 1940).

verbs ἀπολούω, βαπτίζω, ἐκνίπτω (ἐκνίζω), λούω, προσαποπλύνω, the noun λουτρόν, and the adjective ῥαντός. The second group of words has meanings that primarily revolve around cleansing or purifying and that essentially describe a state or consequence of action. These are ἁγνεύω and its related noun ἁγνεία, ἀφαγνίζω, καθαίρω, καθαρεύω, φαιδρύνω. Two very important words straddle the above two types, ἁγνίζω, 'to purify or cleanse primarily with water' and περιρραίνω, 'to purify or cleanse by sprinkling with water' or simply 'to purify oneself'. Whereas the actions described by the first group of terms are assumed to include the use of water, the second group does not and is usually not qualified further. When the latter terms are used, one can only infer, because of the biblical laws, that water has been used to effect the required purification.[56] Several examples will help to clarify these usages.

Philo has a clear predilection for using verbs of bathing/sprinkling to indicate the removal of ritual impurity. Commenting on the Levitical rules of priestly purity, he notes (*Spec. Leg.* 1.119) that a priest cannot eat consecrated food if he is in a ritually impure state, 'but after bathing (λουσάμενος) when sundown has passed he should not be hindered from its use'. A little later (1.191) he qualifies a purifying word with terms of bathing. Using the language of ritual immersion, Philo argues that if the victims of the Temple sacrifices are without blemish then the worshiper's mind should be 'purified and cleansed by baths and lustrations (κεκαθάρθαι...καὶ πεφαιδρύνθαι λουτροῖς καὶ περιρραντηρίοις) which the right reason of nature pours into the souls of those who love God...'

For Josephus the bathing and purifying words seem to be synonymous when applied to ritual actions. While discussing the consecration of the tribe of Levi (*Ant.* 3.258), he notes that God 'purified (ἥγνιζε) it [the tribe] with waters of perennial springs and sacrifices...' In telling the story of David and Jonathan, Josephus notes David's absence from a feast on the new moon (*Ant.* 6.236 narrating 1 Sam. 20.24-26). Josephus relates that King Saul 'purified (ἁγνεύσας) himself [presumably with water] as was the custom', and he surmises that David's absence is because he had not 'finished purifying (καθαρεύσαντα) himself after sexual intercourse'.

Elsewhere, in 2 Macc. 12.38 the Jewish army under Judas 'purified

56. This is especially true because in other Greek literature the purifying agent does not have to be water, but can be fire, sulfur, and the like.

itself [with water] (ἀγνισθέντες) according to custom' in preparation
for keeping the Sabbath. Judith 12.7-8 tells that the heroine, while stay-
ing in the camp of Holofernes, 'went out each night to the valley of
Bethulia and bathed (ἐβαπτίζετο) at the spring in the camp. And when
she came up, she prayed to the Lord God of Israel...Then she returned
purified (καθαρά)...' In this passage Judith bathes/immerses before
prayer, apparently as a ritual act, which effects her purification.

In contrast to rabbinic literature, there is little indication of where
these ritual ablutions were performed, and there is no discussion in this
literature at all of the criteria for valid water for immersion.[57] Sanders's
comment that 'First-century Palestinian Jews seem all to have agreed
that the biblical requirement to bathe after certain impurities should be
fulfilled by immersing in a special pool'[58] seems conditioned by his
understanding of the number of stepped pools extant and his assessment
of those rabbinic traditions which he posits as pre-70. Such a statement
could not be made about Second Temple Greek literature. In almost
every case in these texts, Jews are said to bathe or wash in water in its
natural states. *Aristeas* 305-306, although not about immersion,
describes the translators of the Law washing their hands in the sea.
Judith bathes in a spring, and Josephus notes the purification of the
Levites by 'the waters of perennial springs'.

According to these sources, the reasons for ritual bathing seem to be

57. In *Jos. Asen.* 14.12, 15 Asenath uses 'pure' or 'living waters', the phrase
used in Leviticus to describe what water is to be used by the *zav*, to wash her hands
and face, but no indication is given as to what kind of water might be intended. In
18.8-10 Asenath washes her face with 'pure water from a spring'. The rabbinic
sages, of course, took the phrase 'living water' to mean water that has collected naturally, that was not drawn. Philo is the only writer in this period who might refer in
any way to what 'living water' might mean. In *Spec. Leg.* 1.257ff. he treats the
purity of body and soul. After showing the need for the soul to be pure, he says that
the Law also enjoins the purity of the body. He describes the red heifer ritual
(although he does not explicitly say that the ritual is to remove corpse impurity).
Then in a very confusing passage he tries to demonstrate the wisdom of Moses, who
had the ashes of the heifer mixed in water, by saying that in other instances people
take 'unmixed water for sprinkling. Most [take it] from the sea, some from rivers,
and some draw pitchers from wells'. If by these other people he means Jews who are
performing other purity rites, then the kinds of water he lists would have been used
in Jewish ritual. If, on the other hand, he means non-Jews, then he is holding up
Jewish practice against non-Jewish water purification. I think here the latter may be
intended.

58. Sanders, *Jewish Law*, p. 31.

(1) to remove contracted states of impurity that would prevent access to the Temple and (2) to assure a state of purity for various acts of worship or approach to the divine. The states of impurity are primarily those spoken of in the Jewish scriptures: corpse impurity (Philo, Josephus, Sirach), childbirth (Josephus), sexual intercourse and bodily emissions (Philo, Josephus),[59] touching anything impure (Philo). Diaspora writers recognized that contracting any of these impurities barred one from entering the Temple precincts and so bathing was enjoined before entry to the Temple (Philo), but the 'domestic impurities'[60] (primarily semen and menstrual impurities) seem to have been treated increasingly simply for purity's sake.

Several texts suggest that this attitude toward maintenance of Temple purity was extended to other acts of worship. Judith immerses in a spring before praying, and the translators in *Aristeas* wash their hands while praying. A very interesting text from the *Sib. Or.* 3.591-93 says of the Jews that 'at dawn they lift up holy arms toward heaven, from their beds, always sanctifying their flesh [or other MSS: hands] with water'.[61] Here it may be that washing flesh or hands is to be connected with prayer.[62] 2 Macc. 12.38 notes the army of Judas Maccabeus bathing before Sabbath 'as was customary'.

What these texts tell us, then, is that Jews bathed their bodies in order to remove various states of impurity, primarily those set out in Leviticus 11–15 and Numbers 19. Jews bathed in rivers and streams or washed in the sea, and Justin perhaps witnesses to the use of special pools in the Diaspora. Bathing or washing was probably connected with prayer and Sabbath observance, perhaps as extensions of or a replacement for Temple purity. In any case, ritual bathing was a normal feature of Jewish life. The evidence from Philo may suggest specific sprinkling rituals in Alexandria for corpse impurity and sexual contact,[63] but beyond this prolific writer the evidence is slim. What we do not have, because the

---

59. As Sanders, *Jewish Law*, pp. 29-30 notes, Philo elaborates on the problem of washing after sexual intercourse by saying that the couple should touch nothing before washing.

60. The term is Sanders's. See *Jewish Law*, p. 257.

61. Translation from John J. Collins, *Sibylline Oracles*, in James H. Charlesworth (ed.), *The Old Testament Pseudepigrapha*, vol. 1 (Garden City: Doubleday, 1983).

62. This practice may not be only a Diaspora one. Sanders (*Jewish Law*, p. 231) notes a polemical passage from *t. Yad* 2.20 in which so-called 'morning-bathers' criticize the Pharisees for not immersing before morning prayers.

63. Sanders, *Jewish Law*, p. 257.

texts that we have are not primarily concerned with halakha, are the detailed halakhic treatments of the purity laws; what we think we know must be teased out of a few suggestive texts.

The Literature of the Qumran yaḥad

In comparison to the literature just discussed, the Qumran evidence for purity concerns is an embarrassment of riches. Bathing was an important, daily practice of the community connected, among other things, with the daily meal and prayer, with entrance into the community, and with various impure states.[64] What has recently become clear is that the halakha at Qumran concerning purity has many issues in common with the later discussions of the rabbinic sages, and the study of Qumran halakha is experiencing a heyday with the availability of many new texts from Cave 4.[65] I do not intend to enter that discussion here, but to examine the evidence for the performance of ritual immersion.

The *yaḥad* clearly had as its intention the maintenance of the purity of the entire community as it is delineated in the Jewish scriptures. Bathing before the community meal and the immersion of the novice before formal entry to the community were meant to assure a communal state of continuous purity. Not only the discovery of stepped pools among the ruins of Qumran but also numerous places in the community's literature indicate that this state of purity was achieved and maintained through bathing one's body. 1QS 3.4-9, for example, refers to the one who despises the precepts of God not benefiting from ritual immersion, and the one who does submit to these precepts will 'be sanctified by cleansing water'. In this passage the cleansing or bathing waters (מי רחץ) are distinguished from atonements (כפורים) and sprinkling or purifying

---

64. The most recent treatment of purity issues at Qumran is Hannah K. Harrington, *The Impurity Systems of Qumran and the Rabbis*, SBLDS, 143 (Atlanta: Scholars Press, 1993). Other relevant literature is cited in her bibliography. See also the articles by Joseph Baumgarten, 'The Purification Rituals in *DJD* 7', and 'The Pharisaic-Sadducean Controversies about Purity and the Qumran Texts', *JJS* 31 (1980), pp. 157-70.

65. The work of Lawrence Schiffman has concentrated on issues of halakha. His book-length treatments include *The Halakha at Qumran* (Leiden: Brill, 1975) and *Sectarian Law in the Dead Sea Scrolls: Courts Testimony and the Penal Code*, BJS, 33 (Chico, CA: Scholars Press, 1983). For an extensive bibliography, see 'Bibliography on the Halakha at Qumran', in Elisha Qimron and John Strugnell, *Qumran Cave 4 V, Miqṣat Maʿaśe Ha-Torah* (DJD, 10; Oxford: Clarendon Press, 1994), pp. 124-29.

waters (מי נדה), and thus probably indicate immersion.[66]

I do not have to prove in this essay, however, that the Qumran community practised immersion. But, is there evidence for how they thought it ought to be done? Several texts provide a glimpse. When 1QS 3.4 says of the despiser of God's precepts that he will not be cleansed 'by purifying waters, nor sanctified by seas and rivers, nor washed clean with any ablution',[67] it reveals that natural bodies of water were acceptable for immersion, as we saw in other Second Temple literature. The use of stepped immersion pools at Qumran was almost certainly an accommodation to the dry environment.

An important section in CD 10 provides the basic approach of the community to ritual bathing and is the only text of which I am aware that deals with the performance of bathing.[68]

עַל הַטַּהֵר בַּמַּיִם אַל יִרְחַץ אִישׁ בַּמַּיִם צוֹאִים וּמְעוּטִים מִדֵּי מַרְעִיל
אִישׁ אַל יִטַּהֵר בַּמָּה כְלִי וְכֹל גֶּבֶא בַּסֶּלַע אֲשֶׁר אֵין בּוֹ דֵּי מַרְעִיל
אֲשֶׁר נָגַע בּוֹ הַטָּמֵא וְטִמֵּא מֵימָיו בְּמֵימֵי הַכְּלִי

Concerning the purification with water. No man shall bathe in dirty water or in an amount too shallow to cover a man. He shall not purify himself with water contained in a vessel. And as for the water of every rock-pool too shallow to cover a man, if an unclean man touches it he renders its water as unclean as water contained in a vessel.[69]

66. Rather than the usual rabbinic term טבל 'dip or immerse', the Qumran texts prefer רחץ for washing one's body and כבס for laundering one's clothes.

67. Translation from Geza Vermes, *The Dead Sea Scrolls in English* (New York: Penguin Books, 1987), p. 64.

68. I have examined the list of halakhic texts from Qumran given by Qimron and Strugnell in DJD, 10, p. 123, and have not found any other discussion akin to that of CD 10. Baumgarten in 'The Purification Rituals in *DJD* 7' discusses 4Q512, which apparently concerns a bather standing in the water and reciting the blessing. He also suggests (p. 207) that in 4Q514 col. XII concerning the red heifer, M. Baillet's reconstruction of לוחות עולם 'eternal tablets' should be corrected to ליחות עולם 'permanent streams', a phrase he takes to refer to the source of water for the ritual.

69. Translation from Vermes, *The Dead Sea Scrolls in English*. The text is extant in the Cairo Geniza copy of the work. For a fresh transcription and critical notes from the 4Q fragments, see, Elisha Qimron, 'The Text of CDC', in Magen Broshi (ed.), *The Damascus Document Reconsidered* (Jerusalem: The Israel Exploration Society/The Shrine of the Book, 1992). Theodor Gaster in *The Dead Sea Scriptures* (Garden City, NY: Anchor Books/Doubleday, 1976), p. 111 n. 51 understands מרעיל, whose meaning is uncertain, as מירעל(?) and translates 'water too scant to fill a pail'. Saul Lieberman in *Greek in Jewish Palestine* (New York: The Jewish Theological Seminary of America, 1942), p. 135 n. 151 emends the text to מרחל 'a

In this brief compass, one discovers several important issues. Purity is to be achieved by complete immersion of the body. Some types of water do not remove states of impurity, in this case water that is insufficient to immerse a human body and water contained in a vessel. In the context, I do not understand the prohibition of water in a vessel to be the same problem as the drawn water of the rabbinic regulations, but as the equivalent of water insufficient for full immersion. Thus the water in the shallow rock-pool becomes unclean and cannot of itself render a person pure because, due to the insufficient amount of water contained in it, it is analogous to the water in a vessel.

Is the term rock-pool (גבא בסלע) here a synonym for *miqveh*? The operative word, גבא, denotes a cistern, a pool (Isa. 30.14) or perhaps even a swamp (Ezek. 47.11). It seems generally to indicate naturally occurring pools, but there is no way to tell in CD 10 whether the text indicates a pool dug out of rock or a natural depression or hole that fills with water.

The bottom line, however, is that while the halakha at Qumran concerning states of purity is very complex, the resolution to the problem of impurity seems to be quite straightforward. One needs to immerse in water, the quantity of which should cover the body, and, where the law requires it, one should launder one's clothes.

4. The Consequences for Reconstructing Jewish Life

The irony of the foregoing analysis is that it may not change dramatically our picture of the place and practice of ritual bathing in Second Temple Jewish life. There are parts of the picture that I do think should be looked at a bit differently, however.

It seems clear to me that Sanders's claim that first-century Palestinian Jews all agreed that immersion should be performed in a special pool is somewhat exaggerated. This position can only be derived from two pieces of evidence: the rabbinic literature that he argues witnesses to Pharisaic practice and the identification of the many stepped pools in

---

hamper containing 40 seah of liquid' (see Elisha Qimron, *The Hebrew of the Dead Sea Scrolls* [Harvard Semitic Studies, 29; Atlanta, GA: Scholars Press, 1986], p. 101). I am dubious of this solution since it imputes into the CD text in a rather convoluted manner the rabbinic idea that 40 seah of water is the minimum amount required for a valid *miqveh*, an idea that is not inherent in the text as it stands or evident elsewhere in the sect's literature.

Israel as *miqva'ot*. As I argued above, I am not as sanguine as are Reich and Sanders that all of these pools are assuredly *miqva'ot*, and the literature, both Diaspora and Palestinian, is in agreement that immersion could be conducted in rivers, streams, or even the sea. So, once one moves beyond the rabbinic texts, there are very few extant discussions of how to do it and in what kind of water.

That there may be fewer *miqva'ot* than the number of stepped pools, however, is in some respects irrelevant to whether Jews had a high concern to maintain ritual purity.[70] Since streams, rivers, and seas were all possible options for ritual bathing, we can be sure that people utilized these venues, and the importance of bathing or the frequency with which people bathed is not necessarily dependent on identifying stepped pools as *miqva'ot*. For this problem it seems to me we reach conclusions mainly on the basis of the literary evidence. Certainly, the fact that many halakhic questions about purity in the Qumran literature parallel similar discussions in later rabbinic texts demonstrates that such questions were central *for certain groups* in the Second Temple period.

Sanders takes the existence of *miqva'ot* outside Jerusalem as evidence that certain 'domestic purities' like semen and menstrual contamination were becoming a matter of concern for daily life rather than simply for access to the Temple.[71] If purity for purity's sake is to be seen as extending outside the Holy City, then the families of priests might be a logical context to look for its extension, since priests lived throughout ancient Palestine. Rather than a general concern for purity among the populace, perhaps the presence of *miqva'ot* outside Jerusalem indicates that the idea of maintaining priestly purity for temple service was considered vital to the daily lives of even those priests who were not in the course of their Jerusalem service.

Although I am reluctant to find *miqva'ot* 'more-or-less everywhere', as Sanders articulates it, I do share his view that despite the diversities that are evident in Second Temple Judaism, the fact that different Jews in different places all agreed, probably whether they actually did it or not, that immersion of one's body was the efficient means of removing impurity shows a somewhat surprising degree of unanimity. Indeed, the

70. Reich, '*Miqva'ot* (Jewish Ritual Baths) in the Second Temple Period', English abstract, p. 7, for example, makes the claim that the lack of immersion pools dated to the First Temple period indicates a lack of concern for ritual purity in this period.

71. Sanders, *Jewish Law*, p. 257.

Qumran *yaḥad* did seem to criticize just about everyone else, but they were in agreement with their enemies about the function and importance of immersion. Although these suggestions are not in any sense transformative, the problem of how one approaches reconstructing ancient Jewish life does make a difference. To a great degree, I think it depends on what kind of a picture one sees. If, for example, one looks at Henri Rousseau's painting *The Dream*, the definitive lines and colors allow the viewer to see distinct elements in the picture which together make up the whole. If, on the other hand, one views Claude Monet's *Poplars at Giverny, Sunrise*, clear and distinctive elements are absent. One needs to take a step back and observe the painting in its entirety. The subject begins to stand out despite the lack of a sharp focus or discrete elements. In trying to take a bit of a different look at the practice of ritual bathing in this paper, rather than Rousseau's *Dream*, I have seen Monet's *Poplars*.

ARCHAEOLOGY AND ETHNICITY:
PEOPLES OF ANCIENT CANAAN/ISRAEL

POTS AND PEOPLE REVISITED:
ETHNIC BOUNDARIES IN THE IRON AGE I

Israel Finkelstein

Introduction

The general question of how to determine ethnicity from the material culture of Palestine in the Iron I and the particular problem of the ethnicity of the early Israelites have come to the front line of research in recent years. Especially noteworthy are Bunimovitz's study (1990) on the ethnic identification of the Philistine culture and Dever's article (1993) on ethnicity in the archaeological record and the question of Israelite origin.

Since many of the authorities who attempted to deal with these questions have not addressed some of the theoretical problems related to the creation, maintenance, and identification of ethnicity, a short introduction seems to be relevant here. Especially noteworthy are references to studies on contemporary groups, where *all* data necessary for the investigation of these traits are available.

Ethnicity and Material Culture

Weber (1961) defined ethnicity as a sense of common descent extending beyond kinship, political solidarity vis-à-vis other groups, and common customs, language, religion, values, morality, and etiquette. In Cohen's view, the identities of members in an ethnic group, and categorization of ethnic groups by others, are 'more or less fluid and more or less multiple, forming nesting hierarchies of we/they dichotomizations' (Cohen 1978: 395). Shibutani and Kwan (1965: 47) suggested that an ethnic group consists of those who conceive of themselves as being alike by virtue of their common ancestry, real or fictitious, and who are so regarded by others.

Ringer and Lawless (1989: 1) and Kelly and Kelly (1980: 134-35) argued that ethnicity is created by the dichotomy between an internal set of factors that serve to establish and maintain the group's distinctive we-ness (by its own members) and an external set of factors that serve to shape and designate its they-ness (all non-members). In Barth's words (1969: 13) ethnicity is created by a combination of self-ascription and ascription by others. De Vos and Romanucci-Ross (1975: 378) added that the external force of ascription, by other societies, is as strong as self-identification.

These examples of attempts to define ethnicity, all taken from contemporary cases, show that ethnic lines are fluid, flexible, and changeable; identifying them in the material culture of a given group is therefore a perplexing task. The critical question is how to delineate the boundaries that define a group, rather than the cultural stuff that they enclose. In this connection we have to keep in mind Barth's warning (1969: 15) that these boundaries, which separate the 'we' on one side from the 'they' on the other side, are mainly social boundaries though they may have territorial expression. Ethnicity may be expressed by several cultural characteristics, the most important among them are language, script, ritual behavior (e.g., DeCorse 1989: 138), physical features (e.g., Macdonald 1987 on tattoo patterns in the Philippines), dietary choices, and different aspects of material culture.

Among the many studies on foodways and ethnicity, I would note here Langenwalter's paper on the archaeology of the nineteenth-century China Store in Madera County, California (1980); DeBoer's study on food taboos in Amazonia (1987); and McKee's attempts to delineate ethnicity from the garbage of the Kingsmill Plantation Slave Quarter in Virginia (1987).

In material culture, ethnicity can be expressed in a number of aspects:

1. Architectural forms; valuable case studies are Baldwin's article (1987) on roomsize patterns and ethnic identification in Mesa Verde and the Chaco Canyon in southwest United States, and Paloczi-Horvath's study (1989) on steppe traditions in Hungarian architecture of the thirteenth–fourteenth centuries BCE.

2. Clothing style; for instance, Washburn's study on the Bakuba raffia cloth (1990).

3. Mortuary practices; the case of Pharaohnic Egypt is one of the most celebrated examples and there is no need to elaborate on this here.

4. Style of artifacts, such as pottery, lithics, weaponry, jewelry and basketry; as an illustration one may note Larick's article on the Samburu spears (1986) and Bernick's study on the basketry of the northwest coast of North America (1987; see, in general, Kus 1987).

Even in cases of contemporary societies—when all these traits are traceable and/or visible—it may be difficult to delineate clear boundaries for ethnic groups, because, in Barth's words, 'we can assume no simple one-to-one relationship between ethnic units and cultural similarities and differences' (1969: 13-14). There are several reasons for this situation:

1. Group identity is influenced by complex sociological and psychological factors (Baker 1983: 13).
2. Processes of assimilation and acculturation tend to blur ethnic lines (see Pyszczyk 1987 for the material culture of Ukrainian immigrants in Alberta, Canada).
3. It is difficult to distinguish between expressions of status and manifestation of ethnicity (see, e.g., Cheek and Friedlander [1990] on Afro-American and White households in Washington, DC, in the turn of the century).
4. It is sometimes extremely difficult, or even impossible, to distinguish between the reflection of 'style' and ethnicity in material culture. A good example is Wiessner's work on the Kalahari San (1984; see also Sackett 1982; 1990).

To sum up this short introduction, since ethnicity and ethnic identity 'are concepts that take their form and content from the give and take of human behavior...There is the same continuity and change about them as there is about human behavior' (Peterson Royce 1982: 17). Needless to say, identifying ethnic lines in past cultures is even a more complex and treacherous task.

Ethnicity in Iron Age I Palestine

With some possible exceptions, primarily the Egyptian colonies of the Early Bronze IB in southern Palestine, the Iron Age is the first period in the history of the southern Levant that enables one to deal with ethnicity in the archaeological record. Yet, it is only in the Late Iron II, and especially in the Hellenistic and Roman periods, with the growth in the paleographic material and in reliable textual evidence, that ethnic lines become easier to trace. But ethnic identification is not simple even in periods covered by texts. To quote Shennan's introduction in *Archaeological Approaches to Cultural Identity*, 'ethnic identity is better considered as a subjective and changing phenomenon rather than as an objective and enduring one, and we cannot assume that the "peoples" described in the sources correspond to the self-conscious identity groups that are essential to the definition of ethnicity' (Shennan 1989b: 15).

Dealing with ethnicity in Palestine in the Iron Age I, three points should be stressed from the outset.

The first—the tension between 'ideal' past cultures and 'real' cultural situations—applies mainly to the case of early Israel. The second—that cultural forms may change while the subtler aspects of culture and their meaning may still remain the same over very extended periods of time (in the case of acculturation, e.g., Tax 1960)—applies mainly to the case of the Philistines in the post-formative phase of their settlement in the southern coastal plain. The third—that untraceable social networks may be just as important in describing ethnicity as material culture, because the latter can be shared by several ethnic groups—applies to all groups active on the scene at that time. A good example for this latter point can be found in Hill's study (1989) on the early historic period in Virginia.

A special word should be devoted here to the biblical text and its meaning for the question of ethnicity in the Iron I. It is widely accepted today that historical narratives, especially those dealing with origin myths of early nations, tell us not only how the past led to the present, but also how the present creates the past (on this in ethnicity studies, see Chapman *et al.* 1989: 1). Regarding the early history of Israel, the Bible presents a 'fictional but functional' origin myth. As such, one must remember Cohen's words that

> ethnic group formation is a continuing and often innovative cultural pro-
> cess of boundary maintenance and reconstruction. Once the ethnic identi-
> ties and categories are triggered into being salient, cultural rationalizations
> for the legitimacy of the mobilized grouping are actively sought for and
> created by those involved... The emerging history can be part real part
> fancy (Cohen 1978: 397-98; see also Horowitz 1977).

This applies very well to the biblical account on the origin of early Israel. Though it may have some historical seeds, which are extremely difficult to extract from the myth (Na'aman 1994), it is concealed in the wrap of the ideology and politics of a much later phase in the history of Israel, that of the late-monarchic or even post-exilic period.

In what follows, I wish to examine the most celebrated case of ethnic identification in Iron I Palestine: that of the early Israelites.

The Case of Early Israel: Past and Current Theories

In recent years, scholars have engaged in fierce debates over the question of the identity of the inhabitants of Iron I sites, mainly those located on the margins of what was conceived from the biblical text as the homeland of the early Israelites.

Tel Masos in the Beer-sheba Valley was identified by its excavators—Fritz and Kempinski—with biblical Hormah, and its inhabitants were described as Israelites (Fritz and Kempinski 1983; Fritz 1981; Kempinski 1990). But most scholars rejected this view: Kochavi, and Herzog (1984: 72) proposed to identify the site with the city of Amalek mentioned in 1 Sam. 15 (for a more cautious approach see Herzog 1994: 146-48), B. Mazar suggested an association of the phenomenon of Tel Masos with the floruit of the Philistine coast; and Ahlström argued that 'the site's occupants belonged to the mainstream Canaanite cultural tradition' (1984: 52). According to the author (Finkelstein 1988a), the inhabitants came from different origins, but were dominated by desert people from the south, who established their commercial and political center at the site.

The people of Giloh—a site located to the southwest of Jerusalem—were identified by the excavator, A. Mazar, as Judahites, or Israelites (1981a; a more cautious treatment in 1990: 93-96), while Ahlström (1984b) suggested that they were Canaanites, or more precisely Jebusites, who were related to the people of nearby Jerusalem.

In the final report on the excavations at the small site of Izbet Sartah, located on the western margins of the hill country, overlooking the central coastal plain, the author argued that the inhabitants were Israelites, who expanded westward from the heart of the hill country (Finkelstein 1986: 201-205). But Lederman (1990) and Dever (1991: 79) preferred to see them as displaced Canaanites from the collapsing urban culture of the lowlands.

Aharoni (1957) identified a group of Iron I sites in the Upper Galilee as Israelite. Thirty years later Kochavi (1984: 67-68) suggested that they were built by Phoenicians related to the city of Tyre.

Albright (1943: 36-37) and most scholars after him regarded the builders of stratum B1 at Tell Beit Mirsim in the eastern Shephelah as Israelites. But Greenberg (1987) argued that stratum B1 represents a continuation of the Canaanite occupation of stratum C.

The excavators of Taanach—the large mound on the southern margin of the Jezreel Valley—argued that in the Iron I the site was inhabited by Canaanites (Rast 1978: 55). A. Mazar (1981) suggested that already at that early date the inhabitants can be regarded as Israelites. The identity of the Iron I people of nearby Megiddo has been strongly debated since the 1940s (see summary in Finkelstein 1988b: 92-93), and there is no need to repeat the arguments here.

There were two attempts to tackle directly the question of the ethnicity of the proto-Israelites (Dever's term—1993). In a previous work (Finkelstein 1988b: 27-33) I suggested drawing the ethnic boundaries of the early Israelites and their settlements by a combination of two factors:

1. *The territorial aspect*: an attempt to impose on the Iron I the political map of the early Iron II, that is, the boundaries of the monarchy in its early days, as revealed by supposedly reliable biblical texts. In this regard one should bear in mind that political unification tends ultimately to have ethnicity-creating capabilities.

2. *The socioeconomic aspect*: in the above-mentioned areas, proto-Israelite settlements are those sites which were inhabited by newly settled groups. This argument is important in order to distinguish the proto-Israelite villages from sites with continuity of sedentary occupation in the Late Bronze/Iron I transition.

This solution is not free of flaws. First, the historicity of the biblical texts that deal with the United Monarchy is also questionable (e.g., Davies 1992; Thompson 1992). Second, it is clear today that the differentiation between sedentary and non-sedentary autochthonous people in the LB/Iron I transition for the sake of ethnic identification is meaningless. In any case, even if this suggestion was good enough for the delineation of the general lines of the proto-Israelite settlement, it cannot solve the problem of the ethnic identification of the inhabitants of a single Iron I site.

W.G. Dever has recently engaged the problem of early Israelite ethnicity in a special study (1993). His article is based on four points. The first:

> In 12th century BCE Canaan, there *did* exist, at least on the highland fron-
> tier, a new ethnic entity, which we can recognize in the archaeological
> remains, and which we can distinguish from other known ethnic groups
> such as 'Canaanites' and 'Philistines' (1993: 24).

This is a circular argumentation, which is based on the biblical text
rather than on the archaeological data, because:

A. According to Dever's own view (1991; 1993), there is much
    continuity in the material culture in the Late Bronze/Iron I
    transition; if this is the case, how can one distinguish a new
    ethnic group in the archaeological record?

B. If these people are distinguishable, how can Dever, in the same
    study, cast doubt on the ethnic affiliations of the inhabitants of
    Tell en-Nasbeh and Bethel? Since there are no differences
    between the Iron I finds of these two sites and sites such as
    Shiloh and et-Tell, it is clear that Dever's doubts are rooted in
    nonarchaeological considerations.

C. Even if Dever was right in his claim that we are able to distin-
    guish the highlands people archaeologically from the
    Canaanites and Philistines, there remains the problem of the
    Iron I sites of the Transjordanian plateau. From the material
    culture point of view, they are identical to the hill country sites
    west of the Jordan, though they gave birth to different ethné
    and national identities.

D. If we ignore the Bible, on the same lines of argumentation we
    can easily 'create' ethnic entities in the highlands in the two
    previous waves of settlement that took place there—in the
    Early Bronze and in the Middle Bronze Ages (see Finkelstein
    1994).

In his second point Dever argues that:

> This ethnic group may be presumed to be roughly the same as that which
> had called itself 'Israelite' since the late 13th century BCE, and was thus
> well enough established to be listed as 'Israel'... in the well known
> 'Victory Stele' of Merneptah (1993: 24).

This is a shaky argument, as we know nothing about the size and geographical location of the group named 'Israel' in the Merneptah Stele. In
other words, at least territorially, we cannot make an instinctive connection between the 'Israel' of 1207 and the area where the Israelite
monarchy emerged.

Dever's third argument is that

> Despite our uncertainty as to the full content of the term, these 12th–11th
> century ethnic Israelites... possessed an overall material culture that led
> directly on into the true, full-blown Iron Age culture of the Israelite
> Monarchy... That cultural continuity *alone* would entitle us to regard these
> Iron I villagers as the authentic progenitors of later *biblical* 'Israel' (1993:
> 24).

This is no doubt correct, and I would just add here two statistical aspects
of the dispersal of the Iron I sites in the central hill country, as revealed
by recent surveys: first, only very few Iron I sites south of Shechem
were already inhabited in the Late Bronze Age; second, over 90% of the
Iron I sites continued to be inhabited, undisturbed, until the eighth century BCE. In any event, this argument is good enough for the overall
picture; but for the reasons referred to above, it is meaningless when we
come to scrutinize the results at a single site.

In his fourth point Dever argues that archaeology can comment on

> the technology, subsistence, socio-economic structure, demography and
> other 'material correlates of behavior', including even religion... even
> more reliably than most biblical texts, because the archaeological data are
> contemporary, more numerous and varied, and above all free from the
> biases of the later literary tradition (1993: 24; for a similar view in a dif-
> ferent setting see McGuire 1982: 161-62).

This point, as far as I can judge, is only partially correct. Indeed, archaeology can teach us quite a lot about these characteristics of the proto-
Israelite phenomenon, but I doubt whether ecology and subsistence
strategies can really reveal the ethnicity of ancient people. In any case,
the question is not whether archaeology is more reliable than the biblical
text, but whether it enables us to draw clear ethnic lines in Iron I
Palestine.

Material Culture of the Iron I

The Iron I sites in the hill country and its margins are relatively poor in
finds. With the absence of written material and cemeteries and with the
scarcity of finds related to ritual, the only significant features for this discussion are pottery, architectural forms (both the house and the layout
of the settlement), and foodways as reflected in the faunal assemblages.
These three types of finds are generally discovered in large quantity
and/or vast exposures in every excavated site.

A preliminary word of caution is required here. Binford (1972: 20-25) saw material finds as reflecting varying levels of cultural evolution—functional needs, social traditions, ideas, and symbols. As far as I can judge, the material culture of a given group of people mirrors the environmental background of their habitat, their socioeconomic and sociopolitical systems, the influence of neighboring cultures, the local heritage, traditions of the country of origin in the case of migrating groups, and of course, their cognitive world. In most cases we cannot determine which of these variables is/are the dominant one/s in shaping the material culture of a given community, a fact which further complicates the identification of ethnic lines of past people.

Pottery

Archaeologists tend to put ethnic labels on pottery types, especially when they are decorated with special motives. Thus we relate to 'Philistine', 'Edomite', and 'Midianite' pottery. But doing this, we ignore style, status, and trade factors. Therefore, with so many variables playing behind the scene, in most cases pottery cannot indicate ethnos. This has been demonstrated in numerous examples, especially in cases where reliable historical documents are available, to supplement the archaeological data. Good examples are Adams's studies on the pottery of Medieval Nubia (1968; 1979) and Kramer's insights on the Habur ware and the Hurrians (1977). Both showed the complexity of ceramic evidence in regard to historic, cultural and racial change. Another interesting example comes from the central hill country of Palestine in later periods. There were three different communities there in the Ayyubid/Crusader period—local Muslims, eastern Christians, and Franks. The villages of the latter can easily be identified according to the detailed texts and, as demonstrated by Ellenblum (1992), even by certain architectural characteristics. But pottery is a different story: Cohen Finkelstein's recent study of the pottery collected in these villages (1991) found imported 'Crusader' wares in all three communities. They were apparently distributed according to status and wealth, rather than ethnic lines.

Except for few rare vessels, there are no special features in the pottery of the Iron I highlands sites, either in the assemblages as a whole, or in specific types. The collared rim pithos, once suggested by Albright (1937: 25) and even more boldly by Aharoni (e.g., 1970: 264-65) to be an indicator of 'Israelite' sites, has later been found in lowlands sites, such as Tel Nami on the coast (Artzy 1993) and Megiddo (Esse 1992).

Collared rim pithoi are also abundant in every Iron I site in the Transjordanian plateau—the best-known examples being Sahab (Ibrahim 1978) and Tell el-Umeiri (e.g., Clark 1991: 59) in the Amman-Hesban region. The dominance of this type in central hill country sites should be attributed to economic, environmental, and social factors, such as horticulture-based subsistence and distance of the Iron I communities from stable water sources (Finkelstein 1988b: 275-85; Zertal 1988), rather than to the ethnic background of the population (contra Esse 1992). Incidentally, the significant number of collared rim jars found at Megiddo (Esse 1992) eliminates London's hypothesis (1989) that they are found primarily in rural (as opposed to urban) communities. I believe that the distribution of 'Tyrian' pithoi in the Galilee, which was attributed by Kochavi to Phoenician settlers (1984: 67-68), should also be explained on the basis of geographic, socio-economic, and commercial backgrounds.

The case of the Philistines is even more complicated than that of early Israel, since the Philistines established themselves in a densely settled region and intermingled with significant indigenous populations. It seems reasonable to assume that the early stage of Philistine pottery, that is the monochrome ware, can be taken as an indicator for identifying sites that were inhabited by the newcomers (Dothan 1995; Mazar 1985; Singer 1985; Stager 1995). A singular cooking pot of Aegean origin, which appears at Tel Miqne and other sites of the southern coastal plain with the monochrome pottery, has recently been related to the culinary practices of the new groups (Ann Killebrew, lecture in the ASOR/SBL annual meeting, San Francisco 1992; Yasur-Landau 1992). The unique, unperforated loomweights, also found in early twelfth century strata at Tel Miqne and Ashkelon, complete the evidence for the migration of the Sea People to the Levantine coast (Stager 1991: 15).

Philistine bichrome pottery is a different case. First, it has a long life of over a century; second, it has been unearthed also in non-Philistine regions such as the Jezreel Valley and the highlands. Therefore, even from the territorial point of view it is difficult to decide what percentage of bichrome ware makes a site 'Philistine'.

Bunimovitz (1990) asserted that Philistine bichrome vessels constituted the luxury tableware for the entire heterogeneous population of Philistia in the Iron I. In other words, decorated Philistine vessels were symbols of status and wealth and therefore cannot be used for ethnic labeling.

The same is true for other decorated Iron Age pottery groups that appear in well-defined geographical boundaries. 'Midianite' pottery of the Iron I and 'Edomite' pottery of the Late Iron II represent local traditions, status, and style, but cannot be taken as ethnic demarcators. Knauf (1983) and Parr (1988) were therefore right in suggesting the term 'Midianite' pottery be changed to 'Hejaz ware' or 'Qurayya painted ware.' In the same line of reasoning I would suggest the term 'Buseirah ware' for the so-called 'Edomite' pottery. In any event, the presence of Edomite pottery in sites outside the hub of the Late Iron II Edomite state depicts trade and cultural influence rather than direct Edomite conquest or political domination (contra Beit-Arieh 1988: 41).

Architecture

In certain cases, architectural forms *may* indicate origin and thus ethnos of past people. In medieval Hungary, certain features of the fifteenth–sixteenth century settlements are characteristic of the Cumanian ethnic group and can apparently be traced back to their steppe traditions (Paloczi-Horvath 1989). Ellenblum (1992) argues that mason marks and other construction features found in medieval sites in Israel can distinguish Frankish settlements, even houses, from Muslim communities.

Unfortunately this is not the case in the Iron Age. Shiloh (1973) described the four-room house as an Israelite house-type, but it has later been found also in lowlands and Transjordanian Iron I sites (e.g., Sauer 1986: 10). Its popularity in the central hill country must be linked to environmental and social factors, rather than to the ethnic background of the communities (Stager 1985; Finkelstein 1988b: 254-59).

Several years ago I suggested that the layout of some of the Iron I highlands sites—a large courtyard surrounded by a belt of broad rooms—hints at the pastoral background of their inhabitants (1988b: 237-50). But this is true for Negev Highlands late eleventh century sites as well, not to mention Early Bronze II sites in Sinai and Middle Bronze sites in the Black Desert (Finkelstein 1995); this layout should be attributed to socioeconomic traits of the inhabitants rather than to their ethnic origin.

To sum up this part of the discussion, pottery and architectural forms in Iron I sites on both sides of the Jordan reflect environmental, social, and economic traits of the settlers. They tell us nothing about ethnicity. This leaves us with the third widespread find in the Iron I sites—the faunal assemblage.

Foodways

Foodways, that is, dietary patterns, tend to be conservative symbols of ethnicity. Staski (1990) noted that certain groups resist change in food-ways even in the face of potential assimilation. DeBoer reached similar conclusions in his study on food taboos in Amazonia (1987). What people eat, and how they eat it, is an important aspect of the process of ethnicity. McKee (1987) argued that foodways often rival ideology and religion in terms of cultural conservatism, and that food is one of the primary symbols manipulated by people seeking to maintain their cultural identity and group solidarity.

This notion is wonderfully demonstrated in one of the famous Confucian classics, the Li Chi:

> The people of those five regions... had all their several natures, which they could not be made to alter. The tribes on the east... had their hair unbound, and tattooed their bodies. Some of them ate their food without its being cooked. Those on the south... tattooed their foreheads, and had their feet turned in towards each other. Some of them (also) ate their food without its being cooked. Those on the west... had their hair unbound, and wore skins. Some of them did not eat grain-food. Those on the north... wore skins of animals and birds, and dwelt in caves. Some of them also did not eat grain-food (*Li Chi Book of Rites*, Section III, p. 14).

Clearly, in usual circumstances, archaeology can trace only the foodways component of this description.

But a word of caution is required even here: identifying ethnic groups according to their diet is not devoid of obstacles. In certain cases, processes of acculturation, intercultural contacts, and availability or scarcity of certain food items can influence the culinary practices of a given group (e.g., Langenwalter 1980: 110; DeBoer 1987; Crabtree 1990).

A great body of data on animal husbandry in Bronze and Iron Age Palestine has been accumulated in recent years. Especially important for the study of ethnicity in the Iron Age are the data on the ratio of pig bones in the faunal assemblages. To the information presented by Hesse in his article on patterns of Palestinian pork production (1990), which dealt mainly with Philistine foodways, one should add the following information, which has been published in the last few years.

Middle Bronze Age: At Tel Michal on the coast north of Tel Aviv pig bones make 6.3% of the assemblage (Hellwing and Feig 1989: 239); their share in the Emeq Refaim faunal assemblage, in the highlands southwest of Jerusalem, is 8% (15.2% in the Intermediate Bronze Age,

Kolska Horwitz 1989) and, at Shiloh, 3.5% (Hellwing, Sade and Kishon 1993).

Iron I: Pig bones make only 0.1% of the faunal assemblage at Shiloh (one bone, possibly intrusive [Hellwing, Sade, and Kishon 1993]). No pig bones were found at the Mt Ebal site near Shechem (Kolska Horwitz 1986–87) and at Khirbet Raddana near Ramallah (personal communication from Zvi Lederman). At Hesban, in Jordan southwest of Amman, pigs make 4.8% of the faunal assemblage (LaBianca 1990: 145).

When Hesse compiled his data, the information on the highlands sites was still fragmentary and limited. Hence, it was difficult to reach clear conclusions. It is clear now that in the Bronze Age pigs appear in both the lowlands and the highlands (Figure 1). Their changing ratio in the assemblages reflects the different environmental and socioeconomic

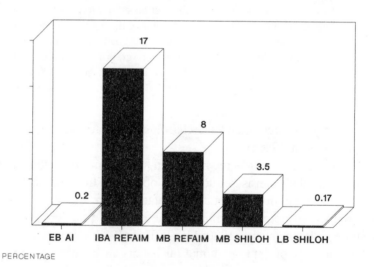

Figure 1. Pig bones in the highlands in the Bronze Age.

backgrounds of a given site. In the Iron I (Figure 2) pigs appear in great numbers in the Shephelah and the southern coastal plain (Tel Miqne, Tel Batash, and Ashkelon) and are quite popular at other lowlands sites. But they disappear from the faunal assemblages of the central hill country. The most interesting fact is that at that time, and in the Iron II, pigs continue to be present in significant numbers at Hesban in Transjordan. The faunal assemblages of the Iron II reflect the same traits (Figure 3).

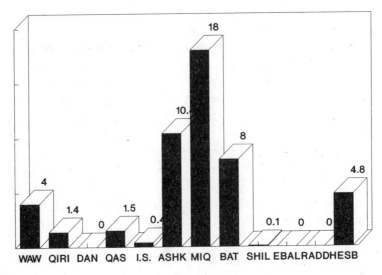

Figure 2. Pig bones in the Iron I (southern sites excluded).

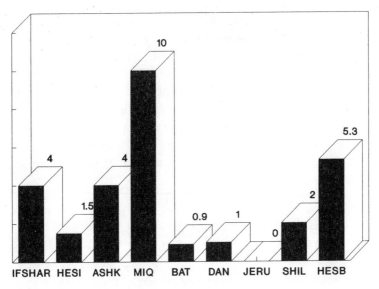

Figure 3. Pig bones in Iron II sites.

Regardless of the factors that may influence pig distribution (Hesse 1990; Wapnish and Hesse in this volume, pp. 238-70), this seems to mean that the taboo on pigs was already practiced in the hill country in the Iron I—pigs were not present in proto-Israelite Iron I sites in the highlands, while they were quite popular in a proto-Amonite site and numerous in Philistine sites. As predicted by Stager several years ago (1991: 9, 19), food taboos, more precisely, pig taboos, are emerging as the main, if not only, avenue that can shed light on ethnic boundaries in the Iron I. This may be the most valuable tool for the study of ethnicity of a given, single Iron I site.

In the case of the Philistines too, foodways and dietary practices are of much help in the search for ethnic boundaries. Hesse (1990: 217-18) has indicated the popularity in pork consumption in the Iron I in the southern coastal plain, and related it to husbandry practices brought from the Philistines' homeland. Killebrew (lecture in the ASOR/SBL annual meeting, San Francisco 1992) and Yasur-Landau (1992) pointed to a unique jar-shaped cooking pot of Aegean origin, which apparently fitted the culinary practices of the Philistine population.

Conclusions

The material culture of Palestine in the Iron I is not rich enough to allow the drawing of clear ethnic boundaries. The main, and in fact only, possible indicator of ethnicity at that period is foodways. It took centuries until distinctive national or ethnic material cultures developed. They seem to have been evolved with the rise of complex political systems and were influenced by the growing conflicts between the emerging polities. In the case of early Israel, most 'ethnic' features in the material culture developed and were introduced by the monarchy, possibly because the new state controlled vast areas with mixed elements. It was essential to unite them by creating a sense of nationalism and ethnic identity.

BIBLIOGRAPHY

Adams, W.Y.
     1968   'Invasion, Diffusion, Evolution?', *Antiquity* 42: 194-215.
     1979   'On the Arguments from Ceramics to History: A Challenge Based on Evidence from Medieval Nubia', *Current Anthropology* 20: 727-34.

Aharoni, Y.
> 1957   *The Settlement of the Israelite Tribes in Upper Galilee* (Jerusalem: Magnes Press) (Hebrew).
> 1970   'New Aspects of the Israelite Occupation in the *North*', in *Near Eastern Archaeology in the Twentieth Century: Essays in Honor of Nelson Glueck* (ed. James A. Sanders; New York: Doubleday): 254-65.

Ahlström, G.W.
> 1984a   'The Early Iron Age Settlers at Hirbet el-Msas (Tel Masos)', *ZDPV* 100: 35-52.
> 1984b   'Giloh: A Judahite or Canaanite Settlement?', *IEJ* 34: 170-72.

Albright, W.F.
> 1937   'Further Light on the History of Israel from Lachish and Megiddo', *BASOR* 68: 22-26.
> 1943   *The Excavation of Tell Beit Mirsim. III. The Iron Age* (AASOR, 21–22; New Haven, CT: American Oriental Society).

Artzy, M.
> 1993   'Nami, Tel', in *The New Encyclopedia of Archaeological Excavations in the Holy Land* (ed. Ephraim Stern; Jerusalem: Israel Exploration Society): 1095-98.

Auger, R. *et al.* (eds.)
> 1987   *Ethnicity and Culture* (Calgary: University of Calgary).

Baker, D.G.
> 1983   *Race Ethnicity and Power* (London: Routledge & Kegan Paul).

Baldwin, S.J.
> 1987   'Roomsize Patterns: A Quantitative Method for Approaching Ethnic Identification in Architecture', in Auger *et al.* 1987: 163-74.

Barth, F.
> 1969   'Introduction', in *Ethnic Groups and Boundaries* (ed. F. Barth; Boston: Little, Brown and Co.): 9-38.

Beit-Arieh, I.
> 1988   'New Light on the Edomites', *BAR* 14.2: 28-41.

Bernick, K.
> 1987   'The Potential of Basketry for Reconstructing Cultural Diversity on the Northwest Coast', in Auger *et al.* 1987: 251-57.

Binford, L.R.
> 1972   *An Archaeological Perspective* (New York: Seminar).

Bunimovitz, S.
> 1990   'Problems in the "Ethnic" Identification of the Philistine Culture', *Tel Aviv* 17: 210-22.

Chapman, M., M. McDonald and E. Tonkin
> 1989   'Introduction', in *History and Ethnicity* (ed. Elizabeth Tonkin, Maryon MacDonald and Malcolm Chapman; London: Routledge): 1-21.

Cheek, C.D., and A. Friedlander
> 1990   'Pottery and Pig's Feet: Space, Ethnicity, and Neighborhood in Washington, DC, 1880–1940', *Historical Archaeology* 24: 34-60.

Clark, D.R.
> 1991   'Field B: The Western Defense System', in *Madaba Plains Project. II. The 1987 Season at Tell el-'Umeiri and Vicinity and Subsequent*

Studies (ed. Larry G. Herr, Lawrence T. Geraty, Oystein S. LaBianca and Randall W. Younker; Berrien Springs: Andrews University Press): 53-73.

Cohen, R.
1978 'Ethnicity: Problem and Focus in Anthropology', *Annual Review of Anthropology* 7: 379-403.

Cohen Finkelstein, J.
1991 'Pottery Distribution, Settlement Patterns and Demographic Oscillations in Southern Samaria in the Islamic Periods' (unpublished MA thesis; Jerusalem: The Hebrew University).

Crabtree, P.J.
1990 'Zooarchaeology and Complex Societies: Some Uses of Faunal Analysis for the Study of Trade, Social Status and Ethnicity', in *Archaeological Method and Theory* (ed. Michael B. Schiffer; Tucson: University of Arizona Press): 155-205.

Davies, P.R.
1992 *In Search of 'Ancient Israel'* (JSOTSup, 148; Sheffield: JSOT Press).

DeBoer, W.R.
1987 'You Are What You Don't Eat: Yet Another Look at Food Taboos in Amazonia.', in Auger *et al.* 1987: 45-54.

DeCorse, C.R.
1989 'Material Aspects of Limba, Yalunka and Kuranko Ethnicity: Archaeological Research in Northeastern Sierra Leone', in Shennan 1989a: 125-40.

Dever, W.G.
1991 'Archaeological Data on the Israelite Settlement: A Review of Two Recent Works', *BASOR* 284: 77-90.
1993 'Cultural Continuity, Ethnicity in the Archaeological Record, and the Question of Israelite Origins', *Eretz-Israel* 24: 22*-33*.

De Vos, G., and L. Romanucci-Ross (eds.)
1975 *Ethnic Identity: Cultural Continuities and Change* (Palo Alto: Mayfield Publication).

Dothan, T.
1995 'Tel Migne-Ekron: The Aegean Affinities of the Sea Peoples' (Philistines') Settlement in Canaan in Iron Age I', in *Recent Excavations in Israel: A View to the West* (ed. Seymour Gitin; Dubuque: Archaeological Institute of America): 41-59.

Ellenblum, R.
1992 'Construction Methods in Frankish Rural Settlements', in *The Horns of Hattin* (ed. Benjamin Z. Kedar; Jerusalem: Yad Izhak Ben-Zvi): 168-89.

Esse, D.L.
1992 'The Collared Pithos at Megiddo: Ceramic Distribution and Ethnicity', *JNES* 51: 81-103.

Finkelstein, I.
1986 *'Izbet Sartah: An Early Iron Age Site Near Rosh Ha'ayin, Israel* (Oxford: *BAR* International Series).

1988a. 'Arabian Trade and Socio-Political Conditions in the Negev in the Twelfth–Eleventh Centuries BCE', *JNES* 47: 241-52.

1988b *The Archaeology of the Israelite Settlement* (Jerusalem: Israel Exploration Society).

1994 'The Emergence of Israel: A Phase in the Cyclic History of Canaan in the Third and Second Millennia BCE', in *From Nomadism to Monarchy: Archaeological and Historical Aspects of Early Israel* (ed. Israel Finkelstein and Nadav Naaman; Jerusalem: Israel Exploration Society): 150-78.

1995 *Living on the Fringe: The Archaeology and History of the Negev, Sinai and Neighboring Regions in the Bronze and Iron Ages* (Sheffield: Sheffield Academic Press).

Fritz, V.
1981 'The Israelite "Conquest" in the Light of Recent Excavations at Khirbet el-Meshash', *BASOR* 241: 61-73.

Fritz, V., and A. Kempinski
1983 *Ergebnisse der Ausgrabungen auf der Hirbet el-Msas (Tel Masos) 1972–1975* (Wiesbaden: Otto Harrassowitz).

Greenberg, R.
1987 'New Light on the Early Iron Age at Tell Beit Mirsim', *BASOR* 265: 55-80.

Hellwing, S., and N. Feig
1989 'Animal Bones', in *Excavations at Tel Michal, Israel* (ed. Zeev Herzog, George Rapp, and Ora Negbi; Tel Aviv: Tel Aviv University): 236-47.

Hellwing, S., M. Sade and V. Kishon
1993 'Faunal Remains', in *Shiloh: the Archaeology of a Biblical Site* (ed. Israel Finkelstein; Tel Aviv: Tel Aviv University): 309-50.

Herzog, Z.
1984 *Beer-Sheba II: The Early Iron Age Settlements* (Tel Aviv: Tel Aviv University).

1994 'The Beer-sheba Valley: From Nomadism to Monarchy', in *From Nomadism to Monarchy: Archaeological and Historical Aspects of Early Israel* (ed. Israel Finkelstein; and Nadav Na'aman; Jerusalem: Yad Izhak Ben-Zvi): 122-49.

Hesse, B.
1990 'Pig Lovers and Pig Haters: Patterns of Palestinian Pork Production', *Journal of Ethnobiology* 10.2: 195-225.

Hill, C.W.
1989 'Who is What? A Preliminary Enquiry into Cultural and Physical Identity', in *Archaeological Approaches to Cultural Identity*, in Shennan 1989a: 233-41.

Horowitz, D.L.
1977 'Cultural Movements and Ethnic Change', in *Ethnic Conflicts in the World Today* (ed. Martin O. Heisler; Philadelphia: American Academy of Political and Social Science): 6-18.

Ibrahim, M.M.
1978   'The Collared-rim Jar of the Early Iron Age', in *Archaeology in the Levant* (ed. Roger Moorey and Peter Parr; Warminster: Aris and Phillips): 116-26.

Kelly, M.C.S., and R.E. Kelly
1980   'Approaches to Ethnic Identification in Historical Archaeology', in Schuyler (ed.) 1980: 133-43.

Kempinski, A.
1990   'L'installation des clans et des tribus dans le bassin de Beersheba', in *La protohistoire d'Israel* (ed. Jacques Briend *et al.*; Paris: Cerf): 299-337.

Knauf, E.A.
1983   'Midianites and Ishmaelites', in *Midian, Moab, and Edom* (ed. John F.A. Sawyer and David J.A. Clines; Sheffield: JSOT Press): 147-62.

Kochavi, M.
1984   'The Period of Israelite Settlement', in *The History of Eretz-Israel,* vol. 2, *Israel and Judah in the Biblical Period* (Jerusalem: Keter Publishing House): 19-84 (Hebrew).

Kolska Horwitz, L.
1986–87   'Faunal Remains from the Early Iron Age Site on Mount Ebal', *Tel Aviv* 13-14: 173-89.
1989   'Diachronic Changes in Rural Husbandry Practices in Bronze Age Settlements from the Refaim Valley, Israel', *PEQ* 121: 44-54.

Kramer, C.
1977   'Pots and People', *In Mountains and Lowlands: Essays in the Archaeology of Greater Mesopotamia* (ed. Louis D. Levine and Cuyler T. Young; Malibu: Undena Publications): 91-112.

Kus, S.
1987   'Notes on and for Friends and Enemies', in Auger *et al.* 1987: 77-81.

LaBianca, O.S.
1990   *Sedentarization and Nomadization: Food System Cycles at Hesban and Vicinity in Transjordan (Hesban 1)* (Berrien Springs: Andrews University Press).

Langenwalter, P.E.
1980   'The Archaeology of 19th Century Chinese Subsistence at the Lower China Store, Madera County, California', in Schuyler (ed.) 1980: 102-11.

Larick, R.
1986   'Age Grading and Ethnicity in Style of Loikop (Samburu) Spears', *World Archaeology* 18: 269-83.

Lederman, Z.
1990   'Nomads they Never Were: A Reevaluation of Izbet Sarta', in *American Academy of Religion/Society of Biblical Literature Annual Meeting 1990,* Abstracts (Atlanta: Scholars Press): 238.

London, G.
1989   'A Comparison of Two Contemporaneous Lifestyles of the Late Second Millennium BC', *BASOR* 273: 37-55.

Macdonald, W.K.
    1987   'Symbols and Skin: Telling Enemies from Friends in Northern Luzon', in Auger *et al.* 1987: 33-43.

Mazar, A.
    1981   'Giloh: An Early Israelite Settlement Site near Jerusalem', *IEJ* 31: 1-36.
    1985   'The Emergence of the Philistine Material Culture', *IEJ* 35: 95-107.
    1990   'Iron Age I and II Towers at Giloh and the Israelite Settlement', *IEJ* 40: 77-101.

McGuire, R.H.
    1982   'The Study of Ethnicity in Historical Archaeology', *Journal of Anthropological Archaeology* 1: 159-78.

McKee, L.W.
    1987   'Delineating Ethnicity from the Garbage of Early Virginians: Faunal Remains from the Kingsmill Plantation Slave Quarter', *American Archaeology* 6.1: 31-39.

Na'aman, N.
    1994   'The "Conquest of Canaan" in the Book of Joshua and in History', in, *From Nomadism to Monarchy: Archaeological and Historical Aspects of Early Israel* (ed. Israel Finkelstein and Nadar Naaman; Jerusalem: Israel Exploration Society): 218-81.

Paloczi-Horvath, A.
    1989   'Steppe Traditions and Cultural Assimilation of a Nomadic People: The Cumanians in Hungary in the Thirteenth–Fourteenth Century', in Shennan 1989a: 291-302.

Parr, P.J.
    1988   'Pottery of the Late Second Millennium BC from North West Arabia and its Historical Implications', in *Araby the Blest, Studies in Arabian Archaeology* (ed. Daniel T. Potts; Copenhagen: University of Copenhagen): 73-89.

Peterson Royce, A.
    1982   *Ethnic Identity Strategies and Diversity* (Bloomington, IN: Indiana University Press).

Pyszczyk, H.
    1987   'Ethnic Persistence and Identity: The Material Culture of Ukrainian Albertans', in Auger *et al.* 1987: 303-308.

Rast, W.E.
    1978   *Taanach I, Studies in the Iron Age Pottery* (Cambridge: American Schools of Oriental Research).

Ringer, B.B., and E.R. Lawless
    1989   *Race Ethnicity and Society* (New York: Routledge).

Sackett, J.R.
    1982   'Approaches to Style in Lithic Archaeology', *Journal of Anthropological Archaeology* 1: 59-112.
    1990   'Style and Ethnicity in Archaeology: The Case for Isochrestism', in *The Uses of Style in Archaeology* (ed. Margaret W. Conkey and Christine A. Hastorf; Cambridge: Cambridge University Press): 32-43.

Sauer, J.A.
    1986   'Transjordan in the Bronze and Iron Ages: A Critique of Glueck's Synthesis', *BASOR* 263: 1-26.
Schuyler, R.L. (ed.)
    1980   *Archaeological Perspectives on Ethnicity in America* (New York: Baywood Publishing Company).
Shennan, S. (ed.)
    1989a   *Archaeological Approaches to Cultural Identity* (London: Unwin Hyman).
Shennan, S.
    1989b   'Introduction: Archaeological Approaches to Cultural Identity', in Shennan 1989a: 1-31.
Shibutani, T. and K.M. Kwan
    1965   *Ethnic Stratification: A Comparative Approach* (New York: Macmillan).
Shiloh, Y.
    1973   'The Four-Room House—the Israelite Type House?', *Eretz-Israel* 11: 277-85 (Hebrew).
Singer, I.
    1985   'The Beginning of Philistine Settlement in Canaan and the Northern Boundary of Philistia', *Tel Aviv* 12: 109-122.
Stager, L.E.
    1985   'The Archaeology of the Family in Ancient Israel', *BASOR* 260: 1-35.
    1991   *Ashkelon Discovered* (Washington, DC: Biblical Archaeology Society).
    1995   'The Impact of the Sea Peoples in Canaan (1185–1050 BCE)', in *The Archaeology of Society in the Holy Land* (ed. Thomas E. Levy; London: Leicester University Press): 332-48.
Staski, E.
    1990   'Studies of Ethnicity in North American Historical Archaeology', *North American Archaeologist* 11.2: 121-45.
Tax, S.
    1960   'Acculturation', in *Men and Culture; Selected Papers of the Fifth International Congress of Anthropological and Ethnological Sciences* (ed. Anthony F.C. Wallace; Philadelphia: University of Pennsylvania Press).
Thompson, T.L.
    1992   *Early History of the Israelite People* (Leiden: Brill).
Washburn, D.K.
    1990   *Style Classification and Ethnicity: Design Categories on Bakuba Raffia Cloth* (Philadelphia: American Philosophical Society).
Weber, M.
    1961   'Ethnic Groups', in *Theories on Society* (ed. Alcott Parsons, Edward Shils, Kaspar D. Naegele, and Jesse R. Pitts; New York: Free Press of Glencoe): 301-309.

Wiessner, P.
1984   'Reconsidering the Behavioral Basis for Style: A Case Study Among the Kalahari San', *Journal of Anthropological Archaeology* 3: 190-234.

Yasur-Landau, A.
1992   'The Philistine Kitchen—Foodways as Ethnic Demarcators', in *Eighteenth Archaeological Conference in Israel, Abstracts* (Tel Aviv): 10.

Zertal, A.
1988   'The Water Factor during the Israelite Settlement Process in Canaan', in *Society and Economy in the Eastern Mediterranean (c. 1500–1000 BC)* (ed. Michael Heltzer and Edward Lipinski; Leuven: Uitgeverij Peeters): 341-52.

CAN PIG REMAINS BE USED FOR ETHNIC DIAGNOSIS IN THE ANCIENT NEAR EAST?

Brian Hesse and Paula Wapnish

1. *Introduction*

If the absence of pig bones in an Iron Age archaeological site is taken as diagnostic for the presence of ethnic Israelites, there were a lot more Israelites in the ancient world than we ever suspected. Beginning some-time late in the second millennium BCE in a wide swath from Anatolia to southern Mesopotamia, from Persia to the Mediterranean, Yahweh's devotees abounded in almost every village and town, swamping the few populations of pork eating non-Israelites still holding out in widely scattered communities. If this sounds unbelievable, it is, but it also reflects the uncritical interpretation biblical historians, theologians, and archaeologists have loaded onto reports of pig bone finds.[1] Zooarchaeology

---

1. A recent case in point is Hess's review (1993) of the evidence for an early Israelite social entity in Canaan. Commendably, he makes an attempt to incorporate animal bone evidence into his argument, but he readily accepts the interpretation of other scholars when a more critical analysis would have served him better. In assessing the faunal reports from the twelfth century BCE hill country sites of Ebal, Shiloh, and ed-Dawwara, he notes the predominance of sheep and goat bones and the absence of pig, and cites Stager (1991) on the surprising lack of pig in an area ecologically well suited for such husbandry. Unfortunately, he also appears to accept Stager's assertion regarding the early date of Israel's prohibition of pork, based on Stager's claim that these (and additional faunal) data undermine 'various theories which require a later date for such dietary legislation among the Israelites as well as attempts to explain the prohibition of pork on the basis of ecological realities...' (Hess 1993: 138). This leads Hess ultimately to conclude that the animal species consumed by hill country inhabitants during the early Iron Age 'correlate in a variety of points with the picture of early Israel's worship as suggested both by Biblical law codes and by the narratives of Joshua, Judges, and the book of Samuel' (Hess 1993: 139). As we will show in the body of the text, pig avoidance or consumption was based on a number of complex interwoven factors and the mere presence or absence

cannot produce a catalog of ethnic index fossils—the linkage between all types of social identities and material culture items is simply too complex for such a straightforward methodology. What can be done, however, is to specify the behavioral conditions under which social interaction took place and provide an understanding of the contextual constraints that structured innovations in animal symbology and their social meanings.

Modern anthropological perspectives on 'ethnicity' stress that the term relates not to static, objective, 'natural' phenomena 'out there' which are readily identifiable by characteristic features, but rather that 'ethnicity', among other principles of group identity, labels dynamic, relational, historically embedded sets of social relations which undergo constant renegotiation of symbolic/cultural content. This shift in theoretical perspective demands a complementary shift in method. We will have to abandon the search for 'index fossils' amongst our bones and explore for the 'contexts' in which animals were deployed, not only alive, but as carcasses, parts of meals, and discarded remains. In what follows we will schematically review some aspects of the evidence for pig use and avoidance from the Chalcolithic to the Medieval periods, concentrating on Levantine sites but placing them in a wider regional framework. A discussion of the multiple 'pig principles' that governed the use of the animal in antiquity provides the tools to understand the incorporation of

of pig bones cannot be taken as *prima facie* evidence of ideological motivation, let alone social identity, *without* providing a detailed analysis of each context that examines all the possibilities. Hess's conclusion about early Israelite worship and use of animals can also be faulted given the nature of the faunal material from Mt Ebal. This site has been interpreted by its excavator (Zertal) as an early Israelite altar, an identification that is disputed among biblical archaeologists. The animal remains were analyzed by Liora Horwitz (1986–87) who noted that the majority of bones derived from sheep, goats, cattle, and fallow deer (96%). Zertal (1986–87) attempted to link these species with the Israelite dietary legislation in Leviticus 11 and Deuteronomy 14. Hess (1993) questions whether or not the 'deer' permitted for consumption in Deuteronomy 14 was the fallow deer (he would have done better to question if Hebrew *yachmur* is in fact firmly identified as deer), and he points out that the congruence of sheep, goats cattle, and (possibly) fallow deer as permissible species and their predominance in the Ebal faunal record does not necessarily identify the site as Israelite. Despite these difficulties he proceeds to his conclusion about the correlation of some points of animal worship in the biblical record and early Iron Age faunal samples. He ignores completely the fact that wild animals, like fallow deer, are never permitted as sacrifice (consumption was permitted with the introduction of profane slaughter), a fact which seriously compromises claims of social identity or biblical correlations.

pigs into various political economies. These historically contingent processes ultimately structured the evolution of the pig's salience as a symbol to Israel and surrounding peoples. This set of understandings will then be evaluated in the light of the rapidly expanding new literature on the nature of ethnicity. We shall find that our task will not be to determine the moment of ethnogenesis—the 'when' question of Israelite origins—but to examine the process of emergence—the 'why' question.

2. The Zooarchaeology of Pigs

Since we believe that religious legislation dealing with food has roots in wider cultural contexts of behavior, the link between 'table and altar' as Walter Houston (1993: 119) puts it, the potential of pig remains as a marker of past social identity must be evaluated empirically as well as theoretically. The exploitation of the pig was one of the most variable aspects of animal use in the ancient Near East. Compared to the dependence on sheep, goats, and cattle, the use of swine was both spotty and episodic, never dominant, always supplemental, and enmeshed in the modes of pastoral production in complex ways. In what follows, distributions of pig bone abundances will be used to illuminate several basic principles or parameters related to the exploitation of the animal. The continua associated with these principles provide a multidimensional context for examining the wide historical swings in pig herding and hunting that characterize the regional picture. Though the animal was incorporated into the neolithic mode of production by the end of the sixth millennium BCE (Flannery 1983), our review will be limited to samples that date no earlier than the Chalcolithic and Early Bronze Age (EBA— Early Dynastic—Old Kingdom), that is, during the emergence of state level political organization that was coincident with the expansion and integration of regional economic systems.

2.1 *Ecology and Political Economy*
2.1.1 *Wetland<—>Dryland & Settled<—>Mobile.* Of the barnyard and pastoral stock of the Middle East, the pig is the least tolerant of arid conditions, though this trait should not be overstated. Wild pigs live throughout the region, even today (Groves 1981), and the subspecies found there are much better adapted to hot, dry regimes than the characteristics of their domestic and wild cousins in Europe and other parts of Asia might suggest. Caroline Grigson (1987) has argued that one limit

to successful swine management in the Levant is rainfall and identifies the 300 mm isohyet as the critical threshold. Marvin Harris (1974, 1985), in a well-known series of publications aimed at linking the biblical legislation against the pig to material concerns facing the early Israelites, also asserted that the reliable presence of moisture was critical to swine management, though he further emphasized the practical difficulties associated with adopting a nomadic migratory lifestyle supported by pig husbandry among other material issues.[2] The distribution map of those archaeological samples in Egypt and the Near East that have produced a significant number of pig specimens[3] provides a picture that crudely confirms those linkages (see Figure 1 and Table 1). It shows that points of abundance[4] are either in the rainier fringes of the Fertile Crescent or

2. See the discussion by LaBianca (1990) for the relationship of settled and mobile communities and its implications for subsistence systems.

3. The segregation of wild and domestic pig bones is done through osteometric techniques, though often supplemented with information about mortality. Unfortunately, in many cases, publication of faunal remains has not been complete enough for us to determine the relative contribution of wild and domestic animals to the meat economy. This inability to segregate the two means of production blurs our historical picture of pig use. It can, however, be noted that in the archaeological samples from historic period sites where the relative contribution of wild and domestic animals has been estimated and pigs are abundant, managed swine are much in the majority.

4. Measures of abundance presented here are expressed in percentage terms based on the total number of identified fragments assigned to *Sus serofa*. They suffer from the multiple biases of differential preservational conditions and variable recovery techniques. Where possible we provide comparisons to sheep/goat abundances since the caprines are both numerous and of closer physical size than cattle, with which a comparison is likely to be strongly affected by differential collection rates. These numbers reflect mortality ratios, not estimates of herd proportions. The high fecundity rate of pigs implies that the number of swine present as means of production at ancient settlements was very much lower than the death estimates suggest (Hesse and Wapnish 1985).

A significant interpretative issue for which only a partial answer may be given relates to the question of how abundant is abundant enough. Some authors have taken even small numbers of pig remains as significant, treating only those samples free of pig bones as usable evidence of adherence to the laws. We are more impressed with the taphonomic complexity of our sites, often phenomena containing numerous layers of occupation that formed through processes that continually buried, uncovered, and reburied remains (Hesse and Wapnish 1985). Thus even perfectly clear and well-excavated stratigraphic features may contain objects from a variety of periods (Hesse and Rosen 1988). For example, a few pig bones were found in Iron

adjacent to the major river systems which structure the region. No examples of impermanent settlements whose occupants were dependent on pigs, wild or domestic, have yet been discovered. From this we may infer, as have other commentators, two pig parameters dichotomized as Wetland<—>Dryland and Settled<—>Mobile.

2.1.2 Domestic Agro-Pastoralism<—>Intensive Agriculture. But this is still not a complete picture. Within those territories where swine husbandry is possible we note considerable historical variation in its application. Houston (1993: 135-40), in a limited review of pig abundances in the Levant, predicted a linkage between cattle and swine management. In his opinion, both species are related to successful agricultural production in more watered areas. He was therefore surprised to discover that cattle and pig abundances are only infrequently linked in the data at his disposal, and that Iron Age samples are mostly contradictory. Such additional explanations as micro-environmental differences in the availability of water or the possibility that deforestation denuded pig habitat were considered and abandoned, forcing him to conclude that pig avoidance has something to do with the husbandry traditions which the settlers brought with them when they populated the later sites. He would have benefited by casting his net for faunal studies further afield.

Pastoral systems are both internally competitive and shaped by external forces. In the Nile Valley, for example, the exploitation of pigs declined sharply after the Old Kingdom period.[5] Richard Redding has argued (1991) that this history is related to changes in the agricultural sector and can be related to other changes in the mode of husbandry coincident with the decline in pigs. In Redding's model, during the Old Kingdom, pigs were a resource aimed at domestic consumption rather than market exchange in a mode of production not strongly influenced

Age contexts in the samples from Ai and Raddana. While these might be contemporary with the stratigraphy, they also might represent contamination from nearby Byzantine deposits as well. Given these problems we prefer to consider samples with less than three or four percent pig remains as representing the economies of societies that utilized swine in only the most marginal of fashions, certainly less than might be expected if use of the animal was salient to outside contemporary observers. Therefore we treat the difference between samples with very low frequencies of pigs and those with absolutely no bones from the animal as not clearly interpretable in cultural or historical terms.

5.   The decline in pig production from a peak in the third millennium BCE was a phenomenon that affected both the Levant and Greater Mesopotamia as well.

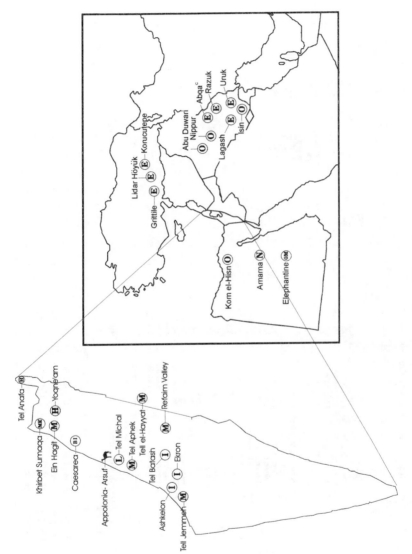

Figure 1 (see over).

Near Eastern Sites With Abundant Pigs

Egypt

Period	Site	Abundance
Old Kingdom	Kom el-Hisn	51%
Old Kingdom	Elephantine	12/14%
Middle Kingdom	Elephantine	20/31%
New Kingdom	Amarna	47%

Eastern Mediterranean

Period	Site	Abundance
Middle Bronze	Tell el-Hayyat	33%
Middle Bronze	Ein Hagit	20%
Middle Bronze	Tell Jemmeh	12%
Middle Bronze	Tel Aphek	7.7%
Middle Bronze	Refaim Valley	8.3%
Late Bronze	Tel Michal	6.3%
Pre-Iron	Ekron	8%
Early Iron	Ashkelon	19%
Early Iron	Ekron	18%
Early Iron	Batash	8%
Hellenistic	Yoqne'am	15.5%
Hellenistic	Tel Anafa	~ 50%
Byzantine	Caesarea	+++
Islamic	Caesarea	+++
Islamic	Appolonia-Arsuf	+++
Medieval	Khirbet Sumaqa	7.5%

Syria/Anatolia

Period	Site	Abundance
Early Bronze	Hassek	51%
Early Bronze	Yarikkaya	33%
Early Bronze	Grittile	18%
Early Bronze	Lidar Höyük	12%
Early Bronze	Hayaz	10%
Early Bronze	Korucutepe	7%
Middle Bronze	Lidar Höyük	20%
Middle Bronze	Korucutepe	11%
Late Bronze/Iron	Lidar Höyük	18%
Late Bronze/Iron	Korucutepe	13%
600–400 BC	Lidar Höyük	20%

Mesopotamia

Period	Site	Abundance
Early Dynastic	Abqa'	30%
Early Dynastic	Uruk	16%
Early Dynastic	Lagash	16%
Early Dynastic	Razuk	10%
Early Dynastic	Lagash	8/16%
Old Babylonian	Abu Duwari	27%
Old Babylonian	Nippur	20%
Old Babylonian	Uruk	18%
Old Babylonian	Isin	31%
800–700BCE	Isin	14%

Table 1. Partial listing of sites in southwest Asia and the Nile Valley with samples containing more than approximately 5% pig remains. Where it was possible to identify the method of estimation a value based on NISP/TNF, the total number of identified bone fragments assigned to a taxon, was selected (note that +++ Abundant; more than one value indicates two contexts were reported).

Figure 1 (over). Location of archaeological sites with abundant pig remains. Only samples dated later than the beginning of the third millennium BCE and containing more than approximately 5% pig bones are included. In the map of the Near East, circled 'O's in Mesopotamia refer to the Old Babylonian Period; in Egypt, the Old Kingdom; circled 'E's refer to the Early Dynastic in Mesopotamia and the Early Bronze Age in Anatolia; the circled 'N' in Egypt indicates the sample is New Kingdom in date; 'OM' that it is both Old and Middle Kingdom. In the map of the eastern Mediterranean 'M' means Middle Bronze Age; 'L' Late Bronze Age; 'I' Iron Age; 'H' Hellenistic; 'BI' Byzantine-Islamic; 'ME' Medieval; Islamic.

by outside demands. However, subsequent intensification of agriculture meant a reduction in the amount of land allocated to pasturage, a change that pressured the mix of stock to favor those species which browse as well as graze, in this case, goats.[6] Intensification also meant plows and plows mean cattle (see, in this regard, Goody 1976; Rosen 1986; Wapnish and Hesse 1991). Cattle compete with sheep for graze, and at the same time, because they yield milk, provide higher rates of protein return than pigs per unit of labor. Thus the changes brought on by the decision to intensify grain production transformed village-based animal husbandry from an emphasis on sheep and pig raising to management that concentrated on cattle and goats. This is a third pig principle: Intensive Agriculture<—>Domestic Agro-Pastoralism.

Parallel results to Redding's Egyptian data can be seen in the zoo-archaeological record of the Levant. Within the scale of potential for swine production set by rainfall and access to water, site size is to some degree negatively correlated with pig abundance in the samples from Middle Bronze Age sites (Hesse 1990; 1995; Figure 1 and Table 1). In the Jordan Valley, for instance, fortified Jericho produced only 1.8% pig remains (Clutton-Brock 1971, 1979) while the small east bank site of Tell el-Hayyat produced about 33% swine from roughly contemporary strata (Metzger 1985). Measured against the abundance of sheep and goats to reduce the impact of collecting bias, the pig to caprine ratios are 1:50 at Jericho and 3:4 at Tell el-Hayyat. On the coastal plain, the small settlement of Ein Hagit produced 20% pig (2:5) while Tel Aphek yielded 7.7% (1:6) (Hellwing and Gophna 1984) and Tell Jemmeh 12% (1:6) (Wapnish and Hesse 1988). The site of Tel Michal is an anomaly. Given the small size of the site, it should have produced more than 6.3% (1:7) pigs (Hellwing and Feig 1989). Perhaps the small size of the sample (110 bones) or the proposed specialized coastal function of the site had some effect. Inland we find samples from larger and more politically significant sites—Shiloh (3.5%, 1:24) and Lachish (3.1 or 0.1%, 1:24 or 1:869) (Hellwing *et al.* 1993)—that contrast with the quantity of pig remains found at rural sites like those reported from the Refaim Valley

6. The situation in Mesopotamia is instructive. Successful habitation of the southern part of the region, where pasturage is at a premium, resulted in the decoupling of different sectors of the pastoral economy—sources of fiber being raised at a distance since they are only infrequently 'harvested', while dairy stock and animals used for traction were maintained in the lowland towns. The whole process is a part of the development of transhumant or purely nomadic systems.

(8.3%, 1:7) (Horwitz 1989).[7] It would seem that there is at least some evidence for the principle that the smaller the site the more extensive the exploitation of pig. If site size can be taken as a measure of the intensity of local agricultural effort then Redding's model explains some of the Levantine evidence as well.

2.1.3 *Rural Subsistence Consumable<—>Urban Market Commodity.* For our purposes it is useful to restate Redding's model of the transformation of pastoral production, from pigs and sheep to cattle and goats (see above Intensive Agriculture<—>Domestic Agro-Pastoralism), in terms of the political economy to provide additional insight. Diener and Robkin (1978), like Redding, suggest that pig production is a local subsistence strategy.[8] They, however, argue that household-based swine husbandry is a strategy designed to reduce a producer's engagement with urban markets, centers controlled by the elites. Since consumables generated domestically replace commodities received through redistributive systems, this tactic conserves a household's precious resources of exchange. Further, pigs have low market potential when the animals are raised at rural locations. Thus the ability to engage in swine husbandry is a measure of economic disengagement and perhaps an expression of political independence. While Diener and Robkin use this notion to provide a logic for the Islamic injunction against pork, suggesting that it served elite interests by tightly binding rural communities to urban centers, we only infer that pig husbandry can be used as a measure of the scope of regional integration in the political economy.[9] In this regard, the

7.   A parallel process has been uncovered by Melinda Zeder (1996). In her evaluation of the Early Bronze Age Tel Halif materials she discovered that the abundance of pig remains, while always small, was inversely related to the scale of the site.

8.   Houston (1993) offers a criticism of our argument based on Diener and Robkin's idea. However, as Houston himself admits, he *has not seen* a copy of an unpublished paper in which we developed a preliminary model of our application, but depended on a reprise of it provided by Horwitz (1989). This despite the fact that we did respond to his request and provided him with copies of our published work, a fact he graciously acknowledges. This has led him to portray our position inaccurately. A general point needs to be made. Archaeological interpretation is now so technically complex that it can only be done co-operatively. The best interpretations of the swirl of texts and artifacts that surround archaeology and the Bible will be achieved by joint effort, not by lone investigators exploiting data they incompletely command, a failing applicable to the authors as well!

9.   Houston (1993) observes, following Patai's comments published in conjunction with Diener and Robkin's article (1978), that central authorities do not care what

contrast which Horwitz (1989) notes in pig abundance between the Early Bronze Age and Middle Bronze Age materials in the Refaim Valley sites, and which she relates to this principle, can be seen as a part of a region-wide increase in intensification and integration of agro-pastoral economies. As we will observe, pigs became less visible in the record as the second millennium BCE proceeded, a pattern that continued through the Iron Age with the exceptions noted. Thus we have another pig principle, expressed as the opposition: Rural Subsistence Consumable<—>Urban Market Commodity.

2.1.4 *Initial Strategy<—>Mature Development.* During the Late Bronze and Iron Ages, extensive exploitation of swine is found only rarely in the archaeological record of the Near East. One center of pig use is in southern Anatolia where samples from the town site of Lidar (Kussinger 1988) and the imperial center of Korucutepe (Boessneck and von den Driesch 1975) contain 18% and 13% pig, respectively. In the southern Levant comparison between sites with Middle Bronze Age and Late Bronze Age samples show both declines (Shiloh 3.5–0.2%, Jemmeh 12–0.3 %; Michal 6.3–1.9% [Hellwing *et al.* 1993]) and at least one modest increase, Lachish 3.1–6% (Tchernov and Drori 1983). To the south at Tell Halif, 3% pig was recovered in a sample deposited during a period when the site served as a trade depot and pastoral production emphasized the raising of donkeys for the transport industry (Zeder 1990).

rural producers do as long as they pay their tax/tribute. Therefore they would have no need to prohibit swine husbandry, and in fact could use surplus extracted from peasants to operate their own urban pigsties. The fact that Christians were allowed to continue to raise pigs while they paid even higher taxes is offered as the clincher. This line ignores the point made above that husbandry is an integrated system—the critical issue is the relative costs associated with different forms of 'carnivorous pastoralism', an equation that will have different parameters in contrasting environmental settings. Pork competes with beef only when the exchange value of meat is high enough to cover the value of dairy products. The little archaeozoological information we have about Hellenistic and Roman animal exploitation suggests that pigs were more available in urban markets than rural settings, and that, therefore, this threshold had been broken in some places for some consumers. Grain surpluses extracted as tax/tribute could be more economically spent fattening hogs than in other pursuits. In earlier periods, with the important exceptions to be noted, this does not seem to have been the case. Thus given the nature of the market, it may make economic sense from the perspective of the urban centers to restrict pork production in favor of the capacity to recirculate larger quantities of beef and grain.

Only once (for further data see Hesse 1990) in the subsequent Iron Age (see Figure 1 and Table 1), does swine husbandry expand in the Levant, and that in the earliest phases.[10] At three sites—Ashkelon, Tel Miqne-Ekron, and Tel Batash—the appearance of Philistine material culture is paralleled by increases in the abundance of pig bones.[11] At Ashkelon twelfth–thirteenth century BCE deposits produced 4% pig (1:15) while the twelfth-century samples yielded 19% (1:2); at Tel Miqne-Ekron, mixed pre-Iron Age/Early Iron Age materials contain 8% pig (1:9), while pure Early Iron Age loci produced 18% (2:5); and at Tel Batash Late Bronze Age rates of 5% (1:13) were replaced with 8% (1:8) in the Early Iron Age. This shift to pig husbandry seems to have been brief. By Iron II, at all three sites, pig use had returned to pre-Iron Age levels. Ashkelon is the one site as yet where we have a clear handle on when pig use began to decline. Pigs were important only in the first century of Philistine occupation (the twelfth century BCE). If this pattern is repeated at the other sites, it might be another case of the 'pig principle' that has been proposed by Pam Crabtree (1989). Based on her work in England at a number of sites, she noted that pig raising is a strategy of new arrivals to a region since it provides rapid protein yields. As the agro-pastoral economy matures, in her view, sheep and cattle come to dominate the economy. If appropriate to apply in the Levant as well, it suggests the dichotomy: Initial Strategy<—>Mature Development as a principle governing swine husbandry.

2.1.5 *Low Intensity Agro-Pastoralism<—>High Intensity Agriculture<—>Carnivorous Pastoralism.* We would also elaborate Redding's developmental model that links shifts in the proportions of different

10. The other important examples are Tell el-Amarna in New Kingdom Egypt, discussed below, two Anatolian sites, Korucutepe (Boessneck and von den Driesch 1975), where, in the Late Bronze Age, when the site was a major imperial center, the exploitation of pig reached its highest peak (13%) and at the town Lidar Höyük on the Euphrates where pig bones contribute 18% to the Late Bronze Age sample and 20% to the 600–400 BCE sample (Kussinger 1988). At the site of Isin in southern Mesopotamia, a small sample of 800–700 BCE date containing 14% pig was recovered (Boessneck 1977). See the summary in Hesse (1995).

11. It is not paralleled at one other important Philistine site, Qasile (Davis 1985), though this site may not be quite as early as the other three. The other large Philistine site, Ashdod, produced a very small animal bone sample with a few wild pig remains (Haas 1971). Since animal bones were not systematically collected during excavation, the significance of this record is moot.

stock to agricultural intensification by extending it into even more focused agro-pastoral systems. What Ingold (1980) has called 'carnivorous pastoralism' or ranching—husbandry aimed at meat production—is an inefficient use of stock, if total caloric yield is the measure of success (Cribb 1984). It is, therefore, only when the exchange value of meat is high or the utility of the secondary products of cattle is low, that the costs associated with this mode of production become acceptable in an intensified agro-pastoral setting. Then the economic edge held by cattle declines. At some threshold of meat demand/price, pork husbandry can expand into the market since swine, as well as fowl, provide extremely effective modes of meat production.

Such would appear to be the case in some regions during phases of the Hellenistic, Roman, Byzantine, and Medieval periods. Though our evidence is extremely sketchy and in some cases anecdotal, examples of urban pig consumption in the Levant can be found.[12] Most personal was our experience during the first year of excavation at Ashkelon. Grid 38, the scene of excavations by one of our colleagues in this symposium, Baruch Halpern, found an enormous pit of Hellenistic/Roman date. The bone sample recovered from this feature, while not yet thoroughly studied, clearly contains a very large proportion of pig and, to a lesser extent, chicken. To the north, also on the coast, at Apollonia-Arsuf, a market place dated to the ninth century CE contained rooms with abundances of pig remains (Roll and Ayalon 1987). Pork seems clearly to have circulated in the market system.

Based on textual materials, Urman (1985: 149) suggested that the Golan probably was used for pork production. The Hellenistic material from Tel Anafa in the Upper Galilee tends to confirm that prediction. Redding (n.d.) reports that in the Hellenistic 2C period pigs are almost as plentiful as sheep and goats and in the subsequent Roman occupation half as frequent. We do not have the comparative samples of faunal remains from contemporary rural settlements so we cannot confirm how Hellenistic/Roman production was organized: rural producers for nearby urban markets, or some form of 'urban pastoralism'. However, Byzantine materials from Kanaf (1.8%) and Qazrin (0.2%) (Grantham 1992: 67) indicate that swine husbandry, if it was there before, did not

---

12. Billy Grantham's dissertation (1995) based on the study of the remains from Sephoris opens important vistas into the relationship between class, community, and the organization of pastoral production in the later periods of antiquity, in particular those related to the pig.

persist as a rural practice, at least in those settlements with known Jewish populations. To these results we may add the report on the remains found at Khirbet Sumaqa on Mount Carmel (Horwitz, Tchernov and Dar 1990). This small site, which contains a synagogue with a cluster of workshops and dwellings, produced 0.6% (1 bone) pig (1:715) in the Roman–Byzantine period and between 4% (1:12) and 7.5% pig (1:8) in the Medieval period, an increase the authors explain as the possible result of the settlement of Christians in the region during the later period.

Pig husbandry may be part of complex political and economic systems without hogs actually flowing through market channels. In later periods some pigs are found in garrisons and important nodes in the trade network in arid regions of the Negev and Jordan. Some military locations had to be provisioned and there the raising of swine could be a useful supplemental subsistence tactic (Toplyn n.d.). In the Negev, swine were apparently a significant component of the diet at the towns of Nessana and Tel-Mampsis during the Roman–Byzantine period, a feat perhaps made possible by the extensive water control facilities built at these sedentary sites located at critical junctions in the political and trade networks of the region.

In sum, for these later periods, in the Hellenistic/Roman period pork consumption was high in urban settings, an archaeological observation in keeping with the prominence of pigs and pork in the writings of the classical authors. The question is how and where this demand was met by production—at urban sties or rural satellites? We know only a little about rural pastoral economies and their engagement in swine husbandry from the archaeological record. During the Roman–Byzantine period there was specialized production at town sites in the Negev but the only information we have on rural pork consumption comes from sites with known Jewish populations where it was in fact absent, so we do not know if a rural mode of swine husbandry was in place elsewhere. From the Medieval period we have evidence of substantial urban consumption and at least one example of small-scale rural production.

We can use the model of agricultural intensification as another pig principle: Low Intensity Agro-Pastoralism<—>High Intensity Agriculture<—>Carnivorous Pastoralism, with pigs emphasized in the husbandry systems at either end of the transformation. However, the degree of agricultural intensity needed to set this process of change in motion and the exact sequences of intermediate strategies and herd mixes that lead from one end to the other are as yet unclear. We suspect that this transformative pattern underlies the course of the macro-regional story of pig production from the Bronze Age to the Byzantine period.

2.2 *Social Identity*

As mentioned above, in the few rural samples from Byzantine and Medieval sites, we have some suggestion that Jewish and Christian social identities may account for the zooarchaeological patterns. This perhaps unsurprising result is important nevertheless, because it demonstrates that social identity expressed in dietary laws regarding the pig is archaeologically recoverable. The question is how far into the past social divisions of this type may be retrojected and under what conditions they are being expressed.

2.2.1 *Ritual<—>Secular.* Much of our picture of pig husbandry may be masked or distorted by the usual practice of reporting animal bone statistics on a site by site basis. When within-site variation is explored some significant differences appear. Early evidence of this is found in both Old Kingdom Egypt and Early Dynastic southern Mesopotamia. At Elephantine on the Nile, roughly contemporary deposits from four sectors of the site produced pig abundances ranging from less than 1% to 14% (Hollmann 1990). Significantly, those samples from the Satet Temple contained very low proportions, a pattern that continued at least into New Kingdom times. On the other side of our region, at Early Dynastic Lagash in southern Mesopotamia, the amount of pig in the administrative residence (16%) sharply exceeds that found in the temple (8%) (Mudar 1982).

Closer to home, at Tell el-Hayyat the proportion of pig remains found in a series of Middle Bronze Age temples was significantly less than that found in the surrounding 'secular' parts of the site (Mary Metzger, pers. comm.). To these negative associations of pigs with ritual contexts, we can contrast the few pig bones found in two Middle Bronze Age tombs at Sasa (Horwitz 1987). We should remark on several widely cited examples of association of pigs with sacred contexts that are not as well documented. De Vaux (1972) wrote extensively on cultic pig use in the eastern Mediterranean, no doubt spurred on by his discovery of pig bones at Tell Far'ah North (Tirzah). In a subterranean structure of the Middle Bronze II period, which he called a sanctuary, bones of young pig were found against one wall and fetal remains were recovered from a jar. Regarding the structure itself, Fowler (1981) effectively refutes an interpretation of it as a locus of cultic activity. At best the evidence is equivocal. De Vaux (1958) also cites evidence from Macalister (1912: 378-79) that pig remains were found in a subterranean cultic situation at Gezer. In the absence of a specialist's report it is impossible to comment on these bone identifications. The same cannot be said for the 'pig bones' reported in Iron Age (tenth century BCE) cultic associations at Megiddo (Locus 2081) and Taanach. We examined these caches in 1984 and they contain no pig remains at all (Hesse 1990).

It is significant that articulated skeletons of pigs have almost never been recovered, as occasionally is found with other domestic and wild stock. The partially dismembered axial skeleton of a pig was found at Hazor on the citadel in a context dated to the second half of the eighth century BCE but there is no reason to suppose a cultic association (Angress 1956). Thus, the recent report of a pig skeleton found outside a Late Bronze Age temple at Beth Shean is particularly interesting (Amihai Mazar, pers. comm. and this volume).

All remaining evidence for cultic use of pigs in conjunction with the worship of a variety of ancient Near Eastern and Egyptian deities is textual (see reviews by Houston [1993] and Milgrom [1991], who emphasizes the Hittite data). The bulk of the behavioral evidence suggests that pigs were a 'secular' animal with only hints of religious associations, expressed here as the pig principle: Secular<—>Cultic.

2.2.2 *Class<—>Class*. Howard Hecker (1982, 1984), in his review of pig use in Egypt and study of the fauna from Tell el-Amarna, demonstrated that the use of the animal in this New Kingdom site was associated with a sector of the site occupied by what he describes as 'workers'. Further he linked the general absence throughout Egyptian history of references to pigs in the texts and of pig imagery in the art to the association of the animal with social classes of low standing, a message also delivered by Herodotus (2.47) in those passages which are descriptive of life along the Nile in the middle of the first millennium BCE.

In the Levant, zooarchaeological evidence of this relationship may be present in some unpublished samples that we have examined. At Tell Jemmeh, the sharp drop in pig bones between Middle Bronze Age materials and those from the Late Bronze Age parallels a shift from a recovery context of household debris in the earlier period to one of an elite residence in the latter (Wapnish 1993). Further reflections of this distinction are present in the preliminary analyses of the Philistine materials from Tel Miqne-Ekron. At Miqne-Ekron pig remains seem much more common in Fields I and III, located along the city wall, than in Field IV, identified as an elite sector (Dothan and Gitin 1990). On this, admittedly slim evidence, we suggest that a final pig principle may be expressed as the opposition: Class<—>Class.[13]

2.3 *Summary*

Our review of the archaeological record relating to the pig uncovered eight 'pig principles'—dichotomies and continua in ancient behaviors and attitudes that structured the exploitation of swine. These principles were expressed in a region-wide historical trend in swine use that saw a steady decline from Early Bronze Age times to the Iron Age with only occasional incidences of intensive exploitation of the animal in the last half of that period. Only with the advent of Hellenistic occupations does pig use return to levels seen in the third millennium BCE. It is evident that there is no clear singular relationship that ties either pig bone abundance or its absence to social identity that we can use as a marker, because other factors can produce similar effects. The next step is to see how these principles affect our search for and understanding of ancient social identities. But what manner of social identity are we talking about?

3. *Anthropological Perspectives on Ethnicity*

The concepts labeled by such terms as 'culture' and 'ethnicity' have been radically reworked in current social scientific thought.[14] This revision has

---

13. Houston's (1993: 169-70) use of the absence of pig remains to establish his supposition that class was responsible for the absence of pig in the diet of the 'elite' at Lachish and in that of artisans in Jerusalem is an example of the complexity of the problem, particularly when working with negative evidence. His argument is circular since it takes the fact that the elite ate beef to prove that they didn't want to eat pork, without demonstrating that market-focused swine husbandry would have been an economically viable alternative in these communities—it all comes down to the decision by the elite as to the best allocation of the surplus that they extract. The absence could be explained by alternative means: by the pig principles related to the environment, the economy of pastoralism, or political control. His notion that 'cultural factors' are more powerful conditioners of cuisine in metropolitan as opposed to rural settings suggests an independence of ideology from material factors that remains to be demonstrated. On the other hand, his notion that the foodways of the poor may be a response to those of the elite might be understood in terms of the use of culinary symbols to effect social promotion, a principle widely documented, as for instance in India.

14. The most up-to-date surveys of the diverse concepts relating to ethnicity as

profound implications for the employment of archaeological data. Cultures and ethnic groups are no longer seen as bounded objective entities whose reality can be taken for granted, but dynamic sets of relations constantly being produced through social structure and practice (Barth 1989). Two questions are paramount: can this new theoretical paradigm incorporate archaeological evidence, and, if so, how?

It is first reasonable to ask whether the modern discourse on ethnicity has relevance to our ancient subject. As Wolf (1982: 381) observes, in the modern world 'ethnic categories express the ways that particular populations come to relate themselves to given segments of the labor market... They are historical products of labor market segmentation under the capitalist mode.' Since that mode of production was absent from ancient Near Eastern political economies, perhaps ethnicity was also. It is our view, however, that while ethnicity has a particular expression generated by the emergence of the working class in the modern era, as a concept that merges social interaction, historical contingency, and world view into a strategy of social identity, it can be generalized to apply in settings dominated by tributary and kin-based modes of production (see the discussion in Friedman 1990). We will emphasize these more widely applicable elements of the modern discussion.

3.1 *Primordial Ethnicity*
Near Eastern archaeologists use what can be labeled the 'primordial' concept of ethnicity, wherein groups are defined by their material/ behavioral content, that is, the symbols and material culture items that serve to reify social entities whose existence is assumed *a priori*. This approach has roots in the 'culture area' idea and diffusionist theories that emerged in the first decades of this century and were used to write 'culture histories' (Trigger 1989). Cultures were defined by overlapping spatial distributions of material culture items. The resultant empirically and inductively generated patterns were understood to be social identities that could be manipulated in historical reconstructions (Kelly and Kelly 1980). Today this approach is criticized for its unreflexive and disintegrative nature. As Wolf (1982: 6) puts it, 'By endowing nations, societies, or cultures with the qualities of internally homogeneous and

they have emerged in social science during the past 30 years can be found in Comaroff and Comaroff (1992) and Eriksen (1993). Their work has served as primary sources in our brief abstract of the issues involved and has informed the methodology we propose.

externally distinctive and bounded objects, we create a model of the world as a global pool hall in which the entities spin off each other like so many hard and round billiard balls'. Further, the primordial approach created social reality and cohesion that on the one hand was thought to be separate from the observer's vision, though in fact it was created by the observer's categories, and on the other, was not necessarily coincident with the native version. The primordial approach survives in modified form in those versions of the 'new archaeology' which eschew concern with systems of meaning and emphasize behavioral systems and their relationship to energy flows.

The hunt for the Israelites of antiquity has existed since the inception of biblical archaeology. Therefore, it is worth reflecting briefly on why scholars now are calling this task a search for an 'Israelite ethnicity' instead of continuing to reference social identity with such well-established terms as 'tribe', 'culture', or 'nation'. We are drawn to this question because, in fact, the analytic emphasis on ethnic identity as opposed to other social identities, and the institutional growth in ethnic studies in the social sciences, is only about 30 years old. There this new emphasis has emerged as a by-product of the reevaluation of such comfortable concepts as social distance, scientific objectivity, and the authority of the ethnographer. This critical task resulted in the demolition of easy confidence in the assumed normalcy as to the boundedness and fixity of social groups. It came to be recognized that what had been described as isolated, independent lifeways—the 'primitive', the 'other', representatives of simpler systems or stages, the usual subjects of ethnographic investigation—were in fact societies powerfully shaped by their unavoidable submergence in regional, and even global, systems of power. What used to be called 'tribes' became 'ethnic groups', a terminological distinction that reflected the new view of human groups as interwoven and interconnected, as products of modern conditions not relics of past evolutionary stages. Further, this intellectual process was encouraged, as Friedman (1989) points out, by the crumbling confidence in modernity expressed in and out of academia. Where modernization was once expected to eliminate sub-national divisions as a by-product of the expansion of rationality and individualism, now ethnicity has been newly mobilized to mediate valid structures on which to build political legitimacy (Kedourie 1988). Given these currents, it is no wonder that the classical concept of an 'ethnos' underwent profound transformation into that of an 'ethnicity'.

One obvious reason that the term 'ethnicity' has come to the fore in Near Eastern archaeology is that the term carries powerful connotations of self-awareness. The biblical accounts about the nature of early Israel's social and political identity have been subjected to widely divergent interpretations. In the absence of a contemporary textual record that could 'resolve' historical claims regarding the emergence of Israel as 'tribes', 'league', 'people', 'nation', etc., some source of material evidence of a self-constructed social identity is desperately sought.[15] After all, nobody is interested in a bunch of Israelites who didn't know they were Israelites.

The danger is that biblical archaeologists see as unproblematic the relationship between the distributions they discover and the meanings they understand to be implicit in those items and their dispersal. Meaning, in this view, simply *is*, rather than being constructed, negotiated, and ongoing within a structure of social relations, a process referred to as praxis. But there is a problem here with the equation of material pattern and social identity, which is empirically reflected in cautionary tales in the ethnographic record of adjacent ethnic groups with indistinguishable material cultures and behaviors (Hodder 1991, Eriksen 1993: 11).[16] Given these newer theories about the dynamics of culture, group identity, and the nature of meaning, it is clear that the assumption of a reliable link between material culture pattern and a group's self-awareness has been broken. If biblical archaeologists continue to pursue the primordial approach, no matter how elegant or nuanced the distribution maps of cultural traits they draw, there is a real risk that a great amount of effort will be devoted to the pursuit of an 'ethnicity' concept that does not contain the ideological connotations that they expect it to hold.

15. McGuire (1982) discusses the straightforward situation in which contemporary records establish the self-awareness of ethnic groups. Thus the methodology which he proposes is largely inapplicable to our problem.

16. Eriksen (1993: 11) makes this clear using the research of Moerman (1965), who worked in Thailand with the Lue. Moerman's 'problem...concerned the boundaries of the group. "Since language, culture, political organization, etc., do not correlate completely, the units delimited by one criterion do not coincide with the units delimited by another" (Moerman 1965: 1215)...Moerman was forced to conclude that "[s]omeone is Lue is by virtue of believing and calling himself Lue and acting in ways that validate his Lueness" (Moerman 1965: 1219). Being unable to argue that this Lueness can be defined with reference to objective cultural features or clear-cut boundaries, Moerman defines it as *an emic category of ascription*'.

This difficulty underlies much of the debate over 'ethnic index fossils'. As each candidate is proposed, contrary examples found outside the 'right' area are brought forward to confound the item's or attribute's utility as a marker of identity. This evidence is then used to deny the existence of the purported ethnic group in the first place. Since material culture is not linked to social identity in this straightforward way, neither argument nor counterargument are couched in the vocabulary necessary to discern a social identity. The problem is the quintessential one of archaeology as a human science, that of, as Mark Leone (1982) put it, 'recovering mind'.

The only solution to the problem of inferring past systems of meaning from ancient material objects that is currently on the table for archaeologists to consider is to, as Hodder (1991) puts it, begin to consider the ancient record a 'text'—to get inside the symbolic, meaningful world of ancient groups through the fullest appreciation of their context (a direction Dever [1993] points to in his insistence on utilizing the widest range of artifactual categories in the exploration of ancient Israelite origins). Hodder (1989) makes an important point about the relationship of material culture to meaning that is relevant in our discussion. He observes that material culture symbols are not as arbitrary as linguistic ones. The properties of items constrain the meanings that they can bear. Therefore the discussion of pig principles developed above is important since it provides the meaningful context of behavior in which the pig developed its salience in regard to social identity.

So what is the modern understanding of 'ethnicity?' Multiple perspectives have emerged, each more or less in concert with a main theme of social science theory. For our purposes we have simplified the arguments into three aspects which we label: Boundary and Hierarchy, Strategy and Contingency, and Ontology and Values. Each of these, we believe, provide useful insight for understanding and employing the pig bone evidence presented above.

3.2 Boundary and Hierarchy

The essential feature of the boundary and hierarchy component of ethnicity is its insistence that ethnic groups emerge from social interaction through the erection and maintenance of social boundaries (Barth 1969; see also Royce 1982 and Eriksen 1993: 58) rather than arising from the mere existence of objective cultural differences. These distinctions tend to form nested structures of identity rather than horizontal divisions of the social landscape. Ethnicities are created rather than expressed and exist only in larger and engulfing systems of social and political relations. This overarching structure in which distinctions emerge may be ideologically egalitarian, in which case John and Jean Comaroff (1992) suggest that the expressed social identity then be labeled 'totemic' rather than 'ethnic', a term they reserve for systems with hierarchical relations. Brackette Williams (1989) goes further, emphasizing the embeddedness of ethnic relations in state-organized polities and the interpenetration of ethnicity with class. For our purposes, the key point is that, even if they are expressed in terms of kinship and descent, ethnic groups are interwoven with political and economic structures. The shared interests of the members in these material spheres of power and resources are foundational in motivating identity. More crudely put for our archaeological purposes, if ethnicity is tied to self-interest, its expression will be deployed by political and economic factors that may condition symbolic content.

Despite the pristine meaning of the Greek *ethnos* as 'nation' (Connor 1994: 100-101), it is important to note that modern concepts of ethnicity are not the same as an ideology of nationhood. The people bearing ethnic identities do not occupy a distinct territory, though attachment to a location may be important to the ideology of the group. Nations are territorial states though much of the supporting ideology that binds people to ethnic groups also fosters loyalty to a nation. In the ideology of either, each may be ancestral to the other. From an archaeological perspective, this further reinforces the point made above that clear-cut macroregional patterns of material culture are unlikely to delineate ethnic groups. Our expectation is that material refractions of ethnic relations should be a complex mosaic of interleaved symbols. Since nations that encompass a single ethnic group are virtually unknown in the present and probably were anomalies in the past (Connor 1994),[17] regionally bounded symbolic clusters are unlikely there as well. Only under political and economic conditions which strictly limit the production and distribution of certain items, like sumptuary laws, will presence/absence patterns of material culture dispersal define nations. Large geographical patterns, particularly of items closely related to subsistence, like animal remains, are often the result of ecological constraints on the means and modes of production rather than reflections of ideological values or

17. Cohen (1990) discusses the multiplicity of ethnic groups in Hellenistic Palestine and the complex links between land and Jews. His discussion demonstrates well the embeddedness of ethnic identities in larger social categories, the multiple shapes of their expression, and the historical contingency of their appearance.

social structures. Distributions crossing environmental zones are more susceptible to interpretation in cultural terms.

3.3 *Strategy and Contingency*

The second perspective on ethnicity emphasizes how it is constructed through social activity—what can be termed praxis or hegemony (see, in particular, the review of Comaroff and Comaroff 1992). This view parallels newer understandings of culture as discourse rather than as the expression of norms, a denial of culture as object (Eriksen 1993). Observed culture is the product of myriad human decisions to think and act, all of which are constrained by the thoughts and actions of others. This very historical idea makes ethnicity a dynamic concept. People manipulate and are in turn manipulated by symbols in producing ethnicity, which results in a constantly shifting language of interaction. The case of the Huron in Canada is instructive (Roosens 1989, in Eriksen 1993: 70-71). The modern presentation of Huron history by the group's leaders bears little resemblance to the documentary record. It is instead, a:

> ...reinterpretation of history in order to create collective identity and political cohesion...This 'culture'...is composed of elements which conform to widespread positive stereotypes of Indians in Euro-Canadian society. The Indians are depicted as being close to nature and full of respect for plants and animals; they are spontaneously hospitable, extremely honest, incorruptible and have great personal integrity; they are tolerant and mild mannered, and are open-minded in respect to foreign cultures. In brief, 'Indian culture' is depicted as superior to the 'white' one in a number of regards.

This despite the fact that the Huron were important intermediaries in the violent development of the fur trade in North America. The implication for archaeology is that the set of symbols exercised by an ethnic group may shift radically and rapidly as circumstances dictate and may have uncertain ties to historical 'fact'. Because ethnic identities are hierarchically structured, the production of ethnicity is shaped by strategies of social mobility and 'getting on' in the world. Germane to our topic is the fact that the adoption of the culinary customs of higher-ranking social identities is one mechanism groups have employed to enhance their social position.

3.4 *Ontology and Values*

The third perspective on ethnicity involves the concept of 'ontology' as developed by Kapferer (1989). He argues that underlying social identity is a deep conceptual structure—basic ideas about the nature of the world and the way things ought to be—which are abstract and not shaped by material processes. When energized by symbols, these ontologies are converted to ideologies and serve as the charter for action. For this to happen, the selected symbols must resonate with some aspect of the deep structure, even when the ontology is only dimly perceived. This is why, Kapferer concludes, leaders are able to activate powerful responses from ethnic groups, though they themselves are not completely trusted or respected. The ontological perspective is useful to us because it provides access to the cosmological, ethical, and theological investigations of Israelite symbolism that have taken as their point of departure (and arrival) the biblical text.

4. *Discussion*

All three perspectives on ethnicity have relevance for our investigation of pig remains through time. The 'boundary and hierarchy' perspective insists that ethnicity is a product of social interaction. Such features as class, neighborhood, household, and community are relevant The 'strategy and contingency' perspective focuses our attention on the negotiated nature of ethnic relations—how symbolic content and significance are shaped by shifting actualities/modes of production. The ontology and values perspective provides access to the process of symbol selection. All three of these poles of interest interact with one another.

When we looked at the behavioral data associated with pig remains we discovered that several principles provided an underlying matrix of oppositions in which the animal can be said to have been understood from our archaeological perspective—that is, based on the idea that the context of an item of material culture constrains the way it can be used symbolically. The most resilient positive themes included the behavioral connotations of rural, moist, settled, household production, and secular, notions which were widespread among the peoples of the entire region. However, at various moments and places the pig also reflected the production schemes of new arrivals, the diet of the working class, and urban cuisine. These meanings were arrayed against an agro-pastoral system that was also experiencing large-scale swings in intensification. These oscillations conditioned the salience of pigs as potential symbols in the negotiation of social identity. Pigs were husbanded extensively only at the opposite ends of the cycle of intensification. Therefore, while their symbolic meaning might have been widely understood, their potency in interaction only occurred irregularly.

Three historical patterns of swine husbandry emerge in the zoo-archaeological data, though it must be emphasized that our samples are neither extensive nor do they cover all periods equally; the relative absence of information about the Late Bronze Age is particularly difficult. The first period is characterized by rural exploitation of the pig and dates to the Middle Bronze Age; the second, urban utilization in the early part of the Iron I period in sites with Philistine material culture; and third, urban use beginning in the Hellenistic period and continuing through the Medieval period.

From the foregoing discussion, it is clear that no human behavioral evidence exists to indicate that pig avoidance was unique to any particular group in the ancient Near East. The fact that complex variables affect the choice to raise swine have confounded attempts to find an origin to the pig prohibition. Lots of people, for lots of reasons, were not eating pork. The bald fact is that there is no date before the Hellenistic period when we can assert with any confidence, based on archaeological and textual evidence, that the religious injunction which enjoined Jews from eating pork was actually followed by them alone as a measure of social distinction. This does not mean that the behavior was not part of the material culture of the Israelites, only that it did not have a context in which it could sharply define a social boundary. This frustrates efforts to set either the onset of the Israelite behavior or, at the very least, a pre-Hellenistic manifestation of it in a specific time frame, forcing research into the origins of the prohibition to be carried out in the absence of a known contextual background.

Outside of the dietary laws in Leviticus and Deuteronomy, the dates for which are widely disputed and range from the mid-eighth century to the fifth/fourth centuries BCE of the postexilic period, two key biblical passages have led many biblical commentators to assume that a community-wide pig prohibition was operative by the postexilic period. Isa. 65.3-5 and Isa. 66.17 both speak of defilement brought about by the eating of swine, among other abominable foods and practices. These texts, however, reflect cultic circumstances and although pigs may have been forbidden at the altar it does not mean it was a generally forbidden food. In the deuterocanonical literature of the Persian period and later, two passages in the story of Judith (11.12 and 12.2) indicate that a non-ritual set of food rules was in place, although no single food is specifically mentioned. Taken together, it would be logical to assume from the Isaiah and Judith passages, and the actual dietary legislation, that Jews were not eating pigs for religious reasons by the postexilic period. Unfortunately, no independent evidence confirms such actual behavior. More important for our purposes in establishing an oppositional reference for Jewish pig avoidance was the fact that most other social groups in the region did not eat pork either.

This situation changes in the Hellenistic period. The famous episodes of defiance to the Syrian king Antiochus IV in the books of Maccabees (1 Macc. 1.47, 1.63; 2 Macc. 6.18-31, 7.1-42) not only portray the pig as a defiling and forbidden animal, in cultic and noncultic situations, for priest and lay person alike, but clearly distinguish it as a food opposing Jew and pagan which both parties recognize. In a perfect world we would have a complete record of archaeological evidence for these two behaviors. Unfortunately the archaeological record confirms only that urban pagans were eating pigs in the Hellenistic period, not that Jews were abstaining from it. That sort of evidence does not emerge until the Roman–Byzantine period. But what makes even this half-a-record significant is the enormous numbers of pigs that were being eaten in (Late) Hellenistic times in such cities as Ashkelon and Anafa, and the fact that a meat market for pigs came on line after an extremely long hiatus (about 700 years) of minimal use.

The rules governing purity and impurity in Israelite society which contain the dietary legislation have recently been subjected to a number of detailed analyses. Naturally, the pig comes in for a good deal of discussion. The most comprehensive treatments by Hübner (1989), Eilberg-Schwartz (1986–87, 1990), Firmage (1990), Milgrom (1991), and Houston (1993) perpetuate the centuries-old dichotomy of two diametrically opposed rationales that guide research into what was fit to eat and what was not. Either the legislation, for whatever reason, established an *a priori* set of criteria governing which foods to eat and which to avoid, or, and this is especially true in the case of the pig, the legislation encoded what had been an already common food avoidance. For advocates of the latter theory, split hooves and cud-chewing were *a posteriori* criteria induced from foods traditionally eaten. But this only pushes the question back a mere step. We know that just about everyone in the region ate sheep, goats and cattle, but can we assume that no proto-Israelites lurked among the pig-eaters of the Middle Bronze Age? On this point all recent expositions come to grief. Even the most sophisticated and comprehensive treatment presented by Houston (1993) operates under the notion of an Israelite pastoral background, one assumed to disdain pig. But pastoral nomadism as the core lifestyle of proto-Israel is by no means assured. The debate over whether the material culture found in the central highlands in the early Iron Age admits of no other explanation than roots in a pastoral tradition is fierce. Indeed, increasing archaeological evidence suggests that Israelite origins were diverse, the only commonality among the various elements probably being a position on the fringes of Bronze Age society (see especially Gottwald 1979 and more recently Dever 1993). Thus the argument that a single traditional foodway lies at the root of the Israelite pig prohibition may be moot.

If, as Dever has recently commented, 'the earliest Israelites seem to have derived from displaced elements of Late Bronze Age Canaanite society—a motley assortment of urban refugees, 'Apiru-like "social bandits", subsistence farmers, small-scale stock breeders, no doubt some pastoral nomads, and adventurers of one sort or another' (1993: 25), the various pig principles suggest that swine were a visceral part of the behavioral and symbolic environments of even so diverse a social matrix. Since this environment generated widespread pig avoidance, the unremarkable nature of this foodway made it an unlikely candidate for establishing a boundary with any specific group, save, perhaps, for the Philistines. But, given the facts that Philistine pig use was both short-lived and associated with nonelites, it would have been a very ephemeral boundary at best. However, the fact that pig disdain did not measure a sharp social boundary does not mean that it was not a shared cultural value within an emerging Israel, one that probably had multiple roots. At a later date this value was mobilized as a boundary-producing mechanism to establish distance and distinction from other groups.

This reflects the situation in the Hellenistic period. The mode of pastoral production had shifted to incorporate extensive consumption of pig in urban settings, a novel development, at least for Palestine. In this context pig avoidance could achieve salience as a boundary marker. Coupled with the complex intermingling of social identities documented for this period (Cohen 1990), pig avoidance marked nothing less than being a Jew, in a social landscape filled with a bewildering array of ideological, national, and social challenges to identity.

To answer our question: Can pig bones be used in ethnic diagnosis?— the answer is yes, but not on a straightforward presence/absence basis.

For each context, that is for each site, the presence or absence of pig bones must be evaluated in terms of the numerous pig principles before the bones will admit to a positive measure of social identity. It is not enough to show that people did not consume pork and disdained pig, as a part of their lifestyle. It has to be demonstrated how those acts were integrated into the social life of the actors as they engaged the larger community in which they lived.

5. *Acknowledgments*

We would like to express our appreciation to the Philip and Muriel Berman Center for Jewish Studies for the invitation to participate in this conference and the support provided by the Center which made our visit possible. Many of the archaeological data reported were collected under a grant to the authors from the National Science Foundation (BNS-8907369) and fellowships from the National Endowment for the Humanities that allowed us to spend a year at the Albright Institute of Archaeological Research in Jerusalem. We would also like to express our appreciation to the many dig directors—Avraham Biran, Trude Dothan, Seymour Gitin, Amihai Mazar, Lawrence Stager, Gus Van Beek, and Sam Wolff, who made materials available for us to study and provided financial support for the work. Joachim Boessneck, Billy Grantham, Susan Henson, Liora Kolska Horwitz, Mary Metzger, Richard Redding, Michael Toplyn, and Melinda Zeder sent us copies of their unpublished manuscripts, information that was invaluable to our project. Donna Cobb prepared Figure 1. Several colleagues on the electronic super-highway came through in the pinch when we lost a bibliographic reference. We offer special thanks to our colleague at the University of Alabama at Birmingham, Thomas McKenna, who guided us in our exploration of the literature on ethnicity and critically reviewed our effort at summation of the issues involved. We, of course, are responsible for any errors of fact or interpretation that remain.

BIBLIOGRAPHY

Angress, S.
1956   'The Pig Skeleton from Area B', in Y. Yadin *et al.* (eds.), *Hazor II* (Jerusalem: Magnes Press): 166-72.

Barth, F.
1969   *Ethnic Groups and Boundaries: the Social Organization of Cultural Difference* (Scandinavian University Press: Oslo).

1989 'The Analysis of Culture in Complex Societies', *Ethnos*, 543.4: 120-42.

Bilde, P. *et al.*
1990 *Religion and Religious Practice in ther Seleucid Kingdom* (Aarhus: Aarhus University Press).

Boessneck, J.
1977 'Tierknochenfunde aus Išān Barḥryāt (Isin)', in B. Hrouda, *Isin-Išan Barḥrīyāt*, I (Munich: Bayerische Akademie der Wissenschaften): 111-33.

Boessneck, J., and A. von den Driesch
1975 Tierknochenfunde vom Korucutepe bei Elâziğ in Ostanatolien, in M.N. Van Loon (ed.), *Korucutepe I* (New York: American Elsevier): 1-220.

Clutton-Brock, J.
1971 'The Primary Food Animals of the Jericho Tell from the Proto-Neolithic to the Byzantine Period', *Levant 3*: 41-55.
1979 'The Mammalian Remains from the Jericho Tell', *Proceedings of the Prehistoric Society* 45: 135-57.

Cohen, S.J.D.
1990 'Religion, Ethnicity, and "Hellenism" in the Emergence of Jewish Identity in Maccabean Palestine', in P. Bilde *et al.* 1990: 204-23.

Comaroff, John, and Jean Comaroff
1992 'Of Totemism and Ethnicity', in J. Comaroff and J. Comaroff (eds.), *Ethnography and the Historical Imagination* (Boulder, CO: Westview Press): 49-67.

Connor, W.
1994 *Ethnonationalism: The Quest for Understanding* (Princeton, NJ: Princeton University Press).

Crabtree, P.J.
1989 'Sheep, Horses, Swine and Kine: A Zooarchaeological Perspective on the Anglo-Saxon Settlement of England', *Journal of Field Archaeology* 16.2: 205-213.

Cribb, R.
1984 'Computer Simulation of Herding Systems as an Interpretive and Heuristic Device in the Study of Kill-off Strategies', in J. Clutton-Brock and C. Grigson (eds.), *Animals and Archaeology. III. Early Herders and their Flocks* (BAR International Series, 202; Oxford: British Archaeological Reports): 161-70.

Davis, S.J.M.
1985 'The Large Mammal Bones', in A. Mazar (ed.), *Excavations at Tell Qasile II. The Philistine Sanctuary: Various Finds, The Pottery, Conclusions, Appendixes*, Appendix 5, Qedem 20 (Jerusalem: The Hebrew University): 148-50.

Dever, W.G.
1993 'Cultural Continuity, Ethnicity in the Archaeological Record and the Question of Israelite Origins', *Eretz Israel* 24: 22*-33*.

Diener, P., and E.E. Robkin
    1978   'Ecology, Evolution and the Search for Cultural Origins: The Ques-
                tion of Islamic Pig Prohibition', *Current Anthropology* 19: 493-540.
Dothan, T., and S. Gitin
    1990   'Ekron of the Philistines: How They Lived, Worked and Worshiped for
                Five Hundred Years', *BARev* 16.1: 21-36.
Eilberg-Schwartz, H.
    1986–87   'Creation and Classification', *Harvard Review* 26: 357-81.
    1990   *The Savage in Judaism* (Bloomington, IN: Indiana University Press).
Eriksen, T.H.
    1993   *Ethnicity and Nationalism: Anthropological Perspectives* (London:
                Pluto Press).
Firmage, E.B.
    1990   'The Biblical Dietary Laws and the Concept of Holiness', in
                J.A. Emerton (ed.), *Studies in the Pentateuch* (VTSup, 41; Leiden:
                Brill): 177-208.
Flannery, K.V.
    1983   'Early Pig Domestication in the Fertile Crescent: A Retrospective
                Look', in T.C. Young Jr, P.E.L. Smith and P. Mortensen (eds.), *The
                Hilly Flanks: Essays on the Prehistory of Southwestern Asia, Studies in
                Ancient Oriental Civilization* 36 (Chicago: The Oriental Institute of the
                University of Chicago): 163-88.
Fowler, M.D.
    1981   'Cultic Community at Tirzah? A Re-examination of the Archaeo-
                logical Evidence', *PEQ* 113.1: 27-31.
Friedman, J.
    1989   'Culture, Identity and World Process', in D. Miller, M. Rowlands and
                C. Tilley (eds.), *Domination and Resistance* (London: Unwin Hyman):
                246-60.
    1990   'Notes on Culture and Identity in Imperial Worlds', in Bilde, *et al.*:
                14-39.
Goody, J.
    1976   *Production and Reproduction* (Cambridge: Cambridge University
                Press).
Gottwald, N.K.
    1979   *The Tribes of Yahweh* (Maryknoll, NY: Orbis Books).
Grantham, B.J.
    1992   *Modern Buqata and Ancient Qasrin: The Ethnoarchaeology of Cuisine
                in the Golan Heights* (MA thesis; Department of Anthropology,
                University of Alabama).
    1996   'Sepphoris: Ethnic Complexity at an Ancient Galilean City' (PhD dis-
                sertation, Northwestern University).
Grigson, C.
    1987   'Shiqmim: Pastoralism and Other Aspects of Animal Management in
                the Chalcolithic of the Northern Negev', *Shiqmin I*, Part (i), BAR
                International Series 356(i) (ed. T.E. Levy; British Archaeological
                Reports: Oxford): 219-41.

Groves, C.
  1981   *Ancestors for the Pigs: Taxonomy and Phylogeny of the Genus Sus*.
            Technical Bulletin No. 3 (Canberra: Department of Prehistory,
            Research School of Pacific Studies, Australian National University.
            Australian National University Press).

Haas, N.
  1971   'Anthropological Observations on the Skeletal Remains from in Area
            D (1962–1963)', in M. Dothan (ed.), *Ashdod II-III, Atiqot 9-10*
            (Jerusalem: Department of Antiquities): 212-13.

Harris, M.
  1974   'Pig Lovers and Pig Haters', in M. Harris (ed.), *Cows, Pigs, Wars and
            Witches: The Riddles of Culture* (New York: Random House): 35-60.

  1985   'The Abominable Pig', in M. Harris (ed.), *Good to Eat: Riddles of
            Food and Culture* (New York: Simon and Schuster): 67-87.

Hecker, H.
  1982   'A Zooarchaeological Inquiry into Pork Consumption in Egypt from
            Predynastic to New Kingdom Times', *Journal of the American
            Research Center in Egypt* 19: 59-69.

  1984   'Preliminary Report on the Faunal Remains from the Workmen's
            Village', in B.J. Kemp (ed.), *Amarna Reports I* (London: The Egypt
            Exploration Society): 154-64.

Hellwing, S., and N. Feig
  1989   'Animal Bones', in Z. Herzog, G. Rapp and O. Negbi (eds.),
            Excavations at Tel Michal, Israel (Minneapolis: University of
            Minnesota Press): 236-48.

Hellwing, S., and R. Gophna
  1984   'The Animal Remains from the Early and Middle Bronze Age at Tel
            Aphek and Tel Dalit: A Comparative Study', *Tel Aviv* 11: 48-59.

Hellwing, S., M. Sade, and V. Kishon
  1993   'Faunal Remains', in I. Finkelstein, S. Bunimovitz and Z. Lederman
            (eds.), *Shiloh: The Archaeology of a Biblical Site* (Monograph Series
            of the Institute of Archaeology; Tel Aviv: Tel Aviv University): 309-
            350.

Herodotus
  1935   The History of Herodotus of Halicarnassus (London: Nonesuch Press).

Hess, R.S.
  1993   'Early Israel in Canaan: A Survey of Recent Evidence and
            Interpretations', *PEQ* 125 (July–December): 125-42.

Hesse, B.
  1990   'Pig Lovers and Pig Haters: Patterns of Palestinian Pork Production',
            Journal of Ethnobiology 10.2: 195-225.

  1995   'Husbandry, Dietary Taboos, and the Bones of the Ancient Near East;
            Zooarchaeology in a Post-processual World', in D.B. Small (ed.),
            *Methods in the Mediterranean: Historical and Archaeological Views
            on Texts and Archaeology* (Leiden: Brill): 197-232.

Hesse, B., and A. Rosen
  1988   'The Detection of Chronological Mixing in Samples from Stratified
            Archaeological Sites', in R.E. Webb (ed.), *Recent Development in*

Environmental Analysis in Old and New World Archaeology (BAR International Series, 416; Oxford: British Archaeological Reports): 117-30.

Hesse, B., and P. Wapnish
1985   *Animal Bone Archeology* (Washington, DC: Taraxacum).

Hodder, I.
1989   'This Is Not an Article about Material Culture as Text', *Journal of Anthropological Archaeology* 8.3: 250-69.
1991   *Reading the Past: Current Approaches to Interpretation in Archaeology* (2nd edn; Cambridge: Cambridge University Press).

Hollmann, A.
1990   *Säugetierknochenfunde aus Elephantine in Oberägypten (8. bis 16. Grabungskampagne, 1978–1987)* (Inaugural dissertation; Munich: Ludwig-Maximilians-Universität).

Horwitz, L.K.
1986/7   'Faunal Remains from the Early Iron Age Site on Mount Ebal', *Tel Aviv* 13/14: 173-98.
1987   'Animal Offerings from Two MBA tombs', *IEJ* 37: 251-55.
1989   'Diachronic Changes in Rural Husbandry Practices in Bronze Age Settlements from the Refaim Valley, Israel', *PEQ* 121: 44-54.

Horwitz, L.K., E. Tchernov, and S. Dar
1990   'Subsistence and Environment on Mount Carmel in the Roman-Byzantine and Medieval Periods: The Evidence from Kh. Sumaqa', *IEJ* 40: 287-304.

Houston, W.
1993   *Purity and Monotheism: Clean and Unclean Animals in Biblical Law* (JSOTSup, 140; Sheffield Academic Press: Sheffield).

Hübner, U.
1989   'Schweine, Schweineknochen und ein Speiseverbot im alten Israel', *VT* 39: 225-36.

Ingold, T.
1980   *Hunters, Pastoralists and Ranchers* (Cambridge: Cambridge University Press).

Kapferer, B.
1989   'Nationalist Ideology and a Comparative Anthropology', *Ethnos* 54.3-4: 2-34.

Kedourie, E.
1988   'Ethnicity, Majority, and Minority in the Middle East', in M.J. Esman and I. Rabinovich (eds.), *Ethnicity, Pluralism and the State in the Middle East* (Ithaca: Cornell University Press): 25-31.

Kelly, M.C.S. and R.E. Kelly
1980   'Approaches to Ethnic Identification in Historical Archaeology', in R.L. Schuyler (ed.), *Archaeological Perspectives on Ethnicity in America* (Farmingdale, New York: Baywood Publishing Company): 133-43.

Kussinger, S.
1988   *Tierknochenfunde vom Lidar Höyük in Südostanatolien* (Inaugural dissertation; Munich: Ludwig-Maximilians-Universität).

LaBianca, O.S.
   1990   *Sedentarization and Nomadization: Food Systems Cycles at Hesban and Vicinity in Transjordan, Hesban, I* (Berrien Springs, MI: Andrews University Press).

Leone, M.
   1982   'Some Opinions about Recovering Mind', *American Antiquity* 47: 742-60.

Macalister, R.A.S.
   1912   *The Excavations of Gezer, 1902–1905 and 1907–1909*, I–III (London: John Murray).

McGuire, R.H.
   1982   'The Study of Ethnicity in Historical Archaeology', *Journal of Anthropological Archaeology* 1: 159-78.

Metzger, M.
   1985   *Tell el-Hayyat in the Late Third Millennium BC: Archaeozoological Perspectives on Cultural Change* (MA thesis; Department of History, University of Alabama at Birmingham).

Milgrom, J.
   1991   *Leviticus 1–16*, AB (New York: Doubleday).

Moerman, M.
   1965   'Who Are the Lue: Ethnic Identification in a Complex Civilization', *American Anthropologist* 67: 1215-29

Mudar, K.
   1982   'Early Dynastic III Animal Utilization in Lagash: A Report on the Fauna of Tell al-Hiba', *JNES* 41.1: 23-34.

Redding, R.
   1991   'The Role of the Pig in the Subsistence System of Ancient Egypt: A Parable on the Potential of Faunal Data', in P.J. Crabtree and K. Ryan (eds.), *Animal Use and Culture Change* (Museum Applied Science Center for Archaeology, Supplement to vol. VIII; Philadelphia: University Museum): 21-30.
   n.d.   'The Vertebrate Fauna from the Excavations at Tel Anafa', MS.

Roll, I., and E. Ayalon
   1987   'The Market Street at Apollonia Arsuf', *BASOR* 267: 61-76.

Rosen, B.
   1986   'Subsistence Economy of Stratum II', in I. Finkelstein (ed.), *Izbet Sartah, An Early Iron Age Site Near Rosh Ha Ha'ayin, Israel* (BAR International Series, 299; Oxford: British Archaeological Reports): 156-85.

Royce, A. Peterson
   1982   *Ethnic Identity: Strategies of Diversity* (Bloomington, IN: Indiana University Press).

Stager, L.E.
   1991   'When Canaanites and Philistines Ruled Ashkelon', *BARev* 17.2: 24-37, 40-43.

Tchernov, E., and I. Drori
  1983   Economic Patterns and Environmental Conditions at Hirbet el-Msas
          During the Early Iron Age', in V. Fritz and A. Kempinski (eds.),
          *Ergebnisse der Ausgrabungen auf der Hirbet el-Mšaš (Tel Masos)
          1972–1975*, I (Wiesbaden: Harrassowitz): 213-22.
Toplyn, M.R.
  n.d.   'Livestock and *Limitanei*: the Zooarchaeological Evidence of the
          Limes Arabicus Project', in S.T. Parker (ed.), *The Roman Frontier in
          Central Jordan; Final Report on the Limes Arabicus Project, 1980–
          1989* (Washington, DC: Dumbarton Oaks, forthcoming).
Trigger, B.
  1989   *A History of Archaeological Theory* (Cambridge: Cambridge
          University Press).
Urman, D.
  1985   *The Golan* (BAR International Series, 269; Oxford: British Archae-
          ological Reports).
Vaux, R. de
  1958   'Las sacrifices de porcs en Palestine et dans l'Ancien Orient' (BZAW,
          77; Berlin: Töpelmann): 250-65.
  1972   *The Bible and the Ancient Near East* (trans. D. McHugh; London:
          Darton, Longman and Todd).
Wapnish, P.
  1993   'Archaeozoology: The Integration of Faunal Data with Biblical
          Archaeology', in A. Biran and J. Aviram (eds.), *Biblical Archaeology
          Today 1990* (Jerusalem: Israel Exploration Society): 426-42.
Wapnish, P., and B. Hesse
  1988   'Urbanization and the Organization of Animal Production at Tell
          Jemmeh in the Middle Bronze Age Levant', *JNES* 47.2: 81-94.
  1991   'Faunal Remains from Tel Dan: Perspectives on Animal Production at
          a Village, Urban and Ritual Center', *Archæozoologia* 4.2: 9-86.
Williams, B.
  1989   'A Class Act: Anthropology and the Race to Nation Across Ethnic
          Terrain', *Annual Review of Anthropology* 18: 401-44.
Wolf, E.
  1982   *Europe and the People without History* (Berkeley, CA: University of
          California Press).
Zeder, M.
  1990   'Animal Exploitation at Tell Halif', BASORSup 26: 24-30.
  1996   'The Role of Pigs in Near Eastern Subsistence: A View from the
          Southern Levant', in J. Seger (ed.), *Retrieving the Past: Essays on
          Archaeological Research and Methodology in Honor of Gus W. Van
          Beek* (Winona Lake, IN: Eisenbrauns): 297-312.
Zertal. A.
  1985   'An Early Iron Age Cult Site on Mount Ebal: Excavation Seasons
          1982–1987', *Tel Aviv* 13-14: 105-65.

GROUP IDENTIFICATION AND ETHNICITY IN THE CONSTRUCTION
OF THE EARLY STATE OF ISRAEL:
FROM THE OUTSIDE LOOKING IN

David B. Small

1. *Introduction*

The contributors to this volume are all known for their continued research into the archaeology of Israel. Although I have worked in the archaeology of Israel and hope to do so again in the future, my academic path has meandered through several different archaeologies, to the point that I now consider myself more cross-cultural than culture-specific in my interests. My contribution to this volume therefore will be an examination from afar, a sideways glance, if you will, at one of the most important questions in Israeli archaeology—ethnicity and the rise of the kingdom of Israel.

The identification of early groups, often loosely termed a search for Israelite 'ethnicity', has been a focal point for research into early Israel since the days of Albright (1924, 1943). From my observational tower there are three issues of archaeological importance in this search for Israelite identity. The first is the question of the appropriate use of the term ethnicity itself in the early dynamics of Israelite state formation (c. thirteenth–tenth centuries BCE). The second is the search for an appropriate methodology for arriving at an identification of those who formed the early state. The third is the impact of research on the role of ethnicity in the developed kingdom of Israel to the larger question of ethnicity and state formation in general. In this final issue, the study of ethnicity in the development of the Israelite state is poised to make a very significant contribution to the archaeology of complex societies.

2. *The Use of the Term Ethnicity in Early State Dynamics in Israel*

Let me turn to the first issue, that of claiming that group identification in the period just before the formation of the Israelite state was ethnic. As this conference has made clear, there are numerous ways in which we could define ethnicity. But even at that, there are some core features to this type of identification, which recur in various studies. Combining the works of Shennan (1989: 14) and Cohen (1978: 387) who have looked at ethnicity in both the past and the present, allows us to filter out these core concepts.

1. Ethnicity is a relationally born definition, coming from a primordial we/they distinction.
2. Ethnicity has two identifying faces: how groups define themselves, and how others define them.
3. Many of the definitional labels used in ethnic marking are descent-conscious, indicating an identity that was inherited.
4. Unlike totemism, which refers to identity born from symmetrical relations between groups, ethnicity is the historical product of asymmetrical relations, opening up investigation to issues of resource competition, and social evolution from simple to complex societies.

Attempts to identify an Israelite 'ethnicity' have focused on isolating groups at the very inception of the formation of the Israelite state (numerous, but see: Finkelstein 1988; Esse 1992; Alt 1968; Chaney 1983; Fritz 1981; Gottwald 1979; Kempinski 1978; Miller 1977). In looking to identify these pre-monarchic groups that were later to amalgamate into the Israelite kingdom, archaeologists have not been seeking to isolate groups in asymmetrical relations, which are the product of complex social evolution, but to isolate groups according to limited early self-identification. As such, they have really been dealing with identifications that do not fit a defining criterion for ethnicity—that it be defined in asymmetrical relationships. It would be best if we were to remove the term ethnicity from the investigation of early groups behind the formation of the Israelite state, and simply refer to our quest as that of searching for group identity, which according to definition would be close to the term totemism.

3. *The Question of an Appropriate Methodology*

There are significant methodological shortcomings in the study of group identification in this important early formative period. To demonstrate just what these problems are, I will focus on a single line of investigation that has sought to identify early Israelites through the appearance of a specific storage jar. The artifact which has been singled out as a hallmark of the emerging Israelites, since its first rocket to stardom by Albright (1924), has been the classic folded rim storage jar (Figure 1). Although I can say nothing more about this jar than has already been written (best summed up in Finkelstein 1988), I would like in my own way to use it as a path to a fuller study of early group identification itself.

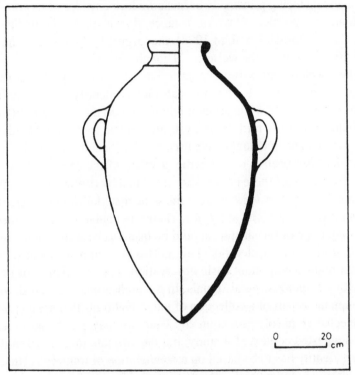

Figure 1. The classic folded rim storage jar (from Ben-Tor 1992, fig. 8.23; by kind permission of Yale University Press)

While I am encouraged by studies such as those of London (1989), Ibrahim (1978), and Finkelstein (this volume, pp. 216-37) that attempt to put this artifact into its socioeconomic contexts, rather than leaving it to more abstract 'ethnic' considerations, we should not dmismiss this artifact as an important avenue into our search for group identification of the early Israelites. The fact remains that even artifacts whose primary functions are economic are also symbols which, taken with others, constitute material cultures that identify specific groups of people. Turning to the storage jar specifically, its distribution does cluster in the region (i.e. the hill country) from which the later Israelite kingdom was to develop. Its use, therefore, by these people can be seen as at least one material manifestation of their identity.

Analyses which use this artifact (Finkelstein 1988) as a type fossil for the presence of early Israelites are now seen as dead-ended (Finkelstein, this volume, pp. 216-37). Attempts to detect Israelites by either the presence or absence of this jar, or its relative frequency on a site, have been unconvincing principally because we lack any idea of its correlation with ancient peoples. Why, for instance, do we see this jar in sites such as Sahab in Jordan (Ibrahim 1978), that arguably do not have the same identity as people in the western hill country at all?[1]

The problem with using this jar to identify specific people is that we think of the artifact, i.e., the jar, as absolutely identifying a group, rather than considering how the group might have used the jar to identify itself. I would thus like to turn the analysis around and try to consider the context in which people might have used this jar for self-identification. This analytical perspective obviates the problem of the appearance or even high frequency of these pots at sites inhabited by demonstrably different people. Different societies can use the same material within different contexts for different social strategies. Therefore neither the distribution nor the frequency of this artifact should be taken to be isomorphic with the distribution of a selected population. This type of analysis also carries with it another important basic observation. The negotiation of identity employs numerous social signals. In the archaeological record, then, it will appear as part of a collection of individual traits that are meaningful in selected archaeological contexts. Thus, we may use the jar to lead us into suggested contexts for study, but the ultimate identification of any group identity has to be based on a *combination* of traits correlated with an identified, understood, ancient context. The jar, then, is only *one* of many objects that was used in combination to identify pre-monarchic Israelites.

What might we suggest as possible contexts within which these people might situationally identify themselves? In order to suggest a likely context for the use of this pot in the identification of pre-monarchic peoples who were later identified with Israel, we must first discuss the

---

1.   The common method of describing the presence of the pot at sites by relative percentages renders site comparison, and therefore meaningful regional analysis, impossible. For example, a record of 30% for this storage jar can be misleading, because it could represent 200 individual pieces out of 600, or 10 out of 30, and when we try to look at its distribution by site percentage, we easily get misled.

characteristics of this pot and the likely means for its production. From the very first then, we are left with an important problem. Was it the jar or was it its contents with which people negotiated their identity? Finkelstein's observant conclusions (1988) that it has been found with greater frequency in upland areas does indicate that it probably was used to store olive oil, wine, and water. But then did people use these liquids or the jar itself to mark themselves? Olive oil and wine are important ethnic markers even today, and the question deserves more attention and research than we can give it here. I will assume, however, that the jar could have contained a variety of goods, and that we can make an argument that its visual presence was an important marker.

The second issue in selecting a context is that of its manufacture and distribution. In a sensitive treatment of the position of this type of jar in selected economic and kinship systems Esse (1992) claimed that the jar was produced by women, as a part-time occupation within the household. Accordingly, the craft was passed on from mother to daughter, and from household to household as brides traveled from family to family in the apparent patrilocal society of the early Israelites. That is, the potter traveled and not the pot.

While I appreciate Esse's attempt to put the presence of this pot into an explainable economic frame, I am afraid that I found his argument less than convincing. First he argued that the size and weight of the jar would argue against its traveling, but even heavier and more cumbersome objects have traveled in the past and still do today (see for example, Hassig 1985). A good example are manos and metates, the corn grinding stones used by Mesoamerican peoples since the late first millennium BCE. Although extremely heavy and of a very awkward shape, these products are still made by hand and transported to periodic markets. Today the beast of burden is a donkey, but in the days before Columbus, because Mexico had no indigenous draft animals, it was a man. Furthermore, as Esse admitted, evidence from Dan has demonstrated that this type of jar was definitely an import, that is, the jar *could* travel. Secondly, Esse's use of ceramic sociology, that is the correlation of ceramic design with social structure, comes from the earlier works of Deetz (1965), who tried to demonstrate social change over time among the Arikara Indians. But studies after Deetz (Hodder 1982, 1983) have clearly demonstrated that this type of work is too naive, assuming some sort of positive relationship between mothers and daughters in the transmission of pottery design, when ethnoarchaeological studies have shown just the opposite. And last, and perhaps most importantly, the jars themselves were wheelmade. Wheelmade pottery demands more than the part-time interest of women in the household. As demonstrated (Peacock 1982), such pottery is most often the product of a larger group of people, usually organized and led by men. Often these groups were extended families or small-scale lineages, as has been clearly demonstrated in the archaeological analysis of Teotihuacan (Storey and Widmer 1989), where whole compounds were occupied by patrilineal and patrilocal families, and engaged in the manufacture of pottery or other goods. While I do not think that the small hamlets of early Israel can compare with the complex urban society of Teotihuacan, I will suggest that this pot might have been manufactured by what Stager (1985) would identify as large families, that appear to have made up certain sections of the early settlements.

If we have identified the large family as a possible producer of this pottery, we are still not yet at a point where we can introduce the concept of larger group identification, since such an identification, to be meaningful in this analytic context, has to be above the family level. Where then might we find a context where these early peoples could use this jar for social identification? The answer lies in looking closely at the ecology and the agricultural profile of the regions they inhabit.

In a careful survey Finkelstein (1988) has given us not only an excellent picture of the topography, but also the productive picture of the territory of Ephraim (Figure 2). In its uneven distribution of the frequency of cereal and olive production, such a territory is a prime example of a region that should be economically interdependent. Rather than relying solely on redistributive patterns embedded in kinship patterns, this type of territory probably witnessed periodic gatherings in which goods, agricultural products as well as manufactured items, were exchanged. The contexts for these periodic gatherings could have been informal markets or, more likely, religious assemblies, where people gathered for religious purposes, but were also engaged in economic activity. A parallel would perhaps be the pilgrimage fairs of the Maya (Freidel 1981), where people would come into the sanctuary from the surrounding territory to engage in religious practices, but also engage in an active barter exchange at the same time. Good candidates for this type of gathering and exchange in early Israel would, of course, be recognized sanctuaries such as *perhaps* Ebal (Zertal 1985) and certainly, in the territory of Ephraim, ancient Shiloh (most recently Finkelstein 1988).

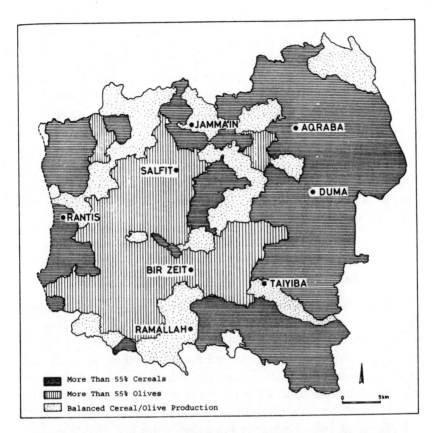

Figure 2. Territory of Ehraim—cereal versus olive-growing areas (1945) (from Finkelstein 1988, ill. 40, by kind permission of the Israel Exploration Society).

The display, the selling, the consumption of goods in these gatherings, would tend to identify a larger group of people, above the level of the village or family. In the case of Israel specifically, we might envision these meetings as providing contexts for the creation of a social identity on par with such groupings as the individual tribes, in this case, as in Shiloh, that is, the tribe of Benjamin. And the tribes' claim on the territory of the tribe would be identified with this group negotiation.

If this conclusion is correct, then I think that I can suggest certain issues for future research into group identification in early Israel at this level of context and regional group identity. First, since we are looking at a context of congregation within which numerous articles could be used to identify the group, textiles, other pottery, food items, and so on, we would have to expand our analysis beyond its limitation to a single artifact. Since pottery is the most durable of artifacts I would suggest that we look for the distribution of similar multivariate pottery assemblages over the landscape as indicators of territorial group identity. Even though we are left with just pottery and do not have the full range of items that we would consider part of this social negotiation, pottery might serve as a sensitive indicator, since food consumption rules were often correlated with this type of identification. This type of analysis, however, would have to take into account issues such as social status and class, since different consumptive habits do vary according to these distinctions as well. In no way is this 'easy archaeology' but it certainly would allow us to set up future research strategies with the aim of identifying local groups, how they identified themselves, and possible correlations with territorial claims.

3. *The Role of Ethnicity in the Early Israelite State and its Impact on the Archaeology of Ethnicity and State Formation*

The early state of Israel does not present an example of state evolution similar to states where the operation of ethnicity in state formation has been studied. Israel supplies an important and necessary example of weak state formation, where we are forced to rethink some already developed concepts of ethnicity and the archaic state. In order to highlight this important point we must first understand the state of current research in ethnicity and the development of the archaic state.

Work on the role of ethnicity in modern states has already strongly indicated that we should equate ethnicity with class (Williams 1989; Eriksen 1993; Brass 1985; Cohen 1978; Comaroff and Comaroff 1992; Shennan 1989). It has been equally argued (Comaroff and Comaroff 1992) that ethnicity should be equated with hierarchical relations, common to state formation. Embedded within the very definition of the modern state, then, is the concept of ethnicity.

3a. *Ethnicity in Other Archaeologies*

While many have been keen to see ethnicity in modern states, there is a good argument that ethnicity can be studied in pre-capitalist societies as well. Scholars in both New and Old World cultures have attempted to use ethnicity as a window into the operation of past societies in general (Baldwin 1987; Grosboll 1987; Santley, Yarborough, and Hall 1987; Friedman 1990; Shennan 1989; Brumfiel 1989; Brumfiel 1994; Pollard 1994; Patterson 1987; Patterson 1991; McGuire 1982. The most often investigated question in this regard is the role of ethnicity in the rise of the archaic state (specifically Brumfiel 1989; Brumfiel 1994; Pollard 1994; Patterson 1987; Patterson 1991; Hesse and Wapnish in this volume). Three recent investigations in the New World have brought forth some common issues. Patterson (1987, 1991) has made the argument that the Inka empire (c. 1430–1532 CE), although it did not share an economic structure common to modern societies, did witness both the creation of an Inkan ethnicity and the death of some regional ethnic identities in the creation of the state. Correlated with a developing political economy, ethnicity in the Inka political empire was based upon a centralized takeover of various forms of land tenure and means of production. Ethnicity was seen as a means of economic negotiation within the empire, with different groups who had a pre-Inka identity being pulled out of their territorial homes and relocated on either imperial farming estates, or in provinces that appeared to have been problematic for the Inka to control. This often involved the forced movement of people from one part of the empire to another and in this transfer different ethnic groups were created by the state, while others were destroyed.

Further north, two recent studies of the role of ethnicity in archaic state formation have been put forth for the Tarascan (c. 1450–1520 CE) (Pollard 1994) and Aztec (1428–1519 CE) (Brumfiel 1989; Brumfiel 1994; Zantwijk 1973) states. Brumfiel outlines that in the Aztec state ethnicity was very much a political tool. As van Zantwijk had earlier observed (1973), in the pre-Aztec period in this part of the basin of Mexico, the land was dotted with different factional groups, *capulli* and *teccalli* which identified with common, somewhat mythical ancestors. To paraphrase Brumfiel (1994: 91-92) the *capulli* was a landholding group composed of commoners '...having economic, political, and ceremonial functions'. The members of this group were 'jointly responsible for paying tribute' and 'serving as a unit in public labor projects and military campaigns'. An elite establishment, a *teccalli* 'was created when a ruler granted lands to a noble in exchange for a pledge of assistance and political support'. Both these groups could and did claim distinctive ethnic identities. The *capulli* in addition was composed of people who cut across class lines, i.e., the group was led by lords that were tied to their subjects by common ethnic identities. These identities were used by these different groups to legitimate use-rights to land. In the Aztec empire these ethnic identities were used by the state in important ways.

First, the state would use the pre-existing *capulli* system as units for taxation and tribute; but in so doing, it often removed the leaders to Tenochtitlàn to prevent the *capulli* being led into rebellion against the state. Second, the state would promote derogatory stereotypes of certain ethnic groups, which kept them out of the running for any position of political power. Brumfiel's most cogent example concerns the Otomi, who were identified as fierce warriors by the Aztec, but at the same time were also said to be too fierce and thus could not be trusted with political authority. Finally, the state created some new ethnic categories in some of its provinces, lumping together several regions into larger state-identified territories. With these new labels the state was attempting to make subjugation appear a natural and legitimate process.

The Tarascan case was somewhat different. As Pollard (1994) argues, the Tarascans were experts at the manipulation of ethnicity for state interests. This was accomplished in two ways: the creation of a common ethnicity in the core area of the state and the manipulation of groups on its borders through the creation of a common self-interest. Pollard argues that a major factor in the creation of a common internal ethnicity was the development of a strong centralizing economic tendency from at least 1350 to the Spanish conquest in 1520, represented in a regional marketing network within the core and the position of administrative centers in areas between it and the border. One way in which this common ethnic identity was achieved was through the development of a shared ethnicity between local leaders in these administrative centers and the Tarascan king. Local leaders were identified as a group by lip plugs that were given to them by the king. Today remnants of that common ethnicity can be seen in the remains of a common language that should be somewhat coterminous with the past ethnic boundaries. On the frontier of the empire the political leaders were carefully manipulating already existing ethnic groups, with the Tarascan king choosing the leaders of border groups with the final goal of protecting the Tarascan frontier.

3b. *Present Operational Features*
These studies have begun to take us on the road to analyzing the role of ethnicity in early states. Two broadly based observations on the role of ethnicity in state development are apparent. The first is the integral role ethnicity has to play in the development of political economies. In each example we can clearly see the use of ethnicity in the construction of a

state-level political economy. For each, the use of ethnicity was strongly embedded in the emerging means of economic control. The Inka created ethnic units in the developing hierarchical and centralizing economic control of their territories, as did the Aztec. For the Tarascans, the creation of a state ethnicity is closely tied to the internal economic network and developing centrality of the Tarascan state.

The second apparent feature of ethnicity in archaic states is its role in the strategies of political domination. Although each state used ethnicity in a different manner to achieve its own political ends, we can clearly see that ethnic identification was an important part of any historical strategy within any of these states. Although each case has to be viewed as a product of its own historical circumstances, it is possible to see how ethnicity can be an effective tool in the strategy of a few to dominate the new power of an emerging state. For the Aztec it was the creation of new provincial ethnicity, plus the use of ethnic labels to deny access to power for possible competing groups within the empire. For the Tarascans it was the construction of a new state-identified ethnicity in its heartland, plus the use of ethnic identification to control border peoples. For the Inka, it was the use of new ethnic identities in their acquired provinces, plus the destruction of pre-imperial ethnic identities by the state. It is therefore quite clear that in these examples ethnicity not only correlates with its defining characteristic as identity within asymmetrical relationships, but shows up as a state means for control, through an evolving strong hierarchy and centralization in developing political economies. Therefore the asymmetrical basis for ethnicity was fully developed in these states, with differences between groups lying at the center of their evolving political economies. To a great extent, these states created ethnicities.

3c. *The Case of Israel*
The study of ethnicity in the dynamics of state creation, although it has made inroads in studies in the New World, is still only in its initial phases. Studies of ethnicity in the dynamics of other states should therefore extend our understanding of its role in state formation. It is here that the study of ethnicity in the rise of the state in early Israel is of utmost importance. Ancient Israel shares an important feature with the New World polities just discussed. Like the Inka, Aztec, and Tarascans, the state of Israel was an amalgamation of corporate groups with pre-state identities. In the New World these identities became ethnic components

in the state as they were embedded into an evolving political economy. Because it is so similar, we should expect the formation of the ancient state of Israel to incorporate similar ethnic generation. However, despite its seemingly fertile bed for ethnic construction, in several ways Israel differs from these other states, and the role of group identification in the formation of the Israelite state is distinctly opposed to the empirical observations and overarching generalities that have been so far constructed.

To present the unusual role of ethnicity in the formation of the state of Israel, it would be best if we were to examine the evidence for ethnicity in early Israel's creation and then turn to a structural analysis that offers some explanation for its different character. Turning to the first, it has to be noted that the documentary history of Israel lacks the telltale signs of the creation or manipulation of ethnic identities in an archaic state (for historical narrative: Miller and Hayes 1986; for social models: Gottwald 1979). Unlike the New World states that we have examined, there is no evidence for the creation of a state ethnic identity. The term 'Israelite' does appear to have been a common term for the people of Israel, used perhaps as early as the ninth century, but it does not seem to have been created by the new state, for it does not bear the hallmarks of an identity embedded in a politicoeconomic strategy of assimilation. Unlike the Aztec, Tarascans, or Inka there is no evidence that a particular ethnic identity, whether new or stemming from pre-monarchic identification, was used in any type of socioeconomic strategy to control territory or the means of production in Israel. Likewise, Israel exhibits no evidence of ethnocide, where any preexisting group lost its original social identity. Pre-monarchic labels, such a Benjaminite, continued.

The reason for this unusual absence of ethnic creation in the kingdom of Israel lies within an internal structure that is distinctly different from states studied so far. Specifically, the political and economic development of this archaic state does not fit accepted models of strong hierarchy and centrality where we would expect ethnicity to be a unit of mediation in state-directed asymmetrical relations. Historical sources (Miller and Hayes 1986) show clearly that the state of Israel, either in its early united form, or later as two separated kingdoms, bears little resemblance to the archaic states of the Inka, Aztec, or Tarascans. Unlike these other more 'traditional' states with more canonical political economies, early Israel appears to have had at best only a weak centrality, weak hierarchy, and poorly developed economic and political institutions.

Political development was weak. Capitals shifted with great rapidity. Saul's headquarters was a Shechem, then David removed it to Jerusalem. Upon the division of the kingdom, Jeroboam moved the northern capital to Tirzah, just outside Shechem, and later Omri moved it again to Samaria. Lines of political transfer were never institutionalized. Succession to power appears to have been based, not upon any state-demarcated path to succession through some recognition of royal kinship, but upon the ability to create one's own power base and seize the throne. This was the method of seizure used by both David and Solomon before the kingdom's split, and a method used at least eight times again in the struggle for power in the northern kingdom. Territorial control largely escaped political and economic crystallization.

Economic control was weak. Power over different areas within the kingdoms appears to have been based more on temporary military force than economic restructuring of the territories, with cities such as Jerusalem resembling more the regal ritual centers of the Maya (Fox 1977), which were more of an extension of the image of the ruling family than a political and economic integrative center (Stager 1985). Rather than state-created ruling systems, power appears to have been a product of patron/client relationships with the house of the ruler incorporating the power itself. (A similar case can be seen in early Rome with the emperor's household becoming the state bureaucracy, but this household agency eventually evolved into a true state administrative apparatus.) Coupled with this is the obvious absence of any centralized priesthood, the Levites rather being attached to different lineages within the territories.

Although different from the Inka, Aztec, and Tarascans, Israel does not represent a minority of one. Parallels may also be seen in the alternative evolutionary paths for some Polynesian societies, such as the Marquesas (Kirch 1991), where central authority and hierarchy were also weak. Here religion never came under the control of the state and there was a noticed power dualism between the chief and the chief priest. In these cases the system of achieved status represented by the positions of the priests survived the rise of chiefly ranking and weakened its authority by serving as an opposing base of power. This scenario is quite like the king–prophet/priest dualism that plagued much of Israel's political development.

The unusual nature of early Israel's internal structure has led some to deny its state level identification. Flanagan (1981) would argue that the situation in early Israel is one of a paramount chief and little regional chiefs that replicated his power. But even this model implies a level of ranking that I think is alien to this early society. Israel was a state, but it was one that belongs to less canonical types, such as the Germanic, argued for by Marx (1965) for early Europe, where the state had little, if any, centralizing and ranking authority, and real power, that is economic, lay within the preexisting lineages.

3d. *Discussion*

The fact that the early state of Israel does not match the commonly held image of archaic states, and therefore does not supply a foundation for the genesis and use of ethnicity in the formation of an archaic state, brings to the forefront an important issue for discussion in the question of ethnic creation and state formation in general: can we assume that state formation always creates ethnicity? It appears to have been so for our New World examples, but Israel, even though it did incorporate multiple corporate groups, did not. Why?

This analysis indicates that a possible reason, and a point that needs to be explored much more fully in the future study of archaic states, is that states can develop with political economies that do not have the assumed prerequisite level of ability to create to any great degree asymmetrical relations between different corporate groups. They can display some astounding weaknesses. In the case of Israel, pre-monarchic groups were not placed into permanent asymmetrical positions either vis-à-vis the state or with one another. It would be better if we were to refer to the group identities of the Israelite monarchy as totemic, a continuation of symmetrical identification that existed in the pre-monarchic period.

This brings up an important cross-cultural comparison. In an investigation of nineteenth-century Ngoni and Zulu political structures (Comaroff and Comaroff 1992), it was argued that a rapid incorporation of various groups into an emerging state allows for each incorporated group to retain a measure of its original totemic identification. That is, the rapidity of this incorporation does not allow for the positioning of these different groups into asymmetrical relationships within the political economy. The case of Israel adds a new field of exploration for this concept. While it may be argued that the kingdom was indeed rapidly created, and therefore similar to the Zulu, ancient Israel does present additional contexts for the study of this type of group incorporation that are absent in both the cases of the Ngoni and Zulu. The history of these African states is very brief, but the history of Israel is much longer, and allows us to study the retention of totemic identification well into the mature development of the state itself.

4. *Conclusion*

From my distanced position the future of research into group identification and ethnicity in early Israel is poised to make some important contributions to the study of group identity and ethnicity in archaic state formation in general. Israel presents an excellent case for the study of the amalgamation of pre-state groups into a larger polity. Although I have described some problems with current approaches, the archaeological record of these early peoples is rapidly expanding and should offer an unparalleled base for the study of identity and social change at this crucial period.

Studies of the role of ethnicity in state formation at present have unfortunately overlooked Israel and other similar examples of polities with weak centralization and hierarchy. It is here, on this cutting edge of exploration into ethnicity and the state, that Israel stands poised to make its most significant contribution.

BIBLIOGRAPHY

Albright, W.F.
    1924   'Excavations and Results at Tell el-Ful (Gibeah of Saul)', *Annual of the American School of Oriental Research* 4.
    1943   'The Excavation of Tell Beit Mirsim III: The Iron Age', *Annual of the American School of Oriental Research* 12: 21-22.

Alt, A.
    1968   'The Settlement of the Israelites in Palestine', in A. Alt (ed.), *Essays on Old Testament History and Religion* (Garden City, NY: Doubleday Press): 172-221.

Auger, R., *et al.*
    1987   *Ethnicity and Culture* (Calgary: University of Calgary Press).

Baldwin, S.
    1987   'Roomsize Patterns: A Quantitative Method for Approaching Ethnic Identification in Architecture', in Auger *et al.* 1987: 163-74.

Ben-Tor, A. (ed.)
    1992   *The Archaeology of Ancient Israel* (trans. R. Greenberg; New Haven: Yale University Press).

Brass, P.
    1985   'Ethnic Groups and the State', in P. Brass (ed.), *Ethnic Groups and the State* (Totowa, NJ: Barnes and Noble): 1-59.

Brumfiel, E.
1989   'Factional Competition in Complex Society', in D. Miller, M. Rowlands and C. Tilley (eds.), *Domination and Resistance* (London: Unwin Hyman): 127-39.
1994   'Ethnic Groups and Political Development in Ancient Mexico', in E. Brumfiel and J. Fox (eds.), *Factional Competition and Political Development in the New World* (Cambridge: Cambridge University Press): 89-102.

Chaney, M.
1983   'Ancient Palestinian Peasant Movements and the Formation of Premonarchic Israel', in D. Freedman and D. Graf (eds.), *Palestine in Transition: The Emergence of Ancient Israel* (SWBA, 2; Sheffield: Almond Press): 39-90.

Cohen, R.
1978   'Ethnicity: Problem and Focus in Anthropology', *Annual Review of Anthropology* 7: 379-403.

Comaroff, J., and J. Comaroff
1992   'Of Totemism and Ethnicity', in J. Comaroff and J. Comaroff (eds.), *Ethnography and the Historical Imagination* (Boulder, CO: Westview Press): 49-67.

Crumley, C.
1987   'A Dialectical Critique of Hierarchy', in C. Gailey and T. Patterson (eds.), *Power Relations and State Formation* (Washington: American Anthropological Association): 155-69.
1990   'A Critique of Cultural Evolutionist Approaches to Ranked Society with Particular Reference to Celtic Polities', paper delivered at annual meeting of the Society for American Archaeology, Las Vegas.

Deetz, J.
1965   'The Dynamics of Stylistic Change in Arikara Ceramics', *Illinois Studies in Anthropology* 4.

Eriksen, T.
1993   'What is Ethnicity?', in T. Eriksen (ed.), *Ethnicity and Nationalism: Anthropological Perspectives* (London: Pluto Press): 1-17.

Esse, D.
1992   'The Collared Pithos at Megiddo', *JNES* 51: 81-106.

Finkelstein, I.
1988   *The Archaeology of the Israelite Settlement* (Jerusalem: Israel Exploration Society).

Flanagan, J.
1981   'Chiefs in Israel', *JSOT* 20: 47-73.

Fox, R.
1977   *Urban Anthropology* (Englewood Cliffs, NJ: Prentice Hall).

Freidel, D.
1981   'The Political Economics of Residential Dispersion among the Lowland Maya', in W. Ashmore (ed.), *Lowland Maya Settlement Patterns* (Albuquerque: University of New Mexico Press): 371-82.

Friedman, J.
1990   'Notes on Culture and Identity in Imperial Worlds', in P. Bilde, *et al.*
(eds.), *Religion and Religious Practice in the Seleucid Kingdom*
(Aarhus: Aarhus University Press): 14-39.

Fritz, V.
1981   'The Israelite "Conquest" in the Light of Recent Excavations at
Khirbet el-Meshâsh', *BASOR* 241: 61-73.

Gilman, A.
1992   'Germanic Social Formations in Europe and Beyond', paper presented at the 57th annual meeting of the Society for American Archaeology, Pittsburgh.

Gottwald, N.
1979   *The Tribes of Yahweh: A Sociology of the Religion of Liberated Israel
1250–1050 BCE* (Maryknoll, NY: Orbis Books).

Grosboll, S.
1987   'Ethnic Boundaries within the Inca Empire: Evidence from Huanuco,
Peru', in Auger *et al.* 1987: 115-24.

Hassig, R.
1985   *Trade, Tribute and Transportation: The Sixteenth Century Political
Economy of the Valley of Mexico* (Norman, OK: University of Okla-
homa Press).

Hess, R.
1993   'Early Israel in Canaan: A Survey of Recent Evidence and
Interpretations', *PEQ* 125: 125-41.

Hodder, I.
1982   *Symbols in Action* (Cambridge: Cambridge University Press).
1983   *The Present Past: An Introduction to Anthropology for Archaeologists*
(New York: Pica Press).

Ibrahim, M.
1978   'The Collared-rim Jar of the Early Iron Age', in R. Moorey and
P. Parr (eds.), *Archaeology in the Levant* (Warminster: Aris & Phillips):
116-26.

Kempinski, A.
1978   'Tel Masos: Its Importance in Relation to the Settlement of the Tribes
of Israel in the Northern Negev', *Expedition* 20: 29-37.

Kirch, P.
1991   'Chiefship and Competitive Involution: The Marquesas Islands of
Eastern Polynesia', in T. Earle (ed.), *Chiefdoms, Power, Economy, and
Ideology* (Cambridge: Cambridge University Press).

London, G.
1989   'A Comparison of Two Contemporaneous Lifestyles of the Late
Second Millennium BC', *BASOR* 273: 43-47.

McGuire, R.
1982   'The Study of Ethnicity in Historical Archaeology', *Journal of
Anthropological Archaeology* 1: 159-78.

Marx, K.
1965   *Pre-capitalist Economic Formations* [1859] (New York: International
Publishers).

Miller, J.
1977   'The Israelite Occupation of Canaan', in J. Hayes and J. Miller (eds.),
        Israelite and Judaean History (Philadelphia: Westminster Press): 213-
        84.

Miller, J., and J. Hayes
1986   *A History of Ancient Israel and Judah* (Philadelphia: Westminster
        Press).

Patterson, T.
1987   'Tribes, Chiefdoms, and Kingdoms in the Inca Empire', in T. Patterson
        and C. Gailey (eds.), *Power Relations and State Formation* (Washington,
        DC: American Anthropological Association): 117-27.
1991   *The Inca Empire: The Formation and Disintegration of a Pre-
        Capitalist State* (Oxford: Berg).

Peacock, D.P.S.
1982   *Pottery in the Roman World* (London: Longman Press).

Pollard, H.
1994   'Ethnicity and Political Control in a Complex Society: The Tarascan
        State of Prehispanic Mexico', in E. Brumfiel and J. Fox (eds.),
        Factional Competition and Development in the New World (Cambridge:
        Cambridge University Press): 79-88.

Santley, R., C. Yarborough, and B. Hall
1987   'Enclaves, Ethnicity, and the Archaeological Record at Matacapan', in
        Auger *et al.* 1987: 85-100.

Shennan, S.
1989   'Introduction: Archaeological Approaches to Cultural Identity', in
        Shennan (ed.), *Archaeological Approaches to Cultural Identity*
        (London: Unwin Hyman).

Small, D.
1994   'City-State Dynamics through a Greek Lens', in D. Nichols and
        T. Charlton (eds.), *Cross-Cultural Approaches to the Small State*
        (Washington: Smithsonian Press, forthcoming).

Stager, L.
1985   'Archaeology of the Family in Ancient Israel', *BASOR* 260: 1-35.

Storey, R. and R. Widmer
1989   'Household and Community Structure of a Teotihuacan Apartment
        Compound: S3WW1:33 of the Tlajinga Barrio', in S. MacEachern,
        D. Archer and R. Garvin (eds.), *Households and Communities* (Calgary:
        University of Calgary Archaeological Association): 407-15.

Williams, B.
1989   'A Class Act: Anthropology and the Race to Nation across Ethnic
        Terrain', *Annual Review of Anthropology* 18: 401-44.

Zantwijk, R. van
1973   'Politics and Ethnicity in a Prehispanic Mexican State between the
        Thirteenth and Fifteenth Centuries', *Plural Societies* 4: 23-52.

Zertal, A.
1985   'Has Joshua's Altar Been Found on Mt. Ebal?', *BARev* 11: 26-43.

IMAGINING THE PAST: THE BIBLE, ISRAELITE HISTORY,
AND ARCHAEOLOGICAL RESEARCH

PHILOLOGY, THEOLOGY, AND ARCHAEOLOGY: WHAT KIND OF HISTORY OF ISRAEL DO WE WANT, AND WHAT IS POSSIBLE?

William G. Dever

Introduction

For the past twenty years or so there has been increasing scholarly discussion of issues in Israelite historiography, yet there is a growing sense of uneasiness that has now reached crisis proportions. Given the problematic nature of our sources in the Hebrew Bible, is it possible to write a satisfactory history of ancient Israel? Or, as Max Miller (1991) has put it recently, 'Is it possible to write a history of Israel *without* the Hebrew Bible?'

In earlier stages of the discussion, it was largely a matter of competing approaches or models, the assumption being apparently that a deliberate choice among various alternatives was necessary, but would then enable the historian to get on with the task. Somewhat later there appeared the first full-scale analyses of the Hebrew Bible as a specifically 'historical' work, in the comparative context of ancient Near Eastern and Greek historiography: John van Seter's *In Search of History: Historiography in the Ancient World and the Origins of Biblical History* (1983); and Baruch Halpern's *The First Historians: The Hebrew Bible and History* (1988).

In the past decade scholars have brought forth several new histories of ancient Israel that mark a turning away from the era of Noth and Bright, with its sharp polarization of 'nihilistic' and 'positivist' histories. Full-scale works of the 'new school' would include J.A. Soggin, *The History of Israel* (1985); N.P. Lemche, *Early Israel: Anthropological and Historical Studies on the Israelite Society before the Monarchy* (1985), and his more popular *Ancient Israel: A New History of Israelite Society* (1988); J.M. Miller and J.H. Hayes, *A History of Ancient Israel and Judah* (1986); and G. Garbini, *History and Ideology in Ancient Israel*

(1988), the latter more an essay on historiography than a history. One could add to this list a number of 'introductions' that included historical sketches of a sort.

These more recent histories of Israel, despite wide divergence, are characterized, I believe, by a rather remarkable consensus, not usually spelled out but recognizable in several common traits, all of course inter-related. (1) The overall assumption is that the texts of the Hebrew Bible are late postexilic, or even Hellenistic, not only in their present edited form, but in content as well, i.e., the literary tradition is largely 'unhistorical'. (2) Much more attention must thus be paid to the role of ideology in history-writing—theirs and ours—including religion and cult. (3) A history of 'Israel' can begin only with the period of the Judges, or even the monarchy, since any prehistory is unrecoverable; but coverage at the other end may extend to the Second Temple period and the for-mation of rabbinic Judaism. (4) Since the tradition is a literary one, not historical, the most fecund approach may be through newer literary-critical methods (narrative history; symbolic-structuralist and other forms of discourse analysis; folklore and ethnohistory; etc.); and the most appropriate models may be those drawn from anthropology. (5) The newer, more comprehensive rubric should be 'social history', rather than religious or political history. (6) Archaeology is acknowledged as a potential source of historical information (usually unexploited, however). (7) The question of the 'emergence' of Israel is one of the most pressing yet controversial issues. (8) Finally, several of the most recent works hint at the possibility of a new 'secular history' of ancient Israel or Palestine that will mark the next major scholarly departure—indeed, I think, a new era in Israelite historiography (below).

In the following remarks, I want to look briefly at three basic approaches to writing a history of ancient Israel, with special emphasis on the unique contribution that I think Syro-Palestinian archaeology as a mature discipline can now make.[1]

1. *The Philological Approach to the History of Ancient Israel*

In many ways philology has been the basic tool of modern critical bib-lical scholarship. The fundamental flaw in the philological approach,

1. For orientation and bibliography on recent trends in Syro-Palestinian archae-ology, see Dever 1985; 1993; for archaeology and problems of Israelite historiogra-phy see Dever 1995a, and especially the review of issues in 1995b.

however, lies in its unexamined positivist presuppositions. It simply assumes (1) that the texts of the Hebrew Bible as they have come down to us, despite the seemingly intractable nature of some passages, taken together constitute an accurate witness to the actual phenomenon of life in ancient Israel; and (2) that the rapid progress of comparative Semitic philology would enable us to read these texts correctly and comprehend their meaning. As Morton Smith put it in his 1968 Presidential Address to the Society of Biblical Literature: 'For a proper understanding of the Israelites we must have the archaeological facts determined quite objectively and independently by competent archaeologists, and the Biblical facts likewise determined by competent philologians, and then we can begin to compare them.'

In other words, philologians were confident that they really could penetrate behind the obfuscation of centuries of theological interpretation to *das Ding an sich*—if not to historical and religious truth then at least to an 'exegetical truth', based not on correct belief but on a correct reading of the texts. Much of the vaunted optimism of classic Protestant Liberalism in its heyday regarding the task of reconstructing Israelite history and religion rested upon the assumed superiority of such an 'objective approach', largely philological (what Burke Long terms the 'logocentric' approach).

Today this seems naive, wistful, and rather sad. Already in the late nineteenth century, as Baruch Halpern (1988: 23) points out, the Greek philologian Burckhardt had castigated then-burgeoning classical philology for its 'spiritual bankruptcy'. It is not simply that the texts—Greek, Latin, Hebrew, or ancient Near Eastern—are not truly representative of the whole gamut of ancient society and culture; or even that such texts are highly symbolic, cryptic 'encoded messages' about past human thought and behavior that can never be fully deciphered.

The more intransigent problem with 'mere philology' is that such an excessively rationalistic, and ultimately literalistic, approach to history can never grasp its 'inner reality', if I may phrase it thus. Or to put it another, less impressionistic way: literature is not life, but rather the product of the intellectual and literary imagination of a creative few. Thus the study of elitist texts of the 'Great Tradition' alone can never enlighten us fully on many matters. In short, in this post-modern, post-positivist era, we ought to acknowledge at last that, even in possession of abundant textual data, we cannot really 'reconstruct the past'. The past is gone irretrievably; and, whatever our data, as Lewis Binford (1983:

31, 32) reminds us, we can only draw inferences about 'what it was like in the past'. All these inferences are indirect and partial; most are untestable; and many are simply modern notions, not derived at all from that past but imposed upon it. What we think we 'know' reveals more about us and our ignorance than about the past that we are proposing to investigate. To counter von Ranke's familiar phrase, we can never really know '*wie es eigentlich gewesen war*', historically or archaeologically.

The minimalist view of Israelite historiography espoused here is not as radical as it would have seemed a generation ago. Indeed, current trends in England and on the Continent are much more extreme. This was borne out for me at a symposium in January 1993 in Bern on mono-theism in ancient Israel, where the consensus of leading European scholars was that the texts of the Hebrew Bible, in their present edited form, are all late and tendentious, of little or no value for the historian.[2] That is a view vigorously championed also by Philip Davies in his recent book *In Search of 'Ancient Israel'* (1992). Though I find this work curious, and certainly not persuasive, Davies does typify the ultimate absurdity to which the exclusive use of the philological method (i.e., his) leads. Davies contends that there was no 'ancient Israel'. This is simply a literary con-struct that has been invented by later rabbinic Judaism (perpetuated by Christianity as well), by a postexilic community seeking an identity, seeking to vindicate itself in the aftermath of national tragedy. Davies' real villains are those he calls a 'scribal class', who finally shaped the lit-erary tradition, who he thinks were temple personnel. But they are not consciously producing Scripture, or even a 'Bible', just propaganda. Even the language of these 'scribal schools' is artificial—not a Hebrew that was ever actually spoken during the monarchy, but an archaizing *Bildungssprache*. In short, all the literature of the Hebrew Bible, based on Davies' philological analysis (certainly not his amateurish theology or historiography), is Hellenistic, even the Prophetic books; a Hasmonean phantasmagoria, worthless as sources of history for any other period. There is no 'ancient Israel'; but Davies is its chronicler.

Davies' nihilism is echoed in both the most recent, comprehensive attempts to write a history of ancient Israel: T.L. Thompson's *Early History of the Israelite People from the Written and Archaeological Sources* (1992); and the late Gösta Ahlström's *The History of Ancient Palestine from the Paleolithic Period to Alexander's Conquest* (1993). These recent works do not in my opinion signal a new approach, much

2.   The proceedings are published in Dietrich and Klopfenstein 1995.

less a breakthrough in writing a history of Israel. Rather they mark a return full-circle to Wellhausen; they simply confirm the intellectual exhaustion, after a century and a half, of the philological method and the classic literary-critical apparatus that accompanied it. In this pessimistic view, I as an archaeologist am neither beyond the pale nor alone. Rolf Rendtorff, in the inaugural issue of the new journal *Biblical Inter-pretation*, in an article entitled 'The Paradigm is Changing: Hopes—and Fears', points out that the classic Documentary hypothesis is dead. 'The question is rather whether the texts are Pre-Exilic or post-Exilic'; and the consensus is for the latter dating. 'We will have to redesign our image of Israel's history and the history of its religion.'[3] Indeed! But *how*?

2. *The Theological Approach to the History of Ancient Israel*

A second traditional approach to the history and religion of ancient Israel has been through theology, either so-called 'biblical' theology, or systematic and dogmatic theology. Whatever the merits of this approach, I would argue that theology is ill-suited to a productive investigation of ancient Israel's history.

Despite a historical thrust of some sort or another, the fact is that the vast majority of Old Testament theologies in the last two centuries have had a frankly confessional character, that is, their goal has been to reconstruct a 'normative' religion of ancient Israel as a foundation for modern belief and morality, largely within the Christian community. That category would certainly include the works of most influential twentieth-century OT theologians.[4]

1. The theological approach may best be characterized as *Heilsgeschichte*: ancient Israel viewed primarily as the first chapter in the history of 'salvation', that is, the story of God's redemption of his people Israel, and then of the Christian church as the 'New Israel'. The dilemma posed by this perspective on Scripture, however, has been with the church since Marcion in the second century of the common era: what to *do* with the OT? Even in its most benign form, reading the Bible as 'salvation-history' overlooks most of the *real* (i.e. secular) his-tory of ancient Israel. Furthermore, when Christians appropriate the

---

3.   This article has no pagination.

4.   For orientation to the vast literature see Hasel 1991—written from a conser-vative perspective, but a good review of the literature and the issues.

Hebrew Bible and Scripture as their own tradition—denying the validity of the tradition for those who created it—this is an enormous piece of hutzpah.

2. In its more extreme forms, however, this kind of 'spiritualizing' leads to typology, which although vigorously opposed by Rudolph Bultmann, Friederich Baumgärtel, G.E. Wright, James Barr, and others, is a methodology with which numerous OT scholars have flirted, either coyly or overtly, among them Walther Eichrodt, Gerhard von Rad, Wilhelm Vischer, and others. Typology may take the form of simply seeing the OT as the 'prophecy' (*Verheissung*) of which the NT is the 'fulfillment' (the familiar Pauline and Lutheran dichotomy of Law vs. Gospel). Or it may become truly pernicious in the form of allegorical interpretation, which denies to the literary tradition—and thus to the experience and faith of ancient Israel—any historical reality at all. In this view, not only were the interpretations of events upon which the writers of the Hebrew Bible based their faith wrong, but any actual 'events' themselves are called into question. That is, they had no intrinsic 'reality', but were merely 'prototypes'—foreshadowings of the Gospel. Secular or 'profane' history, since it is not *Heilsgeschichte*, is not a 'true' history, is in fact no history at all. In this apocalyptic perspective, the *eschaton* in which are living reduces all that precedes it to meaninglessness; *Urzeit* is swallowed up in *Endzeit*. The 'Christ-event' becomes the only 'authentic' event, because it alone is revelatory. But this makes the *real* history of ancient Israel a mere charade.

3. Another way in which Christian OT theology devalues the history of ancient Israel and its religion is an outgrowth of the salvation-history approach, namely the appropriation of the OT as simply the starting point of a *Vergegenwärtigung*, or 're-presentation'. What is involved here is the attempt not merely to 'retell' the story (*nacherzählen*), and thus to contemporize God's saving acts on behalf of Israel, but to 'actualize' these events in the proclamation so as to recreate the (supposedly) biblical faith that was originally inspired by the events. This method of *Vergegenwärtigung* as the most appropriate form of theological discourse was pioneered by von Rad, followed by Westermann, Porteous, Ackroyd, Anderson, Sanders, and many others. The concept is perhaps most accessible in Wright's popular *God Who Acts: Biblical Theology as Recital* (1952). (I still remember the surge of excitement I felt upon discovering that little book as a seminarian nearly 40 years ago.)

Sometimes regarded as an aspect of the traditio-historical method, this approach actually begs the question of historicity, as James Barr has pointed out trenchantly of Wright's work. The 'story' eclipses the 'facts'. 'What really may have happened' in ancient Israel is preempted by the question 'What should I do?' History is less significant than repetition of the biblical writers' interpretations (and ours) of the supposed events. Now confessional recital may be effective theology, but can it claim to be history? Is it even interested in the 'mundane' event? It seems to me that seeing history only *sub specie aeternitatis* may depreciate it to the point where factual history is not worth recovering at all. Allegory makes a farce of history, reduces ancient Israel to a morality play.

4. Whatever and however a selection is made from the many strands of literary traditions regarding Israel's history and religion, the results tend to say more about a given scholar's predilections than the reality. Christian OT theology, for instance, has overwhelmingly preferred the prophetic tradition—despite the fact that it clearly presents a late and perhaps minor tradition within ancient Israel, the Hebrew Bible, and later Judaism—and has pointedly ignored or rejected the priestly tradition with its emphasis on ritual and cult. The Deuteronomistic tradition has been favored by OT scholars secondarily, in my opinion, largely because its theological program, masked by quasi-historical intentions, suits the 'political history' orientation stemming from the Reformation heritage of the Protestant scholars who have dominated OT theology. Indeed, I would argue that the characteristically Protestant mode of OT theology explains many things: its excessively rationalistic preoccupation with ideology, theology, and systematics; its philological penchant in exegesis, stemming from the doctrine of *sola scriptura*; a verbal *Gestalt* that results in a bias against ritual and cult and in favor of the proclamation of the word; a disproportionate emphasis upon faith that stems from Pauline and Lutheran antinomianism, rejects law out of a false dichotomy with gospel, and tends to justify faith by appeals to history and historical proofs; its obsession with what Jon Levenson (1987: 296) calls 'repristinization', which must always find its 'biblical' origins, its continuity with an earlier and thus presumably more 'authentic' religion. Why this compulsion of OT theologians to 'baptize' ancient Israel and the Hebrew Bible, to make Moses and Paul proper Lutherans? Is it not mostly wishful thinking—a 'nostalgia for a biblical past that never was'—and perhaps also a chronic crisis of faith, despite the prevalent slogan *sola fide*?

An observation of Jon Levenson is eloquent: 'In part, biblical theology results from the fact that Christians read the Hebrew Bible through a logic of displacement. It draws much of its energy from the anxieties of the younger sibling' (1987: 296). Levenson also compares Judaism's typical stance with Protestantism's quest for historical certitude and for the systematization of religious beliefs in theology, concluding that Jews today approach the past, even the biblical past, partly in imitation of non-Jews. They do so, however, 'not because of faith, but because of the lack of it, not in hopes of defining a theology, but of finding a replacement for theology' (1987: 290). To be sure, the late Moshe Goshen-Gottstein, a brilliant and seminal Jewish thinker, has proposed a 'Taanakh theology' alongside Christian OT theology (1987). But he conceives this quite frankly as a confessional enterprise, like most OT theology, with no pretensions to descriptive-historical 'objectivity', more typically Jewish philosophy than theology. And he acknowledges that in this enterprise he is entirely alone among Jewish scholars, a maverick. The near-total absence of 'biblical theologies' among Jewish scholars—the community that surely represents the mainstream of continuity with the various tributaries of the Hebrew Bible—should at least give us pause.

3. *Key Issues in the Current Debate—and the Role of Archaeology*

A. *The Historiographical Dilemma*

That there is currently a crisis in Israelite historiography is widely acknowledged by many biblical scholars, and related epistemological issues are at last beginning to be addressed by Syro-Palestinian archaeologists. In the latter field, the replacement of the materialist-functionalist paradigms of the 'new archaeology' of the 1970s–80s by today's 'post-processual' archaeology brings those of us who deal with the archaeology of ancient Israel squarely to face again with ideology and *history*. Meanwhile, we have noted Rolf Rendtorff's conclusion that 'we will have to redesign our image of Israel's history and the history of its religion'. Indeed; but archaeology will then have to play a vital, even dominant role. And very few biblical scholars seem to be aware of that fact, or willing to face its consequences. That is apparently because most biblical scholars still do not understand what today's archaeology is. If not, then we archaeologists are largely at fault.

It is not so much our sources that are flawed, but our approach. Better histories will require better historians, as well as new data and new models. The mere increase in new 'information' will not, in itself, bring a concomitant increase in our understanding of the past, i.e., in genuine historical knowledge. 'Facts' must be converted into 'data' by being placed within a context of meaningful questions.

A beginning might be made by isolating the historiographical questions that biblical philology and exegesis, the writing of Israel's history and religion, and Syro-Palestinian archaeology have in common. What is 'history', and above all what *kind* of history do we want? What are the appropriate, and obtainable, goals and purposes of history-writing? How do we distinguish 'primary' and 'secondary' data, that is, what is the legitimate and most fruitful relationship between textual data and archaeological evidence? What constitutes a workable 'balance of probability', or adequate verification of historical 'facts'? How do we achieve a balance between an empirically based, disinterested, 'objective' history on the one hand, and a dynamic, sympathetic, relevant history on the other? These questions are especially urgent when that history is biblical, Judeo-Christian, and fundamental to so much of the Western tradition— *our* history.

It is to the credit of recent biblical scholars like Thompson, Ahlström, and Davies—and such 'radical' predecessors as Lemche, Garbini, Soggin, Gottwald, and others—that they have raised these historiographical issues so sharply. Of all the above questions, however, I believe that the most crucial is: What *kind* of history do we want? Everything else hinges on that. (1) Clearly the biblical texts, on any other than a minimalist reading, can yield a 'history of ideas', or ideology, as well as an outline of religion-political history—at least for the postexilic period, and I would argue even for much of the monarchy (although not for 'proto-Israel' in the twelfth–eleventh century BCE). (2) Modern, interdisciplinary archaeology, on the other hand, as a mature discipline itself, is now poised to begin writing a technoenvironmental and socioeconomic history—my 'secular history of ancient Palestine' (including 'ancient Israel'); Thompson's larger-scale 'historical (human) geography of Palestine'; or Ernest Axel Knauf's provocative notion of an 'extension of natural history into the specific realm of *homo sapiens*'.[5] It is worth noting also that Knauf has picked up the emphasis of Braudel and the *annales* school on *la longue durée*, which several of us have toyed with, suggesting that we combine

5.   For orientation to the burgeoning literature, see Preucel 1991; and for possible applications to Syro-Palestinian and biblical archaeology, see Dever 1993.

Braudel's long-term history ('structures') and his medium-term history ('conjunctures') into a 'processual history', an approach that he says 'cannot do without archaeology' (1991: 44).

At issue in many recent discussions, at least *implicitly*, is the role of archaeology in writing a history of ancient Israel. But it is curious that that issue has been raised almost exclusively by nonarchaeologists. There are, for example, at least brief, tentative discussions of archaeology's role in writing a history of Israel in several works of biblical scholars, in addition to those reviewed above. Among Syro-Palestinian archaeologists, however—American, European, or Israeli—one can point only to a handful of discussions of 'archaeology, Bible, and history', none much more than dilettantish, and nearly all confined to the early settlement horizon. Until Syro-Palestinian archaeologists who fancy themselves historians engage historiographical issues seriously, there can be no productive dialogue with biblical studies. And archaeologists must contribute precisely *as* historians. Clearly our training is too specialized to allow us any longer to be biblical philologians or exegetes; we rightly eschew theology as a means of appropriating the past on its own terms; and we are, even at best, self-taught as ethnographers, anthropologists, or social theorists. We are thus historians. If Americanist archaeology 'is anthropology or nothing', then Syro-Palestinian archaeology is 'history or nothing'. With all the salutary emphasis today in archaeology on interdisciplinary approaches, the use of socio-anthropological models, and the borrowing of analytical and statistical techniques from the natural sciences, we must not forget that basically we archaeologists working in the historical periods of Israel and the ancient Near East are simply historians who work more with material culture remains than with texts. This brings us to a second issue, that of models drawn from other disciplines and their use.

B. *Appropriate Models in History-Writing*

Socio-anthropological approaches to the study of ancient Israel have been in vogue for some time now and are too well known to need documentation here. In particular, sociological models have been employed for the earlier periods, such as the settlement era and the rise of the monarchy, as in recent works of Mendenhall, Gottwald, Lemche, Frick, Flanagan, Finkelstein and Na'aman, and others. These newer approaches are certainly refreshing; and their specifically anthropological bent makes them congenial, at least in theory, to much of the newer archaeology, especially among the younger generation. Thus there would seem to be a methodological confluence that would bode well for a future dialogue. Yet one can point only to a few studies among archaeologists or biblical scholars that make what I would consider *appropriate* use of socio-anthropological models. Furthermore, the tendency of these efforts to float in the rarified atmosphere of pure theory, the endless controversy, the lack of demonstrable results, and especially the dreadful jargon—all tend to vitiate what might be fruitful approaches and only increase resistance to models among the many remaining skeptics.

We need to remember what 'models', as used elsewhere in the social and natural sciences, are. They are only abstractions, not drawn from the data but imposed upon them in order to manipulate those data experimentally, that is, heuristic devices. As Baruch Halpern says in a devastating critique of Mendenhall (and less so of Gottwald): 'Models teach questions that one might ask, not answers that one must give' (1992: 66). And as Ziony Zevit points out in a recent review of Davies' *History*, '[models] cannot be used to infer unattested data. The shoehorning of archaeological data into a social-theoretical Procrustean bed and using the mangled results to render a verdict on "historical Israel" is unsophisticated, to say the least' (1995). In short, models are rarely explanatory.

It is interesting that Syro-Palestinian archaeologists have made much less use of extreme socio-anthropological models; but inasmuch as that is probably due to their backwardness in general, it does them little credit. Recent models, where employed at all, tend to be simply statistical, as in current Israeli surveys; are drawn from more traditional sources, such as the study of Middle Eastern pastoral nomadism; or are still resolutely (and somewhat naively) confused with 'historical explanations'. I am convinced that sophisticated, modern, interdisciplinary social science models *can* be employed to elucidate textual-historical and archaeological data successfully, just as models from the natural sciences have helped to generate enormous quantities of useful techno-environmental data on the ancient Near East. But we have a long way to go. Meanwhile, inchoate 'social theories' of scholars like Flanagan and Davies, or crypto-theological agendas like that of Boling, get us nowhere.[6] I concur with Halpern, who observes that 'what distinguishes the recent

---

6.   On the possibilities of a 'secular history', see Dever 1991, pp. 108-15; Knauf 1991, p. 44; Thompson 1992, pp. 402-405; and add now the extended discussion in Dever 1995b.

discovery of sociology is a penchant for applying to external typologies to supply the place of hard data' (1992: 65). And I point out that any *new* 'hard data' in ancient Israel will come, by definition, out of the ground—artifacts or texts—not out of the Hebrew Bible, which is a closed *corpus*. In that sense, if in no other, archaeological data will take precedence, will constitute a large proportion of the 'primary' data in future, especially for the pre-monarchic period (as some biblical scholars already recognize). To that issue we now turn.

C. *Archaeology and the Question of Secondary Sources*
Another issue where archaeology can play a role has to do with the nature of the sources: 'primary' or 'secondary'? (1) The first issue is primarily whether the textual sources in the Hebrew Bible are largely of secondary value (if any) for writing the history of the periods of the Judges and the monarchy, since in their final edited form they date to the Persian and Hellenistic eras. In short, what we have here is a *literary*, not a genuinely historical, tradition. Increasingly, biblical scholars such as those we have reviewed here, and especially those on the Continent, conclude that late redaction means late *composition*, and thus sources that are *post factum*, of little historical value.

No responsible scholar today doubts the late date of the final redaction of the tradition. But the question remains whether or not there may be a 'core' within the tradition that comprises earlier, genuinely historical material—some of it possibly contemporary with the events the tradition purports to describe. No one would argue more forcefully than I that archaeology cannot be used to 'prove the Bible'. Nevertheless, there are a number of points at which datable Iron Age archaeological evidence and literary reference in the Bible do 'converge' in such a way as to suggest contemporaneity—a fact that responsible historians cannot deny. If not 'proof', there is weight here on the side of the 'balance of probability', which is what the historian always must work with.

Of the many hundreds of such convergences that might be listed, I mention only a few. (1) Nearly 300 early Iron Age or 'proto-Israelite' villages are now known in the hill country, the settlement type and distribution of which, along with artifactual evidence, provide an 'archaeological assemblage' that agrees remarkably well with conditions described in Joshua–Samuel, as Finkelstein (1988) and Stager (1985) have shown, and enable us to reconstruct a very plausible twelfth–eleventh century socioeconomic and cultural setting for the core of these narratives, 'folk history' or not. (2) The twelfth–eleventh century BCE biblical 'Philistines' are now so well documented archaeologically that we can confidently describe their origins, material culture, and socio-political organization (Dothan 1982). That all this 'fits' the many biblical allusions so well, with no major accommodations needed, shows that a postexilic editor cannot simply have invented these passages, that they are genuinely archaic. (3) The same can be said for the rise of the Israelite state under Solomon (if not David), where the overwhelming indication of the archaeological evidence is for precisely the kind of urbanization and centralization that accompanies the emergence of a state in virtually all cross-cultural comparisons.[7] (4) A fact not often noted is that almost every detail of the sometimes enigmatic descriptions of the Solomonic temple in 1 Kgs 6–9 can now be directly illustrated by reference to actual Bronze and Iron Age temples and their furnishings elsewhere in the southern Levant. A later writer who had never seen the temple could not possibly have given such accurate, detailed descriptions. (4) Finally, we have noted above the emergence of what we may call archaeologically a homogeneous 'Israelite-Judean culture' under the divided monarchy. First, this very well documented material culture is clearly the expression of a well-defined, ethnically distinct 'national character', that is, a people and a nation-state that we can readily distinguish as 'Israel' (precisely the entity that Davies thinks never existed). The evidence is massively documented elsewhere (yet is never surveyed adequately by any biblical scholar):[8] settlement type and distribution; defensive and domestic architecture; household furnishings; ceramic, lithic, and metal implements; ivories, seals and bullae with biblical names; shekel-weights; ostraca and inscriptions; distinctive burials and grave goods; temples, shrines, and cult paraphernalia of all kinds; etc. Again, the point is that this rich panoply of items accords so well with *both* the biblical descriptions of daily life in Israel-Judah and the overall conditions we know in Iron Age Palestine that it simply cannot have been contrived by writers living in the Persian or Hellenistic period—as

7.   I refer here to Flanagan 1988 and Boling 1988; for further critique, see Dever 1995a, 1995b, 1995b.

8.   For a review of 'state formation processes' in early Israel and a critique of some of the literature, see Dever 1995c. The latest work is Finkelstein and Na'aman 1994—certain to be the point of departure for all subsequent studies, despite what in my view is an exaggerated emphasis upon 'nomadic origins'. The view that monarchic Israel basically saw a revival of the old Bronze Age Canaanite city-state system was already elaborated in Fritz 1995.

though to provide a pseudo-historical 'setting' for their theocratic propaganda and program for reform. Any archaeologist could multiply these examples 'on the ground' many times over. These are properly *historical* data; and in future no historian of ancient Israel can afford to ignore them.

D. *What Constitutes a* Sitz im Leben?

As is well known, both form and redaction criticism since Gunkel have sought to comprehend smaller or larger units of biblical texts by attempting to place them in their original context, or *Sitz im Leben*. The notion of 'context', of course, is vital, indeed essential, for every archaeologist, and therefore we readily applaud the search for *Sitze im Leben*. Yet I would observe that in practice, the search produced little more than a *Sitz in Literatur*—a 'setting' that reflected much more the history of the *literature* and its transmission than of 'real life' or history in the usual sense.

To be sure, a few biblical scholars have sensed this deficiency. Rolf Knierim's incisive critique of recent literary criticism of the Hebrew Bible points out:

> For form criticism, the societal settings behind the text are assumed to be the decisive generative forces for the emergence of generative texts. The assumption, however, has always meant that a comprehensive sociological picture of Israel's history is indispensable for form-critical work. The only problem is that we have never had such a comprehensive picture (1985: 144).

Knierim goes on to decry 'dubious reconstructions of settings via dubiously identified text patterns'—which I would characterize simply as a classic circular argument. He concludes:

> A new direction would evolve, however, if the sociological study of Israel's history and the study of the genres of OT literature, each in its own right, would be programmatically correlated. Of such a programmatic correlation we have at best embryonic indications, but neither a program nor an execution (1985: 144).

Exactly; but how about including in that program *archaeology*—the only source of information on society independent of the Hebrew Bible, indeed, I would argue, our best source for a real 'sociology of biblical Israel'.[9]

---

9. Davies cites as his principal archaeological 'authority' T.L. Thompson

Thompson has also addressed this point, although obliquely, in observing that the postexilic 'setting' usually delineated for the final redaction and composition of the Hebrew Bible as a whole is the work of what he terms only 'a handful of tradents': 'One ought not to assume, however, that such *Sitze im Leben* lie *im Leben des Volkes*. Rather we are dealing with scholarly bibliophiles' (1992: 392).

I would say simply that we are dealing with *literature*—a literary rather than a 'real-life' setting. The essential point that many philologians (and theologians) seem to overlook is that literature does not necessarily mirror real life, at least not the life of the masses, but only of the *literati*. The texts reflect the creative, literary imagination of a very few of the elite classes. In ancient Israel, pre- and postexilic, these classes constituted a mere handful of priests, intellectuals sometimes attached to the court writing (?), prophets, and probably scribes. *These* were the people who wrote the Bible, for others like themselves. And while they could write 'disinterested' history or include details on ordinary day-to-day activities when they chose to do so, the fact is that they were simply not interested in what the vast majority of people in ancient Israel thought or did. Only archaeology, as some *annales* historians argue, 'can give history back to the people'.

Perhaps the point is simply: Who *makes* history? And who *writes* it? Which count more, the principal actors, countless individuals over the slow-moving millennia, as with Braudel; or those few who rationalize events, who are often makers of myth more than of history. (If 'history is written by the winners', what constitutes 'winning'?) While I have argued here that there is much more genuine historical information in the biblical texts than supposed by many nowadays (especially if we read skillfully 'between the lines'), the fact is that we are nevertheless almost totally dependent upon *archaeological* data for most of what we shall ever know about most of the people of ancient Israel most of the time.

(1992)—another historian and biblical scholar, who knows the archaeological data only second- or third-hand, and who furthermore is as nihilistic as Davies. For my own critique of both, see Dever 1995a, 1995b. For excellent, authoritative summaries of the archaeological evidence for an 'Israelite material culture', see Weippert 1988, pp. 417-681 (already available to Davies); Mazar 1990, pp. 368-530; and Ben-Tor 1992, pp. 303-73.

4. *Toward a 'Non-Theological' Agenda?*

We have assessed the theological approach above, so only a few further comments are necessary here. The case against Old Testament theology as a surrogate for the study of the history of Israel has also recently found forceful expression in J.D. Levenson's article 'Why Jews Are not Interested in Biblical Theology', which we noted above. Another devastating critique, aimed partly at Mendenhall's and Gottwald's supposedly 'sociological' models, is that of Baruch Halpern, who concludes:

> The study of Israel has bleached, not obliterated, its theological spots...
> Biblical history is not, as Mendenhall claimed, in transition. It remains
> biblical, not Syro-Palestinian, Canaanite, or Israelite... What is wanted is
> a liberation of Israelite history from modern theology... Israelite history
> can engage a disciplined historical imagination. It wants one abjuration for
> it to do so: an abjuration of external doctrine, theological or sociological,
> in favor of the authority of intrinsic data (1992: 54, 66, 67).

My own methodological preferences have been stated in a recent paper entitled 'Archaeology, Philology, Theology and the Pursuit of Ancient Israelite Religion'.[10] One could simply substitute 'History' for 'Religion'. The point is that these more recent 'non-theological' approaches to ancient Israel reveal a shared if largely unarticulated notion that it is possible, and desirable, to write some sort of 'secular history', 'history without the Bible', rather than the typical *Heilsgeschichte* that does such violence to the biblical texts in their context, as well as to the socioeconomic and cultural context for which archaeology increasingly provides empirical data. Despite my criticism here of several biblical scholars who have recently addressed the issues of Israelite historiography, I agree with all of them (and others) on one basic point. We need a fresh approach to the phenomenon of ancient Israel that is truly critical, comparative, generative, synthetic, and ecumenical. In short, let us aspire to 'truer' histories, in the sense of *better* histories—histories, not theologies.[11]

The intent here is not to delegitimize theology, but simply to segregate

10. This paper was delivered at the 1993 inaugural meeting of a new American Schools of Oriental Research 5-year consultation on Archaeology and the Religion of Israel. It will be published in a forthcoming collection of papers from this consultation.

11. Susan Ackerman of Dartmouth College and I are working on a volume tentatively entitled *A Social History of Iron Age Palestine and Ancient Israel.*

it, so as to keep the historical, exegetical, and theological enterprises honest—all of them, each true to its own interests. In approaching the biblical tradition we should follow Krister Stendahl's well-known insistence upon separating the question of 'What *does* it mean?' from the question of 'What *did* it mean?' And I think it is possible to add a third, deeper level of inquiry: 'What really happened?' Despite all the well-taken precautions above, that we can never know *wie es eigentlich gewesen war*, if we do not presuppose that there is some objective reality 'out there', we shall never be moved to investigate and therefore shall learn nothing of what may have transpired. Even the more skeptical archaeologists of the processualist school, for whom 'history' was a bad word, have finally yielded on this point, thanks to the withering critique of Ian Hodder and other 'post-processualists'.[12] Something *did* happen in the past, quite apart from either our conceptualization of its meaning, or even of the perceptions of the original participants in the events. It is our task as historians and archaeologists to penetrate as deeply as possible into past realities, with all means at our disposal, to learn if possible something of 'how it was'.

Conclusion

Baruch Halpern has recently observed of the current state of biblical studies: 'Today the welter of competing claims, the cacophony of methods, betrays the cumulation of the decades. The synthetic eschaton promised in the apocalypse of philological positivism has not arrived' (1992: 65).

The age of positivism in archaeology is similarly over in this post-Albrightian era. Perhaps it is time to liberate the writing of the history of ancient Israel, as well as its literature and religion, from all external dogmas. In particular, we must redefine the relation between our two best sources of information—texts and artifacts—not subsuming one under the dominant paradigm of the other, or leap-frogging back and forth between narrative and archaeology, which will only produce what Knauf aptly calls 'a pseudohistory of nonevents' (1991: 49). The point of departure must be a mutual, honest, critical dialogue between textual studies and the best that archaeology can offer—one that above all is humble, fully aware of what we do not know, and thus open to new insights about the past. Otherwise, as Santyana observed, we are

12. See references in n. 5 above.

doomed to repeat the mistakes of the past, as well as those of past scholarship.

It is my contention that it is *only* in the dialogue between texts and artifacts—pursued rigorously by scholars committed to interdisciplinary inquiry—that we can hope for more comprehensive, better balanced, ultimately more satisfying histories of ancient Israel in all her variety and vitality. The fixed textual data, although of somewhat restricted value historically, can yield an outline of political and theocratic history, of ethnic and religious ideology, together with numerous details of real life embedded in the older materials now incorporated into the literary traditions of the Hebrew Bible—an 'internal history'. The archaeological data—theoretically almost unlimited in extent and variety, more flexible, and less deliberately biased—can yield a broader technoenvironmental and socio-economic history, an 'external, secular' history that is parallel, complementary in many ways, and often corrective. *Both* histories of ancient Israel are now essential, and possible—if scholars in several disciplines are willing to set aside conventional approaches and co-operate in a true dialogue between texts and artifacts.

Let us heed the sage advice of my esteemed colleague, Professor Lou Silberman, to 'listen' to both text and artifact. That means that as historians, when we have been able to read both texts and artifacts as accurately as possible with all means at our disposal, assessing all the data as disinterestedly as possible, we must then be content to sit back and listen—intently, patiently, with a disciplined but sympathetic imagination, and above all with humility. As Ian Hodder (1986: 79) reminds us, in the quest for meaning in history there are always these subjective elements. The role of history is 'to understand human action, rather than events...To get at action is to get at subjective meanings, at the *inside* of events'. By listening perceptively to the human past as it speaks to us today, we may indeed 'imagine', and thus appropriate, that past, and so gain the only insights that we shall ever have into the future.

BIBLIOGRAPHY

Ahlström, G.W.
    1993   *The History of Ancient Palestine from the Paleolithic Period to Alexander's Conquest* (JSOTSup, 146; Sheffield: JSOT Press).
Ben-Tor, A. (ed.)
    1992   *The Archaeology of Ancient Israel* (New Haven: Yale University Press).

Boling, R.G.
1988   *The Early Biblical Community in Transjordan* (SWBA, 6; Sheffield: Almond Press).
Binford, L.R.
1983   *Pursuit of the Past: Decoding the Archaeological Record* (New York: Thames & Hudson).
Davies, P.R.
1992   *In Search of 'Ancient Israel'* (JSOTSup, 148; Sheffield: JSOT Press).
Dever, W.G.
1985   'Syro-Palestinian and Biblical Archaeology', in D.A. Knight and G.M. Tucker 1985: 31-74.
1991   'Archaeology, Material Culture and the Early Monarchical Period', in Edelman 1991: 103-15.
1993   'Biblical Archaeology—Death and Rebirth?', in *Biblical Archaeology Today, 1990: Proceedings of the Second International Congress on Biblical Archaeology, Jerusalem, June 1990* (Jerusalem: Israel Exploration Society): 706-22.
1995a   'Archaeology and the Current Crisis in Israelite Historiography', *Eretz Israel* 25 (the Yosef Aviram volume): 18*-27*.
1995b   'Will the Real Israel Please Stand Up? Archaeology and Israelite Historiography: Part 1', *BASOR* 297: 61-80.
1995c   'From Tribe to Nation: A Critique of State Formation Processes in Ancient Israel', in S. Mazzoni (ed.), *Nouve fondazioni nel Vicino Oriente: realità ed ideologia* (Pisa: University of Pisa): 213-38.
Dietrich, W., and M. Klopfenstein (eds.)
1995   *Ein Gott allein? JHWH-Verehrung und biblischer Monotheismus im Kontext der israelitischen und altorientalischen Religionsgeschichte* (Freiburg: University of Freiburg).
Dothan, T.
1982   *The Philistines and their Material Culture* (New Haven: Yale University Press).
Edelman, D.V. (ed.)
1991   *The Fabric of History: Text, Artifact and Israel's Past* (Sheffield: JSOT Press).
Finkelstein, I.
1988   *The Archaeology of the Israelite Settlement* (Jerusalem: Israel Exploration Society).
Finkelstein, I., and N. Na'aman (eds.)
1994   *From Nomadism to Monarchy: Archaeological and Historical Aspects of Early Israel* (Jerusalem: Israel Exploration Society).
Flanagan, J.W.
1988   *David's Social Drama: A Hologram of Israel's Early Iron Age* (Sheffield: JSOT Press).
Fritz, V.
1995   *The City in Ancient Israel* (The Biblical Seminar, 29; Sheffield: JSOT Press).

Goshen-Gottstein, M.
1987 'Taanakh Theology: The Religion of the Old Testament and the Place of Jewish Biblical Theology', in P.D. Miller, P.D. Hanson and S.D. McBride (eds.), *Ancient Israelite Religion: Essays in Honor of Frank Moore Cross* (Philadelphia: Fortress Press): 617-44.

Halpern, B.
1988 *The First Historians: The Hebrew Bible and History* (San Franciso: Harper & Row).
1992 'Sociological Comparativism and the Theological Imagination: The Case of the Conquest', in M. Fishbane and E. Tov (eds.), *Sha'arei Talmon: Studies in the Bible, Qumran and the Ancient Near East Presented to Shemaryahu Talmon* (Winona Lake, IN: Eisenbrauns).

Hasel, G.
1991 *Old Testament Theology: Basic Issues in the Current Debate* (Grand Rapids: Eerdmans).

Hodder, I.
1986 *Reading the Past: Current Approaches to Interpretation in Archaeology* (Cambridge: Cambridge University Press).

Knauf, E.A.
1991 'From History to Interpretation', in Edelman 1991.

Knierim, R.
1985 'Criticism of Literary Features, Form, Tradition and Redaction', in D.A. Knight and G.M. Tucker (eds.), *The Hebrew Bible and Its Modern Interpreters* (Philadelphia: Fortress Press): 123-65.

Knight, D.A., and G.M. Tucker (eds.)
1985 *The Hebrew Bible and its Modern Interpreters* (Philadelphia: Fortress Press).

Levenson, J.D.
1987 'Why Jews Are Not Interested in Biblical Theology', in J. Neusner (ed.), *Judaic Perspectives on Ancient Israel* (Philadelphia: Fortress Press).

Mazar, A.
1990 *Archaeology of the Land of the Bible 10,000–580 BCE* (New York: Doubleday).

Miller, J.M.
1991 'Is it Possible to Write a History of Israel without Relying on the Hebrew Bible?', in Edelman 1991.

Preucel, R.W. (ed.)
1991 *Processual and Postprocessual Archaeology: Multiple Ways of Knowing the Past* (Carbondale, IL: Southern Illinois University Press).

Rendtorff, R.
1994 'The Paradigm is Changing: Hopes—and Fears', *Biblical Interpretation* 1 (n.p.).

Stager, L.E.
1985 'The Archaeology of the Family in Ancient Israel', *BASOR* 260: 1-35.

Thompson, T.L.
    1992   *Early History of the Israelite People from the Written and Archaeological Sources* (Leiden: Brill).
Weippert, H.
    1988   *Palästina in vorhellenistischer Zeit* (Munich: Beck).
Wright, G.E.
    1952   *God Who Acts: Biblical Theology as Recital* (London: SCM Press).
Zevit, Z.
    1995   Review of P.R. Davies, *'In Search of Ancient Israel'*, *AJS Review* 21: 153-56.

TEXT AND ARTIFACT: TWO MONOLOGUES?*

Baruch Halpern

The short answer to the title of this paper is yes.

But the reasons for that answer merit consideration. Each monologue in turn has limitations.

In 1993, the distinguished analyst of ceramic technology and production Frederick Matson offered a graduate course at Penn State on technological and ethnological approaches to ceramic production. What he instilled in all the students in that course was the strong sense that historical archaeology places too much reliance on ceramic typology and pays insufficient attention to variability and repetition in ceramic production. In addition, ceramic distribution furnishes the basis for theories of demography, and analysis of the product leads to sociological conclusions, the likelihood of which is often overstated, the more so as the conclusions are usually tied to some anthropological theory of social development.[1] It is not surprising, under the circumstances, that Martin Bernals and Peter Jameses—major revisionists—thrive. After all, ceramic evidence is the fundamental building block of archaeological chronology. And a secure chronology is the very integrity of the field. William Lamb, Lord Melbourne once said, 'I wish I were as cocksure of anything as Tom Macaulay is of everything'.[2] In both the positive and

---

*   As the last speaker at the conference, it fell to me to summarize for other participants. The pleasant part of that task was to thank our benefactors, Philip and Muriel Berman, and our hosts, Larry Silberstein, David Small, Robert Cohn, Shirley Ratushny, and Carol Sabo, for the remarkable hospitality and the delightful atmosphere that they cultivated at these proceedings. It remains a pleasure to say so here.

1.   See on such models the discussion by William Dever in this volume.

2.   A contemporary of Byron, whose—unwanted—mistress his wife, Carolyn Lamb, was, and a dandy, Lamb was noted for remarks of this ilk, including the celebrated '11th Commandment' of the Lamb family, 'Thou shalt not bother'. And of course his famous advice solicited by a friend for a young son, 'Get on the public

negative senses, that is how textual scholars feel about archaeologists.

In the world of text, the situation is worse. Textualists have techniques for analysis, some even involving dating. Some are reasonably reliable, like obsidian hydration—it is, for example, definitely possible to date the J (Yahwist) source in the Pentateuch earlier than the P (Priestly) source, since J's renditions of Aramaic names conform to early Old Aramaic systems of consonant representation, while P's conform to late Old Aramaic and Imperial Aramaic phonology.[3] But most are less so, running the gamut from the equivalent of stratified assemblages[4] to ceramic typology[5] to actual cultural typology—the heady notion that certain ideas, as well as social stages, occur in fixed sequence—which was in fact the basis first of de Wette's and then of Wellhausen's reorganization of biblical studies. We have our Frederick Matsons, and then we have our Bernals and Jameses and Velikovskys. In fact, the world of text completely outclasses the world of artifacts—in the production and toleration of lunatics. Some of the most eminent practitioners of biblical studies turn out to be on the field's fringes, and one might even think of the field as consisting only of fringes. This fringe-element gap requires composition: the field of biblical studies needs to trade twelve fringe scholars for Fred Matson.

Despite the similarities on the edges of the fields, important factors separate the disciplines. Obviously the objects of scrutiny differ. The essential skills of textual scholarship differ altogether from those of archaeology—and the skills necessary for publishing significant work

payroll early and stay there'. See Bertram Newman, *Lord Melbourne* (London: Macmillan, 1930).

3.   E.g., J *yqśn* for P *yqṭn*, probably for original edh emphatic (d); J Geshur, P. Geter, probably for original *gtr*. This question is treated at length in my Anchor Bible Reference Library History of Israel, now in progress.

4.   P as the derivative of a literalizing response to JE—most recently, R.E. Friedman, *The Exile and Biblical Narrative* (HSM, 22; Chico, CA: Scholars Press, 1981); Judges 4 as a reifying reconstruction based on Judges 5—Halpern, *The First Historians* (New York: Harper & Row, 1988), pp. 76-103; for a possible alternative approach to Judges 4–5, cf., e.g., K.L. Younger, Jr, '*HEADS! TAILS! OR THE WHOLE COIN?!* Contextual Method & Intertextual Analysis: Judges 4 and 5', in K.L. Younger, W.W. Hallo, and B.F. Batto (eds.), *The Biblical Canon in Comparative Perspective, Scripture in Context*, IV (Lewiston, NY: Edwin Mellen, 1991), pp. 109-46.

5.   Into this class fall most attempts at redaction criticism and many of source criticism. There are a few exceptions with a higher degree of probability, and many exceptions with a lesser degree of probability.

sometimes coincide with neither. Another factor is important in the Late Bronze and the Iron Age: our corpus of artifacts continues to grow, and at a rapid pace; our corpus of texts is all but closed. Will Rogers once quipped, 'Buy land; they're not making any more of it'. Well, buy texts—only Avraham Biran is making them. What this implies is that an archaeologist can truly *test* a hypothesis with fresh data—as Y. Yadin did at Megiddo; a textual scholar can do no more than ground a hypothesis in existing data.[6]

What we have are two cultures. On the one hand there are hard archaeological data, which are somewhat overinterpreted and drastically underpublished by one culture. And on the other hand we have the madness of textual analysis, with its vast range of explications and over-publication, in which standards of evidence vary disastrously, and in which there is a frequent and lamentable tendency for readers to respond to publications without understanding the questions they pose.[7]

In the succeeding treatment, I will exemplify a historian's way of compensating for the limitations on text. The question before us is the historicity of the united monarchy, at first on the basis of direct textual testimony. The text, for the most part, is 2 Samuel. Along with a few chapters to either side of it, it describes the early development of the Israelite state. Two factors play into this choice: first, narratives about state formation are rare, if not otherwise absent, in the ancient Near East; and, second, in the last few years, numerous books have appeared, each of which directly or indirectly questions the existence of David and Solomon.[8] These works have been written from literary, archaeological,

---

6. See the remarks of Dever in this volume; and further discussion below.

7. It would of course be invidious to cite examples. The general principle, however, is sketched out by R.J. Collingwood, *An Autobiography* (Oxford: Oxford University Press, 1939), pp. 29-43.

8. J. Van Seters, *In Search of History* (New Haven: Yale University Press, 1983); *Prologue to History: The Yahwist as Historian in Genesis* (Louiseville, KY: Westminster/John Knox, 1992); T.L. Thompson, *Early History of the Israelite People. From the Written and Archaeological Sources* (Studies in the History of the Ancient Near East, 4; Leiden: Brill, 1992); P.R. Davies, *In Search of Ancient Israel* (JSOTSup, 148; Sheffield: Sheffield Academic Press, 1992); J.W. Flanagan, *David's Social Drama. A Hologram of Israel's Early Iron Age* (Social World of Biblical Antiquity Series, 7; JSOTSup, 73; Sheffield: Sheffield Academic Press, 1988); F. Jamieson-Drake, *Scribes and Schools in Monarchic Judah. A Socio-Archeological Approach* (Social World of Biblical Antiquity Series, 9; JSOTSup, 109; Sheffield: Sheffield Academic Press, 1991). It is not a coincidence that three of

anthropological and philosophical perspectives.[9] What they share is a minimalist approach that denies the presence of a state on any grounds until Assyrian inscriptions, about the year 853, attest a kingship of Ahab. The historicity of the united monarchy looks to be the hot historical topic in biblical studies for the next decade or more, and it may be useful to ask about the nature of historicity in this context.

We no longer need debate the existence of a David, now that the Tel Dan stela—and, this week at least, the Mesha Stele[10]—show that Judah's dynastic name was 'the house of David' already in the ninth century. But the revisionists will continue to contest whether he constructed an empire, which was then administered, and lost, by his son, Solomon. And, while the archaeological evidence for a central state has been called into question more than once, the easiest evidence to deny is that of the biblical text.

The figure of David was as firmly imprinted on the identity of Judah's elite as the Tel Dan stela would suggest. Over and over the books of Kings hold him up as a standard for royal conduct and as the ancestral guarantor of divine favor for Judah's capital city. Yet the David of Samuel, and especially of 2 Samuel, is a not the plaster saint of later memory and messianism. In 2 Samuel, David is a human being.

Scholars have cleared forests writing about the date and purpose of Samuel. But the field today is split. Is Samuel early, roughly contemporary with the events it describes?[11] Or is it, as some critics claim, a late,

these works bear a Sheffield or JSOT imprint. For further works turning away from historical reconstruction to match our actual archaeological remains before textual attestation of the political situation in the land of Israel, see Dever's remarks in this volume.

9. Part of the problem is that the creeping critical rejection of biblical accounts has reached its natural limits. First the patriarchs, then the exodus underwent rejection by historians. Now the conquest has suffered the same fate, and in some cases and in many respects the period of the Judges. Now scholarly skepticism has butted up against the united monarchy, a period for which written records must have been available at least from David's formation of a state bureaucracy forward.

10. A. Lemaire, '"House of David" Restored in Moabite Inscription', *BARev* 20.3 (May/June 1994), pp. 30-37. The traces in the photograph fit Lemaire's reading, but the syntax seems peculiar at this stage.

11. This was the consensus from the early nineteenth century roughly until the 1970s. In fact, it was actions described in Samuel, especially, that enabled de Wette to ascertain that the theology of the Deuteronomic reform had not always been programmatic for Israelite cultic practice.

fictional concoction?[12] What are the nature and purpose of Samuel—and thus its origin?

To my mind, the definitive approach to these questions is that of Kyle McCarter.[13] What strikes a historian on reading the text of Samuel is the number of key actors who die violently in it. Samuel spends a lot of time defending the principal architect of Israelite identity—the agent of the extension of hill-country identity into the lowlands—against what seem to be allegations raised against him by contemporary opponents. In the main, these allegations concern murders or killings. As McCarter observes, the author of the text thus evinces concerns—political concerns—that had to be dead horses, even forgotten horses, within a generation of David's death. For this reason, one should give credence—not unqualified, but nevertheless credence—to many claims that Samuel makes.

In his treatment of David's apology, McCarter identifies the following killings, not as those for which David is responsible, but as those of which he was accused: Saul and Jonathan, in the battle of Jezreel; Abner by Joab and Abishai (2 Sam. 3.27, 30);[14] Ishbaal (2 Sam. 4.6-8);[15] Uriah; Amnon, his eldest son; Absalom, by Joab; and Amasa, also by Joab.

This is not all the fun in the book. In addition to these cases, Naboth, the husband of David's second wife, dies naturally; Abner kills Asahel, Joab's brother, in battle (2 Sam. 2.28).[16] David is avowedly responsible for the killing of seven other Saulides, an Amaleqite who claims to have killed Saul and brings Saul's regalia in token thereof, and the Gibeonites who assassinated Ishbaal and brought David his head (2 Sam. 4.12). The people of Abel kill Sheba at Joab's insistence. Finally, Benaiah kills Adonijah (1 Kgs 2.13-25), Joab (1 Kgs 2.28-35), and Shimei (1 Kgs 2.36-44) on Solomon's order. These are just the highlights. If all this is

---

12. E.g., van Seters, *In Search of History*, pp. 249-91; Davies, *In Search*; Thompson, *Early History*.

13. P.K. McCarter, *II Samuel* (AB 7B; Garden City, NY: Doubleday, 1986); see also his 'The Apology of David', *JBL* 99 (1980), pp. 489-504; cf. J. VanderKam, 'Davidic Complicity in the Deaths of Abner and Eshbaal: A Historical and Redactional Study', *JBL* 99 (1980), pp. 521-39.

14. Note that Joab tells Abner he wants to confer, then plunges a dagger into the 'fifth rib' (? armor?).

15. To the 'fifth rib' again, while he sleeps.

16. Another feature of Samuel that deserves note is the remarkable number of methods used for the killing. Here, Abner kills Asahel by thrusting the butt of his spear backward into the 'fifth rib'.

factitious, we have an author who rolled Hamlet and Richard III into one, the ancient equivalent of Thomas Harris, with the explicit intention of *denying* the existence of Hannibal Lector.

The apology that alibies David for these killings is ham-fisted. But can we reconstruct history from it? David's first providential death is that of Nabal. Abigail has pleaded with David not to kill the man, when he conveniently drops dead of natural causes. This is how David acquires his second wife, who plays no further narrative role. Did Abigail murder her husband to defect to David? The case is hard to call.[17]

For Saul's death, with his three sons, at Gilboa, the agents of death are the Philistines, David's allies at the time and, perhaps, long thereafter. So Samuel distances David from the battle of Gilboa, or Jezreel. One source denies that David *ever* worked for the Philistines (1 Sam. 21.11-16). Another stresses: 1) that Saul drove David to join the Philistines; 2) that David told his overlord, Achish of Gath, he was raiding Judah when he was really raiding desert camps; 3) that David joined the Philistines at a staging zone for their thrust into the Jezreel, but was detailed to the rear as bodyguard for Achish;[18] and, 4) that the other tyrants feared duplicity, so Achish sent him back home. In addition, 5) during the battle, David was off in the south chasing Amaleqites; 6) when he learned from an Amaleqite that Saul was dead, and at Saul's request by the Amaleqite's own hand, David killed Saul's killer; and, 7) David composed a lament to mourn Saul's and Jonathan's deaths publicly (1 Sam. 24–2 Sam. 1).

Protest? This is a dissertation of denial![19] But the alibi does not even completely remove David from the battle: it admits he was in the Philistine camp, arrayed for war; that he was a trusted vassal of Achish, who did fight in the battle. It documents not that David killed Saul, but that the accusation that he helped the Philistines to victory had real

17. One cannot help but think of the occasional topos of the murder suspect who comes to believe that the death of all who cross him/her is a divine judgment. This is the basis of the plot in one of Agatha Christie's novels. A predictable psychological variation would be the beneficiary of violent or providential death who takes on the role of agent after a time. Is Abigail David's catalyst?

18. 1 Sam. 28.1-2; 29.2. As a bodyguard David was thus perhaps unlikely to see frontline action except in the case of a rout in one or another direction, in which case Achish's person might be involved.

19. In the text, David winds up with Saul's regalia. McCarter takes this to be the source of the accusation of complicity in Saul's death. But it may be a purely literary topos foreshadowing his succession.

sting.[20] He was at the front. But the mythmaking machinery of the text portrays him as the great slayer of Philistines in his youth: 'Is this not David, servant of Saul the king of Israel... Is this not David of whom they chant with flutes, saying, "Saul has smitten his thousands, and David his myriads"?' (1 Sam. 29.3, 5). Is the story of David's attachment to Saul's court true, or merely a political convenience—justifying his later attachment to Philistia? We shall probably never know.

Ishbaal's assassins were Gibeonites, persecuted by Saul. The assassins race to David. As in Saul's case, he strings them up. Notably, David keeps Ishbaal's head with Abner's remains in Hebron, away from the house of Saul.[21] In the aftermath, the northern kingdom falls into his lap. If David commissioned the killing, or even put out a contract, his treatment of the assassins is standard mob-style procedure. The text *admits* that the death is so providential for David—it is as providential, we read, as Saul's death (2 Sam. 4.9-10)—that his political opponents *must* have accused him of it.[22] Chances are, he commissioned the hit.

20. A text in Chronicles illustrates how profoundly embarrassing this version of events proved to be. 1 Chron. 12.20 relates that 'From Manasseh, there fell to David when he came with the Philistines against Saul to battle—and he didn't help them, for with counsel the tyrants of the Philistines sent him away, saying, "He will fall upon our heads to his lord, Saul"—When he went to Ziklag, there fell to him from Manasseh PN and PN and PN', etc. There is an epanalepsis here: 'from Manasseh, there fell to him, when he came...' to 'when he went to..., there fell to him from Manasseh...' The intermediate information and the resumption itself is an explanatory gloss—he didn't actually fight Saul, it was only when he returned to Ziklag that these Manassites joined him, while the battle was raging. It seems likely that the original source of this claim did not contain the apophasis, and merely maintained that Manassites joined David at Apheq. The source cannot have reached Chronicles in this form, but the awkward reformulation indicates typical Israelite respect for the source, which could instead have been recast as, 'And in Ziklag, after the death of Saul, there came to him...' Instead, the text mentions defections at the time of the battle of Jezreel! It probably originally mentioned defections just *before* the battle.

21. 2 Sam. 4.6-8, 12. The significance of retaining control over corpses was not lost on David, who never repatriated the remains of Saul and Jonathan from Jabesh Gilead until *after* he had wiped out the remaining Saulides, Meribbaal being the sole exception: in 2 Sam. 21.12-14, Saul and Jonathan and the hanged male heirs are removed to the tomb of Qish. As Meribbaal was confined to Jerusalem, David effectively prevented the development of a royal ancestral cult at Saul's tomb, or, in fact, a tomb specific to the head of the dynasty. It is not reported that he ever removed either Ishbaal's head or Abner's remains to the dynastic tomb.

22. Note the formulation of David's speech: 'As YHWH lives, who redeemed my life from all trouble, when the one who told me, "Lo, Saul is dead", was as an herald

Just earlier, Abner's death is a tidy little bonus. Abner was Ishbaal's Warwick, his second in command. The text describes a quarrel between the two.[23] Abner then acquired Michal, Saul's daughter (2 Sam. 3.13-16), and brought her, *with 20 attendants*, to an allegedly secret assignation in Hebron. At this feast, he promised to dump Ishbaal, and translate Israelite support to David. Abner departed in peace, an ally. But he had earlier killed Joab's brother, Asahel, in open battle. And Joab, without David's knowledge (4.26), therefore exacts vengeance.

The story of the assignation occupies 11 verses (2 Sam. 3.17-27). It requires 12 verses to exculpate David, who declares his innocence, curses the house of Joab's otherwise unnamed father, proclaims mourning, conducts a state funeral, elegizes Abner, eulogizes Abner, fasts all the way to sunset, and, the narrator says, persuades all Israel of his innocence. Rather, Joab and Abishai bushwacked Abner for killing Asahel.[24]

---

of glad tidings in his one view, I seized him and slew him in Ziklag, which was my giving him his reward for glad tidings. But when wicked men have slain an innocent man in his house on his bed, must I not now seek his bloodguilt from your hands, and drive/burn you out from the land?' YHWH has indeed redeemed his life from trouble, both by killing Saul and by killing Ishbaal, without his involvement. Note the response to the incurred bloodguilt: it must be driven out of the land. This is usually thought to be Deuteronomic language, but Deuteronomy speaks only of expunging evil (*r'*) from 'your midst' or 'from Israel' or (Deut. 19.13) of expunging 'innocent blood' (*dm nqy*) 'from Israel' or (Deut. 21.9) 'from your midst'. References outside ritual contexts (Deut. 26.13, 14) are found in Deut. 13.6; 17.7; 19.19; 21.21; 22.21, 24; 24.7 (from your midst); 17.12; 22.22 (from Israel). Usage in Kings in Deuteronomistic contexts is 'burn/drive "after" you' (or, 'the last of you'? 1 Kgs 14.10; 16.3; 21.21) or just 'burn/drive out' (2 Kgs 23.24). In the last instance, the context may imply 'from the land', but this is explicit outside of 2 Sam. 4.11 only in 1 Kgs 22.47, in the evaluation of Jehoshaphat; 2 Chron. 19.3 (a Chronistic speech to Jehoshaphat). The point is that in 2 Sam. 4.11; 1 Kgs 22.47, the land is what is polluted and must be cleansed, whereas in Deuteronomy it is the covenant community that is affected. In most cases in Kings, the question of what is polluted is not addressed.

23. The two fall out over Abner's alleged relations with one of Saul's concubines (2 Sam. 3.7-11). Yet, in 1 Kings 2, Solomon executes his brother, Adonijah, for *asking* for one of David's concubines. 'Ask for him the kingship', he tells Bathsheba, the alleged intermediary of the request, then dispatches the reliable Benaiah to execute him. How believable is this in either instance? As we shall see, it is part of the patterned exculpation strategies that repeatedly characterize this author's work.

24. The argument that 2 Sam. 3.30 is secondary is sometimes based on the allegation that Abishai played no role in the murder of Abner. This is specious

The exculpation is longer than the story. But the story, too, is apology: Abner delivered Michal, giving David a claim on the throne; he campaigned for David among the Israelite elders; he promised to make David king. But Joab gummed up the works: he pursued his vendetta even though Abner had killed Asahel in open battle, and reluctantly at that. The elaborate apparatus of defenses indicates that this murder, like that of Ishbaal, was a very live issue when this text—and probably Joab—were framed.[25]

Even critical readers, such as Gösta Ahlström,[26] take this story at face value. Abner was a fellow that David had every reason to protect. But it is very easy to imagine—and it is a certainty that many ancients did—that a crafty and unctuous David lured Abner to Hebron for a peace conference, and, offering him traditional hospitality, safe conduct, and promises of accommodation, or even submission,[27] turned on him and killed him. This is the technique later employed by Absalom against Amnon—the forgive-and-forget banquet followed by homicide. Lethal deception ran in the family.

David next kills by inspiration. In 2 Samuel 21, YHWH lets it out that

reasoning: Joab plunged the knife in, but someone else must have occupied or restrained Abner's 20 retainers (3.20). Or possibly slaughtered them. This verse is absolutely critical, because it clearly indicates that Abner killed Asahel *in battle*—just as 2 Samuel 2 has him repeatedly warn Asahel before killing him—to make a simple point: Joab killed someone with whom he was in an alliance, with whom he was at peace; Abner, who killed in battle, should have been exempt from blood vengeance. Note the contrast in 3.30: in MT, Joab and Abishai *hrgw*, whereas Abner *hmyt*—here apparently marking a difference between killing in alliance/peace and in war. The theme that Abner left David 'in peace/in alliance' in vv. 21, 22, 23 assumes importance in the account of Joab's death.

25. See McCarter, *II Samuel*, pp. 120-22.

26. *A History of Ancient Palestine* (JSOTSup, 146; Sheffield: Sheffield Academic Press, 1993), p. 465.

27. The concession of Michal might seem to speak against this possibility—the more so in that the author of 2 Samuel 3 adduces it in evidence of the situation. However, it is far from inconceivable that David made it a condition of his submission that he be recognized as a vassal king, and that in token of his special status, he be permitted to marry the king's sister; and that this condition of alliance or submission led naturally to the dispatching of a peace delegation. Abner's group of 20 retainers, on the face of things, resembles such a delegation far more than it does a secret conspiracy. To be sure, Samuel maintains that Abner's traitorous intentions had already been announced publicly at court; but one would think that were Ishbaal powerless to oppose Abner, the latter would have seized the throne himself.

a famine is the result of Saul's killing Gibeonites. The latter demand seven of Saul's male heirs in retribution, and these are hanged—two sons by Rizpah bat-Aia, and five grandsons by Saul's eldest daughter.[28] The Gibeonites had now learned to kill Saulides only on official pretexts, and the seven males were a sort of compensation for the martyrdom of Ishbaal's assassins. David spares Mephiboshet, Jonathan's lame son, and brings him to court permanently—a safe place, betimes, for the lone Saulide heir.[29] David generously left Mephiboshet half Saul's estates in a Solomonic decision after Absalom's revolt.[30]

The killing of Saul's descendants sparked accusations in David's time, and one is preserved. As David abandoned Jerusalem at the start of the Absalom revolt, Shimei, a member of Saul's clan, reviled him, calling, 'Go, go, Man of Blood, and Hellion. YHWH has requited you all the bloodguilt of the house of Saul, whom you succeeded...' (2 Sam. 16.7-8).

Shimei charges that David manipulated the results of oracles so as to rid himself of potential rallying points for resistance. There is direct

28. McCarter (*II Samuel* ad loc) is certainly right that the point of 2 Sam. 6.22 is that Michal remained childless to the day of her death because David broke off relations with her and in effect imprisoned her. So the sister in 2 Sam. 21.8, who is married to Adzriel son of Barzillai the Meholatite (1 Sam. 18.19), not Paltiel ben Laish (2 Sam. 3.15), must be Merab. Barzillai the Meholatite is probably not identical with Barzillai from Roglim in Gilead, but the possibility of their identity is tempting. Abel Mehola was right on the Jordan (1 Kgs 4.12; Judg. 7.22). Another option is to derive this Barzillai from the Manassite clan of Mahlah. Note not just that the taking of Mephiboshet to court is related before the Absalom revolt, but that the disposition of Mephiboshet's (i.e., Saul's—2 Sam. 9.7) estates is decided immediately afterward. Thus the killings must predate the revolt.

29. The presentation of 2 Sam. 9.1-6 is that Mephiboshet, or Meribbaal, is the sole remaining male Saulide with whom David can 'act in good faith for the sake of Jonathan'. Jonathan's lame son is in the house of Machir ben Ammiel in Lo Dabar. Meribbaal's relocation to the court precedes the Absalom revolt, since it is on the basis of his failure to evacuate Jerusalem that David strips him of half of Saul's estates.

30. 2 Samuel 9 presents Ziba as an old retainer of Saul, with 15 sons and a large staff. Regardless of whether this was the case, or whether David appointed him steward, Ziba obviously found common interests with David. The decision to give the steward Saul's estates after the Absalom revolt probably accelerated any tendency toward peculation from Mephiboshet's estates that Ziba may have had. Kickbacks to David were undoubtedly part of this mix—explicitly, in terms of Mephiboshet's maintenance at court, but beyond this, probably, in real terms.

textual linkage in that the story of the killings at Gibeon begins by reference to Saul's house's bloodguilt (2 Sam. 21.1).[31] But Shimei does not say, 'YHWH has requited you for all the blood of the house of Saul which YOU spilled', as distinct from anyone else. He says, 'YHWH has requited you for ALL the blood of the house of Saul'. McCarter accordingly and appropriately therefore includes in the accusation Saul and his sons at Gilboa, Abner, Ishbaal, and the seven grandchildren.[32] David even demanded the return of Saul's daughter Michal from her husband before condemning her to celibacy and executing her sister's children, thus controlling the production of Saulides. Overall, in the aftermath of the battle of Gilboa, he can be said to have adopted a policy of systematic extermination toward the house of Saul, rather like Henry VII knocking off Plantagenets, or like Dennis Price knocking off Alec Guinness 17 times in *Kind Hearts and Coronets*. He even retained Ishbaal's head and Abner's corpse in Hebron, and he repatriated the bodies of Saul and Jonathan from the men of Jabesh Gilead—who stole them from Beth Shan[33]—only on the deaths of all the other heirs (2 Sam. 21.12-14). But David carefully preserved Mephiboshet's life, confining him instead to the court and stripping him of his estates; and, he refrained from killing his accuser, Shimei. He maintained a token hostage and his accuser to show that there was nothing to the accusation. This is one more, reported, alibi (see chart, p. 341).

Now, these are not the only deaths of which David is accused or from which he is exculpated. Uriah's murder is conceded by the text, and taken to be the cause of Absalom's revolt. The latter also has a proximate cause, namely, Amnon's rape of Tamar.

Amnon was David's eldest son, by Ahinoam from Jezreel (2 Sam. 3.2). Two women bear this name: Saul's wife (1 Sam. 14.50), and David's. YHWH also tells David through Nathan, 'I gave you your master's

---

31. For Shimei, David is *'îš had-dāmîm*, responsible for *kōl dᵉmê bêt šā'ûl* (2 Sam. 16.7-8). In 2 Sam. 21.1, YHWH announces, *'el šā'ûl wᵉ-'el bêtô dāmîm*, 'To Saul and to his house there is bloodguilt' because he killed the Gibeonites. The linkage is concrete, and the difference in authority is that the narrator has Shimei speaking in 16.7-8, but YHWH speaking in 21.1. Saul was the one who incurred bloodguilt, not David. However, it must have been somewhat galling to David that Shimei's accusation had the matter out in the open, and it is almost possible to believe that David let him live in order to disprove the allegation, then asked Solomon to murder him.

32. McCarter, *II Samuel* ad loc.

33. Level VI: See Amihai Mazar's contribution to the present volume.

house and your master's women to your bosom' (2 Sam. 12.8). So there is a good chance that David's first wife was Saul's wife first.[34] There are also two Jezreels—one in Israel, the later winter capital (as 2 Kgs 10.1; Hos. 1.4), and scene of Saul's last battle (1 Sam. 29.11), and one in Judah. Josh. 15.56 mentions the site in Judah, which was therefore occupied in the seventh century, but there is no suggestion or likelihood of its earlier occupation.[35] It is likely that Ahinoam, Saul's wife or not, came from the northern Jezreel.

Here, again, is a providence for David. The rapist is the heir-presumptive, representing the most prosperous ambitions of an important political constituency. The sister's constituency is a foreign petty kingdom useful for threatening northern Israel (2 Sam. 3.3). Second, if the rapist was borne by Saul's former wife, his removal eliminates the last vestiges of Saul's legacy from the succession. Possibly David instigated the rape, which is after all suggested to Amnon by David's nephew, Jonadab.[36] Again providential: the avenger is next in line for the succession.[37]

David is politically immobilized. Absalom models himself on David's murder of Abner, and after 2 years invites his brothers to a feast, at

34. See J.D. Levenson and B. Halpern, 'The Political Import of David's Marriages', *JBL* 99 (1980), pp. 507-18.

35. On the date of Joshua 15, see among others A. Alt, 'Judas Gaue unter Josia', *Kleine Schriften zur Geschichte Israels*, 2 (Tübingen: Mohr, 1953), pp. 276-88; F.M. Cross and G.E. Wright 'The Boundary and Province Lists of the Kingdom of Judah', *JBL* 75 (1956), pp. 202-26; Z. Kallai, *Historical Geography of the Bible* (Jerusalem: Magnes Press, 1986), pp. 115-24, 334-97. Alt's position has been repeatedly vindicated by excavations and by surveys (notably, excavations at Ein Gedi, Tel Ira, Hurvat Uzza; surveys by R. Cohen, W.G. Dever). The tenth-century settlements, too, tend to be in areas other than those of the Arava settlements of the seventh century.

36. Of course, Jonadab ben-Shim'a', David's nephew, counselled Amnon, and thereafter remained in good odor in court, according to the text (2 Sam. 13.3-5, 32-33). Provocateur or free agent? His continued good standing inclines one to the former interpretation.

37. The best list of David's early offspring seems to be that in 2 Sam. 3.2-5, which enumerates the eldest sons of six wives in order to imply that Solomon would be the eldest surviving son of the seventh. This list is duplicated in 1 Chron. 3.1-4, but 1 Chron. 3.5 lists Solomon last among four sons of 'Bath-Shua' = Bathsheba, daughter of Ammiel, then enumerates nine more sons before excluding sons of concubines and mentioning Tamar. Chronicles has duplicated the list of 2 Sam. 5.14-16, taking the children of 5.14 (achronologically) as those of Bathshua/Bathsheba. The list in Samuel has no such implications, as 2 Sam. 5.13 makes clear.

which he murders Amnon (2 Sam. 13.23-29). David's alibi is that he first believes Absalom has killed all his brothers and then mourns Amnon demonstratively (2 Sam. 13.30-36).

Unlike Joab, Absalom flees. For murder inside groups, expulsion is a common custom, and attested in the Bible, where Cain, Simeon, and Levi are all landless on the grounds that they have killed—allies—and where the adoptive Egyptian murderer, Moses, flees into the wilderness. In other cultures, the fugitive is repatriated after a period of some years.[38] Absalom spends 3 years with his grandfather, the king of Geshur (2 Sam. 13.38). But Geshur was well within the ambit of David's domination: Absalom could have been extradited easily. And who is the agent of his repatriation? Joab. Joab 'tricks' David into letting the lad come home, even though David is alert to the deception (2 Sam. 14.1-23). David does not readmit Absalom to the court for a period of 2 more years (2 Sam. 14.24, 28); but Joab, who previously had refused to

---

38. See Emrys Peters, 'Some Structural Aspects of the Feud among the Bedouin of Cyrenaica', *Africa* 37 (1967), pp. 261-82. Cf. Oedipus's *miasma* at Thebes. But note also that Moses returns from the wilderness on the death of the king, and that killers resident in 'cities of refuge' can return to their holdings after the death of a high priest in the legal theory of P (Num. 35.9-34; cf. Deut. 19.1-13, which probably contemplates such a return after legal proceedings in the town of origin). The stories about Qen, Simeon, and Levi are of course etymologies for a nomadic lifestyle, nomads being identified in this culture with those who have been driven, for one or another reason, from the settled lands. See latterly, Eckart Otto, 'Gewaltvermeidung und -überwindung in "Recht und Religion Israels"', in J. Niewiadomski and W. Palaver (eds.), *Dramatische Erlösungslehre* (Innsbruck: Tyrolia, 1992), pp. 97-117, 98-99, with further citations and discussion. Otto goes on to observe (p. 100) that the legal strategy of the Covenant Code is to impose death sanctions within the family (Exod. 21.12, 15-17), and this is also indicated by the speech of the Wise Woman of Tekoa in 2 Sam. 14.5-7, where the typical expectation is that fratricide will be punished by death. So one of the causes of the Absalom revolt in the mind of the author of 2 Samuel is David's willingness to take a humanitarian—noncentral—view of crime within a family. However, the indications are that the culture was less than monolithic in this respect, and that the legislation of the Covenant Code regarding the family reflects the interests of the state. Note especially the regulations regarding refuge starting in Exod. 21.13. The same statist ideology presumably underlies 2 Samuel, which, however, portrays David's decision as essentially compassionate and familial. Note Bernard Williams, *Shame and Necessity* (Los Angeles: University of California Press, 1994), arguing that the earliest Greek literary texts presuppose inevitable conflict between human behavior that would later be regarded as 'ethical' and the actual nature of the universe. 2 Samuel would seem to present a parallel instance.

intercede with David (2 Sam. 14.29), does a *volte face* after Absalom torches his crops, and the rehabilitation is complete (2 Sam. 14.30-33).

This looks like a put-up job. David had a problem, which Absalom solved. He took the consequences and returned to court—the return greased by Joab. Yet if there was a deal between David and Absalom, it probably involved assurances that vengeance would bring him nearer the crown. And, after 5 years, Absalom may have found matters at court different than he thought he had left them: our grandson of a foreign kinglet may have faced some pretty stiff fraternal opposition.

Absalom's death, too, is straightforward: David charges the officers in hearing of the troops not to harm the boy, and sends them into battle against him (2 Sam. 18.5); Joab kills him while he is hanging helpless in a tree (2 Sam. 18.9-15); David mourns publicly (2 Sam. 19.1); and, Joab remains on the general staff.

One need not go so far as to say, though I am of course insinuating, that David *intended* to drive Absalom to revolt. For the result of that uprising was to establish the total superiority of David's professional army over the tribal levees.[39] But whatever David's conscious intentions, it is easy enough to see how Absalom might come to rebel. And it is also easy to see how the man of action, who acquitted the family honor, might score points particularly with the state hierarchy, which seems to have stood behind him.

Finally, Amasa. Amasa was the military commander in the Absalom revolt.[40] In a concession to the rebels, David installed him in Joab's place

---

39. And in a way, this is how David created Solomon: he left a legacy of military domination that enabled Solomon to stage an instant coup d'etat, and then cement his grip with a set of bloody murders. See Halpern, *Constitution of the Monarchy in Israel* (HSM, 25; Chico, CA: Scholars Press, 1981), pp. 242-44; 'The Uneasy Compromise: Israel between League and Monarchy', in B. Halpern and J.D. Levenson (eds.), *Traditions in Transformation: Turning-Points in Biblical Faith* (Festschrift F.M. Cross; Winona Lake, IN: Eisenbrauns, 1981), pp. 59-96, 91-95.

40. It is often overlooked that Amasa must also have been a senior officer under David, and was a member of the royal family, being the son of Joab's aunt, Abigail. 1 Chronicles places him in David's army, possibly on this basis, in 12.19. On Amasa, son of Yitra the 'Israelite' or 'Jezreelite' (not 'Ishmaelite'), see Levenson and Halpern, 'Political Import of David's Marriages'. 1 Chron. 2.17 identifies Amasa's father as an Ishmaelite, while MT of 2 Sam. 17.25 has him as an Israelite, and the versions there either as an Israelite (VSS), an Ishmaelite (G-A) or possibly a Jezreelite (G-M). 1 Chron. 12.19, however, names him as a Benjaminite recruit to David's cause, presupposing that the father was an Israelite. This may be derivative.

as commander of the tribal armies (2 Sam. 19.14-15). Immediately after demobilization, however, the revolt of Sheba ben-Bichri broke out. David gave Amasa 3 days to remobilize Judah, *but—mirabile dictu—*Amasa missed the deadline. At that point, David dispatched the standing army, under Abishai. These slouched north to Gibeon—where David hanged Saul's heirs—and encountered Amasa. Joab took this worthy aside for a kiss, and with his left hand thrust a dagger into his belly (2 Sam. 20.1-14).

Again, David stands to benefit. He has just suffered the humiliation of appointing a rebel general his commander-in-chief. And the revolt during which Amasa is killed turns out to consist of one miserable flea, who without resistance is tossed over the wall of a town on the northern border.[41] Joab returns to the general staff.

The repeated exculpation of David for complicity in providential deaths indicates that accusations were contemporary.[42] We all know that in the Manichaean political universe we tend to inhabit, our opponents represent the children of darkness. With the exception of Gerald Ford, no one can even imagine an American president who was not evil incarnate to SOMEbody. And even Ford had his Squeaky Fromm. Not so long ago, fewer Canadians supported then PM Brian Mulroney than believed Elvis was alive.[43] Moving from paranoid demonization of the Other—which establishes that our texts are early—to historical reconstruction presents some difficulties, but the general pattern suggests that murder was an implement of choice in David's strategy for the construction of ethnicity. And the role of states-in-formation in the imposition of ethnicity is more complex and varied than the best state-formation theorists allow.

The *modi operandi* are limited: Joab removes Abner, Absalom, Amasa, Sheba, and, on David's orders, Uriah. He never suffers sanction,

---

See 2 Sam. 17.25; 20.4-12; 1 Kgs 2.32; 1 Chron. 2.17; 12.19; possibly 15.24 = 6.10, 20.

41. As McCarter points out (*II Samuel*, p. 432), the apology, again, blames Amasa's death on Joab, whom David did not even send—it was Abishai who called him. Of course, David may have forgotten that Joab had just killed Absalom, and that Abishai was Joab's brother, and had been complicit in Abner's murder. Appearances, as Pudd'nhead Wilson's calendar remarks of circumstantial evidence, can be misleading.

42. See esp. Vanderkam, 'Davidic Complicity', pp. 521-39; McCarter, 'The Apology of David', pp. 489-504.

43. 12% v 17%. This is taken from a poll by *MacLeans*.

except for a 3-day-long demotion under Amasa.[44] Three times, the killers are aliens: the Philistines kill Saul and three of his sons, and Gibeonites kill the others. Once the killer is David's son. It is convenient for David if somebody dies, and somebody else kills him.[45] Three times, assassins are killed—those of Saul and of Ishbaal, and Absalom, killer of Amnon. In the cases of Saul and Jonathan, Abner, Amnon, and Absalom, David leads public mourning.

These patterns lead to another question: why is the Absalom story told as it is? It exonerates David of Amasa's murder, and justifies the execution of Sheba. It also acquits David of proximate responsibility for the uprising.

But presenting Absalom's revolt as YHWH's way of punishing David for Uriah's death excuses the participants, as YHWH's instruments, for their treason. This element of the apology, like the others, is conciliatory. Even the reasons for the rebellion are obscured—Absalom made extravagant campaign promises, is what we hear.[46] But the real grievances are not articulated, and that, too, stems from the strategy of reconciliation. The apology is irrelevant at any significant remove from Solomon's reign. And this of course coincides with Hayim Tadmor's observation that this sort of elaborate royal apology tends to arise early in the reigns of kings whose mothers were heavily involved in a contested succession.[47]

44. McCarter (*II Samuel*, p. 432) notes that David sends the army out under Abishai, so that Joab does not have command or any way of interdicting Amasa himself. But by the end of the story it is Joab who leads the army and negotiates with the 'wise woman of Abel'. See 2 Sam. 20.15-22; 20:23.

45. This is the case—leaving Nabal aside—with Saul and his three sons (killer: Philistines), Abner (:Joab), Ishbaal (: Gibeonites [from Beeroth]), Saul's heirs (: Gibeonites), Uriah (: Joab), Amnon (: Absalom), Absalom (: Joab), Amasa (: Joab), Sheba (: Maacah acting for Joab). Note that three deaths (Abner, Uriah, Adonijah) involve fallings-out over married women.

46. 2 Sam. 15.1-6. This is almost certainly a code for a promise of lowering popular obligations to the state, or ending corruption, or placing both administration and the means of corruption in the hands of the lineage structures.

47. H. Tadmor, 'Autobiographical Apology in the Royal Assyrian Literature', in H. Tadmor and M. Weinfeld (eds.), *History, Historiography and Interpretation* (Jerusalem: Magnes Press, 1983), pp. 36-57, esp. pp. 54-57. Tadmor is surely wrong, however, to entertain the possibility that the apology is a Davidic document, inasmuch as the exculpation of David for doing Saulides dirty continues through the Absalom revolt—to his Solomonic decision to award half Meribbaal's estates to Ziba—and even into Solomon's reign, when that king finally gives both Joab and

Another pattern confirms this argument. For all the political deaths, David is furnished with an alibi. Nabal, Saul and Jonathan,[48] Abner, Ishbaal, Absalom, Amasa. And a famine and YHWH's oracle forced his hand with the other Saulides.

The flip side of the pattern is more important. The killings for which David *is* made responsible are two executions, of Shimei and of Joab, undertaken by Solomon. The narrator convicts him of one murder only: that of Uriah, the first husband of Solomon's mother. David's elective killings, aside from those that alibi him for other murders, are all tied up with Solomon. For the murder of Uriah, too, he attempts first to alibi his adultery, then to alibi the murder, but is found out by mantic means. For the executions of Shimei and Joab, he is vindicated by dint of personal inaction. Again, David kills only for Solomon.

What is surprising here is that Solomon should have generated concili-atory apology. David spent his career hiding responsibility for his actions. All of 2 Samuel is his Broadway Alibi. David operated, at

Shimei what for. See further below. The image of David projected in the apology— the image mainly of a victim—is not what David himself would have liked. Far more likely is Stefan Heym's intuition, in *Der König–David–Bericht*, that the apology is Solomon's work. Note further that the internal chronology of the Absalom revolt allows 2 years from the rape of Tamar to the murder of Amnon, 3 years of exile and 2 years of house arrest for Absalom, and 4 years (with McCarter, *II Samuel*, p. 355) before the revolt, for a total of 11 years from rape to revolt. Since Absalom was the grandson of a kinglet, it is unlikely that Tamar or he was fathered before David assumed the kingship of Israel in Jerusalem. The earliest date for the apology on these subjects, accordingly, would fall into the latter half of David's alleged 33-year reign in Jerusalem, probably roughly years 16 to 27, with enough time left (6 years) to allow 'all Israel' to expect the next surviving son, Adonijah, to succeed (1 Kgs 2.15, 22). This latter is a remarkable tradition, and although it might be argued that it is a necessary argument for the elimination of Adonijah, the odds are that there is some truth to the characterization here—enough, at least, to convince the original audience of the apology. The regnal dates can be pushed back or forward 2–3 years, but any further adjustment risks bringing the coregency with Solomon into direct contact with the revolt, or bringing the age of Absalom and Tamar at the time of the rape into a tiny minority. If it is true that the siege of Rabbat-Ammon antedates Tamar's rape (and this is not certain), an early date for the latter would locate the siege close to year 10 of David's reign in Jerusalem. This is about as early as one might contemplate the conflict with Aram reported in 2 Sam. 10.15-19, based on other considerations, explored among others by A. Malamat, 'Aspects of the Foreign Policies of David and Solomon' *JNES* 22 (1963), pp. 1-17; esp. 2-3.

48. A second alibi is furnished in 1 Sam. 21.11-15: the rumour that David had been a vassal of Achish of Gath was false!

surface level, according to traditional restraints on the exercise of power. Solomon *projected* power through display, from the imposition of governors over districts of Israel to the press-gang construction of the temple and palace and of fortresses throughout the country. Solomon executed Adonijah for asking for possession of David's concubine, Abishag. He confined Shimei, killing him on David's orders for violating his parole. He banished Abiathar. And, in a very significant episode, he condemned Joab for murdering Amasa and Abner.

This last action speaks legions about the apology in 2 Samuel. David had told Solomon, the text claims, 'You know what Joab did to the two officers of the armies of Israel, to Abner ben-Ner and to Amasa ben-Yeter, that he slew them and introduced the blood of war in *šālôm* (in peace, or in alliance)... Don't send his grey head to hell in *šālôm*', that is, peacefully (1 Kgs 2.5-6). So Solomon killed him (1 Kgs 2.28-35).[49]

Abner's death in 2 Samuel 3 links directly to this text. Three times it stresses that Abner was in *šālôm* with David (vv. 21-23); and it points out that it was because of a deed of Abner in battle, or wartime, the slaying of Asahel, that Joab and Abishai killed him. In other words, they took vengeance inappropriately: they avenged a battle death in time of peace.[50]

Solomon[51] made Joab the chief agent for the violent deaths in David's

49. On the nature of Joab's death in the narrative, see Halpern, *First Historians* (San Francisco: Harper & Row, 1988), p. 146: 'Solomon is passive even in carnage... Joab, "who took the part of Adonijah, though he did not Absalom's" (2.28), dictates his own death even in the sanctuary of YHWH's tent. Bidden to emerge, Joab stymies his executioner, "No, I will die here" (2.28-30); "Do as he says", says the king...' So Benaiah goes back and kills him.

50. Because Joab had killed one with whom he was in alliance, David would later instruct Solomon to execute him: don't send his grey locks to Sheol in peace (1 Kgs 2.6). Thus 1 Kgs 2.5-6 very much picks up the thread of 2 Samuel 3, both explicitly and implicitly, with the contrast of killing in peace and in battle. Peace may mean alliance here. These same texts present the solution to the problem of Huldah's oracle in 2 Kgs 22.15-20 that Josiah would die 'in peace': the exilic editor of Kings reports that Josiah fought Necho, who was assaulting the king of Assyria; the implication is that Josiah was Necho's ally, the opposite of the historical record, which was still known, e.g., to the Chronicler, to Herodotus, and to Josephus. The reason for the reversal in Kings is to infer an ironic fulfillment of Huldah's oracle: Josiah died at the hand of one with whom he was 'at peace'—in alliance. See B. Halpern and D.S. Vanderhooft, 'The Editions of Kings in the 8th–7th Centuries BCE', *HUCA* 62 (1991), pp. 221-29.

51. Or the author of his accession account in 1 Kings 1–2.

reign. This does not imply the writing of 2 Samuel in the first years of Solomon's reign. But the framework of interpretation that the apology draws on was probably the child of that era. Solomon could not, of course, kill David for these murders. His killing of Joab was partisan, since Joab backed Adonijah for the throne. But Solomon could present Joab's execution as that of the trigger-man for all those violent deaths, and, paradigmatically, those of Abner and Amasa—north and south. Ridding himself at once of an adversary and of someone who could relate the truth about David, Solomon remade his father as the political victim of Joab and others, except where he, Solomon, was the beneficiary or agent of the murder. Solomon was the despot David dreamed of being, and his apology sheltered David from the reputation that his adversaries imposed on him—of the devious, rather than the put-upon, politician, whose enemies made a habit of waking up dead.

Why is Solomon, who settles the old and the new accounts draconically, concerned that David should not have done so? Why is he concerned with reconciliation when in year 24 of his reign, on the accession of Shishaq, he will pillage the north—sell the tribe of Asher—to secure the south?[52] The strategy of conciliation in the south, especially in the royal family—about the deaths of Absalom and Amasa—reflects a policy of co-option, of setting Judah apart, always a part of Solomon's administrative strategy. But central is the chronology: early in his reign, Solomon made Absalom's daughter Rehoboam's chief wife, who would bear his successor.[53] Rehoboam was a child at the time, but the war

52. Halpern, 'Sectionalism and the Schism', *JBL* 93 (1974), pp. 519-32.

53. Rehoboam, 41 years old at his accession, reigned 17 years, Abijah 3. The suggestion is that Abijah, who expired peacefully, was not young, although no age at accession for him is provided in the accession formulary. The youngest scions of David to expire peacefully were Ahaz and Jehoiaqim, at age 36 (not allowing for antedating). Allowing Abijah to have reached that age, after 3 years on the throne, would place his birth 16 years before Rehoboam's accession, in year 24 of Solomon. On the significance of that year, see Halpern, 'Sectionalism'. Moreover, the mean lifetime for Davidides whose age at natural death can be calculated is over 51.5 years, and the standard deviation is a little over 3. Allowing Abijah to have reached the mean minus two standard deviations at the time of his death places his birth in year 15 of Solomon, which means in turn that Rehoboam married Absalom's daughter in year 15 at the latest. Allowing Abijah to have reached the mean *plus* two standard deviations places his birth in year 3 of Solomon. There would be a 95% probability of his having been born between year 3, when Rehoboam was 4, and year 15, when Rehoboam was 16, were the sample size actuarially reliable. However the X-squared factor is not good. Taken raw, the figures suggest that the odds of Abijah's dying

wounds had not healed. This is also why Rehoboam, son of an Ammonite princess, was made Solomon's heir: Ammonite collaboration was central to David's victory, and was a stick to the carrot of co-option for the north. The Solomonic schism, now so vividly attested in the Tel Dan stela, was already on the horizon, and all the detail about the actors in Samuel reflects the early Solomonic policy of smoothing relations rather than the later policy of abandoning the north. 2 Samuel is early, and very much in earnest—for after the loss of the north, and after the passage of years, much of its detail would surely have been omitted, as it was later in Chronicles. We know that it is accurate because it is nothing but lies.

This conclusion brings us back to the main question. The foregoing is a very textual overture to some historical issues. And that is the point. Historians, if they exercise their imagination at all—and history without imagination is dead history, or, to be explicit, is philology masquerading as history—can invert the obvious implications of textual data.

Sir Ronald Syme, for example, revolutionized the study of ancient Rome by taking the history of his subject from the Antonine, not

after the age of 50 stand at about 70%. Since any greater age places his birth before year 10 of Solomon, when Rehoboam was 11, it is unlikely that he was older. However, the chances against his birth coming after year 20 of Solomon's reign rise to about 86%.

Ages at reportedly natural death: Rehoboam 58, Jehoshaphat 60, Jehoram 40, Uzziah 68, Jotham 41, Ahaz 36, Hezekiah 54, Manasseh 67, Jehoiaqim 36, Jehoiachin > 55. In addition, Solomon must have lived significantly past the age of 40, and the same is true of Asa. Amaziah was assassinated at age 54, Joash at age 47, Josiah having reached the age of 39. Ages at accession resume with Jehoshaphat (1 Kgs 22.42), who was 35. He was born in year 6 of Asa, which means that that king had his chief wife in place by year 5. So, by the 6th year after Rehoboam's death, or the 23rd year after Rehoboam's accession, Rehoboam had a great-grand-child by a succession of favourite wives. In other words, again, allowing 20 years per generation, schematically, Asa is born in year 3 of Rehoboam, and Abijah in year 23 of Solomon. The implications remain the same, and become more exaggerated as one increases the generational shift figure. Rehoboam was married early in Solomon's reign.

Ages at birth of successors: Solomon: year before accession; Jehoshaphat: 28; Jehoram: 18; Ahaziah (assassinated): 22; Joash: 22; Amaziah (assassinated): 23?; Uzziah: ?; Jotham: 21?; Ahaz: 15; Hezekiah: 42; Manasseh: 45; Amon (killed): 16; Josiah (killed): 16, 14; Jehoiakim: 18.

Augustan, perspective.[54] The task of the ancient historian, of any historian, is in the end to recognize and reconstruct the cacophonous constructions of historical realities, the competing and merely alternative narratives, the possible alternative narratives that were or in some cases might have been pertinent to the historical agents, the human beings, involved in historical transactions. It is also the historian's task to elect his or her own narrative that includes, privileges, excludes, or repudiates elements of all those agents' voices. History is not necessarily accurate, though it must strive to be correct in the proportions it ascribes to causal factors and as accurate as possible. Intentional disregard for evidence, intentional inaccuracy or imagination on the basis of no evidence, distinguishes romance, or even historical fiction, from real history. Thus, even though Mommsen's *Römische Geschichte* is shot through with judgments and allegations from which contemporary historians differ, it remains a work of history. Similarly, in the foregoing account, I have presented David as a serial murderer. Yet other scholars might differ, and even attribute my own predilections as a sign of contemporary Western obsession with serial killers.[55] Neither my own work nor such a riposte would fall outside the category of history, even though the two would be contradictory.

The text, like the artifact, encodes intention. But the intention of the text is to lead the reader in a particular direction. So it makes sense to invert the values and claims of the text and propose alternative scenarios, for which there is no other evidence. Epistemologically, history can be reduced almost to the level of philology, but, oddly, what we know, what we really *know*, is the least interesting part of the field and the easiest to master. History is an art, and what is really important is what we can surmise, but never know. The account I have given you admits of no archaeological verification whatever. But it furnishes a perspective unrepresented in our texts, and that is part of what history is for: done properly, it gives voice to those who do not speak in our texts, who have not left ideologically charged records, who have not successfully manipulated the technologies of persuasion at a temporal remove. Properly undertaken, the art of history is that of imagination, but imagination based on evidence.

54. R. Syme, *The Roman Revolution* (Oxford: Oxford University Press, 1939), p. 1.
55. See J.P. Jenkins, *Using Murder. The Social Construction of Serial Homicide* (New York: Aldine de Gruyter, 1994), esp. pp. 57-78.

And here, too, despite their very different approaches to epistemology, is where archaeology and history properly meet. Of course, they also meet in places that both regard as insignificant: we can identify the biblical name for the little walls projecting outward from various gates, as at Megiddo, Beersheva, or Tel Batashi, *yad haš-ša`ar* (the arm/hand of the gate);[56] we can gauge what a palace looked like and tell from the text how it was used. We can, in effect, illustrate the Bible from the ground, and put vitality in the ground from the text. But in historical archaeology, the two cultures best complement one another in the pursuit of the dog in the night of the underlying structural realities presupposed by and addressed in the texts, and more accessible in the archaeological record. This much has been obvious for years, and there is no need to press the point.

There are, however, problems in both cultures. Historical archaeologists, generally, eschew the methods of prehistoric archaeologists—which is a tremendous historical loss. Second, historical archaeologists tend to rely on texts to furnish their framework of interpretation. To an extent this is justified. But by and large, the archaeologist has little more

---

56. The first scholar to recognize that this term represents an architectural feature of Israelite, and possibly other, gates was P.K. McCarter, in *I Samuel* (AB, 8; Garden City, NY: Doubleday, 1980), p. 114. McCarter identified the feature as the side of the gate, and reconstructed 1 Sam. 4.13-18 to describe Eli falling over into the street between the two sides of the gate. In fact, however, gateways were invariably roofed, as Assyrian depictions indicate: see, e.g., R.D. Barnett and M. Falkner, *The Sculptures of Aššur-naṣir-apli II (883–859 BC) Tiglath-Pileser III (745–727 BC) Esarhaddon (681–669 BC) from the Central and South-West Palaces at Nimrud* (London: Trustees of the British Museum, 1962) pl. LVI, LXX, XCI; R. D. Barnett and Amleto Lorenzini, *Assyrian Sculpture* (Toronto: McClelland and Stewart, 1975), pp. 28, 78 (Lachish). Had Eli been seated atop the gate, the text would therefore have described him not as being on 'the hand', but on 'the roof' of the gate, or even 'in the room above the gate'—cf. 2 Sam. 19.1. Nor could Eli have fallen into the passageway without crashing through the roof or the floor of the upper story, neither of which is described. Rather, Eli's point of observation is probably some highly visible—and thus elevated—seat *outside* the gate, where a large body of men could be addressed (as 2 Sam. 19.9, playing on action 'atop the hand of the gateway' in 2 Sam. 15.2). Further, the side of the gate is called its 'shoulder': e.g., Exod. 27.14-15; 38.14-15; Ezek. 40.18, 40, 41, 44; 46.19; and note 1 Kgs 7.39//2 Chron. 4.10; 2 Kgs 11.11//2 Chron. 23.10; Ezek. 47.1-2. The logic of this terminology seem to be that an entryway has two 'shoulders', as Ezek. 41.2. It is thus the projection from the 'shoulder' that is the 'hand' or 'arm' of the gate—the sort of dromos leading traffic toward the 'outer gate' of some towns.

access to the technologies for analyzing text than the textual scholar has for analyzing ceramic typology. So the tendency is for a scholar who understands one world well and the other imperfectly to rely on the other world, the other academic culture, to furnish the information on which he or she bases interpretation.[57]

This is how scholars who are identified inside a field as marginal manage to put their cases across. Major revisionists, such as Immanuel Velikovsky or Peter James, pick and choose among the interpretations furnished on individual details by specialists, in order to justify elaborate reorganizations of knowledge. Their concern is not with a consistent interpretation of data in a subfield, but with the convenience of some particular observation, divorced from its context, to their point. And where less serious revision is in point, scholars identified in a field as members of the mainstream indulge, if sometimes in lesser measure, in precisely the same sorts of chicanery. By and large, we must all cross fields, and by and large, we do not and cannot do so with the fullest responsibility.

The process of interpretation is circular: the Bible says we had a united monarchy in the tenth century, and monumental architecture and a set of pottery repertoires at lowland sites are then identified with it. Conversely, the textual scholar arrives at the conclusion that there is nothing of value in 2 Samuel, and immediately dismisses the monumental architecture as representative only of city-state forms of organization: we have similar gates not just at the towns named in 1 Kgs 9.13, but also, it is argued, later, at Ashdod.

Now, despite what logicians might claim, there is nothing intrinsically wrong with circular argument; a slight touch of paranoia never hurt anyone, and can sometimes get you across the street alive in Boston. What is important is that the premise is correct—namely that our historical reconstruction based on the text is basically accurate—not as to pedantic detail, necessarily, but as to overall structure; that our archaeological slice of time is in fact synchronous, and the interpretations of the artifacts basically accurate.[58]

57. See W.G. Dever's article in this volume.

58. That synchroneity in archaeology is problematic even on an intrasite basis is not disputed. See, e.g., C. Kramer, *Village Ethnoarchaeology. Rural Iran in Archaeological Perspective* (NY: Academic Press, 1982). Our ability to take a snapshot in time across sites is about the same as physicists' ability to take a snapshot in time across the universe.

But what shows this to be the case? Were it not for Megiddo VA–IVB and IVA, and Hazor X–IX, which seem to be effectively devoid of intramural domestic housing in the Solomonic era and just after,[59] would we, on the basis of archaeology, reconstruct a united monarchy? Probably not, and we might even identify each as some sort of competing regional ritual center in the period. Of course we have the famous gates at Megiddo, Hazor, and Gezer. But Ussishkin lowers these into the ninth century.[60] And, resistance to Holladay's identification of burnished red-slip with the mid-tenth century[61] has the implication that we might raise the dates. These contrary trends would undermine our certainty about the synchroneity of the layers. If Ussishkin is right, much of the

59. On Megiddo, see R.S. Lamon and G.M. Shipton, *Megiddo I: Seasons of 1925–34. Strata I–V* (Oriental Institute Publications XLII; Chicago: University of Chicago Press, 1939) 3-61; G. Loud, *Megiddo II. Seasons of 1935–39* (Oriental Institute Publications, LXII; Chicago: University of Chicago Press, 1948), pp. 45-57, 105, 116. On Hazor, see the paper by Amnon Ben-Tor in this volume, and his edited volume, Y. Yadin, *et al.*, *Hazor III–IV: An Account of the Third and Fourth Seasons of Excavation, 1957–1958* (Jerusalem: Israel Exploration Society and Hebrew University, 1989). The domestic housing in Hazor IX is both well built—essentially elite—and rather sparse. It may well be that this housing is the child of the latter part of the stratum's life, and is roughly synchronous with the early part of Megiddo III, by the end of which, in the Persian era, domestic quarters completely dominate the mound. The shift from Megiddo IVA to Megiddo III need not, therefore, correlate completely to conquest by Tiglath-Pileser III, but may, in some areas, antedate this. Alternatively, the beginnings of the earlier domestic installations on the site may belong not to stratum III, but to IVA. Regardless, Hazor X (and to a lesser extent IX) and Megiddo VA–IVB and IVA seem to reflect a conscious state policy of expelling population from the tells. This is the essential historical conclusion to be drawn about Israelite policy in the Jezreel and Jordan Valley in the united and divided monarchy. Notably, the 1994 excavations in area H of Megiddo came down below the so-called Assyrian palaces of stratum III on what are unquestionably living quarters—and wall thicknesses suggest they are domestic. However, it is also clear that the stratum III palaces were constructed in multiple phases (by my count, three to five). Floors beneath the palace level divulged pottery of the eighth century. This may thus be evidence of stratum IVA domestic architecture, or of an additional phase at the start of stratum III. Notably, there is some suggestion of plaster fall from the ceilings here, as was common in the destruction level of Hazor VI (Yadin, *Hazor III–IV*, p. 44).

60. D. Ussishkin, 'Notes on Megiddo, Gezer, Ashdod, and Tel Batash in the Tenth to Ninth Centuries BC', *BASOR* 277/278 (Feb./May 1990), pp. 71-91.

61. J.S. Holladay, 'Red Slip, Burnish, and the Solomonic Gateway at Gezer', *BASOR* 277/278 (Feb./May 1990), pp. 23-70.

Iron IIA is in fact Iron IIB; the 'Solomonic' gates are all from the ninth century. If Holladay is right, much of Iron I is Iron II or extends into Iron II, and the 'Solomonic' gates are 'Solomonic', i.e., mid-tenth century. And it remains possible that neither is right.[62]

Of course, we now have the Tel Dan stela, which irrefutably tells us there was a dynastic founder named David, sometime before the eighth century.[63] But just as the Merneptah Stele is not persuasive to people bent on denying the existence of a kin-based Israel in the central hills in the late thirteenth century, our reference to a king of 'the house of David' will cut no ice with those determined to deny the reality of the united monarchy.[64]

Archaeologists, typically, respond, why worry about elements on the fringe of the field?[65] The answer is that the epistemology of history,

---

62. It deserves note that Ussishkin's down-dating of the gates would imply that if one accepts Holladay's fine stratigraphy burnished red-slip first dates from the ninth century at most sites. This so ill accords with the historical situation so far as we can know it and so neatly fills one archeological gap (ninth century) while creating another (virtually all of Iron I) as to indicate how incommensurable the two disciplines really are. Those who reject Holladay's overall conclusions need to reckon with their implications for Gezer, where the dating is reasonably firm. In other words, we can reject the identification of the upper gate with Solomon and Shishaq, but this leaves us without textual correlates for the upper gate, and without archaeological correlates for three sets of textual allegations. Accepting the identification on the other hand produces satisfying correlations between archaeology and text for all data related to these particular strata.

63. See the *editio princeps*, A. Biran and J. Naveh, 'An Aramaic Stele Fragment from Tel Dan', *IEJ* 43 (1993), pp. 81-98; B. Halpern, 'The Stela Fragment from Tel Dan: Epigraphic and Historical Considerations', *BASOR* 296 (1994), pp. 63-80. Further fragments, discovered in the summer of 1994, do not alter perspectives gained from the original find. See further, B. Halpern, 'Notes on the Second Fragments of the Stela from Tel Dan', in F. Cryer (ed.), *The Tel Dan Stela* (Sheffield: Sheffield Academic Press, forthcoming).

64. See, e.g., P.R. Davies, '"House of David" Built on Sand', *BARev* 20/4 (July/August 1994), pp. 54-55. Davies takes the reference in the stela to 'the house of David' as a place name, presumably of a village. He would no doubt make the same representation concerning the very probable restoration of the phrase in the Mesha stela, for which see A. Lemaire, '"House of David" Restored in Moabite Inscription', *BARev* 20/3 (April/May, 1994), pp. 30-37. Davies's reading is based entirely on an aversion toward admitting we have a stratified reference to a figure 'about as historical as King Arthur' (p. 55); there is no evidence on his behalf.

65. For an extraordinary and prescient exception, see the article by Dever in this volume.

which is comparable to that of everyday life, involves the softer epistemology of interpreting texts, or human witnesses, or the 'meaning' or implications of behavior.[66] And it is precisely because of this very different epistemology that archaeologists should stick to their stones, and be loath to rely on textual data without either very thorough analysis particularly of the social assumptions in the texts or the understanding that their own constructions are considerably weakened by reliance on them. In dialogue with texts, and I include stratified texts, archaeologists should be careful simply to be less sure of things.

And yet, this does not mean that historical or other knowledge is impossible, merely that its organization is different from that of philology or natural science. History is fiction, and, in fact, even individual people are fictions. We are all physical forces, interacting with the environment, exchanging atoms and electrons with it. But we have evolved as organisms to see the environment not at the atomic level, but at a macro level—we see space as empty, rather than the configurations of atoms that are looser, so we don't run into walls thinking they are doorways—we evolved to distinguish solids from gases sharply, because that furnished the most efficient way to accumulate food without banging into trees. Thus we invent ourselves as individuals in the service of the propagation of the species. And this is a historical act, for it is memory, history, that lends meaning to our existence, history—each one of us a different history—that distinguishes us as individuals. Milan Kundera, in his *Book of Laughter and Forgetting*, makes the case that mass art, popular music, is art without memory. As a collective, as a sociobiological collective, we enable memory to perform its function for the group.[67]

Nor is historical thought solely a human characteristic. Even my Winston, a mix of black labrador and beagle, is a historian: he goes from tree to tree, from lawn to lawn, registering spoors both on the ground and on clothing. By contrast, a wasp is a philologist—a wasp Sphex retrieves food to the entrance of its nest, then drops it to enter and check the nest; ordinarily, it reemerges to drag its prey into the burrow. If a scientist intervenes, however, removing the prey even a few inches from where the wasp deposited it, the wasp reemerges and repeats the

66. See my *First Historians*, pp. 3-32.

67. For a general introduction to the biological issues involved, see E.O. Wilson, *The Diversity of Life* (Cambridge, MA: Belknap Press, 1992). For the philosophical questions, note especially Milic Çapek, *Bergson and Modern Physics: A Reinterpretation and Reevaluation* (Dordrecht: Reidel, 1971).

whole procedure. The wasp is hard-wired to do so—for even 40 repetitions do not alter the wasp's behavior.[68] Perhaps history is not an insect activity, depending on how we decipher social behavior such as the bee dance.[69] It is, however, an invariable feature of mammalian culture.

At the human level, we all have historical knowledge, knowledge of our own and others' lives, which enables some people to keep appointments. In essence, what we commonly refer to as historical knowledge is only a more fragile form of our knowledge of friends, family, institutions, and so on in the present. We are easily led, and so easily mistaken. On the other hand, more often than not, about friends and family, we are right (if we are not insane). Most of us live complacently with uncertainty as to how friends and even drivers of automobiles will behave or react at this or that time, because we have to. A similar level of uncertainty attaches to how we reconstruct history. Why some scholars expect to be as certain about the human past as about the human present, when in both instances we are concerned with humans, is puzzling at best.[70]

All this is not to say that the obstacles to creating fruitful dialogue between an archaeology that aspires to be philological and a history that ascends from philologies are insuperable. On the contrary, I firmly believe we see both archaeological and textual evidence of kinship in decline in seventh century Judah, and of course wonderful evidence for the intensification of agriculture and commerce in the eighth–seventh centuries.[71] The reality is, too, that archaeological remains seem without

68. See D.R. Hofstadter, *Gödel, Escher, Bach: An Eternal Golden Band* (New York: Vintage Books, 1980), pp. 360-61, citing D. Wooldridge, *Mechanical Man— The Physical Basis of Intelligent Life* (New York: McGraw–Hill, 1968), p. 70.

69. See generally for insect social activities, E.O. Wilson, *The Insect Societies* (Cambridge, MA: Belknap Press, 1971); *Success and Dominance in Ecosystems: the Case of the Social Insects* (Oldendorf: Ecology Institute, 1990).

70. I am thinking here both of scholars such as Davies, a self-described historical minimalist, and of those who attack the epistemology of history, denying its theoretical knowability. For further treatment, see my 'Fallacies Intentional and Canonical. On Metalogical Confusion in the Reading of Sacred Text', in J.A. Lassner and P. Machinist (eds.), *The Bible as Literature and as Canon* (Detroit: Wayne State University), forthcoming.

71. Especially at Tel Miqneh, on which see S. Gitin, 'Tel Miqne-Ekron: a Type-Site for the Inner Coastal Plain in the Iron Age II Period', in S. Gitin and W.G. Dever (eds.), *Recent Excavations in Israel: Studies in Iron Age Archaeology* (AASOR, 49; Winona Lake, IN: Eisenbrauns, 1989), pp. 23-58; and the article by Trude Dothan in this volume. My own historical integration of these data is laid out

doubt to confirm the story of a population explosion in the hill country followed by a unified national state, which was not Philistine, controlling highlands and internal valleys, and probably parts of the coast, in the tenth century.[72]

in 'Jerusalem and the Lineages in the Seventh Century BCE: Kinship and the Rise of Individual Moral Liability' in B. Halpern and D.W. Hobson (eds.), *Law and Ideology in Monarchic Israel* (JSOTSup, 124; Sheffield: JSOT Press, 1991), pp. 10-107.

72. See especially Dever, 'Monumental Architecture in Ancient Israel in the Period of the United Monarchy', in T. Ishida (ed.), *Studies in the Period of David and Solomon and Other Essays* (Tokyo: Yamakawa-Shuppansha, 1982), pp. 269-306. See also Dever in this volume; Stern on Dor in this volume, regarding the divided monarchy; A. Mazar on Beth Shan in this volume; Ben-Tor on Hazor, in this volume; the collapse of Miqneh VII in the tenth century. The evidence is even more extensive than this short list indicates, or the context allows. Among other points that might be made is the homology of Megiddo Palace 1723 to the palace of 1 Kings 6; the public buildings of Megiddo VA–IVB and Hazor X; the homologous gates and archaeological and architectural contexts of Gezer, Hazor, and Megiddo; the stratification of the Gezer gate between two destruction layers, one related in 1 Kgs 9.16, the other in 1 Kings 14 and Shishak's Karnak inscriptions; the rise of Lachish V; the end of Egyptian presence in Beth Shan Layer V; the transition to Tell Beit Mirsim A-1, with the arguable construction of the Northwest Gate and Tower complex; the efflorescence of settlement in the Negev highlands, indicating trade, associated with burnished red-slip; public building at Tel en-Nasbeh and Tel el-Far'ah N; the circumvallation of such highlands settlements; and developments at sites such as Tel Dan, including the stela fragments there, and Yoqneam and Hurvat Zayit. On the textual side, Shalmaneser III refers to Hadadezer of Damascus, and to an earlier alleged unifier of Aram—see A. Malamat, 'Aspects of the Foreign Policies of David and Solomon', pp. 2-3—an Aramean king who fought against Asshur-rabi (1012–972) and took lands east as well as west of the Euphrates, about 20 km south of Carchemish. Malamat identifies this earlier king with the Hadadezer of 2 Sam. 10.15-19 (Monolith, Year 3, see D.D. Luckenbill, *Ancient Records of Assyria and Babylonia* (Chicago: University of Chicago, 1926) I.603. For relevant data from the reign of Asshur-Dan II (934–912), see A.K. Grayson, *Assyrian Rulers of the Early First Millennium BC I (1114–859 BC)* (Royal Inscriptions of Mesopotamia Assyrian Periods 2; Toronto: University of Toronto, 1991), pp. 132-35, ll. 6-63. Other references, e.g., to Hiram, Shishaq, Ittobaal, Mesha, Omri, Ahab, Hazael (as usurper) and Jehu, to a later Ben-Hadad, and to a Rezin II roughly contemporary with Jeroboam II, Hiram II, and Sargon II in an era of throne names evoking founders, tend to corroborate the implication of biblical Israelite record-keeping from the turn of the millennium forward. This is not to mention accurate biblical records of campaigns in the West by Tiglath-Pileser III, Shalmaneser III, Sargon, and Sennacherib, and recollections of other foreign kings of the seventh and sixth centuries BCE.

But for the united monarchy, stronger communicable evidence of the simultaneity of things like the introduction of ashlar construction at the end of Iron I, construction of gates, and the like remain desiderata for a credible start: for this enterprise, fine stratification like Holladay's at Gezer is called for, with regression analyses applied to fabrics, tempers, surface treatment and firing atmospheres and temperatures, but with allowance for difference across distance. Social differentiation in the early monarchy has not been the subject of sufficient attention either in texts—what few we have—or in archaeology. Izbet Sartah II, which Holladay's criteria would put smack in the tenth century, is a classic example of it. Sedentarization or state regulation of the Negev is another phenomenon that urgently requires refinement in the field: if Holladay were right, the implication would be a connection with caravaneering. But above all, and for all periods, some basic insight into the history of agriculture as it was experienced in the village, not on the tell, and differential studies of diet—trace element and bone isotope, by gender, age, geography and grave goods—in Iron I and II, would be of utmost service.

In 1983, Larry Stager delivered 'The Archaeology of the Family in Ancient Israel' to a seminar of archaeologists and historians at the Institute for Advanced Studies of the Hebrew University.[73] His description of the compound and house and their functions was anticipated by R.H. Kennett, in the Schweich lectures of 1930. Kennett was working with texts' social assumptions, Stager with the excavated remains. And the two meshed beautifully. Here is a powerful tonic against the fringe elements in Israelite history. The two cultures must be cultivated, each on its own terms, as a check one against the other. The textual scholar can escape the inability to test hypotheses precisely by crossing the lines dividing the fields, and grounding hypotheses in archaeological correlates. The archaeologist can escape the potential atomization of unities—larger kinship groups, nations with variations in local cultures—through appeal to the texts. And one must keep texts, as well as sites, apart and examine each in splendid isolation before pretending that some sort of synthesis, some sort of enforced synchroneity, is possible. It really is not, either archaeologically or textually.

Specialization furnishes key advances in each specialized field. In that respect, Peter Machinist is absolutely correct to insist on maintaining an intellectual separation not just across fields, but even within them—a

73. L.E. Stager, 'The Archaeology of the Family in Ancient Israel', *BASOR* 260 (1985), pp. 1-35.

distinction between different local pottery repertoires, a distinction among different texts about a single event. Similarly, in philology, it seems ludicrous that we have grammars of 'Biblical Hebrew', but none of the book of Hosea, or 2 Samuel, or J. But we need the dialectic of specialized and generalized conversation to provide frameworks for one another. We need to mix separate cultures—in the same petri dish—and then to separate the hybrids over and over for specialized study. And in the end, that is what we are left with, both across the disciplinary divide and within each culture: two monologues, in an endless dialectic.

NOTES TO TABLE ON FOLLOWING PAGE

a.   Shimei is 'from the clan (section?) of the house of Saul', i.e., connected to it up the genealogy. Gera might be a clan.

b.   1 Sam. 16.6; 17.13, 28; 1 Chron. 2.13. In 2 Chron. 11.18, Rehoboam marries Eliab's daughter—his great-uncle's daughter.

c.   1 Sam. 16.8; 17.13; 2 Chron. 2.13.

d.   1 Sam. 16.9; 17.13; 2 Sam. 13.3, 32; 21.21; 1 Chron. 2.13; 20.7.

e.   1 Chron. 2.14 = Nathan the prophet?

f.   1 Chron. 2.14 = Doday = David?

g.   1 Chron. 2.15.

h.   Abigail in 2 Sam. 17.25 is 'the daughter of Nahash the sister of Zeruiah the mother of Joab'. 'Nahash' may be transposed from 17.27; perhaps it replaced 'Jesse': 1 Chron. 2.16-17 names Abigail and Zeruiah as David's sisters. But nothing in Samuel indicates that Abigail was David's sister, rather than his wife. Joab and his brothers enjoy a special status at the court, and are kin to David, but it is unclear that they are his nephews. None of them appears in Samuel until *after* David joins up with Abigail (1 Sam. 26.6). Further, the identification of Abigail as 'the sister of Zeruiah', rather than as David's sister, is at least peculiar, and while it may foreshadow Joab's killing Amasa, only 1 Kgs 11.19-20 otherwise specifies a woman's status by reference to her sister: Hadad's wife is introduced, understandably in the circumstances, as the sister of the Pharoah's chief wife. No text locates a female character by her status as the daughter of her mother. The peculiar locution that Yitra' the GN-ite 'came unto' Abigail signals that the relationship here is not agnatic, so that the emphasis is on Abigail, not Yitra. One way to accommodate MT is to take Abigail and Zeruiah as the daughters of Nahash of Ammon, with whom David allied—cf. the parallel identification in 1 Kgs 11.19. Another is to make Nahash the sister of Zeruiah, and Abigail Zeruiah's niece. Both are weakened by the possibility of textual error; however, 1 Samuel 25 as a story cannot militate against seeing Abigail here as David's wife— Ockham's Razor forbids the unnecessary multiplication of Abigails. Note that in early contexts, Abigail is not identified as 'the Carmelitess' (MT in 1 Sam. 27.3 is in error), but as 'the wife of Nabal the Carmelite'. Contrast Ahinoam, the Jezreelite.

i.   2 Chron. 11.18.

I. Qish

Abiel

Qish

Saul = Ahinoam

Ner — Abner

Gera — Shemei[a]

Jonathan · Abinadab · Malkishua · Ishbaal · Michal = Paltiel · Merab = Ad/zriel

Michal = Paltiel: 1 2 3 4 5 (unnamed)

= Rizpah: Armoni · Mephiboshet

Jonathan: Mephiboshet

II. Jesse

Jesse

Eliab[b] · Abinadab[c] · Shim'a[d] · Netan'el[e] · Radday[f] · Uzm[g] · David · Abigail = Yitra · Zeruiah[h] = ?

Abihayl = Rehoboam · Jonathan

Amasa

Zeruiah = ?: Joab · Abishay · Asahel

Amiel s. of Ahitophel?

David:

= Ahinoam: Amnon

= Abigail (w. Carmel): Kileab

Jezreelite

= Maacah (Talmay k. Geshur): Absalom · Tamar

Absalom: 3 sons · Tamar · Maacah

= Haggith: Adonijah

= Abital: Shphatyah

= Eglah: Yitre'am

= Bathsheba (= Uriah): Solomon · Yerimot[i]

Solomon: Rehoboam = Mahlat

Abijam

III. Assorted Others

Nabal the Carmelite, first husband of Abigail

1 Amaleqite who claimed to kill Saul

Rimmon the Beerothite

Rechab   Baana   the assassins of Ishbaal

Ahitophel f. of Ammiel/Eliam f. of Bathsheba?

Sheba'ben Bichri, of Benjamin

Abiathar the Elid

INDEXES

INDEX OF REFERENCES

OLD TESTAMENT

INDEX OF AUTHORS

Levine, I.L. 59
Levine, L.I. 168, 184, 186, 190, 192
Lewis, B. 63
Lieberman, S. 182, 211
Lifshitz, B. 182
Linder, A. 173
Little, B. 26
Loffreda, S. 175
London, G. 225, 273
Long, B.O. 88
Lorenzini, A. 332
Loud, G. 334
Lowance, M.I. 65
Lowenthal, D. 18, 64, 70
Luckenbill, D.D. 338

MacGregor, J. 48
MacMullen, R. 172
Macalister, R.A.S. 67, 72, 252
Macdonald, W.K. 217
Maier, A. 147
Malamat, A. 109, 126, 327, 338
Marty, M. 87
Marx, K. 284
Mazar, A. 23, 103, 146, 152, 156, 160,
    221, 225, 304, 321, 338
Mazar, B. 65, 182
McCarter, P.K. 315, 316, 319-21, 325-
    27, 332
McGovern, P.E. 146, 153, 156, 162
McGuire, R.H. 18, 223, 256, 278
McKee, L.W. 217, 227
Meshi-Zahav, Y. 71
Meshi-Zahav, Z. 71
Metzger, M. 245
Meyers, C. 202
Meyers, E.M. 175, 202
Milgrom, J. 252, 262
Miller, J.M. 272, 282, 290
Miroschedji, P. de 149
Moerman, M. 256
Morgan, M.A. 188
Morris, B. 70
Morris, I. 23
Mudar, K. 251
Muslih, M. 71
Mylonas, G.E. 102

Na'aman, N. 61, 109, 219, 302
Naveh, J. 168, 335
Netzer, E. 196, 199, 202
Neusner, J. 55, 192
Newman, B. 312
Nielsen, I. 195

Oren, E.D. 146
Otto, E. 323

Paloczi-Horvath, A. 217, 226
Parr, P.J. 226
Patterson, T.C. 18, 51, 62, 63, 278, 279
Peacock, D.P.S. 276
Peress, Y. 48, 49
Persons, S. 87
Peters, E. 323
Peterson Royce, A. 218
Petuchowski, J. 181
Pollard, H. 24, 278-80
Potter, P. 18, 26, 27
Powell, S. 18
Prawer, J. 60, 68
Preucel, R.W. 298
Pyszczyk, H. 218

Qimron, E. 211, 212

Ra'anan, U. 67
Rabinovich, A. 74
Ranger, T. 68
Rast, W.E. 221
Redding, R. 242, 245, 249
Reich, R. 152, 153, 191, 194-96, 199-
    204, 213
Reiner, E. 60
Rendtorff, R. 294, 297
Riedlmayer, A. 71
Ringer, B.B. 216
Robinson, E. 66
Robkin, E.E. 246
Roll, I. 249
Romanucci-Ross, L. 217
Rosen, A. 241
Rosen, B. 245
Rosenzweig, R. 63, 76
Roth-Gerson, L. 168, 184
Rousselle, A. 195